FEAR AND COURAGE

FEAR AND COURAGE

SECOND EDITION

S. J. Rachman

Department of Psychology
University of British Columbia

W. H. FREEMAN AND COMPANY / NEW YORK

A Series of Books in Psychology

Editors
Richard C. Atkinson
Gardner Lindzey
Richard F. Thompson

Library of Congress Cataloging-in-Publication Data

Rachman, Stanley.
    Fear and courage / S. J. Rachman. — 2nd ed.
        p.   cm. — (A Series of books in psychology)
    Bibliography: p.
    Includes index.
    ISBN 0-7167-2061-2
    1. Fear. 2. Courage. I. Title. II. Series.
BF575.F2R29   1990
152.4′6 — dc20   89-11629
                                      CIP

Printed in the United States of America

1 2 3 4 5 6 7 8 9 VB   8 9

To Clare

CONTENTS

THE MODIFICATION OF FEAR

COURAGE

CONCLUSION

PREFACE

My original intention was to carry out a conventional revision of *Fear and Courage*, to bring it up to date, but as the discussion of new findings and ideas began to overshadow the earlier text, the plan changed. It now has six sections: the nature of fear, varieties of fear, acquisition of fear, modification of fear, courage, and a conclusion. Roughly half of the original material has been retained. The remainder has been replaced by new chapters treating the promotion and generality of courage, the nature of panic, the summation of fear, the over-prediction of fear, the unexpected revival of interest in the concept of conditioning, and other topics. Several of the new chapters describe original research.

Psychological writings on the subject of fear tend to exaggerate human vulnerability, and as they are needlessly gloomy, an attempt will be made to introduce a better balance into the consideration of human fear. A significant proportion of my working time, as both a research worker and clinician, has been spent on the psychology of fear, and my interest in courage is comparatively recent. The immediate cause of this interest was the courage shown by severely anxious neurotic patients as they carried out the behavioral training and treatment programs that enabled them to overcome their difficulties. Some of these programs require patients to exercise considerable persistence even while experiencing intense fear, and the courageous manner in which these already fearful people cope with the demands of the training tasks is impressive and thought-provoking. As these people — distressed and often disabled by intense fear — are capable of behaving courageously in clinical circumstances, one begins to wonder if it makes sense to talk of courageous *people*. Perhaps we should talk about courageous acts, rather than courageous actors.

There was little in the scientific libraries to satisfy my curiosity about courage, and a search of *Psychological Abstracts*, the largest repository of psychological references, produced a mere handful of citations. By contrast, references to fear are extremely common. It is a well-researched subject, and a multitude of experiments on animal and human fears have been conducted. There seems to be no logical reason for this disproportionate scientific emphasis, and one wonders if it is merely an additional example of our heightened interest in morbid and distressing events, in preference to the common, ordinary, constructive events of everyday life.

Whatever the cause, the fact remains that we have little scientific information on the nature of courage. Because it is a fascinating subject and one that can be studied with benefit, I collected information from diverse sources, some scientific and others historical, journalistic, or anecdotal, in an attempt to construct a workable view of courage. This attempt was facilitated by applying some of the new ideas on the psychology of fear. The construal of fear as a set of loosely coupled components, originally proposed by Peter Lang and now known as the three systems model of fear, was especially helpful and provided a framework for carrying out a program of research on courage in dangerous military situations. Courage is construed as the persistence of behavior *despite* fear. A good deal of new information about the nature of courage emerged from the study of military samples, especially bomb-disposal operators, and it confirmed that people can indeed be trained to perform courageously. There appear to be a small number of people who are particularly well suited to carrying out dangerous tasks.

Courage, which was described by Socrates as a "very noble quality," appears to be universally admired (even in an enemy), and it is pleasing to report that examples of courage are common and easy to collect.

Some new subjects, such as fear summation, the return of fear, fear inflation, the relationship between fear and pain, and the over-prediction of fear, are introduced and several topics that were included in the First Edition have been given fuller treatment. These include a discussion of the relationship between dangerousness and fear, including the many instances in which they do not coincide, the influence of ideology on the control of fear, fear in solitude, and a fresh appraisal of the concept of fear preparedness. Important developments in the cognitive and conditioning theories of fear are analyzed.

This work is not a comprehensive account of the psychology of fear, but concentrates on interpretations of the new findings and ideas and on fresh assessments of previously established information. It also contains many new questions, and some old ones.

Are some people "naturally" brave? Can people learn to behave courageously? Why do people so often over-predict how frightened they will
feel? Can fears be acquired indirectly? Can temporally remote events
influence fear? Do fears summate? When and why do fears return? Has
the concept of agoraphobia outlived its usefulness? Are some people
frightened of blood? How can we account for the robust efficacy of
behavioral methods for reducing fear? What is panic, and can it be
prevented? Do expectations of cowardice exceed acts of cowardice?

As these are subjects of wide interest, I have tried to make the text
easily readable by minimizing the use of technical terms. Inevitably, some
sections are more suited for professional psychologists, but I trust that
much of the book will be followed with ease by nonpsychologists. In
order to retain the flow of the text, the references and a great deal of
detailed information — as well as some provocative commentaries — have
been placed in the Notes at the end of the book. Whenever possible, I
have tried to draw out some of the practical consequences of our current
understanding of fear and courage.

Before turning to an examination of these questions and the answers,
or interpretations, I wish to express my appreciation of the assistance and
cooperation I have received from numerous people.

Over the years, I have benefitted from collaborating with many col-
leagues, and from conversations and correspondence on the subject of fear
(and courage) with Dick Hallam, Padmal de Silva, Gudrun Sartory,
Martin Seligman, Clare Philips, Marcel van den Hout, Albert Bandura,
Ted Rosenthal, Joseph Wolpe, Hans Eysenck, Raymond Hodgson, Loci
Solyom, Lars Ost, Arnoud Arntz, David Barlow, John Teasdale, David
Clark, Michelle Craske, Paul Salkovskis, Sue Mineka, Tim Beck, Peter
Lang, Arne Ohman, Larry Michelson, Tom Macmillan, Bill Marshall,
Barbara Melamed, and other colleagues. In the recent past I have had
excellent assistance from Cindy Lopatka, Karen Levitt, Richard Booth,
Maureen Whittal, Kim Eyrl, and Sandy Bichard, and welcome encour-
agement in the whole enterprise from Professor M. Gelder and Mr. A. H.
Rogers. Jonathan Cobb and Stephen Wagley at W. H. Freeman and
Company provided excellent editorial guidance.

I wish to thank the following people for permitting me to quote from
their unpublished findings or comments: Dwight Kirkpatrick, Charles
Costello, Martin Seligman, Arnoud Arntz, and Reuven Gal. Dr. David
Stafford Clark kindly permitted me to quote from his paper on air
combat, and Mollie Panter-Downes from her war diary.

The officers and operators of the Royal Army Ordnance Corps have
been extremely cooperative in helping to carry out the research on

fearlessness and courage in the performance of bomb-disposal duties, from 1978 until the present time, and the officers and men of the Parachute Regiment were very helpful in two research projects.

The several research projects described in the book were supported by various agencies, including the Medical Research Council, the Canadian Science and Engineering Council, the European Research Office of the U.S. Army Research Institute, and the British Columbia Health Research Foundation. The preparation of this book was made possible by the award of a Killam Senior Scholarship. I am grateful to all of these agencies for their welcome support. I also wish to thank Tania Deans for her excellent (and modern) assistance in the preparation of the manuscript.

S. Rachman

FEAR AND COURAGE

CHAPTER *1*

HUMAN
FEARS

In the past few years important advances have been made in our ability to reduce human fears. Under controlled conditions, it is now possible to produce substantial and lasting reductions of established fears, even life-long fears, within 30 minutes.[1] It requires greater effort and far more time to reduce complex, intense fears such as agoraphobia, but even these respond reasonably well to training or treatment programs.[2] This welcome progress has also given rise to improvements in our understanding of human fear and courage.

It has become apparent that people are far more resilient than most psychologists have implied. Examples can be seen daily in clinics, counseling centers, and hospitals, as people struggle to overcome their long-standing and severe fears with the help of professional staff. On a larger scale, people display astonishing resilience during wartime; the courage of ambulance crews, fire-fighters, and other service workers during World War II was particularly impressive. These observations promote a better balanced and more hopeful view of human qualities than is conveyed by most psychological writings on emotion, in which we tend to dwell on anxiety, fear, and failure.

Fears do arise, however, and the intense ones can be distressing and disabling. They can dominate the affected person's life. Understandably, intense fears attract the greatest attention, but many milder fears have fascinating and puzzling features that repay consideration. In this book, an attempt is made to cover both types of fear, their causes and variations, and how they can be influenced. It is a book about human fears and few references will be made to the extensive literature describing the results of research on fear in animals. Nevertheless, my views on human fear have been considerably influenced by animal research, particularly on the induction and avoidance of fear.[3]

THE NATURE OF FEAR

The word *fear* is used without difficulty in everyday language to mean the experience of apprehension, but problems arise when it is used as a scientific term. It cannot be assumed that people are always able or even willing to recognize and then describe their experience of fear. Admissions of fear are discouraged in wartime, and in surveys carried out on student populations the admission of certain fears is felt by some men to be socially undesirable. In clinical settings, it is not uncommon to see patients who are unable to identify or recognize even significant fears.

The social influences that obscure the accurate expression of fear complicate the intrinsic difficulty of recognizing and describing our feelings and experiences. For example, many people who say that they are fearful of a particular object or situation are later seen to display fearless behavior when they encounter it. Assessments of the intensity of the fear are limited by the difficulty involved in translating such expressions as "extremely frightened," "terrified," and "slightly anxious" into a quantitative scale with stable properties. For these reasons, among others, psychologists have extended the study of fear beyond an exclusive reliance on subjective reports, by including indexes of physiological change and measures of observable behavior. It is helpful to think of fear as comprising three main components: the subjective experience of apprehension, associated psychophysiological changes, and attempts to avoid or escape[4] from fearful situations. The three components of fear often fail to correspond. Some people experience subjective fear but remain outwardly calm and, if tested, show none of the expected psychophysiological correlates of fear, such as perspiring, trembling, or increased heart rate; others report subjective fear but make no attempt to escape from or avoid the supposedly frightening situation. The existence of these three components of fear, and the fact that they do not always correspond, makes it helpful to specify which component of a fear one is describing.

In everyday exchanges we rely on people telling us of their fears, and we supplement this information with clues provided by their facial and other bodily expressions. Unfortunately, when made in the absence of supporting contextual cues, these interpretations can be misleading.[5] Moreover, the value of observations of facial and other expressions is limited to certain categories of fear, especially the acute fears; chronic, diffuse fears are less visible. For example, we may without difficulty observe signs of fear in an anxious passenger as an aircraft descends, but fail to recognize fear in a person who is intensely apprehensive about aging.

There are many types of fear, but certain categories such as neurotic fears have understandably been studied more intensively than others. Among these varieties, a division can be made between acute and chronic fears. The acute fears are generally provoked by tangible stimuli or situations and subside when the frightening stimulus is removed or avoided. The fear of snakes illustrates this acute type. Chronic fears tend to be more complex but, like the acute type, they may or may not be tied to tangible sources of provocation. The fear of being alone is an example of a chronic, tangible fear; examples of chronic and intangible fears are by their nature difficult to specify. Feelings persistently uneasy and anxious for unidentified reasons is a chronic state of aching fear that has been described better by novelists than by psychologists. The psychiatric term *generalized anxiety disorder* covers some of these diffuse fears, and is now attracting scientific attention.

A distinction is sometimes drawn between fear and anxiety. *Fear* describes feelings of apprehension about tangible and predominantly realistic dangers, and *anxiety* refers to feelings of apprehension that are difficult to relate to tangible sources of stimulation. The inability to identify the source of one's fear is usually regarded as the hallmark of anxiety, and in psychodynamic theories, this inability is said to be a result of repression; the cause of the fear remains unconscious. This distinction between fear and anxiety is common in psychodynamic writings and is not entirely without value, but will not be used in this book.

The origins of fear are still a matter of controversy. The impact of early behaviorism, with its overwhelming emphasis on the importance of acquired behavior, led to the interment of the notion that some fears may be innate. Even the possible existence of such fears in animals was reluctantly conceded. However, the possible occurrence of innately determined fears in human beings is once more under consideration. One of the more prominent and promising accounts of the inherent determinants of fear, Seligman's theory of preparedness, is discussed in Chapter 10. After a series of disappointing experimental findings in the past decade, the early enthusiasm for this theory has dissipated, and many people have discounted the idea prematurely. It will be argued that the experimental methods were not the most appropriate and that the theory warrants a renewed search.

In an introduction, there is a risk of giving an oversimplified summary of the major causes of fear. Nevertheless it may be helpful to set out the main causes that will be discussed in the pages that follow. Useful progress has been made in determining how fears are acquired, and whether or not the concept of "three pathways to fear" is supportable. The first pathway to fear, by conditioning, includes exposure to traumatic stimulation or repeated exposures to subtraumatic sensitizing conditions. The second pathway is vicarious acquisition; direct or indirect observations of people displaying fear. Transmission of fear-inducing information is the third pathway. For a considerable time, explanations of fear acquisition were dominated by the conditioning theory that emphasized the importance of exposure to traumatic stimulation. Recognition of the fact that fears can be acquired vicariously or by the direct transmission of information has helped to produce a fuller account of the causes of fear. In addition, we now have to incorporate the novel idea that fears can be enhanced or inflated by events that occur well after the fear is established, and even by events that are not directly related to the fear. These new findings, which suggest that a fearful connection can be formed between events that are separated in time and space, are compatible with a radically revised and expanded conception of conditioning.

There has also been a radical revision of thinking on the subject of one of the most clinically prominent anxiety disorders, *agoraphobia*. Many writers now reinterpret that disorder as a secondary consequence of a more fundamental problem: panic, episodes of intense fear of sudden onset. (The term *panic* is derived from the terror caused by the shrill and strange noises made by Pan, an unruly and mischievous Greek god, part man and part goat.)

The nature and significance of panic episodes is the subject of one of the most lively debates in psychology for many decades. The argument that episodes of panic underlie most cases of agoraphobia has gained considerable support, but the claim that panic disorders are essentially biological has been the subject of critical scrutiny. Within the last three years, competing psychological interpretations have been put forward and are under vigorous investigation. Clark's cognitive theory states that panics are caused by catastrophic misinterpretations of bodily sensations, such as palpitations and dizziness.[6] People who are predisposed to make negative interpretations of bodily changes are especially prone to develop panic disorders. This plausible theory can deal with an impressive amount of information collected by researchers on both sides of the debate, and already is influential. As will become evident, it has implications that filter into many different aspects of fear.

In keeping with trends in other branches of psychology, there is a growing appreciation of the role of cognitive factors in fearful experiences. For example, it is now argued that fearful avoidance behavior is determined in large part by the affected person's prediction of the probability that he or she will be frightened in a particular situation. Predictions of a high probability of fear are likely to be followed by avoidance behavior, and predictions of zero or low probability of fear are likely to be followed by approach behavior. It is also argued that the expected aversiveness of the fear—and the search for safety signals and reassurance—plays a part in the persistence of avoidance behavior. Previously it was thought that fearful avoidance behavior persists simply because it successfully reduces or avoids fear.

On the practical side, clinicians and researchers now work with greater confidence and efficiency; they have some well-tested and robust techniques. The treatment of anxiety disorders has been refined and the success rates are encouraging, although too many patients are left with residual fear. Promising advances have been made in the development of cognitive techniques for overcoming fear, and it is not unreasonably optimistic to expect that an effective and robust psychological method of treating panic will be available within five years. The findings on courage may give rise to refined methods of selecting and training people to carry out hazardous tasks.

THE IDEA OF TREATMENT

The rationale and status of specific types of treatment will be considered presently, but a few preliminary remarks about the different approaches to reducing fear might be helpful. Fear is a major component of most neurotic disorders, and as a result it is a subject that has greatly occupied clinicians and research workers. A variety of therapeutic methods have been developed and tested. Pharmacological methods are partly successful but fall outside the scope of this book; only the psychological methods for reducing fear will be considered. These can be divided into three main types: direct attempts to reduce the fear or anxiety (as in behavior therapy), attempts to change the person's fearful cognitions (cognitive therapy), and attempts to modify the putative underlying causes of the fear or anxiety (as in psychoanalysis and related techniques).

The direct methods are largely the products of experimental psychology. For nearly a quarter of a century, *desensitization* (graded and gradual exposure to the fear stimulus) was the most extensively used direct method. Some years later, *flooding* (rapid, ungraded exposures) and *modeling* (imitation) techniques were added. Cognitive therapy is in the early stages of development and offers the hope of increasing our grasp of fear. However, the powerful irrational elements in some fears present a major obstacle. The "primacy of affect," the idea that the emotion often occurs *before* the cognition, is another potential obstacle. Psychoanalysis is of course the most famous and influential of the indirect methods and has spawned many derivations. Most of them were, like psychoanalysis itself, developed by clinical psychiatrists or psychologists. The most widely practiced form of indirect treatment is psychotherapy (a confusingly wide term covering many types of activity), not psychoanalysis, which is a far less common form of therapy. Although there are great differences between techniques, the indirect methods are founded on the assumption that a thorough exploration of matters seemingly unrelated to the pertinent fear is a necessary prerequisite for the reduction of fear. In this sense, interpretive psychotherapy stands opposite to the newly established cognitive therapy, which drives directly at the links between cognitions and fears.

Bandura observed that as our treatment techniques become more direct and behavioral, our theories become more cognitive. "It is performance-based treatments that are proving most powerful in effecting psychological changes," but on the other hand, the "explanations of change processes are becoming more cognitive."[7] Plain and direct behavioral techniques, such as *exposure* (repeated, prolonged exposures to the fear stimulus), are robust and act broadly, in the manner of bulldozers. Most fears yield to these repeated exposures. In keeping with the times, however, psychologists are more sensitive to the way in which people construe their problem and how their cognitions influence the response to training or treatment. This sensitivity is reflected in the increasing complexity of the cognitive explanations put forward to explain the effects of some disarmingly simple treatment techniques. Bandura's paradox has not been resolved.

FEAR IS NOT A LUMP

In the course of developing effective techniques for reducing fear, some unexpected and complex findings emerged. Perplexing results also emerged in the clinical application of these techniques. Despite the appearance of marked improvements in behavior — for example, a claustrophobic person acquiring the ability to travel on subway trains — some patients deny that they have benefited. In other patients, the physiological reactions observed during the real or symbolic presentation of a fearful object diminish after treatment, but the person continues to complain of excessive fear. Sometimes the improvements apparent in the person's behavior are followed only weeks later by subjective improvements.

Repeated observations of this type led to the recognition that the three components of fear might show *desynchrony*, or different rates of response to treatment. Recognition that the patient's subjective report tends to be the slowest to change brought relief to therapists as well as to patients. In general, the order of change in response to therapy is first declining physiological reactivity, then behavioral improvements, and finally subjective improvements.

The low correspondence between some measures of fear also led to difficulties in interpreting laboratory findings on fear reduction. It even produced difficulties at the earliest stage of experiments — the selection of suitably fearful subjects. Many potential subjects who rate themselves as being fearful display little or no fear when exposed to the fearful object in a behavioral avoidance test. Some of them walk in, approach the snake (for example), and lift it without hesitation, in spite of having recorded an extreme fear of snakes on a questionnaire. There is a strong tendency for people to overpredict their fears. In laboratory research, as in clinical practice, it is often found that subjective reports of fear diminish more slowly than avoidance behavior and other overt signs of fear.

A major discrepancy between different measures of fear was encountered in an experiment designed to reduce the circumscribed fear of public speaking among a group of university students. Their fear was assessed by a number of self-report measures, two physiological measures, external ratings of fear, and a behavioral test of public speaking. The main aim of the experiment was accomplished, and a good deal of useful subsidiary information was gathered. Gordon Paul found a reasonably high correlation between the self-report measures of therapeutic improvement, but these measures bore little relationship to the physiological indicants of fear.[8] Despite the lack of agreement between some of the outcome measures, all the major ones showed that the treated subjects were significantly less fearful at the termination of the treatment and at follow-up.

Peter Lang, who has been responsible for some of the most valuable research and theorizing on the subject of fear and fear reduction, expressed the new view of fear extremely well: " . . . fear is not some hard phenomenal lump that lives inside people, that we may palpate more or less successfully."[9] He argued convincingly that the components of fear responses are related to each other, but only imperfectly; they are partially independent. In many circumstances, however, they do show corresponding changes. For example, in one of Lang's experiments on desensitization the correspondence between fear reports and heart rate was reassuringly high.[10]

DESYNCHRONOUS PROGRESS IN FEAR REDUCTION

Variations in the pattern of the three components of fear are well illustrated in a series of case studies described by Leitenberg, Agras, Butz, and Wincze.[11] Their careful observations of the therapeutic progress of nine fearful patients showed that behavioral improvements and psychophysiological changes often take independent paths. In some patients the two components changed in synchrony, but in others the behavioral improvements preceded or followed the psychophysiological changes. Desynchronous changes have been reported in other studies. For example, reductions in subjective fear are not necessarily translated into coping behavior,[12] and they occasionally lag behind behavioral changes.[13] Highly demanding procedures such as flooding are likely to produce desynchronous changes: behavioral improvements occur first and most easily, but the person can be left with excessive subjective fear.[14,15,16]

The idea that the three components of fear show a high degree of concordance during periods of high fear or very low fear and that discordances are most likely to occur at intermediate levels of fear[17] received some support.[18] The measures of fear obtained from anxious and nonanxious musicians playing under stressful or nonstressful conditions showed low correlations, but concordance between the three components of fear was "most often observed when intense emotional responses were elicited."[19,20] In a state of deep relaxation it is likely that the self-report will express calmness, the physiological response systems will be reasonably quiescent, there will be no avoidance behavior, and an external observer would describe the person as calm. Evidence in support of the postulated relationship between level of demand and degree of concordance, with high demand producing greater discordance between the components, was produced by Matias and Turner,[21] but low demand was not always followed by response concordance.

In an investigation of fear in parachute jumpers, Fenz and Epstein found evidence of both correspondence and lack of correspondence between different measures.[22] In a group of 10 veteran jumpers, discordant results were obtained. The three physiological measures all showed a steady increase during the entire jumping sequence. This finding was contrary to the pattern observed in the measure of subjective fear, which varied in the following way: increase in fear, then decrease, then another increase. Among the group of 10 novices, however, subjective fear and psychophysiological reactions showed corresponding patterns of increase and decrease. Heart rate, skin conductance, and respiration all built up to a peak shortly before the jump took place (for example, the mean heart rate equalled 145 beats per minute) and then subsided soon after the landing. The veterans experienced only mild increases in heart rate, subjective fear, and other measures, whereas the novices displayed extremely strong reactions. These findings support the idea that the concordance between measures will increase at very high levels of fear and also at the opposite extreme, that is, measures correspond well during states of calm.

CONCORDANCE AND DISCORDANCE

In 1974, Hodgson and Rachman attempted to assemble and integrate the findings on desynchrony, and concluded with several hypotheses.[23] They argued that concordance between the three components of fear (the so-called three systems model) is likely to be high during strong emotional arousal and that discordance will be more evident during moderate emotional arousal. As noted, this hypothesis received partial support, as did the hypotheses that concordance between the three components will be greater under low levels of demand and that high levels of demand will produce discordance between components.[24] It was postulated that the pattern and degree of synchronous change is a function of the therapeutic procedure employed;[25] it was predicted that concordance between components would increase in the follow-up period after a treatment or training program.

It also follows from the three-systems model that if treatment procedures are matched to the patient's fear pattern, the probability of achieving a successful outcome improves. For example, if a phobic patient has a pronounced physiological reaction to the fearful stimulus, training in relaxation is likely to be helpful. In cases characterized by an excessive subjective reaction unaccompanied by physiological disturbance, a cognitive method of treatment is more appropriate. The chosen treatment should be consonant with the observed pattern of fear. Research on this deduction has produced mixed results.[26]

The results of the first two attempts to test the deduction were encouraging. Ost and his colleagues achieved superior results first in a group of social phobics and then with claustrophobic patients by matching the treatment method to the problem.[27] Patients who had a strong physiological reaction to the fearful stimulus benefited more from the treatment involving applied relaxation, and patients with a strong behavioral reaction benefited more from behavioral treatment. In a study of 40 agoraphobic patients carried out in 1984, the consonance effects were in the predicted direction but insignificant.[28] Haug and others found that a consonant treatment method was superior to a nonconsonant method in the treatment of 10 patients with a fear of flying.[29] The differences were evident on the measures of subjective arousal and ratings of the fear of flying, but not on the measures of heartrate or self-ratings of general anxiety. Mackay and Liddell provided partial support in a study of 14 agoraphobic patients; the noncognitive responders did less well than the cognitive responders if they were given cognitive treatment.[30] A positive consonance relationship was also reported by Norton and Johnson,[31] who found that relaxation was more effective for people with somatic anxiety and that meditation was more effective for cognitive reactors. On the other hand, dental phobic patients treated by Jerremalm and other improved significantly, whether the treatment was consonant or not.[32]

A possible explanation for some of the variations in the consonance effect was put forward by Michelson.[33] It appears that the effects may be subject to delay and begin to appear after the completion of treatment, most evidently at follow-up. The agoraphobic patients in his study were divided into three categories, and those who received a consonant treatment (relaxation, exposure, or cognitive therapy) responded significantly better than did those who had a treatment that was not consonant. The differences emerged only after a lag. They became evident after treatment and were more pronounced at the follow-up assessment. "Consonance status appears to manifest its moderating function in a delayed pattern, increasing its influence as the treatment progresses."[34]

Encouraged by the similarity between the results of his own research and those reported by Ost and his colleagues, Michelson feels that tripartite assessments, based on the three-systems model, are an advance and foresees the "distinct possibility of designing individually tailored treatments adapted specifically to the unique tripartite profile of each client."[35] There are grounds for this optimism, but as mentioned, some attempts to find evidence of treatment consonance have been unsuccessful. One explanation for the inconsistency of the results is that such broadly effective methods as exposure may blanket the subtleties of a three-systems analysis. Michelson's suggestion about a delayed effect is worth pursuing.

PROBLEMS IN MEASURING AND DEFINING FEAR

In view of the imperfect coupling between systems, what is the best way to describe and predict fear? After Lang, it is best to avoid relying on a single measure. Self-report measures provide a useful if crude basis for the prediction of fear and have some practical advantages over more elaborate techniques of assessment. Providing that one does not expect too much of these measures, that is, too great a degree of refinement, they can be useful. The inclusion of a behavioral-approach test is highly desirable in most circumstances and provides a check on the predictive value of self-report measures. The ratings of fear made by external judges can also be useful, but they are not free of problems. Some physiological indexes, heart rate in particular, can provide important data. Heart rate acceleration occurs in response to fear stimuli and often increases in unison with increases in subjective intensity of fear.[36] Measures of skin conductance have sometimes been useful, but individual differences in responsiveness are large, and the index is beset with practical and technical problems, including "rapid adaptation," or declining responsiveness as a result of the repeated testing. Measures of muscular tension have added little. In short, total reliance on the self-report can lead us to underestimate a person's degree of courage and total reliance on the observed behavior in a fear test can lead one to underestimate the degree of a person's fear.[37]

Courage and fear

This view of fear as a complex of imperfectly coupled response systems has led to some novel ideas on the nature of courage. A person may be willing to approach a frightening object or situation despite experiencing a high degree of subjective fear and unpleasant bodily reactions. This persistence in the face of subjective and physical sensations of fear suggests a definition of courage—to continue despite one's fear. A psychologist could describe this type of behavior as an example of uncoupling, in which the person's overt behavior advances beyond his subjective discomfort. However, if a person continues to approach a fearful situation—in the absence of any subjective fear or accompanying bodily responses—is he or she also displaying courage? Or is the person displaying fearlessness rather than courage? How then do we describe a person whose physiological system is disturbed as he or she calmly approaches danger? An "autonomic coward"? A person who shows no physiological disturbances when experiencing subjective fear would then be said to possess a brave autonomic system. Perhaps we should reserve the description of "true courage" for people who are willing and able to approach a fearful situation despite the presence of subjective fear and psychophysiological disturbances.

A CONCEPTUAL PROBLEM

Lang's tripartite model of fear was introduced in recognition of the fact that fear consists of more than one component; it is not unitary. However, Lang's new conception may not have escaped the original problem entirely. The three components are loosely coupled, and any one of them can predominate as circumstances change. The absence of a psychophysiological response does not prevent us from concluding that the person is frightened. Nor does the absence of avoidance or escape behavior preclude this conclusion. The experience of fear does not require the presence of all three components, but the presence of a psychophysiological response — or of escape or avoidance behavior or even their combination — is not sufficient to warrant the label of fear. A person might display avoidance behavior and an elevated heart rate as components of the experience of repugnance or rage. However, in the absence of the appropriate verbal report of fear, the meaning of the avoidance behavior and the physiological response is undefined. The behavioral and psychophysiological components of fear usually are prominent, but fear may occur without them. The verbal report, however, is definitional and essential. In this way, the problem that prompted the introduction of the three-system analysis lingers on in a muted form. On the practical side, the unreliability of psychophysiological measures is a continuing source of difficulty.[38,39]

FEAR AND CONTROL

There is a connection between our ability to control potentially threatening situations and the experience of fear. In the face of threats, if a person feels unable to control the probable outcome, he or she is likely to experience fear. If in the same threatening situation this person confidently feels able to control the likelihood of an unfavorable outcome, he or she is not likely to experience fear.

The concept of controllability had a prominent place in Seligman's original theory of learned helplessness, which was formulated to account for depression, but incorporated some aspects of fear. Seligman claimed that helplessness, and therefore depression, resulted from a sense of futility: "Helplessness is the psychological state that frequently results when events are uncontrollable."[40] The sense of helplessness is particularly acute if a person feels that important life events are beyond his or her control, that they will remain beyond control, that the absence of control stems from personal inadequacies, and that the situation is typical. According to Seligman, when "the probability of an outcome is the same whether or not a given response occurs, the outcome is independent of that response. When this is true of all voluntary responses, the outcome is uncontrollable."[41] He went on to postulate that the expectation of uncontrollability "produces fear for as long as the subject is uncertain of the uncontrollability of the outcome" and that this expectation may in turn produce depression.[42] If people perceive that they are in a position to control the outcome of an event, their anxiety is reduced.

Two aspects of Seligman's theory are noteworthy. First, the person's sense of whether or not he can control the situation is a more important determinant of fear than is the objective likelihood of asserting or failing to assert such control; second, a perceived absence of control is likely to lead to fear only when the outcome is expected to be aversive. An absence of control over a desired outcome is not likely to induce fear. In short, the absence of perceived control in a potentially aversive condition generates fear, whereas the acquisition of a perceived sense of mastery reduces fear.

I suggest that what produces self-esteem and a sense of competence, and protects against depression, is not only the absolute quality of experience, but the perception that one's own actions control the experience. To the degree that uncontrollable events occur, either traumatic or positive, depression will be predisposed and ego-strength undermined.[43]

The sense of controllability is related to predictability, and Seligman argued that in most circumstances, people prefer predictable events to unpredictable ones.[44] There is a logical connection between predictability and controllability, and the two often coincide.[45,46]

We can regard the preference for predictability, and the striving to achieve it, as early stages in the process of gaining increased control over a potentially aversive outcome. The more information we have about the expected aversiveness, its likely time of occurrence, its probable duration, and its premonitory signs, the greater the likelihood that we will find ways either to prevent it from occurring or to reduce its consequences if it does occur. The search for predictability in a potentially aversive situation can be seen in the curiosity displayed by children confronting a novel situation (for example, a new animal). If the child's search for relevant information, such as examining the animal, increases his expectation of controllability, any fear that he might have had will subside. But if the new information raises his prediction about the likelihood of the animal behaving aversively, the fear will increase.

Recently, Barlow produced a clever experimental example of the effects of perceived control; in this instance, *illusory* control.[47] When patients with panic disorder were told that they could control the amount of carbon dioxide they were receiving, they experienced significantly fewer panics than did comparable patients who were not given any control over the gas—even though the perceived control was illusory. The belief in control was sufficient.

The concept of controllability and the related notion of predictability encompass several aspects of fear and offer us considerable explanatory power. For our purposes, controllability means the person's sense of whether or not he or she is in a position to reduce the likelihood of an aversive event or its consequences. In most circumstances the perception of inadequate powers of control contributes to fear, whereas the perception of substantial control over events—a sense of mastery if you will—reduces fear, as in Barlow's experiment. Potentially aversive events that are difficult to predict are more likely to produce fear than are predictable events; similarly, behavior or information that increases predictability is likely to contribute to a reduction in fear. Extrapolating from these definitions and concepts, we can argue that people who have a well-developed sense of competence, or, in everyday language, who display considerable self-confidence, will seldom experience fear. People with a poor sense of their own competence, those with little self-confidence, can be expected to experience fear rather frequently.[48]

These variations in fear and the conditions that determine the onset or inhibition of fear need to be considered in the context of a major, overriding fact about human fear. Given the hazards, unpredictability, and uncontrollability of life, there is far less fear than one might expect. Human resistance to fear is nowhere better illustrated than during war.

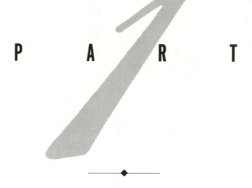

P A R T

FEARS IN WAR

CHAPTER

FEAR UNDER
AIR ATTACK

Before the outbreak of World War II most authorities expected that air attacks on civilian targets would produce widespread panic, enduring terror, and large numbers of psychiatric casualties.

The stimuli presented by a heavy air-raid are far more intense and more terrifying than civilised human beings normally experience. . . . [I]n the summer of 1940 when raids on a large scale seemed imminent in Britain, many of us were apprehensive lest they should lead to widespread panic and hysteria.[1]

These apprehensions, expressed by Philip Vernon, a prominent British psychologist, were typical. They arose from widely held assumptions about human vulnerability and were reinforced by reports of the panicky conduct of the civilian population in Barcelona during raids carried out in the Spanish Civil War and by accounts of frightened crowds fleeing from bombed areas in Flanders and France. A year before the outbreak of World War II, John Rickman, the Editor of the *British Journal of Medical Psychology*, wrote in *The Lancet,* "Since air raids may produce panic in the civilian population it is well to consider the factors that facilitate or diminish panic, and what steps, if any, may be taken against it."[2]

Accordingly, the authorities took into account the psychological as well as the physical dangers when issuing air raid precautions. Arrangements were made for the dispersal of city dwellers, and special psychological clinics were established. However, within a year of the start of the air attacks on Britain, Vernon was relieved to admit, "fortunately we were wrong." What had happened?

To the considerable surprise of almost everyone, the psychological casualties were few, despite the death and destruction caused by the attacks. Of 578 civilian casualties admitted to hospital in a heavily raided area, only two were suffering primarily from psychological disturbance. A report from another heavily bombed area confirmed that only 15 of the 1100 people treated in medical clinics showed psychological disorders. Among 200 admissions to a mental hospital in London during a period of heavy raids, the doctors found that the "air attacks were a major factor in the disorders presented by only five of the total group. Moreover, these five cases responded well to treatment."[3]

Before describing how most people responded to air attacks, it might be helpful to give an account of the kind of disorder that was *expected* to occur on a wide scale but that in fact turned out to be rare.

Dr. E. Stengel, an experienced clinical psychiatrist, provided this description of an air raid phobia: "a persistent and excessive fear of air raids, which was present all the time but steadily increased toward nightfall. The sound of the sirens precipitated an acute anxiety attack."[4] Once established, these phobias persisted long after the air attacks had ceased. The fear of air raids was sometimes accompanied by intense fears of enclosed spaces or of being alone in public places.

However, as Janis noted in his informative study of British reactions to air raids, "the reactions of *most* people generally subsided within one-quarter of an hour after the end of the bombing attack"[5] (original emphasis). For a minority of people these acute reactions took longer to subside: "over a period of days and weeks, there is a gradual return to normality. . . . [C]haracteristic initial symptoms are jitteriness, sensitivity to noise, excessive fatigue, trembling of the hands, and terrifying nightmares in which the traumatic situation is re-experienced."[6]

The resilience that people displayed under air attack was so unexpected and remarkable that surveys and statistical analyses alone cannot convey how people managed to cope. The official reports concentrate mostly on reactions that were expected but did not occur.

Among the many excellent literary accounts of life during the blitz in Britain, the descriptions provided by Mollie Panter-Downes are some of the most vivid and succeed where the official reports fall short.[7]

BLITZ

Panter-Downes's account begins as Londoners prepared for the first air attacks after the declaration of war. "The evacuation of London which is to be spaced over three days began yesterday and was apparently a triumph for all concerned." The BBC provided a Beethoven concert "interspersed with the calm and cultured tones of the BBC telling motorists what to do during air raids, and giving instructions to what the BBC referred to coyly as expectant mothers who are a good deal more than expectant."[8]

"For the first week of the war the weather was superb." In these early stages, people took the official advice about air raid precautions with seriousness and reacted to the first alarms in a prompt manner.

Even Miss Chupp, one of our sub-wardens found that she had not yet been provided with the tin hat promised by a benevolent government for such a contingency. Nothing daunted, she found an aluminum pudding basin, which fitted to a nicety, mounted a bicycle and shot round her section blowing blasts on a whistle with a violence that shook the pince-nez on her mild nose.

After repeated alarms, followed by very little action, the population quickly adapted and apparently showed little concern. The mood is conveyed in this anecdote: "On these fine mornings, London bus-drivers hail each other sardonically by saying, 'Nice day for the blitzkreig, Bill,' but so far nothing has happened."

It should not be thought, however, that people were unaware of the dangers ahead of them. Panter-Downes described the anxiety of parents who were hoping that their children might be evacuated to the safety of America.

The one hope these worried people hang on to is that the overwhelmingly generous offer of hospitality from America may be followed up by the sending of American ships to fetch the children. Britons still have an immense faith in America and the workings of national conscience, but they hope that such gestures will not be delayed much longer. Over here, one gets a new conception of time. It doesn't march on; it hurtles like a dive-bomber.

When the big raids started in the summer of 1940, people continued to display calm behavior. They quickly adapted their daily style of living to the repeated raids and the disturbances of the night. On the frivolous side, there were discussions about the best places to take shelter during a raid. "Shoppers prefer Harrods where chairs are provided and first-aid workers unobtrusively but comfortingly hover about. In the public shelters it is usually a case of standing room only, which becomes hard on the feet after an hour or so." By September, there were many casualties and a great deal of damage had been done. Newspaper announcements of deaths were covered by the euphemistic phrase "died very suddenly."

Life in a bombed city means adapting oneself in all kinds of ways all the time. The calm behavior of the average individual continues to be amazing. Commuting suburbanites, who up to yesterday had experienced worse bombardments than people living in Central London, placidly bragged to fellow passengers on the morning trains about the size of bomb craters in their neighbourhoods, as in a more peaceful summer they would have bragged about their roses and squash.

But the continuing raids began to have their effects. "For Londoners there are no longer such things as good nights; they are only bad nights, worse nights, and better nights. Hardly anyone has slept at all in the past week." Large numbers of people were obliged to sleep each night in the air raid shelters, and on the morning after the raids, "thousands of dazed and weary families patiently trundled their few belongings in perambulators away from the wreckage of their homes."

The Nazi attack bore down heaviest on badly nourished, poorly clothed people —the worst equipped of any to stand the appalling physical strain, if it were not for the stoutness of their cockney hearts. Relief workers sorted them into schools and other centres to be fed, rested, and provided with billets. Subsequent raids killed many of the homeless as they waited.

More and more people were forced by the dangers of the bombing or by the destruction of their homes to seek shelter in the underground railway stations.

Each morning more are leaving their underground sanctuary to go back and find a heap of rubble and splinters where their houses used to be. The bravery of these people has to be seen to be believed. They would be heart-rending to look at if they didn't so conspicuously refuse to appear heart-rending.

And so it went on, with loss of sleep continuing to "be as menacing as bombs (and) the courage, humour and kindliness of ordinary people continued to be astonishing under conditions which possess many of the features of a nightmare."

Panter-Downes, like so many other observers, paid particular tribute to the people who continued to provide essential services during the raids. Firemen, wardens, home guards, and nurses were killed while on duty. "Nurses have been under fire constantly, for several hospitals have been hit more than once. St. Thomas' on the river opposite the Houses of Parliament . . . is a tragic site, its wards ripped open by bombs." By general agreement, these workers performed extraordinarily well despite the dangers and fatigue. Very few of them developed psychological disorders or significant fear reactions.

ADAPTING TO THE RAIDS

Philip Vernon gathered reports from 50 doctors and psychologists (including the young H. J. Eysenck) who had endured the raids and reported that people reacted fearfully to the early threats and raids. "Before the end of 1940, however, Londoners were generally taking no notice of sirens at all unless accompanied by the noise of planes and gunfire or bombs."[9] This rapid *habituation* (adaptation) to the intense stimulation that signaled the imminent appearance of danger is one of the most striking findings to emerge from these experiences. Continuing his professional analysis of the data, Vernon argued,

It might be possible to arrange members of the population along a unidimensional continuum according to their degree of habituation to raids. The average position would be highest in places like London, Merseyside, Bristol and Birmingham and lowest in country villages.

The evidence suggested that emotionally unstable people found it harder to adapt to the raids, as did those who had undergone a particularly intense raid. Furthermore, "a reversion occurs also when there is a long spell of immunity from raids," an early example of the phenomenon of the "return of fear," the re-appearance of a previously reduced fear. He concluded, "there is no doubt that being with others helped the majority of people, and that those who live alone tend to find raids much more trying."[10] This is an early description of the "social buffering" of fear, described in Chapter 18. Like Panter-Downes, Vernon was sure that people with a job to do, such as "civil defense workers, mostly recover their poise readily and set about rescuing casualties, fire-fighting, etc., immediately." Even when people were exposed to intense bombing and near misses, "a good deal of habituation occurs, even to such extreme stimulation." Vernon conceded that "the extent to which people have become habituated to conditions and to noises which were almost unthinkable a year ago, still strikes one as extraordinary."[11]

Much of the information gathered during World War II has been ably reviewed by Janis, but before we consider his conclusions, two reports by British doctors are of unusual interest. Working in the large London Hospital, situated in the most heavily bombed area, Dr. Henry Wilson wrote in 1942 that "the small number of psychiatric casualties that have followed aerial bombardment has been a matter of surprise."[12] Of the 619 civilian casualties brought to first-aid posts after the air raids, 134 were suffering from the acute effects of fear. Within 24 hours, it was possible to discharge all of them, and of these only six returned for further help. Wilson also carried out an interesting comparison between people who had severe reactions to the air raids and a comparable group who had few or no adverse reactions. The surprising feature of the comparison subjects — people who had few adverse reactions — was the large number who suffered from mild fears of an *unrelated* kind. Wilson also mentions that very few people employed in essential services required help for adverse psychological reactions. Not one regular policeman was included, and the divisional police surgeon for the district reported only 1 case among the 900 regular policemen under his care. Wilson himself found it necessary to treat only 1 fireman among a group of 63 within his catchment area, despite the fact that firemen were repeatedly exposed to great danger and intense stimulation.

In his wide-ranging survey of neurotic responses to air raids, Sir Aubrey Lewis, a doyen of British psychiatry, also remarked on the comparative invulnerability of firefighters and other people engaged in essential services.[13] Moreover, the few men who required some assistance after exposure to heavy raids and were suffering from exhaustion recovered rapidly after they had rested. Lewis suggests that engaging in a socially useful occupation might have provided a form of inoculation against stress. Some people who were previously of poor mental health were said to be considerably *improved* after taking up some socially necessary work: "they have a definite and satisfying job." He also adduced some evidence to show that a proportion of chronic neurotics attending outpatient clinics "had improved, since the war has given them interests previously lacking."[14]

Lewis's report, prepared at the request of the British Medical Research Council, is authoritative and thorough. From information gathered in different parts of the country, he concluded that "air raids have not been responsible for any striking increase in neurotic illness." After a period of intense raids, a slight rise in neurotic illness was observed, but it occurred chiefly among those people who had been disturbed before the raids began.

Doctors in Liverpool "trained 18 volunteers as auxiliary mental health workers for service in and after raids but none of the 18 has been required; there was no such work for them to do." In Manchester, which suffered severe raids, there was "no increase in the number of patients attending psychiatric outpatient clinics," nor was there an increased demand for help among the adult evacuees in the quieter areas around Manchester. Various psychiatric departments in the London area confirmed that the number of neurotic illnesses had not increased significantly.

Concerning the effects on children, Lewis concluded that "there is a consensus of opinion that children show great adaptability and recover well from air raid effects, if simple sensible measures are taken. . . . " Moreover, information coming from different sources confirmed the view that "frightened mothers communicated their fears to the children."[15]

The British reactions to repeated air attacks — widespread habituation, unexpected resilience, few phobic reactions, slight or no increased in psychiatric disorders, and the exceptionally competent performance of essential service workers — have been described fully and frequently, but they were not unique. The British were remarkably stoical, in fact as in heroic recollection, and information collected in Japan and Germany after the War shows that people in those countries also displayed great resilience under repeated attacks.

RECENT EXAMPLES

Recent evidence from the Middle East is consistent with reports of the resilience of World War II civilians on both sides. In May 1982, Dr. Philip Saigh of the American University in Beirut was collecting information on the cross-cultural validity of three self-report measures of anxiety.[16] In the following month, Lebanon was invaded by Israeli forces and West Beirut was besieged for 10 weeks, during which time the population was "exposed to intermittent shelling, strafing, and bombing." When the siege was lifted, Saigh located 115 of his original 128 subjects, and 98 of them agreed to fill in the forms a second time. The post-invasion scores on the key measure (an anxiety scale that included items dealing with the conflict, danger, and deprivations of life in Beirut) were significantly lower than the pre-invasion scores (44 versus 53). Moreover, the anxiety scores of the 38 students who had remained in Beirut throughout the siege were no higher than the scores of the 50 students who had evacuated to safety. Six months later, the postinvasion anxiety scores of 55 relocated students were found to be unchanged. No differences had emerged between the students who endured the siege and the evacuees.

In a separate study, Saigh followed the course of self-reported anxiety among 12 students who were in Beirut when the militias started a major offensive in the civil war against the central government in Lebanon.[17] A week after the beginning of the offensive, their Speilberger state-anxiety scores were significantly raised, from 39 to 57, but within a month, the scores had returned to 43. One year later, their scores were 43.9. One of the students developed symptoms of posttraumatic disorder. Consistent with the possibility that exposure to military stresses produces depressive reactions in civilian populations, the students' scores on the Beck Depression Inventory rose from 9.6 to 16.8, a score that is in the clinically significant range. A month later, these scores returned, with the scores on self-rated anxiety, to a nonsignificant level.

This new evidence of human resilience has parallels on the other side of the border. The anxiety scores of 103 Israeli children who had been living in a kibbutz that was exposed to "almost constant shelling," were, like those of 90 control children in a safe area, found to be "uniformly low in the entire sample."[18] Similar results are reported from a sample of bombarded villagers. The agency responsible for providing psychological care for 150 collective farms in Israel reported that the incidence of psychological disorders was no higher in the 2 years after the Yom Kippur war than in the 2 calm years preceeding the war.[19]

Janis concluded from his review of civilian reactions to air raids that most cases of emotional shock with acute anxiety were capable of "fully recovering, either spontaneously or in response to simple forms of psychiatric treatment, within a period of a few days up to a few weeks."[20] Rather than anxiety, it was more common for air-raid victims to display an excessive docility that seems to have verged on a depressive reaction. Contrary to psychologists' expectations, exposure to air raids had little effect on psychosomatic functioning. Air raids "contributed to the wartime increase in various types of psychosomatic disorder, but the proportion of the bombed population displaying such reactions was probably not very large."[21] Surveys carried out in postwar Germany confirmed that psychosomatic casualties were infrequent.

Critics who are skeptical of the significance of psychological stress in producing so-called psychosomatic disorders will not find this observation surprising. Even if the full effects of these wartime events may not have become evident until many years after they took place, it is nevertheless remarkable that such stressful experiences were not followed by an epidemic of psychosomatic illnesses. Certainly most theories of psychosomatic etiology would lead one to predict the occurrence of extensive and intensive problems.

Reports on the reactions of children agree that although transient symptoms were common during the air attacks, "chronic behavioral disturbances following air raids were extremely rare." The evidence on this point which is comprised mainly of anecdotes, is less than satisfactory; the reports attribute fear reactions of the children to the excitement and emotional disturbance displayed by parents or other adults. For example, in his study of the reactions of San Francisco children to blackouts and alerts, the psychiatrist J. Solomon claimed that there was a close relationship between the fear displayed by the adults and the behavior of the observing children. He interpreted the children's fears as the result of "the contagion of anxiety from their parents."[23]

Information of this kind led Janis to conclude, prematurely, that "the incidence of acute emotional disturbances among young children in a community exposed to air raids will tend to vary directly with the incidence of overt excitement and emotional upset among the adults in that community."[24]

HIROSHIMA

The extraordinary resilience demonstrated by people who were subjected to repeated and severe bombing raids is exceeded by the endurance of the victims of the atomic bomb attack on Hiroshima, the most traumatic human event in history. The death, destruction, injuries, and illness caused by the explosion were of a magnitude and intensity without precedent. Given the scale of the trauma, the adverse psychological effects were astonishingly, almost unbelievably, small in extent and intensity. Although the victims experienced sustained apprehension and shock after the disaster, very large numbers of the survivors returned to Hiroshima shortly after the attack — which is remarkable, even given their lack of practical alternatives.

According to Janis, within three months the population was back to about 140,000.

Although apprehensiveness about another attack and fears of contamination may have been fairly frequent, such fears evidently were not so intense as to prevent resettlement in the target cites. From the fact that very large numbers of survivors promptly returned to the destroyed areas, it appears that avoidance of the disaster locale did *not* occur on a mass scale.

The very low incidence of psychiatric disorders was equally remarkable.

Psychoses, traumatic neuroses, and other severe psychiatric disorders appear to have been a rare occurrence following the A-bomb attacks. A small percentage of survivors probably developed some minor neurotic symptoms that were evoked or precipitated by disaster experiences, such as excessive fatigue, recurrent bodily complaints, and persistent phobias.[25]

I can think of no psychological theory — naive or sophisticated, commonsensical or scientific — that would have predicted the prompt return of the Hiroshima survivors or their extraordinary psychological resistance.

HABITUATION

Fears tend to habituate with repeated exposures to the fear-provoking situation, and powerful evidence of this phenomenon comes from observations of people exposed to air raids. The data on the British were summarized by Janis. "One important point which emerges very clearly is that there was a definite decline in overt fear-reactions as the air blitz continued, even though the raids became heavier and more destructive."[26] The bombed population displayed increasing indifference towards the air attacks, and warning signals tended to be disregarded unless attacking places were in the immediate vicinity. The emotional adaptation of the British population is consistent with that described in bombed populations in Japan and Germany.[27] It is particularly interesting that urban people, who endured more air raids, became better adapted as their experiences increased. In contrast, rural civilians, who had less direct and less frequent experience, tended to become more afraid.

Two other observations are in keeping with the habituation account. First, "variable and wide intervals between successive raids tend to have a more disturbing effect than regular, short intervals." Under most circumstances habituation is facilitated by regular and short presentations of the stimulus. Second, "during prolonged quiet intervals between dangerous raids, there tends to be a loss of emotional adaptation (or spontaneous recovery of former fear reactions)."[28] This observation too is in keeping with what we know of the habituation process (see Chapter 15).

In all, the information assembled by Janis supports an habituation interpretation of the widespread adaptation displayed by people subjected to air raids. Fear reactions are subject to a process of habituation (and probably of the associated process of sensitization) and furthermore, habituation can occur even when the fearful stimulation is intense. It has been assumed that habituation to fear-provoking stimuli, if it occurs at all, is confined to those stimuli which provoke only the mildest degrees of fear. Indeed, this assumption, which is almost certainly erroneous, was put forward as one of the major reasons for discounting the possibility that the newly developed clinical techniques of fear-reduction achieve their effects by a process of habituation.

The progressive habituation of fear reactions, despite repeated exposure to intense stimulation, contradicts expectations generated by the traditional conditioning theory of fear acquisition (see Chapter 11). According to that theory, fears are acquired by repeated associations between a neutral stimulus and an aversive event, and therefore repeated exposure to air raids should result in an increase, not a decrease, in fear reactions. Instead,

among a large proportion of the British population, exposure to a series of relatively dangerous raids during the air blitz evidently produced a gradual extinction of fear reactions, just as occurred in the earlier period when the population experienced a series of relatively non-dangerous alerts.[29]

Nor could the differing reactions of urban and rural civilians have been predicted. According to the conditioning theory of fear acquisition, the urban population, having endured more frequent exposures to the putatively conditioning experiences, should have experienced *more*, not less, fear than the rural population, who underwent fewer exposures.

It must be remembered, however, that the evidence does not point to a uniform process of habituation. The majority of people appear to have adapted astonishingly well to repeated bombing raids, but a proportion (according to Janis, 26 percent of a German sample) reported that they became *more* frightened as the number of raids increased. The increase in fear is deducible from the conditioning theory but is also compatible with an habituation explanation. Given exposure to intensely fear-provoking situations, one would anticipate that some people might become sensitized rather than habituated. For example, people who are fearful of enclosed spaces tend to habituate to repeated exposures unless they have strongly frightening cognitions, in which case they may even show increasing fear, or sensitization.[30] Bearing in mind these exceptions, we can accept Janis's conclusion that there is a "general tendency toward emotional adaptation under conditions of repeated danger exposures."[31]

We also have some information about the conditions (in addition to adverse cognitions) that might interfere with the usual pattern of increasing habituation to danger. To put it another way, sensitization to fear stimuli might be facilitated by

prolonged fatigue, hunger, and other incessant deprivations. . . . What is most often singled out as the primary source of emotional stress, however, is a type of traumatic event that corresponds closely to the *near miss* experiences described in connection with air raid reactions.[32]

MacCurdy also drew attention to the powerful effects of an exposure to a near miss.[33] Proximity to an extremely dangerous situation generates fear, whereas *remote* misses appear to reduce fears. People who were exposed to remote misses reported immense relief at the conclusion of the raid. MacCurdy attributes great importance to this experience, which he calls "successful escape." People who are exposed to remote misses develop an increased tolerance for the emotional stress of subsequent air raids; an example of "learned irrelevance." In addition to near misses and adverse cognitions, potentially disruptive factors include fatigue, heightened arousal, irregularity of stimulation, and novel stimulation.

CONTROLLABILITY AND DISTRACTION

Some evidence suggests that people who regarded the protection and relief measures as inadequate experienced greater fear than those who considered the measures to be adequate, a finding in keeping with the controllability theory. Similarly, the majority of German civilians reported that they were more frightened by night raids than by daytime ones. Assuming that people have a greater sense of control during the daytime, the reasons given for fearing night raids are compatible with the controllability explanation. The victims complained that at night it was more difficult to flee from fires and destruction because their orientation was hampered. It is also conceivable that people exaggerate the flashes and noises of the bombs at night. Noises and flashes of bombs perceived against a dark and silent nighttime background are perceptually more intense, and produce more fear.

Janis supposes that "people who face danger tend to feel less fearful if they are able to engage in some form of useful overt activity."[34] Assuming that this view can be substantiated, and Gal and Lazarus present support for the idea,[35] the controllability theory leads to the suggestion that if people engage in activities which they interpret as increasing their control over the possibility (or effects) of an aversive event, such behavior should be helpful in controlling fear. A distraction theory might lead us to predict that the fear-controlling value of the activity will be proportional to its distracting powers, rather than to the extent to which it is felt to contribute to a person's potential control.

In addition to the value of distraction and control, it is claimed that work undertaken as a part of one's responsibility toward other people is valuable in reducing one's own fears. Rakos and Schroeder showed that snake-phobic subjects who were required to help other phobics overcome their fear of snakes benefited from the experience.[36] The significant reductions in the fears of these helpers were attributed to the demands of their helping role and to the beneficial effects of modeling the appropriate coping behavior. There are other examples of the fear-reducing effects of what has been described as "required helpfulness."[37]

In conclusion, the wartime observations support the view that fear reactions can be controlled to an extent if during exposure to stress, the person engages in some form of activity. Furthermore, activities in which the actor takes responsibility for other people appear to have particularly useful fear-reducing or fear-preventing properties.

THE SIGNIFICANCE OF HABITUATION TO FEAR

The psychological effects of air raids provide important evidence of human resilience, and of the operation of an habituation process even when dangerous and intense stimulation is involved. Human habituation is not confined to harmless repetitive stimulation, such as the traditional auditory signals presented in the unchanging context of a laboratory.

The widespread occurrence of habituation led Janis to discount the role of uncertainty in producing fear. He argued that uncertainty and suspense "are not generally effective in producing tense and prolonged fear reactions." Rather, the "high degree of uncertainty and suspense characteristic of periods when air attacks are expected, probably elicits active fear symptoms in only a relatively small proportion of the population."[38] The great majority habituated to the raids and showed declining fear. The facts of habituation are important, but Janis may have been misled by assuming that the raids continued to pose a high degree of uncertainty. Habituation may have occurred as part of a process of decreasing uncertainty, or even as the *result* of decreasing uncertainty. It is common for people to begin by overpredicting how much fear they will experience in a novel or alarming situation,[39] but with repeated disconfirmations of their overpredictions, the estimates become increasingly accurate.

As noted earlier, military experts, politicians, journalists, and presumably the population at large began by overpredicting the fear, panic, and hysteria that would be provoked by the expected air raids. Their predictions became more accurate as the raids continued; the uncertainty was reduced, and the population became habituated to the raids. The degree of habituation increased with increasing exposure to the raids, even when the raids became heavier, as in London during the blitz. During the first three months of the blitz, the emergency services that had been introduced to deal with the anticipated rush of cases of "bomb neuroses" treated an average of two people per week. Urban dwellers showed greater habituation than rural people, who had far fewer raids and therefore less opportunity to learn how to reduce the uncertainties of a raid. Laboratory research has demonstrated that with practice, people learn to predict their fear responses more accurately.

Seligman's theory of depression,[40] with its emphasis on feelings of uncontrollability, might lead one to predict that depression rather than fear can be expected after repeated exposures to the uncontrollable events of an air raid. As we have seen, some of the evidence is consistent with such a prediction. Among many victims of bombing raids, the emotional consequences were apathy and docility rather than fear. To quote Vernon, "There is widespread lethargy and lack of energy, even after lost sleep has been made up, and pessimistic feelings about the future."[41] In Japan as well as in England, there was "a high incidence of excessive docility among air raid victims which suggests that acute apathy . . . may occur fairly often."[42]

CAN IT BE CONDITIONING?

The conditioning theory of fear acquisition, discussed in Chapter 11, is embarrassed by the fact that so few victims of air raids developed significant and lasting fears, but it is not sufficient merely to point out how and where the available theories of fear fall short. Any and all of them would have predicted that people subjected to air raids will develop intense fears, and the failure of this prediction leaves a vacuum. Seligman's theory of prepared fears, the idea that we are pre-disposed to acquire fears to certain objects but not to others, provides some insight (see Chapter 10).[43] He distinguished between prepared and nonprepared fears; the prepared fears are said to be of biological significance, easily acquired, unusually stable, and prone to spread. Our information on reactions to air raids does not fit this description of "prepared fears." For the most part, the fears that were provoked by air raids were acute but short-lived. There were few signs of stable, generalized fears, and we must therefore conclude that the air raids were, in Seligman's terms, nonprepared-fear situations.

Seligman maintains that prepared fears are survivals from pretechnological times and that their biological significance has to be seen in evolutionary terms. Air raids, based as they are on modern technology, have no evolutionary history, and for this reason, human beings are not predisposed to acquire fears when they are exposed to the bizarre phenomenon of bombs dropped on them from aircraft overhead. Whether such an explanation offers satisfaction or not, it does at least provide some unusual perspectives on the subject of fear. For me, it emphasizes the curious nature of a species that readily displays intense fear of harmless spiders and snakes, but has the psychological resilience to endure danger and destruction from bombing attacks, repeated by day and by night.

CHAPTER 3

FEAR IN
COMBAT

Is there a difference between active courage and passive fearlessness? Did the combatants and civilians respond differently to the dangers of war? Far more information was collected from and about the combatants than the civilians, and the U.S. military authorities in particular went about the task of studying their soldiers with unmatched energy.

In broad terms, the soldiers were as resilient as the civilians. They had higher rates of psychological breakdown and reported considerable fear in combat, but these differences can be understood as the consequences of the extraordinary demands that were made of them. They served in active offensive roles, many were repeatedly exposed to great dangers, and some faced almost certain death (for example, Royal Air Force bomber crews in the 1942 campaign). Despite the perils and fear, the large majority coped extraordinarily well.

Shaffer observed that the war provided an "unparalleled opportunity to interrogate a large group of healthy young men who faced the imminent danger of death,"[1] and hoped that an improved understanding of fear would emerge. It did, and the information is unusually consistent. The significance attached to this information is not misplaced, but because the troops were an unrepresentative sample of the population, the data do not provide a basis for unequivocal generalizations about fear. For some purposes, the information is best read against the background of knowledge about civilian reactions, especially to air raids.

THE PERFORMANCE OF AIR CREWS IN COMBAT

The combat troops were young, vigorous, healthy people. They were selected in the belief that they would be resistant to breakdown, and the training was designed to increase their tolerance for fear and stressful experiences. The resilience which most of them displayed can be attributed to a combination of youthful strength and effective training. As we have seen, however, untrained civilians of various ages and states of health showed great resilience under air attack; youth, health, and training are not essential for the display of resilience under stress. The civilians and the soldiers exhibited strength under severe stress, but the specialized training and the inherent qualities of the troops enabled them to do more than "heroically endure". They were required to carry out skilled activities in dangerous conditions, and encouraged to do so even while attempting to ensure their own protection. Most of the civilians played a passive part, in which endurance was more important than initiative.

In the introduction to his 17-volume report on the performance of U.S. combat aircrews, Flanagan, who was responsible for organizing and co-ordinating much of this remarkable research, offered a piece of military understatement: "It was definitely a hazardous business."[2] In some theaters of the war, an airman's chance of completing a tour of operational duty was little better than 50 percent. For a period in 1942, RAF (Royal Air Force) bomber crews had no more than 10 percent chance of surviving a full tour of operations.[3]

Dr. David Stafford-Clark, who acted as a medical officer attached to RAF bomber squadrons for over four years and participated in some missions, wrote a vivid and memorable description of the dangers and stresses of these flights.

The air crew flew in darkness relieved only by the dim orange glow of a lamp over the navigator's table and the faintly green luminosity of the pilot's instruments, three or four miles high, through bitter cold over hundreds of miles of sea and hostile land, with the thunderous roaring of the engines shutting out all other sounds except when the crackling metallic voice of one member of the crew echoed in the others' earphones. For each man there was a constant awareness of danger; danger from the enemy, from sudden blinding convergence of searchlights accompanied by heavy, accurate, and torrential flak, from packs of night fighters seeking unceasingly to find and penetrate the bomber stream; of danger from collision, from ice in the cloud, from becoming lost or isolated, from a chance hit in a petrol tank leading to loss of fuel, and a forced descent into the sea on the way back, if nothing worse. There was no single moment of security from take-off to touch down, but often the sight of other aircraft hit by flak and exploding in the air, or plummeting down blazing to strike the ground an incandescent wreck, even when a crew's own aircraft had escaped attention. These were familiar aspects of the flying man's experience.[4]

Stafford-Clark quotes the official statistics for RAF Bomber Command, for the entire war. In this flying force of 125,000, there was an overall casualty rate of 64 percent, of whom 44,000 were killed. The incidence of psychological breakdown was less than 5 percent.

The most striking fact to emerge from combat studies is that these healthy, highly trained young people were capable of performing remarkable feats of skill and enterprise, despite repeated and prolonged exposures to danger and stress. Summarizing the information obtained from U.S. air crews, Flanagan observed that their morale remained "generally high" and that there was "very little breakdown of personnel." Most of the information testifies to the overwhelming importance of social bonds and approval. Thousands of people repeatedly risked serious injury or death rather than ostracism. The most important source of motivation was the small social group of which each soldier or airman became a part.

The primary motivating force which more than anything else kept these men flying and fighting was that they were members of a group in which flying and fighting was the only accepted way of behaving. The aircrew combat personnel were closely knit together. First because they flew, and second because they fought. In combat operations they lived together and had little contact with people outside the groups. . . . The individual identified himself very closely with the group and took great pride in his membership of the group.[5]

An important theme in this information is the significance of a person's sense of controllability and personal competence. Fear seems to feed on a sense of uncontrollability; it arises and persists when a person finds himself in a threatening situation over which he feels he has little or no control. But a sense of personal competence, self-confidence if you will, appears to provide protection against fear. The data also illustrate the superiority of a three-system model of fear over the lump theory. Combat fears were ubiquitous, but avoidance behavior was rare. These observations are an illustration of the independence of subjective fear and the escape from or avoidance of the threatening situation. Fear and avoidance were uncoupled. The persistence of these soldiers and airmen despite frequent and intense subjective fear exemplifies courageous behavior.

As we shall see, some of the information conflicts with prevailing psychological theories of fear. One of the major weaknesses of all psychological theories is the assumption that people are highly vulnerable to threats and stress. The theories are designed for creatures more timorous than human beings.

Flanagan's one percent

As part of Flanagan's series, Shaffer and others administered a fear questionnaire to 4500 airmen who had combat experience in the European theater of war in 1944.[6] The major part of this study was then repeated on an additional 2000 experienced fliers. All but 1 percent of the airmen reported that they had experienced fear on at least some of the missions. Moreover, one-third to one-half reported that they had experienced fear on almost every mission. There was some correspondence between the objective danger of the mission and the amount of fear experienced, but other factors played a part (see Chapter 4). For example, fliers who took part in the 1945 campaign, during which the combat missions were less dangerous, experienced greater frequency and intensity of fears than fliers who took part in the most punishing period of 1944.

Sheer exposure to danger is not the sole determinant of fear; the greater fear experienced by the 1945 cohort probably reflected the approaching end of the European battle. The airmen said that a time-limited tour of operational duty helped them to persevere and that their fear increased as they approached the concluding missions of a tour of duty. It is possible that advance information about the duration of fear or about other aversive experiences, such as pain, may make the experience more tolerable.[7]

The majority of airmen reported that having a commitment to fly a specified number of missions or hours was helpful in controlling combat fear and that the fear of death or injury increased as they approached the end of a tour. This finding of a type of "negative emotional goal-gradient," has been reported on a number of occasions but is not fully understood.

The symptoms of fear experienced during combat included palpitations, dryness of the mouth, sweating, stomach discomfort, urinary pressure, trembling, tension, and irritability. The most persistent of these symptoms were tension, tremor, and sleep disturbance. The most commonly reported cumulative effect of repeated exposure was a mixture of fatigue and restlessness. Many of the airmen experienced ruminations and disturbing dreams. Shaffer provided no details of the content of the dreams, but we know from other sources, such as Grinker and Spiegel[8] and Lidz,[9] that the theme of helplessness was common. Lidz described some common themes:

The soldier is helpless in the face of an attack, and if he attempts to defend himself, he is impotent. While attempting to flee he awakens with a terrified scream.

Helplessness is said by Seligman to arise from a sense of the uncontrollability of important aversive events and to cause fear and then depression.[10]

A survey of 6000 airmen suggests that the factors of helplessness and hopelessness were indeed responsible for increments in fear.

Being in danger when one cannot fight back or take any other effective action, being idle or being insecure of the future were the elements that tended to aggravate a fear in combat.[11]

The three factors rated as being most fear-provoking were being fired upon when you had no chance to shoot back, hearing a report of an enemy aircraft that you could not see, and the sight of enemy tracer bullets.

The fliers reported a change in the content of their fears as their experience of combat increased. On their first mission their greatest fear was that they might not be able to carry out their duties satisfactorily, and specifically that they might behave in a cowardly manner. On later missions these fears of personal failure were surpassed by fears of being killed or wounded. The fear of being a coward has been described by many writers, including Harold Macmillan.[12] *Expectations* of cowardice exceed acts of cowardice, and this can now be interpreted as one more example of the strong tendency to overpredict one's fears (see Chapter 17).

Breakdown

Despite a tendency to make too much of their material, Grinker and Spiegel's detailed clinical accounts of how U.S. aircrew reacted to combat are a useful source of information. The case excerpts are vivid, distressing, sometimes horrifying, and often illuminating. Their major conclusion is that the air combat was extremely stressful and that after prolonged exposure, most airmen began to show adverse psychological effects. The case descriptions demonstrate that major breakdowns can be precipitated by exposure to a traumatic event, by repeated exposure to minor stress, or by a combination of these conditions, in which prolonged combat experience is terminated by exposure to a particularly distressing event.

The onset of intense anxiety after exposure to a traumatic event is illustrated by the experience of a 22-year-old American air gunner. On his twelfth bombing mission, the aircraft sustained a direct hit and his fellow gunner received a mortal wound. After trying unsuccessfully to save his friend

he went to pieces . . . and began to tremble all over. . . . He swung his loaded gun back into the plane and tried to bail out . . . but the tail gunner caught him just in time to save him from jumping out over the target.[13]

His immediate reactions were intense and uncontrolled.

He sat down and began to smoke one cigarette after another. Thoughts tumbled through his mind without any order. He thought of his home, and then began to pray with tears running down his face. He again wanted to bail out and was restrained by the tail gunner. He felt he would never get back alive and . . . when the plane at last landed, he swung his legs out of the gun hatch and had to be prevented from jumping out of the aircraft before it had come to a stop. He explained afterwards that he was afraid of an explosion and could not get out of the aircraft fast enough. When it finally halted, he jumped out, ran a short distance, and then stopped, trembling all over.

The gunner's posttraumatic reactions are described as follows.

During the days following his return to his base, he continued to have intense anxiety. He seemed to be afraid of everything, especially of the dark. He could not shake off the feeling that someone was following him. There was severe insomnia, with terror dreams in which he saw the dead turret gunner with blood pouring from his neck. During one nightmare, he dreamed that someone, an unknown figure, was standing stooped over the end of his bed.

As in a number of comparable cases, the anxiety reactions were followed by depression. The most common pattern was for air-crew members to show a gradual accumulation of adverse effects, such as insomnia, loss of appetite, tremor, extreme startle reactions, irritability, and tension. These reactions appeared to follow a cumulative pattern, and although the great majority of fliers retained enough control to complete their prescribed tour of duty, some were unable to continue.

The psychological significance of the dangers to which they were being repeatedly exposed and their declining control over their own reactions are well described by Grinker and Spiegel. "With the growing lack of control over the mental and physical reactions came a grouchiness and irritability that interfered with good relations among men."[14] Muscular coordination was replaced by uncontrollable tremors, jerky movements, and tension. Their "anxiety may be related for a time only to a reaction limited to the most dangerous moments over the target, but it has the tendency to spread until it is continuous or is stimulated by only trivial sounds." Their ability to sleep was impaired and they started to experience nightmares. Various gastric symptoms such as nausea, vomiting, and diarrhea appeared. They also reported a loss of appetite and various pains and aches, with headaches and backaches being particularly common.

Following Seligman's theory, it is understandable that the fliers' diminishing control over their own reactions and the objective dangers to which they were exposed resulted in deficits in motivation, emotion, and cognition.[15] The shift in motivation was manifested as a decline in willingness, which was replaced by a weariness of battle; the fliers endured because they had no choice. Their transient fears grew into constant apprehension, and anxiety spread ever more widely. Cognitively, they suffered a growing pessimism about their chances of surviving. Some airmen became depressed and secluded themselves from their friends. Their thinking and behavior deteriorated; forgetfulness, pre-occupation, and brooding became frequent and ultimately even the most purposeful activities were disrupted.

Breakdowns were uncommon, but the fear that most combatants experienced was generally accompanied by a range of adverse bodily reactions. The reactions of combat infantry troops in the Pacific theater of war, reported in a survey of 6000 soldiers were, in descending order, palpitations, a sinking feeling in the stomach, trembling, nausea, cold sweat, and feelings of faintness.[16]

The military authorities distinguished between combat fatigue and anxiety neurosis. Combat fatigue, manifested by excessive tiredness, irritability, and restlessness, usually dissipated after a period of rest. Anxiety reactions were more intense, affected a wider range of psychological functions, and persisted. Quite commonly the onset of an anxiety condition was preceded by an episode of combat fatigue.

Vulnerability to breakdown

In an attempt to determine the nature of vulnerability to breakdown, Hastings, Wright, and Glueck collected data on 150 successful airmen who had completed a tour of demanding combat duty.[17] Entirely contrary to expectation, they found that nearly half of these successful airmen had family histories of emotional instability. Moreover, there was evidence of emotional instability in half of the fliers themselves, including neurotic tendencies in nearly a third of them. However, "their life patterns [were] not marked by asocial acts . . . [but were] characterized by vigor, persistence, and physical health."[18] All of these successful airmen experienced fear during combat. A large majority of them reported having suffered from combat fatigue, and some of them suffered severely. After a raid, ruminations were common. They also said that during their tour of duty, they had become more aggressive outside of combat. Almost without exception, they claimed that their accumulated tension was released by the action of combat. Thirty-five percent of these airmen had been wounded or had crashed during their duty; 80 percent had flown in severely damaged aircraft, had flown with wounded members of their crew, or both. Nearly two-thirds of them came from squadrons that had suffered very heavy losses. After enduring a traumatic incident, they felt that they could prevent the development of fear or other adverse consequences if they slept for 12 to 24 hours. It was assumed that it is easier to adjust to a terrifying experience some days after its occurrence rather than immediately after it has happened. This potentially important belief remains to be evaluated.

The results of the survey argue against any simple account of the relationship between emotional instability and the likelihood of breakdown under combat stress. Lepley found that the correlations between combat ratings and emotional stability were low, ranging between 0.14 and 0.49 but with most correlations falling in the twenties.[19] The characteristic that correlated most highly with combat ratings was flying skill. Among a group of fighter pilots, the correlation between flying skill and combat efficiency was 0.77; among heavy-bomber pilots, 0.94; and among transport pilots, 0.83.

In light of these findings it is not surprising that attempts to predict which airman would be vulnerable to breakdown had scant success. For example, Wickert was unable to find any significant relationships between the pre-combat test records of an airman and the occurrence of anxiety reactions during or after combat.[20] Moreover, the officers' selection test results did not relate to the development of anxiety reactions. In assessing the significance of these failures, we should remember that the air combat crews on whom these ideas were tested were unrepresentative: the relationship between these predictive measures and the emergence of anxiety may have been obscured by the fact that the airmen were highly selected. However, an analysis of 218 military bomb-disposal operators carried out by Hallam gives a consistent outcome.[21] There was no relationship between psychometric or psychiatric results and the performance of dangerous duties, and the few cases of psychological disturbance were not predicted by psychological tests or by psychiatric interview.

Wickert found

no relationship between anxiety reaction and conventional tests of aptitude and achievement, whether the tests are given before combat or after combat . . . [and] no relationship between anxiety reaction and pre-combat psychomotor tests, even though both these and the pre-combat printed tests were given under somewhat stress-provoking conditions.[22]

It is nevertheless of interest that "men with greater intellectual ability are better able to control their emotional reactions."[23] A relation between general intellectual ability and specific types of military competence is also seen in the results of a study on paratroop training reported by Stouffer.[24] Whereas 60 percent of trainees from the group with the highest intelligence scores completed the parachuting jumping course without error, only 11 percent of the recruits who formed the group with the lowest intelligence scores achieved errorless performance. In addition, whereas only 14 percent of the brightest recruits failed the parachute course, the failure rate among those in the lowest group was 44 percent.

Overall the studies show that flying and combat performance depend heavily on skill, aptitude, and motivation. Problems of personality, temperament, and adjustment seem to play a minor part in combat performance.

TRAUMA, AVOIDANCE BEHAVIOR, AND ADAPTATION

Despite the fact that their casualty rate was extremely high, fighter pilots were significantly more willing than any other group to accept another tour of combat duty.[25] Among the navigators and bombardiers only 17 percent expressed such a willingness, whereas 48 percent of the unmarried fighter pilots were agreeable to returning to combat duty. All types of pilots were more willing than other crew members to return to combat, and those who flew fighter aircraft were more willing to volunteer than were the pilots who flew bomber aircraft. Unmarried officers and men were more favorably disposed than married ones toward returning.

The willingness of a large minority of airmen to return to combat duty, despite the dangers, fears, and fatigue, emphasizes the complex relationship between fear and avoidance (see Chapter 18). Persisting with a difficult and dangerous task despite subjective fear, an example of the discordance between the components of fear, is the definition of courageous behavior elaborated in this book.

There were correlations between the frequency and the strength of combat fears, and a willingness to return to combat, but the relationships were not strong. The willingness of the pilots to return to combat was not related to the severity of their combat experiences; that is, to their experiences of crash landings, injuries, bail-outs, or fatalities among fellow crewmen. The relationship between fear and willingness to return to combat was positive, but so weak that even among those airmen who were afraid on every combat mission, as many as 72 percent were willing to return to combat. The willingness of wounded or injured and frightened pilots to return to duty attests to their resilience and provides one more reason for dissatisfaction with contemporary theories of fear. There was more courage and considerably less fear than our theories allow.

The remarkable absence of a connection between trauma and the willingness to return to combat is overshadowed by the even more remarkable absence of a connection between wounds or injuries and the emergence of fear. The absence of a link between wounds or injuries and fear was also noted among U.S. infantry soldiers and in civilians who were injured in bombing raids (Chapter 2). Airmen who had suffered a severe bout of combat fatigue were more reluctant than other airmen to return to combat.

Repeated exposures to combat were followed by alterations in the content of fear, a decline in the frequency and intensity of fear responses, and an accumulation of combat fatigue. The airmen's fears of personal failure soon diminished and were replaced by a fear of being killed or wounded.[26] The fear of cowardice declined from 17 percent on the first mission to 6 percent on subsequent missions, and the fear of death or injury rose from 12 percent to 30 percent. Similar changes in the content of fear were reported among infantrymen.[27] Before going into action for the first time, 36 percent were frightened of being cowardly, but the number dropped to 8 percent as they accumulated combat experience. As with the airmen, their fears of being wounded or killed became more common with increased exposure. Among the infantrymen, 64 percent experienced *decreasing* fear with increasing exposure, perhaps because of habituation. A much smaller number (14 percent) reported increased fear, or sensitization, with repeated exposures to battle. Other factors being constant (especially an absence of traumatic experiences), the majority habituated to combat conditions and experienced a decreasing degree of fear.

The occurrence of a traumatic episode, a decline in physical condition, or the accumulation of excessive levels of combat fatigue can contribute to increasing sensitization, that is, to a reversal of the usual pattern of decreasing fear. One should also remember that mild fear can improve efficiency. For example, in one of the U.S. Air Force studies, it was found that 50 percent of the airmen reported that fear sometimes improved their efficiency and that they were more accurate in their work. A large number of the airmen, 37 percent, reported that even strong fear increased their efficiency, and only 14 percent claimed that it had adverse effects on their efficiency.[28]

THE CONTROL OF FEAR

There are no absolute standards, even satisfactory comparative ones, against which we can judge the courageous performance of battalions, divisions, or squadrons, and still less entire armies. However, few will disagree with the claim that the U.S. military forces performed well during World War II. The policy for preventing and controlling disruptive fear under combat conditions seems justified in the light of present understanding, but we are not in a position to evaluate the particular measures that were taken to control fear. The information accumulated since the end of World War II is for the most part consistent with the three major policies adopted by the military authorities at the time. First, the soldiers were allowed to acknowledge their feelings of fear in the face of danger. Second, care was taken to exclude men who were thought to be psychologically unfit to endure combat conditions. Third and perhaps most important, specialized training and instruction were provided. The soldiers were drilled in the appropriate actions to take under combat, and their training generally included exposure to realistic battle conditions.

There is little evidence on which to base a judgment on the first policy, the adoption of a novel, more permissive attitude about fear. The information gathered during the war seems to be equivocal. The evidence pertaining to the second policy, the exclusion of vulnerable people, suggests that it may have been successful. Observing someone display an excessive fear reaction can produce fear in the observers, and the military research confirms that fear contagion did take place. However, given the poor predictive value of psychiatric or psychological screening for specific military duties, some of these exclusions may have been unnecessary. The third policy, based on the belief that training can play a vital part in preparing people to endure combat and other forms of stress, is probably as old as the institution of military combat. If a sense of controllability in coping with fear is indeed valuable, the traditional belief in the utility of simulated combat training will receive modern support.

There is no danger that combat training would have been dispensed with in the absence of support from psychologists, but modifying the training procedures in an attempt to achieve greater controllability over anticipated threats may be of value in teaching people to cope with a range of dangerous jobs. Clinical research into the reduction of fear confirms the value of encouraging fearful people to practice coping with situations that they perceive as threatening, over and above the benefit of teaching them to cope with representations of these threats.[29] In a survey carried out on infantry troops in the Pacific theater, there was a positive correlation between their perceived adequacy and their fear reactions during combat. In a comparable study carried out during the North African campaign in 1943, the troops attached special importance to training under realistic battle conditions. In a third study, carried out in the Italian theater, 81 percent of the troops ranked realistic combat training as the most important type of preparation to provide for new recruits.[30]

In 1977, Professor Albert Bandura of Stanford University argued that therapeutic behavioral changes result from an improved sense of self-efficacy.[31] Almost as if anticipating Bandura's theory, the military authorities based their combat training policy on two major premises. In Stouffer's words, "the general level of anxiety in combat would tend to be reduced insofar as the men derived from their training a high degree of self-confidence about their ability to take care of themselves and to handle almost any kind of contingency that might threaten them with sudden danger; and the intensity of fear reactions in specific danger situations would tend to be reduced once the man began to carry out a plan of action in a skilled manner."[32]

However, some of the findings are awkward. For example, 38 percent of the troops who expressed a great deal of confidence subsequently experienced a high degree of fear in combat. The converse was also noted. Six percent of the troops who rated themselves as having little or no self-confidence beforehand experienced little or no fear during battle. Even more puzzling are the 18 percent of the soldiers who said that they were losing self-confidence with increasing exposure to combat, even though they continued to report low levels of fear. Here, too, the converse was also observed: 17 percent of the troops who reported that they had gained in self-confidence as their combat experience increased nevertheless continued to report high levels of combat fear. During operational duties, military bomb-disposal operators showed the expected negative correlation between self-efficacy and fear, but notable exceptions were also encountered.[33]

The general trend of the information is consistent with the policy that was adopted, and indeed with the views expressed by Bandura, but a substantial minority of the troops described experiences that contradict views based on the assumption of a direct, invariant relationship between self-confidence and reported fear. In summary, soldiers who expressed a high degree of self-confidence before combat were more likely to perform with relatively mild fear during battle, but a minority who expressed little confidence also performed well. Another minority, about whom one would feel special concern, consisted of soldiers who expressed a high degree of self-confidence before combat but experienced intense fear during combat. This type of overconfidence was recently encountered in 7.5 percent of 105 trainee paratroop soldiers.[34]

THE THREE SYSTEMS IN COMBAT

Some of the puzzling observations reported during the war are more easily understood with the three-system analysis than with the lump theory of fear. Recognizing that the three components of fear, which comprise the three systems, are only loosely coupled, we can expect independent trends; the three components sometimes are discordant and they can also change at differing speeds. With this perspective in mind, some of the awkward examples are less puzzling. During battle, two of the three major components, subjective fear and physiological disturbance, are commonly reported, whereas avoidance behavior, which is generally associated with subjective fear, does not occur.

In the most interesting minority of cases, there is a discordance between the subjective experience of fear, especially the anticipation of these feelings, and the psychophysiological disturbances characteristic of fear. If these psychophysiological aspects of fear are most susceptible to habituation training, this component will decline as combat experience increases, providing that the soldier has managed to avoid traumatic exposures. The subjective component of fear is largely modified by the person's perceived self-efficacy—a combination of his actual competence and his confidence in this competence. The growth of perceived self-efficacy is facilitated by skillful instruction and training, and given a few exposures to combat, it should reach its maximum level and then remain reasonably stable. Evidence of this progression was obtained in a study of the training of military bomb-disposal operators.[35] So, providing that other factors remain reasonably constant, desynchronous changes in the components of fear are most likely to take place in the middle stages of a soldier's combat career.

Insofar as fear is at least partly a product of a sense of uncontrollability over a potentially aversive situation, the competence of the person in danger is likely to be an important determinant of whether fear will arise. As noted, there is a correspondence between self-confidence and fear experienced during combat, and the factor that correlated most highly with air combat performance was flying skill. Evidence gathered from studies of astronauts (see Chapter 20), confirms the value of confidence in one's own skill, as does the research on the training and performance of bomb-disposal operators. One of the major conclusions of the large study of U.S. Air Force personnel carried out in World War II was that if adequate aptitude and motivation are ensured, the problems of temperament, personality, and individual adjustment are relatively minor.[36] The possibility of a correlation between general intellectual ability and competence during dangerous situations is strengthened by the study of the Mercury astronauts, who were men of superior intelligence and wide competence.[37]

The outcome of the extensive study of the control of fear that was carried out on U.S. air crews is admirably summed up by Shaffer.

The study suggests that there is no royal road and no short cut towards the control of fear. The greatest factor that reduces fear is confidence in the equipment, in fellow crew members, and in leaders. Good equipment is a material problem but confidence in it is psychological. The study suggests that deliberate training procedures be set up to create confidence. . . . Next to confidence, concentration on effective activity is the biggest antidote to fear.

Men can be trained to keep busy while in the air, with meaningful tasks that are pertinent to the difficulties encountered. Social stimulation is also of great value. "A . . . commander can help to control fear by being calm himself, and by keeping all of the crew in touch with what is going on."[38] The important factors for controlling fear are confidence in equipment, confidence in the crew, confidence in leaders, continued activity, observation of calm models, and circumscribed tours of duty.

The factors found to be of less value in controlling fear should also be mentioned. Pay, promotion, hatred of the enemy, and ideological commitment played little or no part in controlling fear. Praying in combat was said by three-quarters of an infantry sample to help, especially when they were in greatest danger, but only three-fifths of the air men felt that it had helped them. It does not follow that the power of prayer diminishes with proximity to heaven.

Before turning to an examination of some of the other determinants of fear and its control, it may be helpful to summarize the major points. In face of the dangers and discomforts of combat, soldiers and airmen were resilient and performed well, even then they experienced intense fear reactions, as almost all of them did at some time. Despite repeated exposures to dangers, stress, and wounds or injuries, their fears continued to undergo habituation. Subjective fear was common; avoidance behavior was not. A small minority of the combatants developed persisting fears of pathological intensity or quality; attempts to identify signs that might predict vulnerability to breakdown were not particularly successful. Among methods of fear control, improving the person's real and perceived efficacy under realistic training conditions, as Bandura's work suggested, was especially helpful. The provision of effective, calm leaders and the support of a cohesive group made important contributions to the control of fear.

CHAPTER 4

INFLUENCES
ON FEAR
IN COMBAT

The factors that contribute to fear in combat have been the subject of study and speculation, and at present we know most about the influence of ideology, social contagion, the sense of controllability, isolation, and the imperfect relationship between objective danger and fear.

OBJECTIVE DANGER AND FEAR

There is a strong relationship between the danger encountered in battle and the degree of fear experienced, but fear is not determined solely by objective threats. In a survey of infantry veterans carried out in the Pacific theater of war, high levels of combat fear were reported even by those soldiers (20 percent of the total) who had experienced comparatively little danger. Among those who had been engaged in dangerous battles, and had observed a large number of casualties, only 40 percent reported a high degree of combat fear. Twenty-two percent of those who had endured very severe battle experiences nevertheless reported low levels of fear during combat. Some troops experienced considerable fear in the presence of minimal danger, and others had little fear even under the most threatening conditions.[1] The relationship between objective danger and the amount of fear is strong, but exceptions are found at either end of the scale of fears.

Information gathered from U.S. airmen who took part in combat during the 1944 campaign in Europe confirms the role of objective danger in determining fear. They were acutely aware of the danger of the combat missions, and Royal Air Force (RAF) bomber crews also "were aware of this grim actuarial outlook." In 1942, their chances of surviving a tour of duty were 10 percent.[2] In general, the more dangerous the task they were given, the more frightened they were. The dangers posed by flying in heavy bombers were extremely high, especially during the first six months of 1944. During this period the casualty rate among heavy bomber crews reached 70 percent,[3] and they reported significantly more fear than airmen in medium bomber crews or fighter pilots. However, even when they were in *less* danger than the U.S. fighter pilots (who had a casualty rate of 48 percent at the time in question), the crew of U.S. bombers reported greater fear. Moreover, U.S. combat fliers operating under the safer conditions of the 1945 campaign experienced more fear than had their 1944 comrades who had flown under conditions of extreme danger. The evidence of fear levels among combat air crew confirms the strong relationship between danger and fear, but other factors must have come into play. Given the mortal danger in which they operated, there was insufficient fear.

Reports on the airmen of the Royal Air Force are consistent with the observations of the U.S. airmen. In their most dangerous phase of the war, RAF crews had survival statistics that were even more grim than those of the U.S. Army Air Force in 1944, but the psychological breakdown rate among RAF bomber crews remained low.[4] When they did occur, breakdowns usually took the form of uncontrolled fear, as they did in the U.S. crews. The psychological breakdown rate in the RAF was higher among air gunners than among pilots, and four times more common in bomber crews than in fighter pilots (whose chances of survival were also very low at the period in question).

Why did the fighter pilots consistently report less combat fear and have lower psychological breakdown rates than members of bomber crews, even including bomber pilots? The greater degree of controllability that the fighter pilots exercised may have inhibited fear, and they were after all highly trained, self-confident men who had sole control over their aircraft. Sadly, this control over the performance of the aircraft was not sufficient to ensure their safety, as the catastrophically high casualty rates prove. They had almost no control over their attackers or over events. Seemingly, their greater control over the performance of the aircraft helped to suppress some of their fear even when the objective dangers rose to critical levels, but they were not without fear. Men in the bomber crews, especially the least active among them, such as the rear gunners, had less control and also greater fear; even when they were in relative safety the passive combatants were more frightened than those who had some measure of control.

The interpretation of the fear reported by combat airmen as a combination of danger and perceived controllability seems to go part of the way toward explaining the pattern of combat fears reported by different types of airmen, but whatever the full explanation, the astonishing fact is that despite the horrifying casualty rates, the airmen reported fear that was not proportional to the dangers involved.

THE INFLUENCE OF IDEOLOGY

One of the surprising findings to emerge from the extensive studies of U.S. soldiers during World War II was the insignificant influence of ideological factors on their combat fears and on performance generally. The most important combat incentive was a desire to get the war over with and return home. The second most important incentive was the need to support and assist one's immediate comrades. Idealistic and patriotic reasons were not regarded as important. For example, a mere 5 percent of infantry veterans reported that a belief in war aims was an important combat incentive.[5] A sample of officers returned a slightly higher percentage of idealistic replies (10 percent), but their primary motivation was similar to that of the enlisted men.

Even among some soldiers who were saturated with ideological propaganda, political and ethical convictions appear to have had little influence on their fears or their combat conduct. Studies of German troops carried out by Shils and Janowitz during the European campaign of World War II showed that "the solidarity of the German Army . . . was based only very indirectly and very partially on political convictions or broader ethical beliefs."[6] The information was gathered from repeated polls carried out on large numbers of prisoners of war, interrogation of recently captured prisoners, and the use of captured documents. Despite the evident fact that in the closing stages of the war they were being defeated, the German soldiers persevered in the face of rapidly increasing casualties and danger and maintained a high degree of integrity and fighting effectiveness. Desertion and surrender were uncommon. On the basis of the data that they gathered, Shils and Janowitz dispute the view that the "extraordinary tenacity of the German Army" can be attributed to the Nazi convictions of the German soldiers. They argue that the integrity of that army was "sustained only to a very slight extent by the National Socialist political convictions of its members, and that the more important motivation of the determined resistance of the German soldier was the steady satisfaction of the certain primary personality demands afforded by the social organization of the Army." The most important group was what they call the primary unit, consisting of that small group of fellow soldiers, headed by a noncommissioned officer, with whom most time was spent, in and out of combat. When this primary unit

developed a high degree of cohesion, morale was high and resistance effective . . . regardless in the main of the political attitudes of the soldiers. The conditions of primary group life were related to spatial proximity, the capacity for intimate communication, the provision of paternal protectiveness by NCOs and junior officers.

The effectiveness of this primary unit was supported by the firm structure of the larger army unit. In the German Army an important additional factor was the widespread devotion to Hitler. This devotion "remained at a very high level even after the beginning of the serious reversals in France and Germany." In monthly opinion polls of German prisoners of war carried out from D-Day until January 1945, in all but two samples, over 60 percent expressed confidence in Hitler. The authors point out that the soldiers' confidence was attached to Hitler the powerful leader and was not an endorsement of the political views that Hitler expressed.

The few criticisms that were made of Hitler's conduct were technical, not moral. With the exception of Nazis, the German soldiers were only slightly influenced by political or ethical considerations. Very few men expressed repugnance at the massacres carried out, the atrocities committed, or the initiation of destructive, aggressive war. For example, the attitude of the average German soldier toward the SS troops was not unfavorable, despite the fact that they were known to commit atrocities on civilian populations and soldiers. As Shils and Janowitz remark, the Waffen-SS units were highly esteemed, not for their Nazi connections, but because of their fighting qualities. The ordinary soldiers felt safer when there was a Waffen-SS unit on their flank.

The Spanish Civil War

The significance of these findings on the influence of ideological factors is illuminated by comparing the data collected from World War II recruits with that collected by John Dollard from American veterans of the Spanish Civil War. The majority of these 300 volunteers had spent more than six months in the front line, and 58 percent of them had been wounded at least once. They differed from the regular U.S. soldiers studied by Stouffer and his colleagues in a number of important respects. In addition to risking official and unofficial disapproval by fighting for a foreign country — one that was embroiled in an ideological civil war — they were exposed to the considerable dangers of warfare. Their training and material were inferior, they were demographically different from the ordinary U.S. troops, and they formed an exceptional part of the poorly organized, poorly equipped, and often ramshackle Republican Army. Above all, they volunteered for ideological reasons.

It is not surprising therefore that they attributed considerably more importance to ideological beliefs. In reply to the question of what they considered to be the most important factors to help a man overcome his fear in battle, 77 percent endorsed "a belief in war aims."[7] The comparable question put to regular U.S. troops[8] produced a response of only 6 percent. Even the more highly motivated airmen studied by Wickert and his colleagues regarded ideological commitment as a relatively minor determinant of their combat performance.[9] In their responses to a questionnaire dealing with the factors that help to overcome fear, ideological commitment was not among the first 20 times endorsed, although it did feature as a component of their "broad motivation." This is not to say that ideology was of no importance. The causes of the war and the war aims must have had an influence on the soldiers involved, but they do not appear to have any significant influence on the immediate determinants of fear or of courageous behavior.

Approximately three-quarters of the Spanish Civil War volunteers experienced fear when going into battle for the first time, a figure similar to that reported by regular airmen and soldiers. The volunteers in the Spanish Civil War also described the same pattern of habituation with repeated exposures to battle. They confirmed the predominantly anticipatory nature of combat fears and the occurrence of post-combat disturbances, including nightmares.

The overwhelming majority of the men felt that they "fought better after observing other men behaving calmly in a dangerous situation."[10] Moreover, 75 percent of them expressed the view that fear can be contagious, that it can be transmitted from one soldier to the next.

As in other studies, these volunteers found that concentrating on a task was helpful in counteracting fear. Interestingly, the soldiers reported that trying to set a courageous example was a useful way of reducing one's own fears (an early observation of the effects of "required helpfulness"). Their attitudes toward soldiers who finally cracked up were as lenient as those of the regular soldiers in World War II. However, for volunteers who espoused progressive idealistic aims, the veterans of the Spanish Civil War expressed harshly punitive attitudes toward deserters; 70 percent of the respondents felt that a man who deserts several times should be shot. By comparison, only 2 percent of U.S. combat fliers recommended a penalty of death.

The regular airmen and soldiers attached particular importance to the quality of their training and equipment, but the Spanish volunteers attached twice as much importance to the value of ideological beliefs in overcoming fear. They also attached far more importance to the value of hatred.

No fewer than 83 percent of the Spanish Civil War volunteers said that a strong feeling of hatred for the enemy enabled them to fight more effectively. Expressions of hatred for the enemy were not common among U.S. regular troops, and they considered it to be unimportant. Only 7 percent of 5000 U.S. airmen expressed significant hatred of the enemy.[11]

Anger as an inhibitor of fear

In passing, it might be mentioned that although we have little further information about the effects of hatred on the control of fear, there are indications that anger can act as a potent inhibitor of fear. Two clinical examples of the inhibitory power of anger were provided by patients suffering from agoraphobia. In the first case, seen some years ago, a highly competent, successful engineer became virtually housebound after he had experienced panics and developed agoraphobic fears. He was immobilized unless accompanied by his wife, on whom he had become thoroughly dependent. In her absence he was unable to walk further than 20 yards from the front gate of his house. However, he was amazed to discover that on those few occasions when he became extremely angry with his wife, he was able to travel without fear. These bursts of free mobility gradually seeped away, and after an hour or two, as his anger diminished, the fear returned.

According to Clark,[12] panics are caused by catastrophic misinterpretations of bodily sensations, and this particular patient consistently misinterpreted his elevations of arousal (especially palpitations) as signals of an impending heart attack. Presumably the temporary freedom from fear was caused by a significant change in his interpretation of the increased bodily sensations; when he took them to be manifestations of his anger, rather than signs of a heart attack, he was fearless.

In the second case, the slow but steady progress of a housebound agoraphobic woman underwent a dramatic change. Throughout the treatment, she had demanded constant reassurance and support for each small step in her retraining program. An attempt was made to fade out this excessive support, and eventually the patient was advised that she had reached the point at which she should take over the main responsibility for the remainder of the program. She took great offense at what she interpreted as withdrawal of interest and left the session in a state of anger that took several days to subside. At the peak of her anger, she succeeded in traveling home alone, for the first time in many years, and fearlessly. She decided that she was now capable of "doing everything" without further therapy and proceeded to demonstrate the truth of her conclusion by traveling widely and without fear for several days. When her anger toward the therapist decreased, she became aware of the return of a moderate amount of fear. In both of these cases, a state of anger "inhibited" severe and chronic fears, which then returned as the anger declined. The fascinating relation between fear and anger, reciprocally inhibiting at times, has yet to be clarified. The possibility that in cases of panic, and perhaps other fears, the change from fear to anger is mediated by a change in the interpretation of bodily sensations, is worth considering.

Courageous behavior and allegiance

Despite its volume, the evidence collected during World War II on the negligible role of ideological factors in controlling fear is not universally applicable. In certain conditions, ideological factors can promote courageous behavior. The evidence collected by Alexander

George from Chinese soldiers captured during the Korean War suggests that the barrage of intensive political indoctrination successfully motivated the troops of this communist army.[13] The Chinese soldiers performed with exceptional persistence under extremely adverse conditions, but when they suffered major defeats, their morale disintegrated rapidly and large numbers surrendered. Apparently the powerful effects of their political indoctrination were eroded by combat defeats. It is of interest that after these military defeats, the policy-makers in the Chinese Communist Army shifted the emphasis from political indoctrination to the development of professional military skills. In his analysis of this and related material, George aptly remarks that in many circumstances there is an indivisible connection between shared political beliefs and allegiance to and trust in the primary military unit. As far as the U.S. regular troops are concerned, it is possible that ideological determinants of their behavior were active but were embedded in other factors and that expression of them was inhibited by a resistance to conspicuous displays of patriotism. Nevertheless the evidence does indicate that *explicit* attempts at political indoctrination are of slight value in promoting courageous behavior, at least in Western armies. This conclusion is perhaps unexpected and therefore requires consideration.

Is it merely another example of the observation that the immediate antecedents of our behavior are to a large extent governed by our relations with a small number of familiar people, rather than by our broad associations with or allegiances to much larger groups? Even if this plausible assumption can be supported, it may be confined to cultures that emphasize the value of the individual, even above the needs of the community. In postrevolutionary China the wishes of the individual were subordinated to the perceived needs of the nation. The communist ideology of the Chinese government governed military conduct as well as civilian behavior, in a way that is not dissimilar from the manner in which religious ideology has governed military and other conduct in Iran since the deposition of the Shah. Unlike that of soldiers from other cultures, the fearless or courageous behavior of soldiers from ideologically driven states appears to be directly and strongly influenced by abstractions and by allegiance to large groups.

It is easy to see how courageous behavior that is promoted by allegiance to a small, familiar group can survive military defeats; the attachment to the small group is not necessarily altered by defeat of the army. However, it would be most unwise to assume that courageous behavior that is driven by ideology is always more brittle. Certainly there are examples of confusion and demoralization following the defeat of "ideological armies," but ideological beliefs and attachments are not renowned for their responsiveness to changing circumstances. The pervasiveness and historical roots of religious ideologies may make them more resistant to military reverses than are political ideologies, which are changeable and usually of comparatively short duration.

FEARS IN SOLITUDE

There is consistent evidence that membership in a small, cohesive group can play an important part in controlling fear. Military examples of the power of cohesive groups are provided by studies of combat airmen[14,15,16] and of military bomb-disposal teams.[17] With a few interesting exceptions, most people appear to be more susceptible to fear when they are alone. When they were isolated in battle, even experienced combat veterans tended to perform badly and were far more inclined to surrender. Prolonged isolation had the effect of reinforcing the soldiers' fears and lessened their resistance.[18] Civilians experienced more fear when they were caught alone during an air raid. Even the veteran war historian S. L. A. Marshall, who specialized in providing a worm's eye view of battles, experienced panic when he was isolated for a brief period during the Korean War.

So I took off afoot across the stretch with not another person in sight. Half way, three mortar shells came in, exploding within fifty or so yards of me. The terror I knew was almost overwhelming. I ran until I was exhausted. It always happens that way. Be a man ever so accustomed to fire, experiencing it when he is alone and unobserved produces shock that is indescribable. Whether the difference comes of some atavistic fear or is more truly a reflex of the purely selfish, though human, feeling that if one must die one should at least get public credit for it, is a question for the psychiatrists. I don't know the answer, I only know what happens.[19]

Harold MacMillan, who was noted for his courageous behavior in World War I, interpreted his own experience of isolation panic as an indication of the social pressure to behave courageously. He had been wounded and was making his way toward the nearest rest station, accompanied by another injured officer.

In the darkness, and the confusion of the bombardment, we became separated. At that point, fear, not to say panic, seized me. I suppose that courage is mainly, if not wholly, the result of vanity or pride. When one is in action—especially when one is responsible for men under one's command—proper behavior, even acts of gallantry, are part of the show. One moves and behaves almost automatically, as a member of a team or an actor on the stage. But now it was all over; I was alone and nobody to see me. There was no need to keep up appearances and I was frightened.[20]

MacMillan's explanation of his near panic is plausible but unlikely to provide a full account of isolation fears. At least two other factors can play a part. First, fears can be inhibited by the mere presence of other people, a phenomenon known as "social buffering" and considered in Chapter 18. Second, the presence of another person increases the possibility of control. Even if the key person is unable to reduce the probability of an aversive outcome, his companion might be able to do so, or at least contribute to reducing the odds. Failing that, the presence of another person may be of critical value in controlling the effects of the aversive event itself, or in dealing with the consequences of the event. Many agoraphobic patients who are unable to venture beyond the garden gate can move freely if they are accompanied by a trusted person. Their freedom of movement is rarely enhanced by the company of a child or of a stranger. The usual explanation for this discriminative behavior is that if the worst happens (for example, fainting), a trusted companion will take steps to ensure that the patient is protected and returned to safety. The companion increases the probability of controlling *at least* the consequences of the fear reactions.

Just as the presence of another person often is sufficient to inhibit fear, regardless of possible control, for most people who participate in programs intended to desensitize their fears (see Chapter 14), even *imagining* a feared situation is less distressing if they think of themselves as being accompanied rather than alone. It is reasonable to expect that the direct inhibitory influence of another person and the possibility of increased control interact. The powerful fear-reducing effects of parental presence are of course well known and provide a good example of the combination of increased control and social buffering of fear. In passing it is worth noting that the presence of other people can have an inhibiting effect on pain reactions, even when the factor of controllability is excluded.

The introduction of two additional factors in the social inhibition of fear is not intended to contest MacMillan's claim that social influences strongly modify the overt expression of fear and that full fear reactions are more likely to occur when social restraints are absent. The fear-inhibiting effects of these factors lead one to expect that people are likely to be more fearful when alone. Adding the assumption that people are in their most psychologically isolated state in the early hours of the morning leads to a fresh view of Napoleon's famous remark: "I have very rarely met with two o'clock in the morning courage."[21]

Solitude is not always and everywhere the breeding ground for fear. Some people experience little or no fear when confronting extremely dangerous situations alone, and indeed some prefer to meet dangers unaccompanied. The majority of U.S. fighter pilots studied in World War II preferred their solitary role and performed very well. They reported the least fear of any air combat personnel. They were particularly self-confident and competent young men, and it seems that their own confidence in their flying and combat skills, coupled with a sense of control over events, inhibited excessive fear. By contrast, the gunners and heavy bomber crewmen, who had far less control of events, reported greater fear. Symonds and Williams attributed the elevated fear of RAF air gunners to their "relative isolation from the rest of the crew."[22] The difference between pilots and gunners can be illustrated by an experience common to most of us. Driving a car under difficult road conditions is less frightening than being a passenger. The ability to exert some control in a potentially dangerous situation can help to inhibit fear reactions.

For certain purposes it might be worthwhile to distinguish between solitary and group fear on the one hand, and solitary and group courage on the other. Presumably those people who are most strongly influenced by social approval will show the largest variation in their conduct in solitary and in group situations. But people who are relatively unresponsive to social influences should show little difference in their fearful or courageous behavior when alone or in company. It seems likely too that people who are described as fearless performers, discussed in Chapter 21, should be well represented among those who are comparatively unresponsive to social influences and perform fearlessly alone or in company.

To conclude, we are more susceptible to fear when alone, but when in a group, we are open to fear by contagion. Even though we have the capacity to collect fears, alone or in company, it remains one of our underused capacities.

FEAR AND COURAGE BY CONTAGION

Fear can be inhibited by the presence of other people, by social buffering, but only by the correct people displaying the appropriate behavior. Intimidating or unfamiliar people are as likely to promote fear as trusted companions are to inhibit it. Even trusted companions, including fellow soldiers, can promote fear if they display fearful behavior. Fears are susceptible to social influences in either direction—promotion or inhibition. The effects of contagion depend on the person's history and the nature of the contact; contagion can promote fear or courage, and even a measure of immunity to fear.

Seventy percent of a sample of 1700 infantry veterans in the Italian theater of war reported that they had experienced a negative reaction to seeing a comrade "crack up."[23] Half of the total sample added that the experience had increased their susceptibility to fear. Equally high figures on the contagious effects of fear were reported by Dollard;[24] 75 percent of his Spanish Civil War volunteers reported a susceptibility to fear contagion. The strong ideological beliefs of these soldiers did not protect them from this form of acquisition of fear.

Most of our information about combat troops indicates that they attached great importance to personal leadership in helping them to cope with dangerous circumstances. A courageous example encouraged them to imitate that behavior and boosted their self-confidence. More than twenty years after the cessation of World War II, laboratory research demonstrated that the sight of a live and courageous model is more effective that hearing about one;[25] in keeping with this result, the troops benefited most from what they saw their officers *do* rather than what their officers *said*.[26] The troops rated courageous behavior as the most important characteristic to look for in their comrades.

Increases in fear or in courageous behavior through social contagion were also observed in civilian populations. Observers of civilian reactions during air attacks, as described in Chapter 2, frequently commented on the power of imitation. Parental models were especially important in determining whether children did or did not react fearfully to air attacks.

The power and pervasiveness of observational learning, a concept reintroduced and creatively elaborated by Bandura,[27] underlines the importance of courageous leaders. Skilled models are of great value in the preparation for and execution of dangerous and difficult tasks. Frightened people, especially leaders, can trigger widespread fear. This is a powerful reason for excluding from the conduct of difficult and dangerous tasks any people—especially leaders—who are likely to display uncontrolled fear reactions.

CONTROLLABILITY AND UNCONTROLLABILITY

Controlled behavior in dangerous situations is valuable in itself and helps to promote courageous behavior in other members of the group. As discussed above, controllability is an important determinant of courageous or fearless behavior, and uncontrollability or the loss of control can be important determinants of fear.[28] In a substantial cross-sectional survey carried out in the Pacific area, Stouffer and his colleagues found that combat air crew had four times as many satisfied members as were found in infantry divisions. The airmen consistently reported higher morale and expressed more favorable attitudes than did men in other combat units.[29] Among the air crews, fighter pilots expressed the most satisfaction (93 percent). In all three categories of bomber crew, bomber pilots were always top of the list of satisfied members. Light-bomber pilots scored the highest on satisfaction (91 percent), and pilots of heavy bombers scored the lowest (70 percent).

In another survey by Stouffer,[30] the average number of awards for combat air crew was ten times greater than for ground troops. One has to remember, however, that the actions of air crew members were more easily recognized. In the midst of a large and confusing ground battle, the contributions of individual participants are seldom clear. In addition, the air crews participated in discrete episodes of combat, which made it easier to rate their performance under stressful conditions. Despite suggestions that the Air Force was generous in awarding decorations, it seems likely that more combat airmen displayed acts of courage than did their counterparts on the ground. The courage of the airmen may have been promoted by a number of factors, such as the highly selective composition of the crews, their high morale, and their membership in small, close-knit fighting groups with strong group identity. The factor of controllability may also have played a significant part.

Some of the findings, such as the comparative distress experienced by bomber and by fighter crews and the differences between pilots, navigators, and gunners, can be interpreted in terms of the person's degree of control. Given that a person's sense of controllability in a potentially or actually dangerous situation is an important determinant of his fear, then combatants who had appropriate competence and confidence should have suffered less disruption from fear. Variations in the degree of fear experienced by different members of an air crew can be summarized in ascending order: fighter pilots, light-bomber pilots, heavy-bomber pilots, heavy-bomber navigators, heavy-bomber rear gunners. Discussing these findings, Stouffer and his colleagues postulated that the heavy-bomber crews experienced more fear because of the "necessity to fly in rigid formation and the restrictions upon evasive action when exposed to flak and enemy fighter attacks . . . [and] conditions which probably tended to augment anxiety reactions in all of the members of the crew."[31] The ascending order of fearfulness corresponds roughly to the descending order of control in dangerous situations. Fighter pilots, in sole control of highly maneuverable aircraft, were encouraged to operate with a degree of automony. By contrast, the pilots of heavy bombers had incomplete control of their large, slow and cumbersome aircraft; furthermore, they often were under instructions to fly in a direct and unchanging path, in tight formation, regardless of enemy attacks.

The gunners in heavy-bomber crews were exposed to the same danger, with evasive actions proscribed and with even less control over impending events. Prolonged inactivity "may have tended to augment the feelings of helplessness on combat missions,"[32] and crew members complained of the immobility enforced by long flights in cramped aircraft. During these flights they were in danger for several hours at a time, with little possibility of reducing the threats surrounding them. They complained that in addition to the emotional strain, they developed considerable muscular tension and the flying conditions precluded the release of this accumulating tension. Similar complaints about congested living conditions and the inability to carry out physical exercise were voiced by members of bomb-disposal units on operational duty.[33] If the release of physical tension is one way of achieving a reduction of fear, the cramped conditions of the air crew may have contributed to the persistence of their fears.

Fighter pilots reported less fear than other airmen, even though their combat conditions were similarly cramped. Working under cramped conditions does not preclude the exercise of a considerable degree of control, and presumably in the case of the fighter pilots, the sense of control was sufficient to counteract the effects of immobility. Furthermore, the members of bomber crews had to operate in their cramped conditions for prolonged periods of up to several hours at a time, whereas the fighter pilots were required to endure physical restriction for short periods at a time.

Another factor that might have helped to inhibit fear in the fighter pilots, despite the high casualty rates, was the need for them to concentrate intensely. In his analysis of the results obtained from U.S. fliers, Flanagan concluded that "engaging in effective activity is a frequently indicated factor in reducing fear . . . even activities that merely keep a man busy, although they may not be very effective in avoiding the real danger, tended to decrease fear."[34]

Hastings and his colleagues reported similar findings on combat pilots,[35] and Stouffer and his colleagues observed that during infantry combat the "person's mobility may literally be reduced to zero, as when a soldier was pinned in his foxhole for hours or days . . . many men have testified that the severest fear-producing situation they encountered in combat was just such immobilization under artillery or mortar fire."[36] Immobilization usually precludes the possibility of achieving control, and it also precludes a release of tension through activity. A large majority of combat airmen complained of high levels of tension and fatigue, and claimed that their tension was relieved by the action of combat. They also said that in the periods between combat they carried out an increased number of aggressive acts.

To summarize, the scattered military information on the subject is consistent with the view that perceived control inhibits fear and that a sense of uncontrollability in a potentially aversive situation contributes to fear. Most troops experience fear in combat. Nevertheless, the overwhelming majority perform their tasks satisfactorily, and serious breakdowns are uncommon. The discordance between fear and avoidance behavior fits the present definition of courage and is best construed in terms of a three-system analysis. There is a close but imperfect relationship between the presence of danger and the experience of fear, with several important exceptions in which the covariance between danger and fear does not prevail (for example, the less than intense fear of highly vulnerable fighter pilots).

With some exceptions, ideological factors had little influence in generating or controlling combat fear. Surprisingly weak avoidance behavior was generated by repeated and prolonged exposures to danger or by the repeated experience of fear in combat. Individual differences in vulnerability to excessive combat fear are difficult to predict. Most soldiers were more vulnerable to intense fear when alone.

Having drawn attention to the remarkable resilience that enables people to endure danger, injury, and distress and having expressed surprise that people are not more fearful than they are, we can now consider the curious pattern of the fears which they do manifest.

P A R T 2

VARIETIES OF FEAR

CHAPTER

TYPES AND BOUNDARIES OF FEAR

Human fears present several puzzles, and some odd fluctuations. For example, there is no obvious reason why panic disorders should arise in a person's mid to late twenties or why the incidence of agoraphobia should increase after bereavements.

THE PUZZLING DISTRIBUTION OF HUMAN FEARS

Unexplained aspects of the distribution of fears abound. Some fears are irrationally disproportionate to the stimuli that provoke them. Large numbers of people are frightened by the sight of small, harmless spiders, but comparatively few significant fears were evoked by exposure to repeated aerial bombing raids. In the first example there is too much fear, and in the second, too little fear.

Some of the most common fears are irrational, in that the object or the situation feared is neither dangerous nor thought by the affected person to be dangerous; these fears appear to have no biological significance. On the other hand, certain rational fears, which may threaten survival, are oddly uncommon. Given the great danger of driving at speed, surprisingly few people are frightened to do so.

The most evident and most important feature of the distribution of human fears is that it is *not* random; some fears are very common and others extremely rare. This non-random distribution requires an explanation, and any theory that fails to account for this mighty fact is unsatisfactory.

Nonclinical fears

In one of the earliest attempts to discover the types and degrees of fear that exist in a normal population, Agras and his colleagues interviewed 325 randomly chosen adult residents of Burlington, Vermont.[1] The classification system they used and their reliance on interview material have been criticized, but their findings are nevertheless useful and interesting. Agras and his colleagues classified the responses into four categories: mild fears, intense fears, phobias, and clinical phobias (most severe). (As is evident from this classification, Agras and coworkers distinguished between fears and phobias on the grounds of severity. This is a common practice, but the need for separate categories rather than a continuum of severity, is not convincing, and has drawbacks. It implies that at a certain point of severity, a break in continuity occurs, and it suggests the existence of other differences.) The most commonly reported type was a fear of snakes, with no less than 25 percent of the sample expressing an intense fear of this reptile. Of the total sample, 39 percent reported at least a mild fear of snakes. The second most common fear was that of heights. Among the severe fears, agoraphobia (fear and avoidance of public places and transport) was the most common, with the fear of injury or illness a close second.

Two patterns emerged from this study of adult fears. The majority of fears reach peak incidence in early adulthood and decline in the succeeding years. Examples of this pattern include fears of animals and of the dark. The second, less common pattern was that of a gradual increase in the fear, reaching its peak in middle adulthood, and is illustrated by fears of illness, injury, and crowds.

On the basis of their findings, Agras and his colleagues cautioned that theories of fears that are based on clinical psychiatric experience, with small numbers of phobic patients, "cannot be generalized to all phobias," because psychiatrists see a small, non-random sample of self-selected patients. Three-quarters of the people who were rated as having disabling phobias were not receiving psychiatric care, and they concluded that "psychiatrists do not see the milder cases of phobia, nor do they see a representative sample of the different types of phobia".[2] Their figures on disabling phobias indicate that clinicians see only a minority of even the severe cases, and these are unlikely to be representative.

The results of a community study of fear carried out by Costello[3] and of population surveys suggest a similar conclusion. Costello found a high prevalence of mild fears (244 per 1000 population) and of phobias (190 per 1000 population) in a sample of 449 women. Animal fears were most prevalent, followed by fears of tunnels, heights, and enclosed spaces, then social fears, fears of mutilation, and fears of separation. With the exception of social fears, these are not the fears, however prevalent and intense, that are commonly seen in clinical settings. Agoraphobia and social fears have the highest clinical incidence.

These findings show that clinicians see only a partial and unrepresentative distribution of human fears and raise doubts about the validity of reaching conclusions about the psychology of fear on the basis of clinical samples.

Is research on psychiatric samples a suitable analog for the study of fear?

In addition to the dangers of overgeneralizing about the nature of fear and phobias on the basis of clinical samples, reliance on these small, unrepresentative samples restricts the value of theories of fear established purely on clinical data, including the theory of psychoanalysis.

Given that fears are extremely common but seldom seen in clinics and that people who receive treatment for phobias are a minority of the affected people, one begins to question whether the importance attached to fear research carried out on psychiatric samples is justified. Do studies of psychiatric patients provide a suitable analog for the study of fear?

It has been asserted that research carried out on non-psychiatric fearful subjects is of little value, because their fears are significantly different from clinically relevant fears, usually described as phobias.[4] If this argument is accepted, it follows that most of the research on psychiatrically-defined phobias is of little value in helping to understand the psychology of fear. Fortunately, most of the differences between the fears reported by people with psychiatric problems and other people are not of great significance. Provided that the type and intensity of the fears are similar, the psychiatric state of the patient is of minor significance.[5] It has to be conceded, however, that even when the key features of intensity and type are held constant, research carried out on non-psychiatric samples will in most instances be more representative and therefore superior to research carried out on clinical samples.

Samples of normal people provide a more balanced representation of the phenomenon of fear. Undue reliance on findings obtained from people who have been diagnosed in clinics as having significant phobias is best avoided. In seeking to answer questions about specifically clinical phobias — usually defined as fears that are persistent, unadaptive, and disabling or distressing — the selection of a clinical sample is preferable, providing that it is representative of the population in question.

It need hardly be said that the fears of psychiatric patients are not *ipso facto* pathological; most are normal fears. Moreover, distinctions between pathological fears and normal fears should not rest on the clinical status of the person who is frightened. Distinctions are easily made when comparing extreme examples, but in practice the differences between the two usually rest on shades of intensity. If the intensity of the fear is graded on a continuum, as seems unavoidable, it is difficult to agree on a cut-off point between normal and pathological. This definitional difficulty does not preclude decisions, however, and intense fear reactions that are indeed persistent, unadaptive, and distressing or disabling generally are regarded as phobic, or pathological. All five of these adjectives are relative terms, and the definition assumes a unitary type of fear reaction. Despite these difficulties, the classification of some fears as pathological has clinical utility even if purists grimace. Costello found that animal fears were the most prevalent in his sample, and by adopting strict criteria, 12.5 percent of them were classified as phobic.[6] The more intense was the person's affective response to the animals, the more likely he or she was to avoid them. Interestingly, there was no significant relationship between the severity of the affective response to agoraphobic situations and the probability of avoidance. The relationship between fear and avoidance is discussed in Chapter 18.

The snake puzzle

Another puzzle arises from the distribution of different *types* of fears. Some people who live in an area containing few snakes, for example, Hawaii, nevertheless report that they are frightened of snakes. A weaker, but relevant example is also provided by the results of a survey carried out in North Indiana by Kirkpatrick; 74 percent of his subjects reported that they were frightened of snakes, even though "snakes are too rare in Northern Indiana to account for 74% of them having this fear."[7] Even allowing for a high percentage of immigrants to North Indiana in this sample, the figure is high. Is it perhaps possible to be frightened of something that one has never encountered? This question is addressed in Chapter 10, but for the present it is sufficient to observe that no theory of human fear acquisition can succeed unless it accommodates the expected and the unexpected distributions of fear.

Age and fears

Most age-related fears of adults appear to be understandable. The ability to cope with threats varies with age, and these changes tend to be reflected in the distribution of fears. For example, Kirkpatrick found that with the approach of old age, people begin to show an increased fear of heights and water.[8] Over the same period, their earlier fears of insects and animals declined. With decreasing visual acuity and physical strength it is not surprising that elderly people begin to fear heights; with the growth of their strength and competence children begin to shed their fears of animals and of the dark.

The emergence of agoraphobia in early adulthood is one of the age-related changes that is less easy to explain. Why should people begin to experience a fear of public places and travel between the ages of 18 and 25? They will have had very many fearless experiences in such places over a period of many years. It often emerges out of a background of fearless familiarity.

As the public places remain relatively unchanged, at least part of the reason for the increasing incidence of agoraphobia must be sought elsewhere. Internal changes that might mediate the emergence of a fear include ill health or a misinterpretation of an aversive event, such as fainting or overbreathing. The strengths and weaknesses of this approach are examined at length in Chapter 7, but it must be conceded that at present we have no direct explanation for the onset of agoraphobia in middle age.

The fear of insects and animals

The high incidence of the fear of insects and animals presents a severe test for cognitive explanations of fear. Even harmless snakes and spiders are extremely common objects of fear, and many people who are frightened of them readily acknowledge that their fear is senseless. Often they experience additional embarrassment from the fact that their fears are so irrational. The fears are also irrationally intense. In keeping with these two manifestations of irrational fears, it is remarkable that fears of this kind are common even in countries or areas that are free of harmful snakes or spiders. To borrow a phrase from Seligman, the fears are non-cognitive.[9]

If irrationality and intensity are adopted as the defining characteristics of abnormal fears, then the fears of harmless snakes and spiders are prime examples of such abnormality. As this definition implies, abnormal fears are not necessarily pathological, or even of clinical significance.

People can develop fears, even intense and persisting fears of animals or insects that have never harmed them. They can develop fears of animals that are incapable of harming them, and even of animals which they recognize as being incapable of harming them. Such fears can arise and persist in the acknowledged absence of any threat or danger.

To add to the mystery, people can develop intense and lasting fears of insects or animals which they have never encountered. For example, schoolchildren who have never left their virtually snake-free island of Hawaii express a fear of snakes, even of harmless snakes. Immediately, one thinks of the possibility that they might have acquired their fear of snakes by watching films or television, or read in books about frightening experiences with snakes, and it is probable that indirect experiences of this kind are largely responsible for their fears. However, it may go deeper than this because it was suggested to me by some elderly inhabitants of this almost snake-free island, that a fear of snakes was not uncommon even before the introduction of television and movies. It is possible that in those ancient times before the introduction of television, a fear of snakes was acquired and transmitted informationally. Certainly, fears can be acquired by the transmission of frightening information (see Chapter 12) but we should not preclude the possibility that people are inherently predisposed to fear certain objects, and if this is so, then snakes and spiders are very likely candidates for the "release" of these inherent deeply rooted tendencies.

However, if there is such an inherent tendency, we then have to deal with the fact that the fear of snakes, spiders, and so forth, are not universally expressed or displayed. There is no reason to presume that inherent tendencies are rigid and unmodifiable.

Fearless familiarity

In the case of the fear of snakes it is possible that people start with the inherent tendency to respond fearfully, but learn by various means, especially by disconfirmatory experiences, that snakes do not harm them. Counter-intuitively, we can argue that people who live in areas that allow many opportunities for disconfirmatory experiences should show a *lower* incidence of snake fears than people who live in areas where there are no snakes.[10] The fearful people who live in snake-free areas have few opportunities to learn fearlessness by direct confirmation. They may, however, come to regard this as one of life's more tolerable deprivations. The increasing use of satellites to beam television programs across the world may remedy this inequity, and facilitate the transmission of fears to all corners of the world.

The non-random distribution of the fear of spiders and snakes, and the irrational element in these fears, present problems for a conditioning theory of fear and some other theories. In an attempt to deal with these problems and others, Seligman introduced the concept of "prepared phobias."[11] The idea is that these insects/reptiles/animals are prepared stimuli and that human beings are predisposed to acquire strong, non-cognitive and persisting fears of them, with ease and rapidity.

There is a rational element in some of these fears, in that some spiders and snakes are indeed harmful. The second rational component is that people who are frightened of snakes and spiders, even harmless ones, learn to dislike and perhaps even fear their own reactions to the appearance of spiders or snakes. These reactions, which may include trembling, sweating, and choking, can be extremely unpleasant and are regularly provoked by the objects in question. It is rational for people to expect — and to dislike and therefore attempt to avoid — these unpleasant reactions to the appearance of snakes and spiders. This should not however distract attention from the irrationality of the original response.

At the outset it was suggested that fears of insects and animals, such as snakes and spiders, provide a severe test for cognitive explanations of fear, and so they do. However, it should be mentioned that so far no concerted attempt has been made to provide an explanation. It is possible that snake-fearful people are having "automatic thoughts," those fleeting but potentially damaging thoughts that are said to play an important part in certain kinds of intense fear and in depression. At present, we have no evidence to suppose that this is what is happening.

DO FEARS SUMMATE?

What is the relationship between the various types of fear? Are they connected in some way, and is a person who has two or more fears more frightened than a person with a single fear? Do a person's fears overlap or are they separate? We have some idea about how to answer these questions, but need a method for delineating the boundaries of fear, and the structure of fears. Some steps in this direction have been made, and it is convenient to begin by asking whether or not fears summate.

If fears do summate, how do the separate "blocks" combine and what binds them?[12] Which components of the fears come together? The question can be tackled most simply by arranging for the simultaneous presentation of two different types of fear-evoking stimuli. If stimulus A provokes fear and stimulus B provokes fear, what is the product of A and B presented simultaneously? The method of presenting two or more fear stimuli in *succession* has not yet been used systematically, but would take this form. For example, if stimulus A promotes a fear of 60, and is then followed by stimulus B, which previously provoked a fear of 50 when presented alone, will the two summate to produce a fear in excess of 60? Does A followed by B equal A+?

For our first experiment we used a simple method: two discrete and manipulable fear stimuli—snakes and spiders—were chosen for study.[13] Thirty subjects who reported that they were fearful of snakes *and* spiders, and whose fears were confirmed in behavioral tests, were exposed to each stimulus separately and then simultaneously. As can be seen from Figure 1, the fear responses did summate. By balancing the order of presentation, it was learned that neither content nor order (snake first or spider first) had any significant effect on the summation.

However, a pattern of match-mismatch emerged, in which summation was seen to occur if the first stimulus provoked less fear than the second stimulus. When they were then presented simultaneously, they summated. On the other hand, if the first stimulus was reported to be more fearful than the second stimulus, the simultaneous presentation resulted

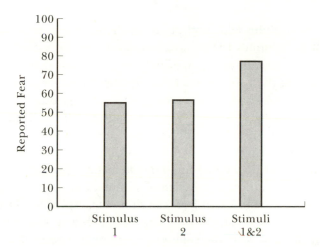

Figure 1 *Fear reported after single and combined presentations of the two stimuli, snake and spider (Rachman and Lopatka, 1986c, p. 655. Reprinted with permission of Pergamon Press.)*

in a *subtraction*. The fear reported in the presence of both of these stimuli was weaker than the fear provoked by the first stimulus acting alone.

The occurrence of summation may mean that the two fears share important attributes and therefore, when the two are presented simultaneously, the quantity of these attributes increases (adding apples to apples). On the other hand, summation might also be interpreted to mean that the two fears *differ* on an important attribute. If the fears are very similar or if the larger fear incorporates the smaller fear, then their simultaneous provocation should produce little or no additional fear. In contemporary parlance we might say that if the two fears are highly similar, then fear stimulus A should fully predict fear stimulus B, and there will be no summation. The results of the experiment, implying the operation of some form of matching or contrast effect, is consistent with such an interpretation. They also fit remarkably well into the new and expanded view of conditioning, which emphasizes the importance of the predictive value of conditioned stimuli (see Chapter 11).

The occurrence of subtraction can be explained in the same manner. If the two fears are highly similar, and therefore fear A fully predicts fear B, their simultaneous presentation should produce no summation, but only the degree of habituation that is usual when a fear stimulus is presented repeatedly. If the first stimulus evokes fear to the magnitude of X, and the second stimulus adds nothing new, then the simultaneous presentation will be X minus the habituation effect, giving a subtraction.

Other interpretations are possible, including one that emphasizes the importance of the first report of fear. If this first report acts as a pivot or an anchor, it might be given a disproportionately strong value, and prove resistant to change.[14] Hence, fear summation will be influenced by the magnitude of the first report of fear. In a preliminary experiment, Rachman and Lopatka were able to "stake out" high or low pivotal points in fear subjects, but they could find no systematic influence of the pivot on the occurrence or non-occurrence of summation.

At present, we know that fears can summate, especially if the second or subsequent fear is greater that the first. If the second or subsequent fear is less than the first fear, then subtraction is likely. Fears do summate, or subtract, but they do not do so in a simple, arithmetic manner.

The boundaries of fears

In a continuing attempt to describe the boundaries of fear, a simple method was developed for determining the interrelatedness of two discrete fears. It can also be used for separating out two or more fears. Following the investigation of summation, it was argued that if two fears are functionally dependent, then a deliberate change in one fear should be followed by a change in the second fear. If a person responds fearfully to two physically distinguishable stimuli, and we then reduce or eliminate the fear response to one of these stimuli, the person's subsequent reaction to the "untreated" remaining fear should provide an index of the extent to which the two fears were originally related. If on the other hand the two fears are not functionally related, a deliberately induced change in one of the fears should leave the second unchanged.

A fresh group of 28 subjects who were frightened of both snakes and spiders were recruited. The results of the experiment showed that the method is workable, in that it proved possible to separate pairs of fears that were and pairs that were not inter-related.[15] Contrary to expectation, however, the functional inter-relatedness that emerged after the experimental treatment did *not* match the subjects' self-estimated judgments of the similarity of their fears. There was no relationship between their estimations of similarity and the response of the two fears to experimental manipulation.

Whether we should regard this as yet one more example of the extent to which we falsely believe that we have accurate information about ourselves[16] or whether we should simply concede that the information comes from two domains that are but loosely connected is open to debate. Whatever the explanation, there is a practical lesson here. Clinicians might wish to be more cautious in their interpretation of their patients' estimations of the extent to which their different fears are connected; at any rate, these estimations may have little predictive value for the course of therapy.[17] From a scientific point of view, a method for determining the functional relationships between two or more fears should help to establish a topography of fears, and perhaps tell us something about their structure and flexibility.[18]

A fear of blood?

Efforts to determine the structural boundaries of a fear are related to means for analyzing the content of a fear. Is the negative reaction to blood a fear? It is common knowledge that some people faint when they see blood, and it sometimes gives rise to ridicule and embarrassment. The sight of operations, injections, deformities, or mutilations can also provoke fainting. For the affected people these sights are aversive, perhaps nauseating and usually repugnant. As a result they tend to avoid gory films, hospitals, and the like. It is probable that their avoidance behavior is strengthened by a fear that they might faint or feel nauseous or that they might be ridiculed for their squeamishness.

This combination of faintness, subjective aversiveness, and avoidance behavior has come to be described as a phobia. It was given the cumbersome label of "blood-injury-illness phobia," but for the sake of brevity, it will be described here simply as a "blood phobia."

This fear, if it is a fear, is of particular interest, not merely because it is common, but because it raises questions of theoretical importance. Indeed it forces us to consider exactly what we mean by the concept of *fear*, in contrast to other unpleasant affective states. A full analysis of the "fear" of blood is therefore necessary.

In the fear survey carried out in Burlington, 3 percent of a random sample of 325 people reported a fear of illness or injury.[19] The figures from a Canadian study are consistent: 4.5 percent of 499 females in Calgary reported a fear of mutilations, which in this survey had similar features to blood phobia.[20] Blood phobia is well represented in fear questionnaires that are in common use, and often comes out as a separate factor.[21]

In 1976, Connolly, Hallam, and Marks reported an odd feature of this newly labeled phobia. Unlike people with other phobias, their four patients did not show the expected pattern of psychophysiological arousal when presented with the relevant stimulus, that is, blood. Instead, they showed a bi-phasic response, in which a brief initial elevation of heart rate response was followed by a large, sudden drop in rate.[22] As Thyer and his colleagues point out, the only exception to the phobic "pattern of consistent sympathetic activation appears to be the phobic anxiety evoked by stimuli that pertain to blood, injury, or illness."[23] The occurrence of this bi-phasic response was confirmed in the laboratory by Ost, Sterner, and Lindahl.[24] Blood phobia is closely associated with fainting in response to blood or injuries, but also occurs without fainting.[25]

Many people who have a phobia for blood avoid exposure to blood or injuries,[26] but some nevertheless continue to donate their blood. The occurrence of fainting, or fear of fainting, is, however, one of the most common obstacles encountered in collecting blood in transfusion centers.[27]

Given the occurrence of avoidance behavior and the observation of physiological reactivity to the stimulus, albeit a unique pattern, why is there a doubt about whether this pattern is a phobia of blood?

First, people who are affected by the sight of blood do not describe their reaction as one of fear; rather they express a strong aversion to it. It is quite unlike the psychological experience described by people who feel they are about to be attacked by a threatening dog or who feel trapped in an underground tunnel. Their reactions to the sight of blood come closer to the aversions that people might describe when they come into contact with nauseating sights or smells. These give rise to strong avoidance behavior, but the occurrence of avoidance behavior should not be interpreted mistakenly as fear, or as an index of fear. It appears instead to be some from of repugnance, or squeamishness. Second, the physiological reactions are dissimilar to those evoked by exposure to frightening stimuli. Third, blood phobics display a characteristic form of behavior that is quite unlike any other fear reaction. Their response to the sight of blood can be muted or blocked if they adopt a recumbent position. There is no other fear stimulus that loses its power to evoke a phobic reaction when the affected person changes his or her posture.

We are left then with only one component of fear. The only manifestation of fear is the attempt to avoid the aversive stimulus. However, the occurrence of avoidance behavior is not sufficient to define fear. It can be caused by and is associated with a wide range of aversive reactions. People avoid physical discomfort, unnecessary effort, embarrassing social situations, unpleasant smells, and a range of potentially unpleasant circumstances and events.

This is not to say that "blood phobias" are without interest. Fainting at the sight of blood or injury can be dramatic and troublesome and is a psychological phenomenon that merits study in its own right. It has indeed been the subject of determined and fruitful investigations by Ost and his colleagues in Sweden.[28] Why should the visual perception of blood, injury, deformity, or mutilation (the use of the word "illness" is misleading) produce such a strong physical reaction,[29] and why is it restricted to only certain members of the population? (Other kinds of aversive stimuli, such as the smell of putrefaction for example, can also produce a strong physical reaction, nausea, and subsequent avoidance. It remains to be seen whether nausea or repugnance is accompanied by the same biphasic physiological reaction.) We also need to know what purpose is served by this apparently unadaptive response. Ethological or evolutionary explanations—which emphasize the survival value of immobilization in the face of threat or the notion that the sight of blood or mutilations signals an attacker or the threat of attack—are plausible but perhaps far-fetched.

If the people who respond adversely to blood are not phobic, how should we construe their behavior? Even though they are not frightened of blood, they find it aversive and express apprehension about their possible reactions to it. But the unpleasant psychological reaction is closer to repugnance (nausea/disgust?) than to fear. These aversive reactions are sufficient cause for the development of avoidance behavior.

If any fear is involved, it may be the fear of their own reactions to the stimulus and not the stimulus itself. It is even possible to reconstrue blood phobias as a fear of fainting; it then becomes possible to open a connection with other types of fears and phobias. If panics are caused by catastrophic misinterpretations of bodily sensations,[30] we can begin to forge a connection between panics and blood phobia. In both cases, the intense fear is provoked by a misinterpretation, or possibly a correct interpretation, of an unpleasant bodily sensation. A cognition that is probably common to both is the fear of passing out. This cognition is also commonly reported by people experiencing claustrophobic panic episodes.[31]

There is a place for such a revised concept of blood phobia. The term "blood-injury-illness phobia" is a misnomer because the affected people do not *fear* either the blood or the sight of an injury or illness; instead, they fear that they might faint, lose control, or pass out when they see blood or bodily damage. However, there is an important difference between blood phobias and panics that might prove useful in thinking about the role of irrational thinking in the genesis and maintenance of intense fears.

Panics are said to be caused by *misinterpretations* of bodily sensations, but in blood phobias there often is a rational basis for apprehension. The sight of blood or injuries produces a vasovagal reaction in most of the affected people, and this reaction often gives rise to feelings of faintness or actual fainting: 12 of the 15 blood-phobic patients described by Thyer and others[32] had a history of fainting, and 14 of the 18 described by Ost and others had "fainted in the phobic situation, and the majority had fainted many times."[33] If the fear of fainting or expectations of repugnance provide the basis for "blood phobias," it is a rational basis.

Fainting at the sight of blood or damage is not uncommon; no less than 11 percent of a student population reported having fainted at the site of blood or damage.[34] Information of this type led Thyer and others to suggest that "the clinical entity may represent an exaggeration of a response that is relatively prevalent in the general population."[35] Indeed, and most people tolerate their adverse reactions or arrange to avoid encountering blood or bodily damage.

Career planning. In a comparison of the fears of monozygotic and dizygotic twins, Torgersen obtained results which are suggestive of a genetic contribution to blood phobia. The monozygotic twins showed a significant positive correlation of 0.35 on "mutilation fears," in which blood, wounds, hospital smells, and so on featured prominently.[36] In contrast, the dizygotic twins showed a slight negative correlation on this fear pattern. Given the unique physiological pattern associated with blood phobia, demonstration of a genetic contribution would come as no surprise. The children from aspirant families who share this predisposition to react strongly to the sight of blood help to swell the ranks of lawyers. The reaction to blood is common among children and appears to be more intense among girls than among boys. The early appearance of the adverse reaction is consistent with the idea of a predisposition to react adversely to blood,[37] and the fact that it is detectable at an early age is helpful to parents who are planning careers for their children.

Onset and modification. Most of the blood phobics studied by Ost and Hugdhal[38] attributed the onset of the problem to a conditioning experience (45 percent) or a vicarious experience (41 percent). Only 9 percent said that they had acquired the reaction as a result of information received. Contrary to prediction,[39] the person's attributed mode of acquisition was found to be unrelated to the strength of the different components of the fear.[40]

Ost and his colleagues went on to provide the first controlled evaluation of the effects of psychological treatment. The group of nine patients who received nine individual treatment sessions at weekly intervals showed significant improvements that were sustained at the 6-month follow-up assessment.[41]

The adverse reaction to the sight of blood is modifiable, perhaps lastingly.[42] The manner in which the phobia is acquired needs further consideration, for although the majority of Ost's respondents attributed the onset of their problem to psychological causes, we should not lose sight of Torgersen's suggestion of a genetic contribution, or of the fact that the reaction is detectable at an early age. It may be a highly prepared (nonphobic) adverse reaction (comparable perhaps to certain kinds of food aversion), widely represented in the population, and in sensitive people very easily triggered by a conditioning event.

If the aversive reactions to blood come closest to a feeling of repugnance or nausea, the practical problem is one of assisting the person to overcome this repugnance and to cease avoiding. In the short term, the aversive reactions can be dampened by adopting a recumbent position, but over the longer term, the person's reactions may need to be dealt with by special training. In order to avoid an unwanted and inconvenient dependence on the adoption of a recumbent position, Ost and his colleagues carried out the training while the person was upright. The two methods of treatment were exposure and applied relaxation. The subjects in the relaxation group were also provided with exposure to bloody stimuli, and therefore the specific value of the relaxation is unknown. If relaxation alone produces therapeutic improvement, it would be interesting to discover whether this is achieved by some deep change in the relationship between the visual stimulus of blood and the vasovagal response. Given the lasting efficacy of exposure treatment, perhaps we are seeing a habituation of the vasovagal response. If so, it would not be surprising to find occasional recurrences, especially during episodes of elevated arousal or novel stimulation. These are empirical questions.

The construal of the adverse reactions to the sight of blood as a blood phobia, even if mistaken, as it probably is, can nevertheless lead to a happy conclusion. Some years ago, a young woman who complained of feeling faint whenever she saw blood, injuries, or hypodermic equipment was successfully treated by the use of a fear-reduction technique. The problem was construed as an unusual fear reaction, but one that would nevertheless respond to desensitization, the method in use at the time. In retrospect, it seems probable that the benefit that the patient experienced was achieved inadvertently. Following the standard procedures, she was exposed to blood and hypodermic needles while relaxed in a recumbent position. Her reactions to imaginal and then real presentations of blood and hypodermics steadily reduced. As the vasovagal reaction to the sight of such stimuli is dampened when the person is in a recumbent position, she may have derived more benefit from the *position* in which the treatment was provided than from the desensitization itself.

It is suggested that the blood-injury-illness phobia be reconstrued as an adverse psychophysiological reaction to blood and bodily damage and that it should no longer be regarded as a phobia. There is no obvious alternative label, but perhaps "blood/damage sensitivity" will do.[43] The mistaken classification of this reaction probably arose from over-generalizing the significance of the avoidance component of the reaction.

SUMMARY

Studies of samples of people who are free of psychiatric disorders provide a better balanced and more accurate representation of fear than the more common studies of the fears of psychiatric patients. Certain types of fear are markedly more common than others, and this non-random distribution of fears presents problems of interpretation; the connection between fear and experiences with the feared object is neither direct nor simple. The distribution of fears and the irrational elements in many fears suggest that non-cognitive, prepared factors play a major part in the emergence and persistence of some of the most intense and common fears.

It is now possible to map the boundaries of fears, and to assess the extent to which different fears summate, or diminish when they co-occur.

An adverse reaction to the sight of blood or damage is common and often is associated with avoidance behavior. The subjective reaction is probably one of repugnance or disgust rather than fear; a fear of blood is absent in most cases, and the physiological reaction is unlike that observed in response to fear stimuli. The physical and psychological reactions to the sight of blood or damage are unpleasant and therefore contribute to avoidance behavior. If these reactions are intense or particularly inconvenient, they can present a problem for the affected person. There may be a genetic contribution to this excessive sensitivity to blood or damage; the reactions are common in children and can be observed at an early age. Conditioning events are said to be implicated in many instances and may serve to release an existing predisposition to react adversely. Fortunately, progress has been made in developing training methods that are capable of producing substantial improvements. It is anticipated that progress in understanding this curious behavior will follow if the problem is reconstrued as an aversive, but not phobic, reaction. It is a heightened sensitivity to the sight of blood or damage.

CHAPTER 6

CLAUSTROPHOBIA AND THE FEAR OF SUFFOCATION

Many people are frightened of being confined in a closed space (*claustro* means "closed"). Small rooms, locked rooms, tunnels, cellars, elevators, subway trains, and crowded areas are all capable of provoking the fear, and people who fear one of these situations tend to fear them all. Fears of restriction and entrapment, such as sitting in a barber's chair, or waiting in line at a supermarket, are associated with a fear of being enclosed, and usually are regarded as signs of claustrophobia.

Claustrophobia is notable for the speed with which people obtain relief from particular episodes of fear. With the exception of traumatic or prolonged experiences, the fear subsides as soon as the person leaves the enclosure.

The prospect of entering a closed space causes anxiety, and affected people engage in extensive avoidance behavior. It is not uncommon to hear of people who walk up 10 or more flights of steps rather than use the elevator, or who follow extremely devious routes in order to avoid tunnels. Before considering the distribution and associations of claustrophobia, it is worthwhile asking what precisely is frightening these people.

A person who has claustrophobic reactions is not frightened of an elevator, as elevator, but is frightened of what might happen to him or her while in it. We then go on to ask what exactly the person fears might happen in the enclosed space. For just as agoraphobia is increasingly being regarded as a fear of what might happen to one in a public place, rather than as a fear of the place itself, so too claustrophobia can be re-analyzed in this manner.

The subjective feeling of being trapped may be important and certainly features in the accounts given by many claustrophobic people. Most closed spaces entail a degree of entrapment, sometimes total entrapment. Enclosed places also entail a restriction of movement. Some claustrophobics feel excessively vulnerable when their movements are restricted. The fear reaction resembles the one animals display when their flight is prevented, and it is possible that the human fear of enclosed spaces is a vestigial fear of being trapped in a way that prevents escape when threatened. It should be borne in mind that animals certainly, and people probably, are more vulnerable "in conditions of confined space"; experimental neuroses are far more easily induced when the animal is confined.[1]

The fear of suffocating is prominent in claustrophobia, and is also reported by many people who are not troubled by enclosed spaces.[2] This extremely intense but remarkably common fear has evaded the attention of psychologists for too long. At least three types of suffocation fear can be distinguished, but at present we have little information about these variations: a fear of suffocation may arise from the belief that there is insufficient air available, that adequate access to the air is blocked (for example, by a mask), or that there is adequate air but a psychophysiological dysfunction is impeding normal breathing (e.g., an airway is blocked).

Being confined in an enclosed space might well be interpreted as a threat to one's breathing, and it is therefore understandable that for those people who are especially frightened of suffocation, enclosed spaces present a serious threat. A large majority of claustrophobics express a fear of suffocating in the closed space, and in experimental investigations this fearful cognition was closely associated to the bodily sensation of shortness of breath.[3] Even though the large majority of fears of suffocation are exaggerated, they are at least understandable in the sense that very many people, not only claustrophobics, overestimate how much oxygen is needed in order to survive. For example, a group of highly educated students greatly overestimated how much oxygen they would need in order to survive in a small, enclosed room that is not airtight; in fact, it is possible to survive indefinitely in such a room. Even in an airtight small room, a person can survive for several days.[4]

There are fears of enclosure in which suffocation plays no part. There is no danger of suffocation while sitting in a barber's chair, and other than the risk of losing a piece of one's ear,[5] there is no rational basis for being frightened. The fear of crowds, which often is associated with claustrophobia, brings little risk of suffocation when the crowds are gathered in the open air.

Attempts to elicit from claustrophobic people the fundamental basis of their fear of closed spaces are seldom rewarding. Quite soon, the affected person runs out of explanations, and expresses puzzlement about quite what it is that he or she is frightened might happen. "I just feel trapped." The difficulty in finding an explanation and the persistence of the fear even in the face of credible and reassuring information, are indications of a non-cognitive quality in claustrophobia.

PANIC

Some guidance about the nature of the underlying fear can be provided by the results of recent experiments carried out on claustrophobic subjects. Under laboratory conditions, the most commonly endorsed fearful cognitions reported during an episode of panic were a fear of suffocating, passing out, panicking, running out of air, and losing control (in descending order of frequency).[6] These cognitions were linked in understandable connections with bodily sensations that commonly occur during high levels of fear. The most common fearful cognition, suffocating, was positively correlated with shortness of breath, and the fear of passing out was highly correlated with faintness and with chest pain. It was also found that certain combinations of bodily sensations and cognitions had an increased probability of ending in, or being associated with, panic. For example, a combination of two of the three sensations of choking, shortness of breath, and dizziness, when associated with a cognition of suffocation, occurred frequently during episodes of panic. Very many more cognitions were reported on the 50 trials during which a panic occurred than on the 64 no-panic trials. On every episode of panic the subjects reported at least one fearful cognition. These findings on the frequency of fearful cognitions and their close association with particular sensations, especially during episodes of panic,[7] can be interpreted as support for Clark's theory[8] that panics are caused by the misinterpretation of bodily sensations.

Most of the claustrophobic panics were associated with shortness of breath and an exaggerated fear of suffocation: a catastrophic misinterpretation of bodily sensations. However, in many instances, the occurrence of a fearful cognition, even of suffocating, was not associated with an episode of panic. The occurrence of these cognitions does not inevitably lead to a panic, and the suggestion is that it is the combination of unpleasant bodily sensations and matching cognitions that is responsible for producing a panic.

However, the research suffers from two weaknesses. The list of cognitions used in the investigations was adapted from the list prepared by Chambless[9] for use with agoraphobic subjects, and the feelings of being trapped or restricted, which now seem to be important contributors to claustrophobia, were not included in that list. It is also necessary to exercise caution because these findings are associations, and not causal relationships. The simple co-occurrence of bodily sensations and fearful cognitions with an episode of panic, does not permit causal inferences. The absence of physiological measurements during the test trials is another weakness. We have little information about this aspect of claustrophobia.

A significant elevation of heart rate occurs when a claustrophobic subject enters a closed test room.[10] In a study by Johansson and Ost, the heart rate of subjects also increased significantly, from 73 beats per minute to 79, when they were in the experimental test room. In both studies, the increases in heart rate did not vary in correspondence with subjective fear.[11] Apparently, claustrophobics experience a moderate increase in heart rate when they are in an enclosed space, but these changes are not concordant with self-rated fear or with escape behavior. Interestingly, even though the subjects who participated in the experiments on claustrophobic cognitions reported a higher incidence of palpitations and chest pain during episodes of panic, none of them endorsed the fearful cognition of having a heart attack.[12] The enclosed test room presents no "cardiac threat," and the subjects were young and healthy.

Given the frequency with which claustrophobic subjects experienced a shortness of breath (on 80 percent of all panic episodes) and the significant correlation of this sensation with a fear of suffocation,[13] it is perhaps surprising that Miller and Bernstein found no evidence of respiratory disturbances in their subjects. Possibly the occurrence of respiratory disturbance (rapid, shallow breathing?) is evident only or most strongly in association with the fearful cognition of suffocating. There is no reason to suppose that disturbances in respiration are any more or less likely than other bodily sensations to be associated with the fearful cognition of being trapped. In future studies of the changes that take place during periods in an enclosed space, all three components of fear should be assessed. The behavioral component has not been studied methodically, but we know that affected people go to great lengths in order to avoid enclosed spaces. As will be described presently, therapeutic blocking of an escape from an enclosed space is most often followed by a steady decline in the fear.

CLAUSTROPHOBIA AND AGORAPHOBIA

There is an association between agoraphobia and claustrophobia, and part of the connection might be the common fear of entrapment and restriction. It is a curious fact that many people who are fearful of small, enclosed spaces are also frightened of being in large open spaces. This puzzle reflects neither confusion nor perversity, and probably can be understood as two manifestations of a fear of being trapped. There is *no escape* route available if a threat should arise. The persistence of these fears in modern man may be a vestige of the way in which primitive people reacted to the danger of being attacked while in a small enclosure or in a large unsheltered space—flight is impeded.

Situations involving confinement or restriction of movement can evoke intense feelings of anxiety or panic . . . examples include sitting in a barber's or dentist's chair, queueing in a shop, sitting in a bus, or talking to a neighbour. In these and similar situations, the agoraphobic feels trapped, with no appropriate line of escape available. Many agoraphobics appear to plan escape routes in advance.[14]

Much of this description applies equally well to claustrophobics and supports the idea that there might be common elements in these fears.

In addition to the fear of entrapment, there is a common fear of panicking. In both types of fear, the person is frightened by the absence of an escape route and by the significance of internal stimulation. When they make a catastrophic misinterpretation of bodily sensations, they are inclined to panic. These panics, triggered as they are by internal events, can occur in public places or enclosed spaces. Indeed, any place or event that produces an increase in bodily sensations provides the opportunity for a catastrophic misinterpretation, and hence for a panic. Given the importance of shortness of breath and a fear of suffocating in the generation of claustrophobic panics, and the emphasis placed on overbreathing as a cause of agoraphobic and other panics, it should be possible to map out the bodily sensations and fearful cognitions that are common to agoraphobia and claustrophobia.

In both phobias there is a (usually realistic) fear of experiencing a panic; as Barlow has shown, episodes of panic are reported by patients with all the variations of anxiety disorder.[15] Despite the overlap with agoraphobia, some distinctive characteristics of claustrophobia have been identified.[16] Unlike agoraphobics, claustrophobics rarely have trouble walking out in the fresh air. Moreover, the difficulties which claustrophobics experience are unaffected by their distance from home, whereas agoraphobic problems are exacerbated by increasing distance from home or a safe place. Neiger and others have also pointed out that claustrophobia is unaffected by the presence of a trusted person, whereas most people with agoraphobia derive some comfort by the presence of another person.

HOW COMMON IS CLAUSTROPHOBIA?

There is a notable discrepancy between the common occurrence of claustrophobia in the general population and the small number of people who seek professional help in overcoming their problem. Presumably, most people with claustrophobia manage to avoid enclosed spaces or have learned to endure them. In roughly three out of four cases the claustrophobia is not severe,[17] and there is no need for professional help, but the gap between the prevalence of claustrophobia in the population and the small number seeking help cannot be attributed entirely to low levels of fear. Survey data indicate that severe claustrophobia may affect as many as 2 percent to 5 percent of the population, but very few of this large total seek assistance. The incidence of claustrophobia in clinics is low.[18] In part this reflects ignorance, for few people appear to know that in most instances claustrophobia declines smoothly with appropriate training.

Costello found a high prevalence of mild fears and of phobias among women in Calgary.[19] Of the 449 women who took part in his study, 66 (12 percent) reported that they had a fear of enclosed spaces, crowds, or elevators. Of this group, 18 (4 percent) said that their fears were severe. The figures reported in a study carried out in Indiana by Kirkpatrick are slightly higher.[20] Among 342 women, 77 (22.5 percent) reported a fear of enclosed spaces, and of these, 46 (13.4 percent) said that it was a severe fear (that is, very much fear or terror). Another 25 women reported a fear of elevators, and 16 of them said it reached severe intensity. The 200 men in the sample reported fewer and less intense fears. Fifteen of them said that they were frightened of enclosed spaces, but only six said the fear was intense. The highest frequency of fear was reported in the age groups 18 to 25, and least fear was reported by men between the ages of 25 and 45 years.

The related fear of suffocation was found to be even more common than the fear of enclosed spaces, especially in young females. No less than 17.6 percent of the 188 females below the age of 24 said that they had an intense fear or terror of suffocating. Nine percent of the men below 24 expressed this degree of fear. These figures are remarkable, and because there is no explanation for them at present, it points to the need for attention to be directed toward this relatively un-noticed but serious fear. The peak period for the fear of suffocation was early adulthood, but people of all ages were affected to some extent.

The results of the large NIMH survey[21] of five communities are consistent with those of Costello and Kirkpatrick, given that the questions asked of the 18,572 respondents were more restricted. "Being in a closed place" was the eighth commonest fear, and "tunnels or bridges" the ninth commonest. Twice as many women as men endorsed these fears, but there were no gender differences in age of onset of any of the fears.

It is worth mentioning that in Kirkpatrick's study, the fear of suffocating was one of the most commonly reported of all fears.[22] The incidence of the fear of suffocating was twice as common as the fear of enclosed spaces, and it is therefore evident that the fear can occur in a range of different circumstances and in response to different types of hazard.

Notwithstanding the evident importance of a fear of suffocation, two other features appear to play a significant part in claustrophobia. The fear of being trapped and the fear of physical restriction can occur alone or in combination with each other and with a fear of suffocation. The fear of being trapped and the fear of physical restriction remain to be investigated.

THE ONSET OF CLAUSTROPHOBIA

The best information about the acquisition of claustrophobia comes from a retrospective study carried out by Ost and Hugdahl.[23] Notwithstanding the weaknesses of the method of collecting the information, and a small sample, with its unsatisfactory reliance on the patients' recall of their experiences and their interpretation of that information, their comparison of three different types of phobia is most enlightening. Just over two-thirds of the 23 claustrophobic people in their sample of 106 phobic patients reported that their problem had been acquired as a result of a conditioning experience. Relative to the two comparison phobias, social and animal, significantly fewer of the claustrophobics said that they had acquired their problem vicariously. During laboratory testing, the people who said that they had acquired their fear by conditioning had a significantly larger increase in heartrate than those who had acquired their fears indirectly. Contrary to expectation,[24] the indirectly acquired phobias were not milder than those obtained through conditioning.

The presence of claustrophobia early in life, 37 percent by the age of 14,[25] is not incompatible with a conditioning explanation, but does raise the possibility of innate determination in a proportion of cases. The conditioning events that generally are thought to be responsible consist of aversive experiences in an enclosed space. This idea, drawn from clinical experience, is consistent with the conclusion from experiments on the induction of neuroses in animals, in which confinement can make an important contribution to the onset of fear.[26] There is in addition some evidence from naturally occurring disasters.

Ploeger studied 10 miners who survived an underground disaster and remained trapped underground for 14 days. Of the 21 miners who had taken refuge at the time of the accident, 6 were suffocated. Ten of the survivors were studied for up to 10 years, and according to Ploeger, all but one of them experienced important personality changes. "Phobias were observed in 6 out of the 10 surviving miners. In particular, they feared darkness, loneliness, murmuring of water . . . and confining or limiting situations. In addition, most of them complained of intrusive memories and nightmares."[27] Bearing in mind the wartime evidence of the fear-preventing effects of a responsible job and of required helpfulness, it is noteworthy that the miner who functioned as leader both before and after the catastrophe developed no symptoms.

A recent example of the probable genesis of claustrophobia by indirect experiences was seen after the tragic fire that destroyed a large section of the King's Cross underground station in the London subway system. The intense heat and dense smoke trapped many travellers, and 31 people were killed and many injured. For some weeks after the tragedy, many people avoided the system and used other forms of transport. Many expressions of claustrophobia—new, revived, and inflated—were reported in the newspapers and on radio and television.[28] On the available evidence of the extensive avoidance and expressions of fear, it is not possible to tease out the instances of vicarious acquisition (especially the fear acquired by observing television pictures of frightened survivors) from the instances of fear acquired by the processing of non-visual information about the disaster. It is likely that both of these indirect pathways, vicarious and informational, were involved. Claustrophobia probably can be acquired indirectly.

It is not possible to make definitive statements about the onset of claustrophobia, but it is probable that many people develop the fear as a consequence of enduring an aversive experience in an enclosed space. Others acquire the fear indirectly, vicariously, or informationally. Also the wide distribution of the fear, its relatively early onset and seemingly easy acquisition (one nasty experience usually is sufficient), and its non-cognitive features introduce the possibility that it might be a prepared phobia. The fact that claustrophobia is easily reduced goes against the deduction from the theory of prepared phobias but is not fatal to the essential propositions of the theory (see p. 151). On the present evidence, it is not possible to be certain about the ease with which claustrophobia is acquired, and because this is a key feature of prepared phobias, it is necessary to await further information.

SYMBOLIC FEAR

We have also to consider whether anxiety that is not provoked by enclosed spaces can nevertheless give rise to a sense of *psychological* entrapment, symbolic entrapment. Such feelings often are associated with or arise out of unsatisfactory personal relationships. In a well-known example, Dr. Joseph Wolpe described "the spread of anxiety to new stimuli based upon 'symbolism,'" in a 30-year-old claustrophobic patient. "The onset . . . turned out to be related to a marriage in which she felt 'caught like a rat in a trap.' Many years earlier she had had a frightening experience in a confined space, and this had led to slight uneasiness in such places as elevators. Her marital situation now generated a chronic undertone of 'shut-in' feeling with which the physical enclosement of elevators now summated to produce a substantial fear reaction."[29] (Incidentally, this is an interesting use of the concept of fear summation. The question of whether or not fears do ever summate is considered in Chapter 5. It also provides an example of the way in which an "unrelated" aversive event can generate a fear.)

With respect to fear symbolism, at present we have little to work on other than case descriptions. Some of these are illuminating and even persuasive, but they do not provide a satisfactory basis for deciding on the validity and nature of symbolic forms of claustrophobia. We require evidence that is collected deliberately and systematically. The investigation of symbolic aspects of fear is an inviting but complex task, and notwithstanding the scarcity of dependable evidence, most writers acknowledge the occurrence of some form of symbolic fear. The explanations range from Jung's anthropological speculations about ageless, collective symbols, through the psychosexual interpretations of Freud, to Wolpe's conditioning theory, and most recently to Lang's emerging theory of emotion.[30]

IS CLAUSTROPHOBIA A SUITABLE CASE FOR TREATMENT?

In a series of experiments, we attempted to modify claustrophobia by rational means and by repeated exposures in a small enclosed room.[31] Having learned that a fear of suffocating is the most common cognition during claustrophobic panics, we tackled it early and with deliberate naivete. We informed our volunteers as fully and convincingly as we could that there was sufficient oxygen in the test room and that they would be safe while inside it. The subjects were given written information and were told that the room was not airtight and that they could survive indefinitely. They were also told that even if the room were airtight, which it was not, they would have sufficient oxygen for 4 to 7 days. The provision of this accurate and reassuring information had little effect on the subjects' fear even though they found the information to be credible. The provision of lighting in the test room failed to produce any consistent effects on fear; some of the subjects felt less frightened when a light was provided, but others felt more frightened.

We made three attempts to suppress or prevent claustrophobic panics by providing safety signals, either in the form of conditioned signals or by the provision of reassuring information, but had limited success. The safety signals did reduce the fears to a significant but only very small extent. It is not yet possible to decide whether all safety signals have a weak influence on claustrophobia or whether we simply have not developed appropriate and sufficiently powerful safety procedures. Given the preceding analysis, the best safety signals should be those that signal access to sufficient oxygen or access to escape.

Two of the three safety procedures entailed at least some indirect modification of the fearful cognitions, but we have yet to attempt a direct modification of these cognitions. As there were no claustrophobic panics in the absence of a fearful cognition, some success might be expected from the direct modification of the fearful cognitions. However, there are growing indications of non-cognitive elements in claustrophobia, and these give grounds for caution. Are rational methods capable of changing the non-cognitive elements of a fear? Can we use reasoning to change a fear that was not acquired by reasoning?

There was some habituation of fear over successive trials, regardless of safety signals or information, and that is encouraging, particularly as the process appears to operate robustly and independently of our tactics. The subjects' reports of fear declined with scant respect for our experimental intentions. Although most of the subjects showed evidence of considerable habituation, between 15 percent and 30 percent showed an increase in fear.

In order to track down the causes of this sensitization, we reanalyzed the information from the four relevant experiments and found that there were significant differences between the fearful cognitions of those subjects who did and those who did not show habituation of fear.[32] Of the nonhabituators and those who showed no change, 86 percent endorsed the cognitive items "I am going to pass out" and "I am going to suffocate." The comparable figures for the habituators were 23 percent and 31 percent. The nonhabituators also endorsed such bodily sensations as shortness of breath far more frequently than did the habituators. Certain cognitions might have impeded the habituation of fear, but that possibility has to be examined in prospective experimental analyses.

The best information on the effects of psychological treatment comes from Ost and his colleagues, Johansson and Jerremalm.[33] Influenced by the pioneering case studies carried out by Leitenberg, Agras, Butz, and Wincze,[34] they carried out a controlled evaluation of exposure therapy and of their own method of applied relaxation. Thirty-four outpatients with claustrophobia were randomly assigned to one of the two treatment methods or to a waiting-list control group. The patients were treated individually in eight sessions and were given homework exercises to carry out. Both methods of treatment produced significant benefits, and the exposure treatment gave better results for patients in whom the behavioral component of fear was most evident; patients in whom the physiological disturbance was most prominent responded better to the relaxation procedure. This difference was interpreted as supporting the hypothesis that "greater effects are achieved when the method used fits the patient's response pattern than when it does not,"[35] a plus for the concept of treatment consonance.

The successful and stable reductions of claustrophobia achieved by Ost and his colleagues require interpretation. Given that their success can be replicated, and the incidental findings of habituation that emerged in our experimental investigations suggest that this is likely, what are we to make of the relative ease with which claustrophobia can be reduced? In those instances in which the underlying fear is one of suffocation, presumably this cognition is amenable to modification. (The cognitions associated with the *reduction* of claustrophobia have yet to be determined. For example, we still do not know if the fear of suffocation diminishes with successful treatment.) As mentioned earlier, the mere provision of accurate information is a weak method for achieving such modifications. As in other examples of fear modification, the disconfirmation might be most effective when the person repeatedly experiences the absence of any aversive outcome. "I did not suffocate." In the study by Ost, as in our experimental investigations, repeated exposures to the fear-provoking situation were part of the procedure, and they almost certainly facilitated the reduction of fear. The question to be decided is whether the exposures achieve their effects directly, and independently, or through their influence on fearful cognitions.

Insofar as the feeling of being trapped contributes to claustrophobia, it is less obvious why relaxation, or even repeated exposures, should reduce this feeling of entrapment. Relaxation regulates breathing and should overcome shortness of breath, and presumably reduce the fear of suffocation. But the role of relaxation in dealing with other types of claustrophobic fears is unclear. When trapped, a relaxed person is as vulnerable as a tense person. Breathing smoothly opens no doors.

Perhaps the claustrophobic person learns by repetition that no aversive events take place in the potential trap. Even if the person continues to feel vulnerable, he or she learns that there is no threat in that particular circumstance. The weakness of this argument is that the person would need to learn afresh in each new potential trap that he or she is not in danger of experiencing an aversive event. There should be little or no generalization from one trap to the next.

However, the results obtained by Ost suggest that the benefits did generalize; otherwise, the patients would have complained that their improvements were too narrow and unsatisfactory. In addition, there is a small piece of direct evidence to indicate that generalization of improvement did occur. At the follow-up assessments, which took place between 12 and 16 months after the end of treatment, the patients were tested in two situations that had not featured in the treatment, and the large majority of them passed both of the tests. One wonders whether those people who had started out concerned about shortness of breath and a fear of suffocating still had these sensations and cognitions.

The occurrence of generalization suggests either that the fear of being trapped played little or no part in the fears of these patients or that a fear of entrapment is modifiable by therapy and that the effects generalize. Does learning to endure one trap build up one's resistance to other traps? In order to answer these questions, the cognitive and behavioral changes that take place at each stage must be measured.

At present our grasp of the reduction of claustrophobia is an uneasy mixture of an effective behavioral procedure for reducing the fear and a groping toward a cognitive explanation for the process by which the changes occur. It is a good example of Bandura's paradox.

THE NATURE OF CLAUSTROPHOBIA: AN INTERPRETATION

Returning to the original question, what is it that claustrophobic people fear? This interpretation will concentrate on a fear of suffocating because we know most about this particular aspect of the fear and it is assumed to be an important constituent of claustrophobia. The interpretation is presented in recognition of the occurrence of claustrophobia in which a concern about suffocation plays little or no part (for example, when the underlying fear is one of entrapment or of physical restriction).

The importance of a fear of suffocation is indicated by the very high frequency with which claustrophobic subjects endorse this fear in experimental conditions.[36] Additionally, in 80 percent of the episodes of claustrophobic panic, a fear of suffocation was reported. We also know that a fear of suffocation, is associated with the bodily sensations of shortness of breath and dizziness. Furthermore, the evidence from the Indiana survey indicates that fears of enclosed spaces and of suffocation are correlated, and that the fear of suffocation is one of the most frequently reported fears in a general population.

Given that a fear of suffocation constitutes a fear of an "internal event," it is not surprising that the presence or absence of other people has little effect on claustrophobia. The only exception is the increase in fear that can be caused by the arrival of extra people; if the new people are thought to be competitors for the potentially insufficient quantity of air, then their presence adds to the threat. With the exceptions of social phobias and fears of contamination, there are no other fears in which the arrival of other people increases fear.

If the underlying fear is indeed one of possible suffocation, then the distance from home is irrelevant. The determining factor in the increase or decrease in fear is the availability of sufficient air and regular breathing. The quick relief that claustrophobic people experience when they leave the enclosed space is consistent with the idea that many of them are frightened of suffocation. Access to ample quantities of fresh air is sufficient to remove the danger speedily.

The effects of treatment are consistent with the idea that a fear of suffocation plays a part in most cases of claustrophobia. Certainly, the effectiveness of applied relaxation, in which practice in regulated breathing is included, should have a beneficial effect. The therapeutic effects of exposure are less easily accommodated, and one has to resort to speculating that the exposure trials consist of a series of disconfirmations of the threat of suffocation.

The evidence to support the importance of a fear of suffocating is substantial and well connected. However, there are reasons against accepting it as a comprehensive explanation. To begin with, a minority of claustrophobic people deny that they are frightened of suffocation. Second, Miller and Bernstein[37] found no evidence of respiratory disturbance when claustrophobic subjects entered the enclosed test room. (This finding is surprising but not too damaging because it is possible for people to feel short of breath even though their respiration is normal. It is a question of misinterpreting one's bodily sensations.) Third, the occurrence of claustrophobic fears in situations where there is no threat or actual shortage of fresh air suggests that other types of fear might underlie claustrophobia. (Here too, however, one could argue that people who are vulnerable might well misinterpret their bodily sensations of shortness of breath, even when fresh air is freely available, but this defense seems lame.) Fourth, in some types of claustrophobia, the element of entrapment might be paramount. As mentioned earlier, it seems most unlikely that people who get frightened while waiting in a barber's chair or similar circumstances are fearful of suffocating. In these situations, the fear seems to be provoked by physical restriction or by a feeling of being trapped. A feeling of being trapped, even when fresh air is plentiful, can give rise to a claustrophobic reaction.

The fact that claustrophobic fear is so little responsive to the provision of reassurance about the availability of oxygen either may count against an interpretation based on suffocation or, preferably, can be regarded as another example of the resistance of intense fears to rational persuasion.

All of this leads to the conclusion that a fear of suffocation is a prominent feature of most instances of claustrophobia but that in a minority of instances, other types of fear underlie it (entrapment and physical restriction are likely alternatives). The present interpretation is open to evaluation, and some preliminary attempts have been made to put it to experimental test. The provision of reassuring information about the availability of oxygen had little effect, and that counts against the interpretation. However, a more direct and severe test can be carried out by providing easy access to supplies of oxygen over which the claustrophobic person has personal control, given some preliminary training. If in cases of claustrophobia that are based on a fear of suffocation, this personal control of oxygen supplies proves to be effective, it will provide some support for the present interpretation. If the provision of oxygen fails to bring about a reduction in fear, at least two explanations are possible. The interpretation is wrong, or the interpretation is correct but the fear is not amenable to rational modification, and therefore would require further sifting and experimenting.

We have, however, a more direct and preferable way to test this interpretation. Any information or action that significantly reduces or eliminates the identified fear of suffocation should be followed by a reduction in fear. On the same lines, any procedures that leave the fear of suffocation unchanged should not be followed by a reduction of fear. In tests of this kind, it will be essential to ensure that the subjects are selected for the presence of a significant fear of suffocating. The methods of producing the changes, whether they are cognitive or relaxation or exposure practice, are of secondary importance. Any intervention that significantly alters the fear of suffocation will do.

SUMMARY

Claustrophobia is a stable fear of a variety of enclosed spaces. Approximately 10 percent of the population experience the fear, and for roughly 2 percent of them, the fear is severe. The peak age for the fear is 18 to 25 years, more women than men experience it, and in approximately a third of the instances the onset can be traced to childhood. A majority report that they acquired a fear as the result of an unpleasant (conditioning) experience. The second most common attribution is to vicarious experiences. Claustrophobia is associated with extensive avoidance behavior, but only a small number of affected people seek professional help.

A fear of suffocating appears to be an important element of claustrophobia. It is the most commonly endorsed fearful cognition and is reported in 80 percent of episodes of experimental panic. It frequently is associated with shortness of breath and dizziness during episodes of panic. A fear of entrapment and a fear of restriction may also play a part in a proportion of claustrophobic fears.

Given the wide distribution of the fear, its relatively early onset, its apparent ease of acquisition, and its non-cognitive features, claustrophobia may be a prepared phobia. The fear is not easily reduced by cognitive methods, but it does undergo a smooth and regular decline with repeated and controlled experiences of periods in selected enclosures.

CHAPTER 7

AGORAPHOBIA: CORE OR CONTEXT?

The concept of agoraphobia—the prototypical modern neurosis because it is so common and because its features contain the essence of neurotic behavior—has been severely criticized in the past few years and may not survive. The main features of agoraphobia are a fear and avoidance of public places and of traveling, especially in public transport.[1] These features sometimes are associated with a fear of being alone, even at home. Affected people report that they are frightened of passing out, having a heart attack, being trapped, losing control, or experiencing some other aversive outcome.[2] They describe unpleasant bodily sensations in anticipation of and during excursions away from safety, which is in most cases their own home. In severe cases the person is immobilized unless accompanied by a trusted companion, and even then his or her mobility may be tightly constricted. The disorder usually emerges in early adulthood and is at least twice as common in women as in men. Agoraphobia is the most common neurosis seen in psychological and psychiatric clinics, ranging from 2 percent to 10 percent of neurotic patients, and the number of people in the general population who are agoraphobic varies from survey to survey, but the range is from 1 in 1000, at a specific point in time, to as high as 3 in 100 (over a 6-month period), with a lifetime prevalence of 7.7 percent in women and 2.9 percent in men.[3]

Agoraphobia often is associated with claustrophobia or other psychological problems, but most frequently with depression. Agoraphobics have high levels of general anxiety.[4] Their levels of fear and avoidance show daily or weekly fluctuations, but the essential fear and avoidance often persist for many years. A proportion of agoraphobics improve spontaneously,[5] and the problem responds moderately well to treatment.[6] Repeated practice in which the person methodically enters situations that provoke the fear, the so-called exposure treatment method, is a dependable way of achieving improvements but tends to leave the patient with residual fear.

AGORAPHOBIA AS A TEST CASE

The subject of agoraphobia rose to prominence in the early 1950s because of its common appearance in clinics. The fear was well suited for treatment by the newly emerging methods of behavior therapy and presented a welcome challenge to proponents of the radically new "learning theory" of neurosis, from which the behavioral methods of treatment were derived.[7] Learning theorists such as Eysenck and Wolpe, strongly influenced by behaviorist theories, with their empirical basis and insistence on the study of observable behavior, were early to recognize that agoraphobia could be used as a valuable testing ground for their radical views.

Unadaptive avoidance *behavior* is a central, major, and accessible feature of agoraphobia, a common, severe neurosis that was resistant to the treatments available at the time. The hope then was to modify the unadaptive behavior, which certainly was open to observation and could be measured. Agoraphobia was an apt choice for another reason. The learning theory that Eysenck, Wolpe, and others were attempting to apply to clinical problems arose out of and was supported by a large collection of information on the behavior of small animals that had been collected by laboratory investigators intent on understanding the nature of avoidance learning. The proponents of the clinical application of learning theory were familiar with the concepts and methods of studying avoidance behavior, and they readily construed agoraphobia in these terms. What promotes avoidance behavior? Why is it so persistent? Can it be extinguished or modified? These were familiar questions to laboratory psychologists, and writers such as Eysenck and Wolpe began to direct the same questions to the neuroses, especially agoraphobia.

The *acquisition* of agoraphobia was also approached in this style. If agoraphobia is construed largely as a problem of persistent, maladaptive avoidance behavior, one needs to know why such avoidance arises in the first place. Another important component of agoraphobia is the person's description and display of *fear*. Here too there were experimental guides, some of them originating in Pavlov's own laboratory.[8] In particular, it was known that experimental neuroses can be induced in animals by the methods of conditioning, and the ideas underlying this work were introduced into the study and treatment of agoraphobia and other neuroses.[9]

Conditioned fear was thought to be a central component of most neuroses, including agoraphobia, and was an integral part of Wolpe's comprehensive theory.[10] Along similar lines, Eysenck asserted that it is "very difficult to deny that neurotic reactions, like all others are *learned* reactions, and must obey the rules of learning" (original emphasis).[11] He viewed neurotic problems as conditioned reactions, and agoraphobia fell into the first of two classes of such reactions, which he labeled "surplus." In agoraphobia, it was argued, the conditioned stimuli that evoke fear consist of public places, public transport, and so on. It was argued furthermore that the conditioned fear gives rise to avoidance behavior, for people learn to avoid places in which they have experienced fear or pain.

For a period this approach was valuable, and it supported and promoted novel methods of treatment. The theory was simple but ambitious. It was derived from and connected to experimental findings, and many psychologists found it to be plausible. In part because of the encouraging results of the new treatments, the theory attracted attention and support.

The treatment methods and the results were not predictable from the main competing theory, which was psychodynamic. To the contrary, psychodynamic theorists argued that the whole enterprise was misguided, at the very least, and predicted that behavior therapy was bound to fail. It was said that at its (poor) best, the therapy is superficial, might be harmful, and certainly would be followed by substitute symptoms.[12] These pessimistic expectations were disconfirmed.

Despite its appeal and progress, however, the conditioning theory of neuroses began to strike problems. The theory of fear acquisition, discussed in Chapter 11, was criticized on the grounds of insufficient clinical evidence, among other problems, and it became clear that the assumption of a simple connection between fear and avoidance behavior could not be sustained. Important exceptions to this postulated connection were noted. The conditioning account of agoraphobia encountered particular difficulties, and a wrangle developed over what counts as a "precipitating event." If agoraphobia is a conditioned response to public places and arises from an association between a fearful event and a public setting, can it then be satisfactorily regarded as a conditioned form of acquisition? Some critics argued that this explanation begs the question because one needs to know why the original fear occurred in the first place.

Whatever the dispute about the nature of the precipitating fearful event, there was and remains agreement that after such an event or series of frightening events, it is highly probable that the person will develop conditioned fear reactions to the context in which the fear was evoked. This view received partial confirmation from the reports given by agoraphobic patients, many of whom attribute the onset of their problems to a precipitating event of a fearful type. For example, Ost and Hugdahl found that 81 percent of their 88 agoraphobic patients attributed the onset of their fear to a conditioning experience.[13] Reports form other groups of patients produced lower figures. Seventy percent of Thorpe and Burns's 963 agoraphobics reported a precipitating event, but only 38 percent of the total described the precipitating event in a way consistent with a conditioning explanation.[14] Mathews, Gelder, and Johnston put the figure even lower.[15] Even if it is possible to encompass the onset of agoraphobia within the conditioning theory, other difficulties remain. For example, it is difficult to account for agoraphobia that arises after a non-fearful event, such as a bereavement. In the series described by Thorpe and Burns, up to 10 percent of the patients reported that their problems began after a death.[16] It is also difficult to explain why a proportion of agoraphobic patients fear being left alone at home if their problem is construed as a fear of public places or public transport. There is little danger, after all, of the No. 24 bus turning up in one's kitchen.

The argument that agoraphobia arises as the result of a conditioned fear developed in a public place after a precipitating fearful event is plausible, but leaves the nature of the precipitating event unclear. Even at its most successful, the conditioning theory of agoraphobia is silent on a number of questions, including the following. What accounts for the age distribution of the disorder (why are females over-represented)? Is agoraphobia a distinct illness, is it an illness at all? Are agoraphobics really frightened of public places, and if they are not, what is the basic fear? What accounts for the daily fluctuations and the spontaneous remission rate? These questions will be tackled in due course, but first it is worthwhile to point out that the term *agoraphobia* is regarded as a misnomer. According to Hallam, "Agoraphobia is not a central core feature of a phobic syndrome, but a variable feature of patients with neurotic anxieties."[17]

AGORAPHOBIA AND ANXIETY

In his challenging critique, Hallam argued that agoraphobia is not a phobia "in the sense of fear attached to a discrete set of cues" and claimed that agoraphobia is indistinguishable from states of *general* anxiety.[18] The fears that are said to be typical of agoraphobia usually are found to be correlated and tend to emerge as a connected set or cluster when a factor analysis is carried out.[19] Hallam concedes that the statistical studies are "reasonably consistent in demonstrating the existence of a factor loaded for items measuring fears of public situations and various forms of somatic distress."[20] The strongest and most consistent associations are between fears of public places, public transport, and shopping. These fears tend to be positively, but weakly, correlated with a fear of being alone. The statistical associations are broadly consistent with clinical descriptions.

What then is the problem? On close inspection, it turns out that agoraphobic people might be frightened not of public places, or buses, or department stores as such, but of what might happen to them in such places. These places are the context, not the core.

If agoraphobics are frightened of these places as discrete phobic cues, why is the fear partly suppressed by the presence of a trusted companion? Why do the fears show such notable fluctuations, day by day and week by week? The buses, buildings, and department stores do not change from day to day or week to week, at least not in tune with the person's fluctuating fear of them.

Hallam's questioning of the discreteness of these phobic cues is well taken, and he emphasizes the presence of *general* anxiety in agoraphobia. He prefers to regard agoraphobia as part of a generalized state of anxiety in which the already anxious person responds to certain cues that spark off a stronger fear reaction. An alternative, which acknowledges that most agoraphobics report elevated levels of general anxiety, is that the fear of public places and transport are indeed cues for fear, but they are secondary to and conditional upon more basic fears.

What is the core?

The idea that there is an underlying fear was prompted by the recognition that the large majority of agoraphobics have a history of panic episodes. It is probable that the agoraphobic avoidance develops as a consequence of these panics. The cognitions that promote the panics and, in turn, the fear of the panics are the basis for the observed agoraphobic avoidance. These ideas are discussed in Chapter 8 and are mentioned here in order to explain one of the major reasons for the reconsideration of agoraphobia.

The idea that agoraphobics have an underlying fear is used by several theorists (for example, by Chambless and Goldstein, in their concept of "fear and fear" and by Clark[21] in his cognitive theory of panic), but the common idea is that fundamentally agoraphobics are frightened about what might happen to *them*, to their minds and their bodies. If the fear is imminent and intense, a panic might result. If a person is frightened of having a heart attack or passing out, then excursions into crowded public places take on a threatening quality. If the underlying fear is that of having a heart attack, then traveling alone, far from medical help, is particularly dangerous. If the underlying fear is of going crazy, then the person might take particular care to avoid public gatherings in enclosed spaces, such as busy cinemas or theaters.

The fear-reducing effect of a trusted companion becomes intelligible in this context: the presence of another person might help to reduce the danger, or at very least, ensure that if something awful does happen, steps will be taken to ensure the affected person's safety. The idea can also be used to explain why there is a correlation, however weak, between the fear of public places and the fear of being alone at home. For if the underlying fear is of a threat to one's health, such as having a heart attack, then public places *and* being alone at home are unsafe. It follows that in those cases where the person is afraid of being alone in public places and of being alone at home, it should be possible to identify a threat to health or well-being, and the manifestations of fear should vary in relation to the speed of and security of access to medical or other safety.

Even if the core fear is a threat to one's health or well-being and if the fear of public places and transport are secondary and conditional to this core fear, it does not preclude the possibility that the affected person will also learn to fear the secondary cues, by a process of conditioning. For example, entering a department store in which a panic has been experienced might provoke a conditioned reaction (trembling, sweating) that is interpreted as evidence of an imminent threat. The development of secondary cues might obscure the core fear. In most cases, the removal of the core fear should be followed by a weakening or elimination of the secondary cues, but this process may be disconcertingly slow, particularly if the person continues to avoid public places and transport even after the core fear has diminished. An effective means of extinguishing the secondary associations is by repeated practice, in which the person enters the feared places in a planned and controlled manner.

Is there a coherent structure?

Fears of illness and death are prominent among the types of anxieties reported by agoraphobic patients,[22] and there is evidence to show that they are at least as anxious as other neurotic patients.[23] Continuing his argument that agoraphobia is essentially an anxiety state, Hallam contests the view that "agoraphobia has an underlying unity and coherence based on a fear of public places."[24] Agoraphobics report elevated levels of anxiety, but they also score well above the average on depression and other neurotic problems. Agoraphobia is not a distinct and coherent, separable disorder. It is a diffuse set of fears, and it lacks the coherence of more typical phobias, such as those of heights and animals. Support for the idea that these other phobias are more coherent than agoraphobia has come from an unexpected source. In the course of his protracted research into the psychophysiology of fear, Lang found that the connections between the verbal report of fear and the physiological reactivity were weaker and less stable in agoraphobic patients than in patients with other types of phobias.[25] These other types of fear are more easily and dependably evoked by images or verbal description than are the fears of agoraphobic subjects.

These results are consistent with Hallam's arguments, but another explanation, which draws on Clark's theory,[26] is possible. If we pursue the idea that the fear of public places or transport is secondary and conditional to a core fear of harm occurring to one in these places, then Lang's results can be interpreted as reflecting the verbal and visual cues that are secondary and conditional to the core fear. Well-knit, coherent, dependable responses will be evoked more easily in agoraphobic subjects, it is now suggested, if the verbal and visual cues that tap the *core* fear are used. For example, if it is determined that the core fear of an agoraphobic patient is the threat of having a heart attack, he might then be presented with cues that provoke an immediate threat to his cardiovascular system, not with cues of public places or transport. To take a second example, if the core fear of the subject is a threat of losing control, then the cues should be tailored to that fear, rather than to buses or department stores. The coherence of the emitted fear-response components should increase in proportion to the salience of the cue material to the core fear.

The presentation of material secondary to the core fear reduces the chance of provoking a coherent fear response because the cue material is degraded. Material that is pertinent to the core fear, on the other hand, should produce a coherent response. In most cases of agoraphobia, the best combination would be the stimulation of the appropriate bodily sensations and the appropriate, personal, misinterpretation of these sensations — appropriate in the sense that the interpretation would lead to an expectation of a catastrophic outcome. If the person's core fear is that he might pass out, then the material should concentrate on evoking feelings of dizziness and the interpretation that the person is about to pass out. Following some of Lang's findings, cue material that concentrates on the evocation of bodily sensations rather than on static descriptions or pictures should be more effective in eliciting coherent responses. It will be appreciated that there are ethical limits to the type of provocation that can be justified in these laboratory conditions.

The deductions drawn from the alternative view of the agoraphobic have been anticipated to some extent by Lang's own research. His findings have led him to the conclusion that what he calls the "response propositions" are more effective than "stimulus propositions" in eliciting fear responses, and this distinction is particularly clear when dealing with agoraphobic subjects. The revised view of agoraphobia, which opposes the conventional idea that the person is frightened of public places, makes it easier to absorb these results and conclusions, but the differences that he found in the fear responses elicited by response and stimulus propositions can be interpreted in a slightly different way. In agoraphobic patients, at least, the differences in response to the two types of proposition might have resulted from the use of more pertinent stimuli rather than from different types of proposition (that is, stimulus or response propositions). The response propositions used by Lang come closer to eliciting the core fear than do the stimulus propositions, which presumably contain more in the way of descriptions of public places, transport, and so on.

Pursuing this interpretation of agoraphobia might help to explain the outcome of treatment studies. They have been broadly effective but tend to leave some residual fear, presumably because they have been slightly off target. Removal of the core fear—fear for one's health and well-being—should be followed by the total removal of the "agoraphobia." No less.

COGNITIONS

The growing importance attached to the role of cognitions in agoraphobia has produced a demand for more information about these phenomena. The fearful cognitions tend to fall into two major groups: a fear of illness or harm and a fear of public scrutiny or embarrassment. To this we may add that the experience of intense fear, especially of panic, is intrinsically unpleasant. The view that agoraphobics are frightened of what might happen to them, rather than of places as such, makes intelligible the connection between agoraphobia and a fear of being alone at home. If the most important fearful cognition is that of impending harm or illness, then being left at home leaves one in a vulnerable position. In these cases, the amount and range of the fear should bear a close relationship to the person's distance from medical or other safety, both in distance and in time. Thus, going on holiday in a remote area is frightening, as is being too distant from one's physician. The difference between a fear of places and a fear of personal harm is well illustrated in the example of an agoraphobic who is anxious when his physician is not easily accessible. The agoraphobic's fear will increase if he, the patient, travels away from the physician, but he will experience roughly the same increase in fear if he remains in the same place but the physician travels away! The key element is access to safety. And safety will be construed in each case by the nature of the central fear-cognition.

AGE AND GENDER

Two major facts about age and gender must be integrated into a comprehensive account of agoraphobia. The disorder is more than twice as common in women as it is in men,[27] and the ratio in some samples has reached as high as 4:1.[28] In addition, the onset of agoraphobia usually occurs in early adulthood. Learning theorists are obliged to explain why people should be so prone to develop these maladaptive conditioned responses in early adulthood. Cognitive theorists also are required to explain why people, especially women, should develop such vulnerable cognitions at this particular stage in their lives. And those who advocate a biological explanation of agoraphobia, in which the underlying disorder is a biologically induced panic, need to explain why this vulnerability should turn critical in early adulthood. The explanations must also take into account the fact that in a significant minority of cases, the onset of agoraphobia is associated with a significant loss.

SAFETY SIGNALS

Some progress in dealing with the question of the age of onset can be made by introducing what has been called a "safety perspective."[29] If we regard agoraphobia as constituting a balance between danger and safety signals, the problem can be restated not as the emergence of a new fear, but rather as a loss of safety. The theme of a loss of safety and of striving to regain it is common in descriptions of agoraphobia.[30] The survey carried out on 963 agoraphobics produced some evidence of the role of safety, for agoraphobics reported feeling their greatest distress when trapped and deriving the greatest comfort when they knew that they had easy access to safety, or were accompanied by a safe person.[31] Aspects of agoraphobia can be construed as a function of the frightened person's perception of access to and speed of return to safety.[32]

Broadly speaking, any important event that threatens one's security or health and well-being is capable of tilting the balance between danger and safety. Among people who are concerned about traveling or being alone, presumably because of fear of ill health or catastrophe, the loss of a spouse, relative, or friend on whom they depend for security and support might give rise to agoraphobic fears. On the question of the mode of onset, bereavement or loss onsets of agoraphobia are far more likely to occur in over-protected, over-dependent people. Traumatic onsets can occur in over-dependent or normally dependent people.

The next question is why agoraphobia tends to develop in a person's twenties, and why especially in women and at this age? Young agoraphobic women, having overcome whatever fears they had of independent mobility and of being alone, are likely to go through a period when they are relatively housebound (especially after childbirth), and as a result, there is an elevated risk of these fears returning in the late twenties. Their safety signals and procedures are weakened by lack of repetition and practice. We also know that if a person's mastery skills are not used for a period, there is an increased risk of experiencing a return of fear (see Chapter 16). At these times and in these circumstances (for example, bereavement), young agoraphobic women suffer a loss of safety, and the balance tilts toward danger.

IS AGORAPHOBIA DIMENSIONAL OR CATEGORICAL?

Many writers have argued that agoraphobia is a category, that is, a separate problem that is discontinuous from ordinary fear and not merely an extreme version of fear. The category view is implicit in medical diagnostic systems that include agoraphobia. Arrindell presented statistical evidence and arguments to support Roth's claim that agoraphobia is indeed a separate, delimited syndrome and not a graded, affective response.[33] Arrindell argues that agoraphobia does indeed have an all-or-none nature and that it is "not common in a mild form." Thorpe and Burns also argue that there is "little continuity between non-phobic populations and fears in agoraphobic populations. Although there was some continuity between the fears of the specific phobics and the normal population, no such continuity appeared to exist with the agoraphobic fears."[34]

The fact that fears of public places and public transport have been shown to intercorrelate, to hang together, is used in favor of the idea that agoraphobia is a separate category. Moreover, the emergence of agoraphobia in early adulthood and its somewhat predictable course are taken as evidence in favor of the categorical view.[35] Other evidence is the tendency for agoraphobics to respond similarly to the same form of treatment. Evidence of a specific cause, in the absence of which no agoraphobia develops, would clinch matters, but we are not in sight of discovering such a cause. Hallam and others would argue that there is no such cause to be discovered.

The dimensional view of fear, usually but not necessarily contrasted with the concept of pathological fears, is that most fears can be found in the general, non-clinical population, albeit in a skewed distribution.[36] The identification of mild forms of agoraphobia, restrictions of mobility in non-clinical samples, and the not infrequent occurrence of panics in non-clinical groups are all consistent with the view that agoraphobia, like other fears, is a matter of degree and does not constitute a qualitatively distinct category. In a survey of the prevalence of fears in the general population, 13.2 percent of 449 female respondents reported that they had fears of an agoraphobic character. These fears were "sub-clinical forms of agoraphobia" and included fears of being alone, traveling, and being in crowds, as described in the standard psychiatric classification, the *Diagnostic and Statistical Manual* (DSM-IIIR). But Costello adds that "not one had the degree of constriction of normal activities that DSM-III lists as a diagnostic criterion for agoraphobia."[37] In a Canadian study, limits on mobility were reported by elderly people and by students.[38] Given the close association between agoraphobia and panic disorder, the report by Norton and others[39] that a large percentage of the population experience occasional panic attacks is consistent with the view that mild agoraphobia does occur. They found that approximately 35 percent of the 186 normal young adults had experienced one or more panic attacks within the past year. The figures from the study by Craske were lower, but not inconsistent: 24 percent of the students and 5 percent of the elderly reported having experienced a panic within the past week.[40] This new evidence is insufficient, but it does suggest that agoraphobia and episodes of panic do occur in the general population, in mild forms. In addition, we now have evidence of restricted mobility in normal samples.

The question of categorical distinctions can be approached in a novel manner by setting a different question. Is agoraphobia distinct from other fears or does it overlap with them? What are the boundaries of fear and how can we tell where one fear ends and another begins? The conventional ways of separating different fears are clinical investigation and statistical analysis, particularly factor analysis. The raw material used for both types of investigation consists of the affected person's self-report of his fears. However, these self-reports comprise only one of the three components of fear, and a dependence on this single component may give rise to a one-sided conclusion. By combining verbal reports of fear with psychophysiological data, Lang has started to map the inter-relationships between these two components in various types of fear,[41] and his early results indicate that phobias of circumscribed objects such as snakes are more coherent than agoraphobia.

Another approach to the delineation of the boundaries of fear is based on the notion of the "functional dependence" of different fears. It is argued that if a person has more than one fear, the deliberate manipulation of one of these will bring about changes in the person's other fear—if they are dependent. If the deliberate removal of a fear of snakes is followed by a reduction in the person's fear of spiders, we can conclude that the two fears were functionally dependent to some degree (see Chapter 5). Although evidence of the functional dependence or independence of agoraphobia is indirect, it is not uncommon for successfully treated agoraphobic patients to report a reduction in some of their seemingly unrelated fears. Such reports suggest that agoraphobia is not always functionally independent and therefore not always categorical.

Why then do so many patients in clinical interviews, and when responding to fear questionnaires, give information that suggests a categorical disorder? The apparent conflict is open to the following interpretation. In an experimental study of subjects who were frightened of snakes and spiders, it was found that their self-reported judgments of the similarity of the two fears bore no relationship to the behavioral evidence of functional dependence. Fears that were subjectively similar were not behaviorally similar. If a fearful patient or subject describes two of his fears as being unrelated, it is not possible to predict whether the two fears will show functional independence or not. Agoraphobic patients therefore might describe their problem as being unrelated to any other fear, but go on to benefit from treatment that successfully reduces these apparently unrelated fears (for example, social fears). Equally, a person might describe his or her agoraphobia as being closely related to social fears, but then derive benefit only from a reduction of the social fear, while the agoraphobia persists unaltered.

Fears can be categorical within the domain of self-report but not coherent in the behavioral sense. The general lesson is that mapping the boundaries of different fears is likely to be complex, and we should not be surprised to find that two or more fears might be linked subjectively, but vary behaviorally in unrelated directions.

Verbal descriptions of the boundaries of fear are accessible and important, but this onion has more than one skin.

IS AGORAPHOBIA AN ILLNESS?

Categorical classification and pathology often overlap, but some illnesses, such as hypoglycemia and hypertension, are dimensional. Exceptions to the view that agoraphobia is best regarded in dimensional terms does not preclude the possibility that it is an illness. As Hallam has pointed out, the idea that agoraphobia is an illness is so deeply imbedded in medical and lay constructions that it is exceedingly difficult to talk about the phenomenon in terms that do not imply an illness.[42] It is customary to talk about the symptoms of agoraphobia, suitable forms of treatment, diagnosis, and prognosis. He correctly observes that the absence of an alternative vocabulary is a handicap to the introduction of alternative views on the nature of agoraphobia. It is difficult to clarify the relationship between abnormal behavior and illness, and that large task will not be undertaken here except to remark that Hallam and others have questioned the idea that agoraphobia is an illness.

If agoraphobia is regarded as an extreme of normal behavior, not necessarily pathological, it is preferable to talk about the task of retraining excessively fearful people, rather than to prescribe tablets and treatment for people with a mental disorder called agoraphobia, as is implied in the prevailing classification of psychiatric problems, DSM-IIIR.

CONCLUSION

For over 30 years agoraphobia was regarded as the prototypical neurosis, and theories of neurosis that were unable to provide a plausible explanation of the concept of agoraphobia attracted little support. Therapists were quick to lose interest in new methods of treating neurosis if they failed to produce useful effects in the management of agoraphobia. The search progressed steadily, and although we now possess reasonably effective methods of treatment, there is room for dissatisfaction. The majority of patients derive considerable benefit from the prevailing methods of treatment, but many are left with residual fear and disability. Moreover, progress in understanding the disorder has not kept pace with therapeutic advances, and many problems remain unsolved. The demographic features of agoraphobia, particularly those relating to age and gender, are not well understood, and there is continuing debate about whether agoraphobia is a distinct category or an extreme fear at one end of the continuum. Doubts have been raised about whether agoraphobia should be construed as an illness or not, and the idea that agoraphobics are frightened by public places and transport has been challenged. The recently recognized importance of the concept of panic disorder has initiated a major reconsideration of the concept of agoraphobia. Many aspects of the concept will need to be re-examined, some re-cast, and others modified. Some aspects of the concept of agoraphobia will cease to be relevant, and it is probable that the concept will lose much of its significance and interest. Agoraphobia has been demoted.

CHAPTER

8

PANIC: BIOLOGICAL AND COGNITIVE EXPLANATIONS

Largely as a result of Donald Klein's powerful advocacy, panic disorder has replaced agoraphobia as the neurotic disorder of greatest interest. For the most part, agoraphobia is now regarded as a secondary manifestation of panics.[1] Klein argues that panic disorder is a distinctive type of anxiety disorder and that it is essentially biological in nature. People who suffer from panic disorder are prone to develop a fear of public and other places in which they might experience panic attacks, and they therefore tend to avoid such places.

His views have given rise to lively debate about the nature of panic, and arguments for and against the biological and psychobiological explanations have been batted about so energetically that sometimes the debate resembles trench warfare.[2] The occasional dust-ups should not obscure the fact that "we are participating in a debate between two models of psychopathology with panic disorder as the centerpiece."[3] Seligman has described the opposing points of view in this way. "One model, biomedical, claims essentially that panic is a disorder of the body, is biochemical, with genetic vulnerability, and appropriately treated by drug therapy. The other, cognitive-behavioral, claims that it is a disorder of the mind based on misinterpretation, with a cognitive diathesis, and suitable for psychotherapy."[4]

The work of Klein and his colleagues gave rise to important changes in the U.S. psychiatric diagnostic system, and in the revised third edition of the *Diagnostic and Statistical Manual* (DSM-IIIR) of the American Psychiatric Association, the essential features of a panic attack are described as discrete periods of intense fear or discomfort, accompanied by at least four symptoms (for example, palpitations, trembling, sweating, dizziness).[5] If a person experiences these attacks recurrently, at least four times within a 4-week period, and if one or more of them is followed by a period of at least a month of persistent fear of a repetition, then a diagnosis of panic disorder should be considered. The DSM-IIIR classification contains two types of panic disorder, those that are associated with agoraphobia and those that are not. It is implied that there is a small number of cases in which agoraphobia is not associated with a panic disorder.

As Gelder points out, the recognition of panic episodes is not novel, and a variety of biological explanations have been proposed to account for their occurrence.[6] None of these explanations (that panics are the result of low blood-sugar levels, thyroid deficiency, and so on) has been confirmed, and episodes of panic attracted little attention until Klein began his advocacy. He argued that panic disorders are an important and distinctive type of anxiety disorder and that "almost all agoraphobia . . . is initiated by spontaneous panics."[7]

KLEIN'S ARGUMENT

Klein based his claim for the distinctiveness and importance of panic disorder on two main arguments. Patients with a history of panic attacks do not respond to the drugs that produce improvements in patients with other kinds of anxiety disorders, but they do respond well to imipramine, an antidepressant drug. "Spontaneous panics respond to imipramine whereas generalized and anticipatory anxiety do not."[8] Klein happened on the antipanic effects of imipramine in 1959 when he was stumped by the failure of phobic patients to respond to powerful tranquilizing drugs such as benzodiazepines.

The happy thought struck us that perhaps these patients might benefit from imipramine (a newly introduced anti-depressant(?) drug). The logic behind this was not exactly coercive: it was more a case of our not knowing what else to do for them, and thinking that perhaps this strange, new, safe agent with peculiar tranquilizing powers might work. Several patients volunteered for a pilot trial, primarily because anything was better than being sent home unimproved.[9]

Klein's frank explanation of the origin of his work on panic is best appreciated in light of the disdainful disapproval of biological approaches that was typical of the psychodynamic spirit of U.S. psychiatry during the 25 years after World War II.

The second piece of evidence on which he based his argument arose from the demonstration that panic attacks can be induced in the laboratory by the infusion of lactate into patients who have a history of panic attacks. These two pieces of evidence were combined to reach the conclusion that panic disorders are distinctive: panic patients respond differentially to drug treatment, and panics can be provoked in these patients by a specific drug that leaves other patients unaffected. These are the two main pillars on which the concept of panic disorder was established.

Moreover, the connection between the two pillars is strengthened by the fact that the induction of a panic by lactate infusion can be blocked by the prior administration of imipramine. Additional arguments were introduced later, but they are secondary in importance and timing to the two main arguments.[10] It then became apparent that there is a close connection between panic attacks and agoraphobia. A high proportion of agoraphobic patients describe experiences that fit into the experiences of panic attacks.

Klein interpreted the evidence to mean that panic disorder is essentially biological, but its exact properties were left unidentified. In an attempt to improve on this unsatisfactorily vague position, Klein and Klein recently proposed that "spontaneous panics are due to the pathological central discharge of an evolved alarm mechanism, possibly linked to separation anxiety or asphyxia."[11] In this definition and throughout the development of the concept, Klein has emphasized the distinction between spontaneous and situational panics. The spontaneous attacks are those which are said by the patient to "come out of the blue," and differ from the situational panics in which a probable external threat can be identified.

Klein has assembled a good deal of evidence to support the main pillars of his argument, and most writers accept that imipramine does have anti-panic effects.[12] There is no dispute about the fact that a high proportion of people with a history of panic attacks respond positively to the lactate infusion laboratory test. However, for reasons that will be set out shortly, Klein and others are now attaching less significance to the results of the lactate test; it was originally claimed that the overwhelming majority of panic patients respond positively, but the latest figures are that "lactate infusions cause panics in only about 60% of panic patients, and 5% carbon dioxide inhalation causes panic in a subset of these."[13]

Klein quotes six studies[14] to support the idea that panic initiates agoraphobia: 97 percent of 32 patients reported becoming phobic after panics (Uhde); 88 percent of 42 agoraphobics said that panics antedated their phobias (Argyle and Roth); 94 percent of 36 agoraphobics developed phobic behavior after panic attacks (Aronson and Logue); all 12 of the agoraphobics described by Garvey and Tuason said that panics preceded or coincided with the onset of their agoraphobia; 79 percent of 28 agoraphobics attributed their agoraphobia to panic attacks (Thyer and Himle); 87 percent of 57 agoraphobics started with spontaneous panics (Lelliott and Marks).

DEBATE

The biological theory has been subjected to four types of criticism. The numerous attempts to find a biological substrate or foundation for the disorder have been unsuccessful, the theory is unsatisfactorily vague on critical points, there is positive evidence that contradicts the theory or its implications, and finally, some critics consider the whole enterprise to be misguided.

The basis for the original argument, the two main pillars, has been challenged. The biological interpretation of the induction of panics by lactate infusions has come under particularly severe criticism. The responses to lactate are not as specific to panic disorder patients as was originally suggested. For example, Ehlers and others noted that the "panic rates for panic patients and patients with generalized anxiety disorders or major depression with secondary panic attacks did not differ."[15] As conceded by Klein, a large number of panic disorder patients (40 percent) do not respond positively. The response to lactate infusion lacks specificity and sensitivity. In a wry comment on the non-exclusive connection between lactate and induced panics, Gorman[16] noted that so many chemical agents have been shown to produce the effect that one begins to wonder if there is "any active agent that does not cause a panic." Clark comments that these active agents do not have a common chemical property.[17] If panic disorder is a biological dysfunction, it is one that is easily provoked, and by diverse chemical agents.

Margraf and his colleagues have argued that the evidence on lactate infusion is open to several interpretations, not least because of a failure to take into account significant differences in the baseline status of the patients tested.[18] In addition, the instructions given to the patients during the test can have a crucial effect on the outcome. The extremely high rates of positive response that were reported in the early research can be accounted for by failures to control for baseline responding, by the use of uncontrolled and suggestive instructions, and bias introduced by the fact that the experimenters knew the identity of the patients and the drug being infused. These aspects of the procedure are described by one of Klein's colleagues in this way: "The physician who attended the lactate procedure knew the diagnosis of the subject and knew that . . . lactate was in fact the infusion substance." After the introduction of "blind conditions," the panic rate dropped from "about 3 in 4 to about 2 in 4."[19]

The specificity of the action of imipramine (and other anti-depressant drugs) on spontaneous panics has not been confirmed.[20] According to Tyrer, imipramine produces broad spectrum effects. The case for specificity of action is weakened by the fact that "several classes of medication have the specific property of blocking spontaneous panic attacks. These include the tricyclic anti-depressants, monoamine oxidase inhibitors, and alprazolam."[21] The same view was expressed by Zitrin, and other collaborators of Klein, who pointed out that there are "three classes of medication that effectively stop the panic attacks."[22] The claim of an exclusive connection between imipramine and panics has been disconfirmed. The debate about the exact dose of imipramine that is required to demonstrate the panic-blocking effects of imipramine is now beside the point.[23]

All three classes of anti-panic drugs have unwanted effects. According to Zitrin, they produce refusals, defections, adverse side-effects, and relapses. Between 18 percent and 25 percent are "exquisitely sensitive to tricyclics, and have poor tolerance for these drugs."[24]

Unfortunately it remains true that Klein's theory still lacks specificity. The original notion that there is some underlying biological dysfunction has failed to attract support despite numerous investigations and the energetic use of all of the most advanced biochemical and imaging diagnostic techniques. The trawl for a biological cause of panic has led to repeated disappointments and should be more discouraging than it has been.

Klein's recently introduced explanation of the causes of spontaneous panics, which postulates a pathological central discharge, leaves the essential properties of the dysfunction unidentified, and there is no explanation for each separate part of the statement or the total product.[25] In addition, the distinction between spontaneous and original panics, which Klein regards as "crucial,"[26] is fuzzy, and appears to be too subtle for such a broadly stated explanation. Attempts to distinguish between spontaneous and situational panics have not always been successful.[27] It also has been objected that patients with panic disorder are not as distinctly different as Klein postulated. For example, Barlow and others have shown that panics are commonly reported by all categories of anxiety disorder patients.[28]

Some of the positive evidence that the biological theory might have difficulty in accommodating includes the following. Panics can be induced by purely psychological procedures. Behavioral treatments are followed by significant reductions in the frequency of panic, and there are early signs that the newly developed cognitive therapy might be more, and dramatically more, effective in abolishing panics. There certainly is no reason why psychological treatments should not be effective in modifying biological disorders, but these results are not deducible from Klein's theory. The evidence of common fearful cognitions before and during panic attacks presents no direct challenge to Klein's theory, and they can be regarded as mere accompaniments of the panic, but they also are not deducible from the theory. The observed links between the bodily symptoms and cognitions (see p. 128) are similarly awkward for the theory.

The major demographic features of panic disorders remain unexplained. There is nothing in the biological theory to explain why women are so much more vulnerable to this putative biological disorder, and there is no reason to explain why it should occur most frequently in the person's late twenties. As mentioned earlier, the argument that panic disorders are distinctive has come under challenge because it appears that episodes of panic are common to all anxiety disorders. The decreasing likelihood of a panic being induced by lactate observed after *repeated* inductions, a sort of adaptation effect, does not smack of a biological dysfunction, and if it is such a dysfunction, it shows the curious quality of diminishing with repeated tests.[29]

The most sweeping rejection of Klein's views has come from Marks, who continues to support the view that agoraphobia is a separable and coherent disorder.[30] He argues that panic occurs in such a wide range of disorders that the term *panic disorder* "might best be abandoned inasmuch as it covers such a wide range of conditions."[31]

"Close scrutiny indicates that panic disorder has no distinct etiology, genetic background, biological markers, or treatment that separates it from other anxiety disorders."[32] These views do not have an immediate appeal for Klein.

Marks contests the claim that there is a drug with specific anti-panic effects: "There is no drug that exclusively helps panic disorder and no other syndrome".[33] In regard to the genetic evidence, he argues that there is a "familial loading" for a variety of anxiety disorders and depression, but not for panic disorder as such. In the course of a lengthy and detailed rebuttal of these and other objections, Klein appears to make some concessions on the question of the anti-panic effects of imipramine and acknowledges that a benzodiazepine drug can reduce panics.[34] Given that the inefficacy of benzodiazepines (and other anxiolytic drugs) in reducing panics, in contrast to the anti-panic effects of imipramine, was such an important factor in Klein's original "pharmacological dissection," this is a significant change of view.[35]

It should be mentioned that the interpretation of the results of some of the drug trials is contested. For example, the authors of the three reports on the outcome of the largest and most ambitious of these trials, a "multicenter trial" of the effects of alprazolam versus placebo in panic disorder and agoraphobia, concluded that taking the drug is "effective and well tolerated."[36] In order to prevent relapses, they recommended that patients be given the drug for a "longer period, at least six months."

My interpretation of their results leads to an opposite conclusion. In a competition between alprazolam and a placebo, the patients should be given placebos rather than alprazolam.

It is true that midway through the 8-week drug trial, the patients receiving alprazolam had benefited more than those receiving the placebo. By the fourth week, the panic rate for the drug group had been reduced from 5.60 per week to 2.14. The weekly panic rate for the placebo group had declined from 6.15 to 3.80. However, by the end of the drug trial, at 8 weeks, there was no longer any difference between the placebo and drug-treated groups. An analysis of a subgroup of 126 patients revealed that when the drug was discontinued at the end of the 8 weeks, "some, in fact most, (drug-treated) patients experienced relapse." The drug-treated patients were left worse off after the drug was tapered off than they had been before treatment began. At the "first post-taper" period they had an average of 8.22 panics per week — more than four times as many as the patients who had been treated by placebos, and more than their own original weekly average of 6.61. Furthermore, the drugs produced many side-effects and in 10 out of the original 263 patients, "potentially serious" adverse reactions occurred (hepatitis, mania, intoxication).

Except for a brief initial period, the placebos produced equal or better results than the drugs, and were followed by fewer rebounds, withdrawal problems, side-effects, or adverse reactions. When the placebos were discontinued, the significant improvements achieved during the 8-week trial period were maintained without change. The placebos were safer and better tolerated. The problem is that 37.7 percent of the placebo patients dropped out of treatment, and this indicates a need to reduce the noncompliance rate among patients receiving these safe tablets. Rather than keep patients on alprazolam for lengthy periods, ways should be found to ensure that patients take the placebos as prescribed. At the very least, patients should complete a trial of placebos before alprazolam is even considered. Overall, the mixed results produced by drugs makes it imperative to find superior alternatives.

LASTING VALUE

In light of this catalog of problems and objections, what is the current status of the biological theory? It is difficult to defend the theory in detail because it has never been stated fully, in a formal and specific manner. Nevertheless, the general idea that panic disorder is a distinctive illness and is essentially biological can be assessed. The two main pillars on which Klein rested his principal argument have been undermined and no longer are defensible.

Nevertheless, part of Klein's work is of lasting value. The two pillars are best regarded as scaffolding that served a temporary purpose and left behind a welcome recognition of the considerable importance of episodes of panic. He also has drawn attention to the "panic sensitivity" of certain people, and the evidence on the effects of lactate infusion, although considerably reduced in scope, supports the idea that there are differences in individual vulnerability. Klein has also made it possible to carry out a fundamental re-assessment of the concept of agoraphobia and has helped to replace it with a view that probably comes closer to the true state of affairs. It cannot be coincidental that such a large proportion of people who display agoraphobic fear and avoidance attribute the onset of their problems to episodes of panic. The possibility of a causal link between panic episodes and agoraphobia deserves to be taken very seriously. However, we have to address the question of why it is that the many other people who experience episodes of panic do not develop agoraphobia. Klein's work has prepared the way for a better understanding of the consequences of panic, which in many cases can be more serious and disabling than the episodes of panic. Finally, Klein's introduction of the concept of panic disorder, and his determined advocacy of a biological explanation, acted as grist and led to the formulation of competing, psychological explanations.

COGNITIVE EXPLANATIONS

"Panic attacks result from the catastrophic misinterpretation of certain bodily sensations," according to Clark.[37] This psychological explanation, the most specific and comprehensive of its type, is a sharp contrast to Klein's explanation that panics are "due to" a pathological central discharge.

"The catastrophic misinterpretation involves perceiving these sensations (palpitations, dizziness) as much more dangerous than they really are."[38] For example, a person might misinterpret palpitations as evidence of an impending heart attack. Other examples include the misperception of breathlessness as evidence of incipient respiratory arrest, or perceiving dizziness as evidence of impending loss of control. According to Clark, a wide range of stimuli are capable of provoking panic attacks, and include the external stimuli that are typical of agoraphobia (for example, supermarkets, buses), but more often the stimuli are internal (bodily sensations or thoughts).[39] Unless the misinterpretation is "impending," in the sense that the threat is immediate, it is more likely to arouse anxiety than an episode of panic. Disturbing misinterpretations of bodily sensations that give rise to anxiety about one's health, but of a kind that pose no immediate threat, are the raw material for hypochondriasis.[40]

In support of the cognitive theory, there is evidence that panic patients have a higher frequency of the cognitions that lend themselves to catastrophic misinterpretations.[41] They are more likely to experience thoughts of impending loss of control, loss of consciousness, heart attack, and so on than are people who have anxiety that is not associated with a panic experiences. Clark also cites evidence to show that the changes in bodily sensations usually precede a panic attack. Experimental studies have shown that panic patients are significantly more likely to interpret their bodily sensations in a mistaken and catastrophic manner than are people who do not experience panic attacks. Furthermore, there are early indications that if a catastrophic misinterpretation is activated, the probability of experiencing a panic is significantly increased.[42]

The cognitive theory of panic entails a causal link between bodily sensations and fearful cognitions, and as a first step in seeking the presence of the link, panic episodes were induced in claustrophobic volunteer subjects and in patients with a diagnosis of panic disorder.[43] The data were searched for meaningful links between the fearful cognitions and the bodily sensations that were reported to have occurred during episodes of panic.

As deduced from the theory, panic episodes were indeed accompanied by many more bodily symptoms and fearful cognitions than were the non-panic episodes, and several understandable links between the sensations and cognitions emerged. The links between *combinations* of bodily sensations and cognitions were even clearer than the links between single sensations and single cognitions. For example, when claustrophobic subjects reported bodily symptoms of dizziness, choking, and shortness of breath in association with the cognition of "suffocation," a panic was almost always recorded. Among panic disorder patients, the combination of palpitations, dizziness, and shortness of breath accompanied by the cognition of "passing out" usually was associated with a panic. As expected, the links observed in the group of panic disorder patients were different to the links observed in the group of claustrophobic subjects. Having noted that the observed links were meaningful, it must be said that there were fewer than might have been expected. The overall number of links fell below expectation, but this might simply reflect the stringent criteria that were adopted in the analysis. Among the claustrophobic subjects, there were no instances in which a panic was reported in the absence of a fearful cognition, but contrary to expectation, a number of panics were recorded by the panic disorder patients even in the absence of an associated fearful cognition. For technical reasons[44] it is premature to draw any conclusion from these "non-cognitive panics," but if the finding is replicated in a way that puts the matter beyond question, it will limit the explanatory value of the cognitive theory.

The pattern of detected links can be illustrated by the following examples. Among the claustrophobic subjects, a report of the sensation of choking plus the feeling of shortness of breath was never associated with a panic, in the absence of an accompanying fearful cognition. However, when the same bodily symptoms occurred in association with the cognition "I am going to suffocate," then a panic was recorded on 25 out of 31 occasions. Among the panic disorder patients, a combination of breathlessness and dizziness, accompanied by the fear of passing out or losing control, was associated with panic on 11 out of 13 occasions. By contrast, the combination of breathlessness and dizziness, *not* accompanied by a fearful cognition, was never associated with a panic. Some interesting information about the significance of specific cognitions was also detected. Among the claustrophobics, 60 percent of all panic episodes were accompanied by the bodily sensation of choking. One-third of all the panic episodes reported by the claustrophobics were associated with fear of choking to death. By contrast, when the panic disorder patients reported choking sensations, they never had the accompanying cognition that they might choke to death.

The fearful cognitions endorsed most frequently by the panic disorder patients on those occasions when they had a panic episode were the fear of passing out or acting foolishly. The fear of suffocation, which was endorsed on 80 percent of all claustrophobic panic trials, was seldom reported by the panic disorder patients (on less than 10 percent of all panic trials). These and the other examples of the specificity of the connections between the particular bodily sensations and the associated cognition sit very well with the cognitive theory. The findings certainly do not contradict the biological theory of panic, but neither do they offer any support, and it has to be conceded that they are not deducible the biological theory. The links are of interest and certainly consistent with the cognitive theory, but they can tell us nothing about the claimed causality of the connections.

Clark's theory is causal, and it is no easy matter to demonstrate that the observed associations between fearful cognitions and panic are more than co-effects. It is possible that the cognitions described by panic disorder patients are epiphenomena;[45] perhaps they are mere accompaniments of a fundamentally biological disorder or accompaniments of conditioned panic reactions. The question remains to be resolved, but the proponents of the cognitive theory have reason to feel hopeful about the outcome. Reports of specific connections between the catastrophic cognitions and the occurrence of panic are accumulating in case histories. In some of the clearest examples, the panics were eliminated shortly after the patient's cognitions had been corrected, and in some other examples, the patient's panics were not significantly reduced by established treatments unless and until the cognitions were altered. These reports are insufficient, but they do provide a useful building block.

The argument that cognitions play an important part in the occurrence of panics is supported by several pieces of evidence. First, the instructions given to vulnerable subjects are important determinants of the occurrence or non-occurrence of panic. For example, when subjects are told that the physiological provocation (lactate infusion or carbon dioxide inhalation) might produce panic, the panic rate increases. Under the same provocation, when the subjects are given a "neutral" instruction (for example, "You will experience tingling sensations which some people find pleasant"), there is a low rate of panic production.[46] Second, links between bodily sensations, fearful cognitions, and panic have been demonstrated in experiments with panic disorder patients and with claustrophobic subjects. The panics were associated with a significant elevation of fearful cognitions. Third, the claustrophobics' panics declined when subjects engaged in a distracting task; in contrast, when comparable subjects succeeded in concentrating on their bodily sensations while remaining in an enclosed space, panic increased.[47] Fourth, the presence of a doctor makes it difficult to produce laboratory panics by physiological means,[48] and this presumably is the consequence of cognitive appraisal. Fifth, the introduction of a degree of personal control, by access to a lever which can control the experimental conditions, reduced the probability of a panic occurring during the inhalation of carbon dioxide.[49]

Cognitions alone?

Can catastrophic cognitions, in the absence of bodily sensations, produce a panic? There are three reasons for insisting on the inclusion of bodily sensations in the production of panic and on linking them to the frightening cognitions. These bodily sensations frequently are reported by patients describing their episodes of panic, the production of panic by hyperventilation is best explained as a misinterpretation of the bodily sensations that arise from overbreathing,[50] and the cognitive theory is better able to explain the evidence of biological provocation of panic in terms of a postulated *link* between bodily sensations and cognitions. There is a technical problem here because the DSM-IIIR definition of panic disorder includes the occurrence of at least four of the bodily symptoms on a 14-item checklist as an essential criterion for the occurrence of panic. Therefore, episodes of panic that are not accompanied by at least four of these bodily symptoms are definitionally excluded from the diagnosis of panic disorder. Adherence to the DSM-IIIR system of classification precludes the possibility that some episodes of panic occur even in the absence of bodily symptoms. For purposes of addressing the present question, the DSM-IIIR classification can be ignored.

We have evidence of significant connections between the bodily symptoms, the fearful cognition, and the occurrence of panic (for example, the occurrence of a claustrophobic panic is strongly associated with the fearful cognition that one might suffocate, and the bodily sensations of choking, dizziness, and shortness of breath).[51] For these and other reasons, the inclusion of a link between bodily symptoms and fearful cognitions is justifiable. However, it remains possible that panics can occur even in the absence of such links.

The emphasis, indeed insistence, on the catastrophic misinterpretations of *bodily sensations* appears to be necessary in accounting for the "spontaneous" episodes of panic, which are the core of Klein's conception of panic disorders.[52] These episodes are spontaneous in the sense that they "occur from within"; there is no identifiable external trigger. And if spontaneous panic attacks are the result of internal events, then they can be either biological malfunctions, as postulated by Klein, or internal events that give rise to psychological misinterpretations, as in Clark's theory. Bodily sensations, especially significant changes in bodily sensations, are the internal events that are misinterpreted and produce spontaneous panics. But we cannot exclude the possibility that other internal events also provide opportunities for misinterpretation.

It follows that some "situational panics," those in which a trigger stimulus is identified, can be explained without a resort to internal events; neither biological malfunctions nor intrusive bodily sensations are required to explain these episodes.

Episodes of panic that do not fall into the "spontaneous" category—

which would include panics that are reported in the full range of anxiety disorders and in the circumscribed phobias — can be encompassed in a simplified extension of Clark's theory. It can be said that these panics are the result of catastrophic cognitions, and the raw material for these cognitions can come from many sources. The restriction to "catastrophic misinterpretations of *bodily sensations*" can be omitted.

An advantage of the cognitive theory of panic is that it enables one to accommodate much of the current information on panic, including the evidence collected and assembled by proponents of the biological theory. As Clark has argued, the fact that a variety of biochemical and physiological manipulations can induce panic attacks suggests that it is not the specificity of the biochemical or physical agent that is important.[53] The common element should be sought in the person's understanding of the procedure and his or her expectation of the effects of the manipulation. Clark advances some evidence that this is so, and the induction of panics by psychological methods provides additional support. The chemical techniques for inducing panic achieve their affects indirectly, and only provoke a panic if the bodily sensations which they induce are interpreted as a sign of immediate threat.

It follows therefore that if a person is given repeated infusions or other physiological provocations, he or she will learn that catastrophic consequences are unlikely (unless an extremely aversive experience occurs). Thus, the repetition of the procedure leads to a decrease in the frequency of panic episodes,[54] as also occurs with psychologically induced panics.[55] The cognitive theory also accommodates the fact that in a minority of instances panic episodes can be induced by relaxation an outcome not predictable from the biological theory of panic. If the induction of relaxation gives rise to a catastrophic misinterpretation of the changes in bodily sensation, a panic can occur. If, for example, the person is frightened of losing consciousness or suffocating or dying, then the bodily sensations of slowed breathing, tingling, and faintness might well be interpreted in a threatening manner and give rise to a panic. Heide and Borkovec concluded that relaxation-induced anxiety is caused by a "fear of somatic anxiety cues and fear of loss of control."[56] The therapeutic effects of drug treatment are obtained either by directly blocking the bodily sensations that provide the material for a misinterpretation or by changing the person's interpretation of his bodily sensations. If the patient's tendency to misinterpret bodily sensations in a catastrophic fashion is not altered during the period of drug administration, relapse is likely to occur when the drug is withdrawn.

Vulnerability to panic

Clark postulates that certain people are vulnerable to panic in the sense that they have an enduring tendency to misinterpret bodily symptoms.[57] There are at least three forms of vulnerability. The person may be disposed to experience intense or frequent bodily sensations,[58] he or she may be disposed to make catastrophic misinterpretations, or both. So far, the second possibility, the inclination to "catastrophize," has received most attention, and rightly so. One needs to know why A makes such alarming interpretations and then panics, and why B makes benign interpretations and does not panic. In addition, there is a need to find out why A has a panic in some circumstances but not in others. The opportunities for panic are almost limitless and can arise at any time of any day or night.

The idea that people are inclined to be consistent in their interpretations of significant events features prominently in most psychological theories of depression, and indeed the progress achieved in that line of research has been a valuable prompt and encouragement for the formation of the new theories of panic.[59] It has been proposed that some people make consistently gloomy interpretations of events, of themselves, and of their status. They over-estimate the significance and the probabilities of unpleasant events, and play down the value of positive events, or fail even to perceive that they are positive. Ironically, these card-carrying pessimists may be more in tune with the world than are the rest of the population, for it turns out that their gloomy estimations of probable success and of their control over events often are more accurate than those of the non-pessimists. Depressed people tend to display what has been described as *depressive realism* and tend to be accurate when they say that they have little control over aversive events—unlike non-depressed people who may overestimate their degree of control. They have a comforting "illusion of control."[60]

Clark and his colleagues are testing the postulated tendency to misinterpret, and have shown that when they are asked to interpret ambiguous situations, patients with panic disorder are significantly more likely than normal control subjects or patients with other types of anxiety to interpret their bodily sensations in a negative fashion.[61] Successfully treated panic patients show a marked reduction in their tendency to make these catastrophic misinterpretations.

In a second experiment, they demonstrated that panic disorder patients are primed to use negative words, such as "choking" and "dying," when presented with verbal tasks. They have also shown that panic patients are inclined to respond anxiously to word combinations that link bodily sensations to catastrophies (for example, breathlessness to suffocating). As predicted, 10 out of 12 panic patients, but no recovered patients or normal controls, reported sudden increases in anxiety when exposed to these combinations. Some of the panic patients even experienced an episode of panic while reading the cards.

If the tendency to make these catastrophic misinterpretations is indeed "a relatively enduring tendency," then in order to be effective, treatment procedures must bring about a reduction in this predisposition. Clark and his colleagues have accumulated some small pieces of information that support this idea. The effects of drugs on episodes of panic provide a useful test case, for if the vulnerability is psychological in the sense in which Clark sees it, then the use of drugs should at best produce a small degree of incidental reductions in the predisposition. In the majority of cases, the enduring tendency should remain unaffected by the drugs, and therefore when medication ceases, a recurrence of panic episodes is to be expected. In contrast, any psychological treatment that produces a stable reduction in the predisposition should ensure that new relapses will occur, and these should be confined to patients who continue to make, or revert to, catastrophic misinterpretations. According to the biological theory, the administration of an adequate amount of the effective drug, such as imipramine, should be effective, regardless of whether the patient is making correct or incorrect interpretations of his bodily sensations.

The timing and context of episodes of panic

Why does a vulnerable person, say someone who has a panic disorder, experience a panic at time A and in place B and not at other times in other places? In addressing this question, we need to bear in mind that most people who experience episodes of panic do not have a panic disorder. It will be assumed here that the causes of the episodes of panic reported by patients with panic disorder are essentially similar to those reported by people who are free of this disorder.

Following Clark's theory, the search for the determinants of particular episodes should be directed toward the factors that provoke the bodily sensations that provide the opportunity for misinterpretation. Hyperventilation (over-breathing) causes an increase in the relevant bodily sensations and is known to be involved in many instances of panic.[62] Hyperventilation, in turn, can be caused by strenuous exercise or by distress.

The ingestion of caffeine produces the relevant bodily sensations and therefore can provoke a panic. Broadly, any event or information that increases the bodily sensations provides an opportunity for misinterpretation, and hence for panic.

An important if uncommon variation should not be overlooked. It is not only increments in bodily sensations that can lead to a misinterpretation. The perception of a decrease in bodily sensations, such as a slowing of heart rate or a decrease in respiratory rate, can be misinterpreted as impending disaster: perhaps a loss of control or even death. The occurrence of relaxation-induced anxiety is well documented.[63]

Strictly speaking, it is the perception of a significant *change* in sensations that sets the opportunity for a misinterpretation. So the list of initiating causes of an episode of panic must include events that decrease the sensations. Panic can be induced by over-breathing, by taking psychoactive drugs, by experiencing unwanted feelings of relaxation, by meditational states, and so on.

The second part of the chain is the *misinterpretation* of the perceived changes in sensations. Even the most frequent panicker experiences very few episodes of panic relative to the occasions on which he or she perceives changes in bodily sensations. If a perceived increase in heart rate is always attributed to a benign cause, such as running to catch a bus, there will be no panic. In experimental analyses of claustrophobic panic, the perception of relevant bodily sensations in the absence of a fearful cognition did not end in panic.[64] Panic disorder patients are less likely to experience a panic during the infusion of lactate if they feel safe in the presence of a physician or if they are given reassuring safety information about the sensations produced by the drug.

Cognitive vulnerability to an episode of a panic is determined by the person's interpretation of the particular sensations and by the threatening quality of the context (frightening department store or reassuring hospital clinic). Safety signals reduce the person's vulnerability. The context and particular interpretation probably are subject to priming. People who are feeling apprehensive about their health or psychological control before they enter the situation, be it a store or a hospital, will be more vulnerable.

People can be primed by receiving alarming information about their own or other people's health (for example, George had a heart attack) and by adverse life events. The incidence of panic episodes increases after such events, and the onset of panic disorders often is linked to adverse life events.[65] In addition, some people are consistently primed to misinterpret their bodily sensations. Before turning to a consideration of such people, the factors that increase vulnerability to a particular episode of panic are summarized.

Any factors that bring about significant changes in bodily sensation increase the opportunity for catastrophic misinterpretations. The common factors include over-breathing, strenuous exertion, taking stimulants such as caffeine, drugs, and unwanted relaxation. The priming conditions that increase the likelihood of a person misinterpreting these changes in sensation include adverse life events, alarming information, and a consistently negative style of attributions. The eliciting conditions are a threatening context and the absence or withdrawal of safety signals.

Leaving aside drug treatments, the vulnerability to an episode of panic can be reduced by avoiding actions that provoke excessive bodily sensations (for example, caffeine intake), by adopting or developing safety signals and procedures, and best of all by making correct interpretations of the changes that do take place.

Critique

Even at so early a stage, a number of interesting critiques are emerging. The problems include the temporal relation between cognitions and panic, the elusiveness of the "responsible" cognitions, the nature and causes of nocturnal panics, the occurrence of noncognitive panics, and the differences between the cognitive theory and the conditioning theory.

The demographic features of panic disorders (onset in early adulthood, female preponderance) also remain to be explained. Why should people begin to "catastrophize" in early adulthood? Why are women two to four times more likely to "catastrophize"? Why do so few elderly people develop panic or agoraphobia? They have greater reason than young adults to be concerned about their bodily sensations and health.

In its favor, the theory is bold and simply stated and has wide explanatory value as well as functional value. However, it has been criticized on a number of grounds. Seligman argues that the concept of "catastrophic misinterpretation" is too loose and bears little relationship to conventional cognitive psychology.[66] He also observes that Clark's cognitive theory is no sufficiently different from non-cognitive explanations and seems to overlap the conditioning explanation of panic. Seligman reminds us of the persistently troublesome problem of why it is that certain kinds of fear appear to defy disconfirmation. Why, he asks, does a person who has experienced hundreds of panic attacks fail to learn that his heart is *not* failing? Why does he continue to believe that he is about to have a heart attack? "Under all laws of disconfirmation of which I am aware, he has received ample evidence that what he believed was false, and he should have abandoned it."[67] Teasdale notes that cognitive therapy often is of limited effectiveness unless it is backed up by "experiential" evidence.[68] Even when they produce changes in thinking, cognitive interventions need to be backed up by direct experience. And if this is so, why are cognitive changes insufficient, and if they are insufficient, where does the cognitive theory stand?

A satisfactory explanation is required for nocturnal panics, a not uncommon experience.[69] It is possible that a proportion of these are induced by disturbing dreams and that in other cases the person is awakened and then becomes aware of a disturbing bodily sensation. Collecting the information necessary to test these ideas, with the need for precision, accuracy of reporting, and timing, is no easy task. One more potential problem is the occurrence of the "non-cognitive panics," in which the affected person reports having experienced a panic without the accompaniment of a fearful cognition.[70] These are the panics that in the fullest sense may be described as coming "out of the blue." They may be failures to identify the appropriate thought, but it should be said that each of the patients who reported a non-cognitive panic had on at least one other occasion reported a so-called cognitive panic. It is not a matter of dealing with people who are incapable of recognizing and reporting fearful cognitions.

WHAT NEXT?

A useful start has been made in discovering the conditions that are associated with the occurrence of panic, and some tentative steps have been taken toward answering the principal question: What conditions promote episodes of panic? The ancillary question is: What conditions inhibit the occurrence of panic?

Cognitive theorists offer a direct answer to these questions, and phenomenological inquiries have produced evidence that is consistent with the hypothesis that panics are caused by catastrophic misinterpretations. The study of naturally occurring panics will take us at least part of the

way toward answering the fundamental questions. Given specifiable setting conditions, or specific prompts, the probability of a vulnerable person experiencing an episode of panic can be significantly increased or
decreased. Any setting or prompt that increases the opportunity for catastrophic misinterpretations, or that increases the probability of a misinterpretation occurring, will raise the probability of a panic occurring. In
practice, this would involve increasing the number and intensity of relevant bodily sensations and/or encouraging the person to interpret these
bodily sensations as indicators of imminent danger. For ethical reasons a
strong test of the main hypothesis cannot be carried out, as it would
require that the affected person be persuaded that he or she truly is in
imminent danger.

A second tier of questions will need to be addressed. Given support for
the fundamental hypothesis, we need to know why only a select minority
of people experience episodes of panic. Virtually everybody experiences
the bodily sensations that provide the opportunities for catastrophic misinterpretations, but very few people make the misinterpretations that
induce panic. Clark and his colleagues have made a useful start in searching for the psychological characteristics that predispose people toward
making these catastrophic misinterpretations, and it is a short step from
there to learning which characteristics *reduce* a person's vulnerability. A
guide can be extracted from recent studies of soldiers who regularly carry
out hazardous duties, and one can anticipate matters by pointing out that
a group of the least vulnerable people reported that they had no physical
or mental complaints whatsoever (Chapter 21).

We will also need to explain what brings a panic episode to an end.
Presumably the duration of each episode is a function of the operative
cognition, and as the intensity or threat of the cognition wanes, so the
panic declines. This explanation remains to be tested.

CHAPTER

PANIC: CONDITIONING, EXPECTATIONS AND AVOIDANCE

Seligman argued that there is an overlap between the cognitive and conditioning theories of panic, and comparisons are possible now that Wolpe and Rowan have formulated a conditioning alternative.[1] They argue that the development of panic disorder is a two-stage process.

The initial panic attacks are

unprecedented, excruciating experiences that no one would ever want to have repeated . . . in most cases, it starts with a combination of strange and unpleasant sensations for which hyperventilation is responsible, and which precipitates unexampled levels of anxiety . . . fears of insanity or death . . . arise afterwards—probably as attempts by the subject to rationalize what has happened to him.[2]

The first panic is "an unconditioned response to a disturbing set" of events. The development of a panic disorder, in the second stage, is due to a conditioning of the evoked anxiety to stimuli that are contiguous with it. Panic disorders are the result of "contiguous stimuli, especially endogenous stimuli, being conditioned to the elicited anxiety."[3]

Their argument is illustrated by an analysis of reports given by 10 patients with panic disorder who said that their attributions *followed* the onset of panic. According to Wolpe and Rowan, in the great majority of cases of panic, the first attack is "set off by purely psychological events."[4] The attack is said to be a climactic consequence of unusually high or prolonged anxiety, and careful examination usually reveals "undercurrents of neurotic anxiety." The occurrence of the initial panic attack often is preceded by stressful life events.[5] Very high levels of anxiety do not always lead to panic, and hence, "something more than a linear anxiety is apparently indicated."[6] When the anxiety produces hyperventilation, a panic attack may be triggered; it is well demonstrated that deliberate hyperventilation can produce episodes of panic in people who have a history of such experiences.

Wolpe and Rowan believe that the cognitive theory, despite its plausibility, is contradicted by the reports given by their patients. The cognitions are not causally relevant, but are "in effect an epiphenomenon."[7] Their criticism that people do not panic or develop panic disorders when they are faced with serious threats undoubtedly would draw the reply that it is only threats of immediate catastrophe that induce a panic. Wolpe and Rowan point out that even the "most authoritative verbal assurances" have little effect on panics or panic disorder, and these failures are contrary to the cognitive theory. To this criticism the cognitive theorists might reply that the reassurance might be inappropriate, the provision of reassurance is not always accepted, and even when it is, a reduction in the intense bodily sensations that give rise to the feeling of panic does not necessarily follow. However, if the reassurance succeeds in reducing or eliminating the key fearful cognition, then panics should be prevented or at least reduced. This is a testable idea.

This conditioning theory shares the assumption made by Levitt and

Lopatka that the quality of the panic episodes changes over time.[8] The factors responsible for the initial episodes of panic, whether they are fearful cognitions or unconditioned stimuli, are not necessarily the factors that promote the development of a sustained panic disorder. The initial panic that is experienced in response to an unconditioned stimulus (for example, a toxic substance) or to a fearful cognition of impending death might be succeeded by the development of a fear of future panics. In a case described by Wolpe and Rowan, "later attacks were dreaded, not because of implications of death or insanity, but because the attacks were 'a terrible experience.'"

Wolpe and Rowan deduce guidelines for an effective form of therapy.[10] In the first place, steps must be taken to prevent the occurrence of hyperventilation, and the patient has to be taught how to deal with overbreathing should it occur. The second stage of the treatment is to extinguish the anxiety responses to the effects of hyperventilation, and this generally involves *in vivo* desensitization. The patient is taught to inhale a low concentration of carbon dioxide until the fearful symptoms appear. With repetition, the symptoms cease to be fearful, and after progressively strong evocations have been given, "the patient eventually tolerates maximal symptoms without fear."[11]

There is some overlap between the conditioning and cognitive theories, and there is agreement on the importance of disturbing bodily sensations, especially those produced by hyperventilation, and on the cognitions that are associated with them. There is also some overlap in the proposed methods of treatment. The crucial divergence between the two theories arises from the role attributed to the fearful cognitions. In the cognitive theory they are causally implicated, but in the conditioning theory they are regarded as epiphenomena. As described in Chapter 11, the conditioning theory of fear acquisition faces numerous problems.

These competing explanations can be used to generate competing predictions, and Seligman has proposed some examples.[12] The cognitive theory predicts that misinterpretations are necessary to produce a panic, and the conditioning theory predicts that they are not; the cognitive theory predicts that mere exposures will not produce decrements in panic, but the conditioning theory predicts that they will. Actually, in the Wolpe–Rowan version the exposures must be preceded by the correction of overbreathing. With that addition, the differences between conditioning therapy and cognitive therapy shrink.

CONSEQUENCES OF PANIC

There are disagreements between the proponents of the cognitive and conditioning theories, and both disagree with the biological theory, but all sides appear to share the assumption that there is a close and necessary connection between the occurrence of panic and the development of extensive avoidance behavior. This plausible view rests mainly on the evidence of clinical reports and the general expectation that fear will be followed by avoidance behavior, as is often the case. However, the clinical reports are retrospective and should be treated with reserve. It is likely that in a proportion of cases, probably the majority, the occurrence of panic is indeed followed by the development of avoidance behavior, but there are important exceptions.

Panics are not always followed by avoidance, and avoidance is not always preceded by panic.[13] A significant minority of agoraphobic patients report the development of avoidance behavior after events in which there was no panic (for example, bereavements). We also have numerous instances of patients who experience panic but do not subsequently display avoidance behavior, and evidence of a small group of people who continue to show normal approach behavior despite having experienced some panics.[14] There is a significant minority of people who experience panics but remain free of apparent psychological problems.[15]

Having noted the exceptions, we can now consider the strong relationship between the predictability of panic and subsequent avoidance. When a person predicts that a panic is likely to be experienced, he or she will take steps to avoid the situation in which it is likely to occur. The expectation of panic is a powerful determinant of avoidance. Also, the onset or increase of avoidance behavior is more probable after an unpredicted panic than after a predicted panic. After predicted panics there should be little change in avoidance behavior, especially among veteran panickers. Similarly, when a person predicts that he or she will not have a panic in a particular situation, and this prediction is confirmed, no changes follow. This gives rise to the possibility that exposure treatments will produce little or no change on patients' "good days," and that in turn leads to the seemingly paradoxical idea that panic patients, especially those with agoraphobic avoidance, will benefit most from treatment sessions that are carried out on their "bad days." On these days, there is a greater opportunity for a disconfirmation of fearful expectations. Using a bus on a "good day" confirms that it was a correctly predicted "good day." Worse still, if a panic occurs on a predicted "good day," it will produce the undesirable consequences of an under-prediction of fear. The idea that treatment on "good days" is a no-win action is counter-intuitive but may well be correct, especially early in a program of treatment.

The experience of panic often is distressing, and the consequences can be disabling. Some patients report that they are left exhausted and incapacitated for as long as 24 hours after an episode, but more important in the long run is the effect that experiences of panic have on their freedom of movement and their freedom from fear. The evidence emerging from laboratory investigations of the relationship between panic and its consequences suggests that panic-related avoidance is determined mainly by the estimated probability of the panic. The expected aversiveness of the event, the cognitions associated with panic and safety, and the operation of safety signals, also contribute, but to a lesser degree.[16] The cognitive consequences of a panic can be substantial and include significant increases in the prediction of future panics. Interestingly, although panics are followed by increases in expected fear, they are not commonly followed by increases in reported fear. In this respect, panics have a larger effect on expectations than on behavior.

The evidence also suggests that unexpected, so-called unpredicted panics, contribute most to these changes in expectation.[17] If a person expects to panic and the expectation is confirmed, there is little effect on subsequent reports or predictions of fear or safety. If, however, the person's expectation of panic is disconfirmed, a reduction in fear usually follows. (These findings recall Rescorla's revision of conditioning theory;[18] changes in responsiveness occur only after mismatches in which the expected does not occur — conditioning occurs as a result of "surprises". When the event is expected, or as he describes it, fully predicted, then little change follows. See page 180 for a full account.) Under laboratory conditions, subjects correctly predict roughly one in three panics, but they show a high rate of over-prediction. With increasing experience of panics, their ability to predict accurately shows an improvement.

To sum up, avoidance behavior develops or strengthens if a person predicts that there is a high probability of experiencing panic. The contributory factors include the expected aversiveness, associated cognitions, and the availability of safety signals. Avoidance behavior will be weakened if the person predicts that there is a low probability of having a panic.

THERAPY

A verdict on the efficacy of conditioning therapy must await clinical trials, but there is sufficient evidence about the effects of cognitive therapy to permit a preliminary evaluation.

The fate of cognitive therapy for panic disorders is important for a number of reasons. It is the first theory-driven therapy for this disorder, and deserves special attention for this reason. Moreover, the outcome of the tests of the therapy will have an important bearing on the status of the theory. A positive result would provide a boost for the theory, but not a full validation—at least not without supporting evidence.[19] Confirmation of the efficacy of the therapy would be welcome because it shows promise of turning into a powerful and apt procedure. The early claims are that complete improvement is achieved in many cases.[20]

The most highly developed form of cognitive therapy for panic,[21] generated by Clark and Salkovskis from Clark's theory, is undergoing testing at the Warneford Hospital in Oxford.[22] The therapy involves "identifying patients' negative interpretations of the bodily sensations which they experience in panic attacks; suggesting alternative noncatastrophic interpretations of these sensations; and then helping the patient to test the validity of these alternative interpretations by discussion and behavioral experiments."[23] The associated behavioral treatment is conventional and consists of repeated, gradual exposure to situations in which panics are expected or experienced. The behavioral experiments are designed to test the validity of a particular cognition, and the rationale for their use differs from the role they play in conditioning therapy.

The general approach can be illustrated by a brief case excerpt. It was determined that a young man was experiencing episodes of panic because of his fear of having a heart attack. He was given full information about the nature of panic disorders and how they differed from cardiac disorders, and then shown how his overbreathing produced physical symptoms similar to those which he experienced during panics. He was then given repeated practice in overbreathing and taught to reinterpret these physical sensations in a correct manner, by attributing them to the overbreathing as such. Having learned to interpret the sensations correctly, he accepted that the palpitations which he had found so disturbing were a result of exertion, entirely normal, and unrelated to the symptoms of a heart attack. They were re-interpreted as a sign of health, not of danger. When these changes in interpretation had brought some relief, he was given a number of exposure exercises to carry out between sessions. In this way, he gradually acquired the ability to travel freely and without fear, and he resumed his tennis and other activities.[24]

In their first attempt at evaluating the derived treatment, Clark, Salkovskis, and Chalkley selected subjects who perceived a similarity between their natural panic attacks and the effects of overbreathing.[25] Patients were given repeated experiences of overbreathing, and learned that the elicited symptoms were not dangerous. Their catastrophic interpretations were diminished or removed. "Substantial reductions in panic attack frequency were observed during the first weeks of treatment. These initial gains, which occurred in the absence of exposure to feared external situations were improved upon with further treatment, including exposure to feared situations if appropriate, and were maintained at two-year follow-up."[26]

The origin of the therapy is important. Clark's theory was "initially derived from the observation that the effects of hyperventilation . . . are similar to naturally occurring panic attacks, together with the finding that individual differences are important in determining the affective response to hyperventilation. Hyperventilation was conceptualized as one of a range of possible sources of symptoms which could be interpreted."[27] In order to help patients whose symptoms were not reproducible by hyperventilation, they expanded their procedure, and the results of their study carried out on seven panic disorder patients are promising. "All patients showed substantial reductions in panic frequency, with 6 out of 7 becoming panic-free at or before the twelfth session."[28] The expanded and refined procedure is now under evaluation in a large controlled trial.[29] In addition, attempts are being made to analyze the mechanisms thought to be involved in producing the therapeutic changes.

Salkovskis and Clark are investigating in detail the temporal connections between the cognitive intervention and the experience of panic.[30] No conclusions are possible at this early stage, but in a number of single-case analyses, it was found that the frequency of panic episodes declined shortly after the key specific maladaptive cognition had been altered. The improvements that took place after treatment that was less closely focused on the faulty cognitions were slower and less pronounced. Thus far, it appears that the focused intervention is more effective, and more immediately effective than the non-focused intervention. The reductions in panic frequency, including their total elimination in some cases, were accomplished even though the patients received no "exposure" treatment. Confirmation of this finding would be of considerable importance in evaluating the cognitive and conditioning theories.[31]

Indirect evidence

It was remarked earlier that one of the strengths of the cognitive theory is that it enables one to subsume a good deal of information, including much that has been collected by proponents of the biological theory. Clark has used the theory adroitly to account for the effects of behavioral and pharmacological treatments.[32] Most of our knowledge about the effects of behavioral treatment on panic is indirect and is drawn from findings on the efficacy of this treatment in dealing with agoraphobia. If it is assumed, as seems reasonable, that a high proportion of agoraphobic patients who took part in these studies were experiencing episodes of panic, then it is possible to draw some general conclusions.

According to cognitive theory, behavioral therapy should be effective insofar as the information and explanation provided by the therapist, plus the exposure exercises, lead to significant changes in the person's interpretations of his bodily sensations. In the simplest case, if a patient who has been experiencing episodes of panic can be encouraged to resume normal travel, he or she will then discover during these excursions that the dreaded heart attack does not occur, and the frequency of panics should reduce. The connection between the disturbing bodily sensations and the expected heart attack is repeatedly disconfirmed. However, as the behavioral treatment deals only indirectly, if at all, with the catastrophic misinterpretations, its therapeutic value should be limited. And it is the fact that although behavioral treatments for agoraphobia are generally effective, they often leave the patients with residual fear. For example, Michelson and others found that nearly half of the agoraphobic patients who received benefit from exposure therapy continued to experience occasional panic attacks.[33] Behavioral therapy might also serve to reduce panic attacks by reducing the opportunities for misinterpretations — if the bodily sensations undergo extinction by repeated exposure to the fearful situation, there will be fewer occasions on which the person can misinterpret these unpleasant sensations.

So far so good, but the reduction of opportunities for panic is not a sufficient answer. If the person experiences fewer bodily symptoms and fewer opportunities to panic, but nevertheless fails to correct his or her misinterpretations, it is to be expected that occasional panics will take place. A failure to tackle the catastrophic misinterpretation directly leaves the person vulnerable to future episodes. All of this leads to a differential prediction. Relative to behavioral treatment, cognitive therapy should be followed by a greater number of cases in which the panic episodes are *eliminated*. Recent results, although preliminary, tend in this direction; reports of 80 percent or more patients becoming panic-free are typical.

Whether one accepts a cognitive interpretation of the therapeutic effects of behavioral treatment for panic disorder or not, the occurrence of such improvements is a significant fact in its own right. In a review of treatment outcome studies, including his own, Michelson found that moderate but significant improvements in agoraphobia and in the frequency and intensity of panic attacks have been achieved by a variety of psychological methods, which include programmed exposure practice, psychosocial treatment, and relaxation treatment.[33] The fact that a useful degree of improvement can be achieved with various types of psychological procedure suggests that if panic is indeed a biological disorder, it is an unusually obliging one.[34]

Zitrin, who collaborated with Klein on treatment and other studies, concluded in 1986 that "since a majority of patients who have panic disorder with phobic avoidance make significant gains solely with psychological therapy (behavioral or supportive therapy), in clinical practice a trial of psychotherapy alone is indicated before one considers medication to block panic attacks."[35]

It is too early to expect independent verifications of the effects of cognitive therapy, but the reports provided by Barlow, Beck, and Kopp are consistent with the findings described by Clark and his colleagues.[36] Beck reported an outstandingly good result from a preliminary study of 25 patients with panic disorder. "All of the patients reported a total elimination of panic attacks by the end of treatment. This improvement persisted for 6 months post-treatment in those patients who had already completed treatment and entered the follow-up phase."[37] Barlow and Cerny[38] also have had excellent results. Using a method that combines cognitive and behavioral procedures, they obtained "substantial reductions in panic frequency" in 20 patients, of whom "fully 82% (reported) no panic at post-treatment." On this measure, and on the clinician's ratings of severity, the treated patients did significantly and substantially better than non-treated control patients. A degree of caution is always in order when evaluating the claims made for new forms of treatment, especially when they are not supported by the appropriate clinical controls,[39] but Beck, Barlow, and Clark have reported the increase in power that is demanded by Clark's theory.

Given that cognitive techniques have been in use for some time and have proved to be disappointingly weak in dealing with anxiety disorders, the cause of the new optimism is questioned. In addition to undoubted improvements in technique and understanding, I suspect that a major reason for the extremely promising results now being reported can be found in the infectious confidence of the leading therapist-researchers. "It can be done, it works, and it works thoroughly and dependably." One measure of their enthusiasm and confidence, reminiscent of the spirit of the clinical researchers who developed behavior therapy 25 years ago, is seen in the way they eagerly trawl for more and more cases. As with behavior therapy, the acid test will come when independent and detached clinicans take up the methods.

We already know that exposure has powerful fear-reducing effects, and now it is essential to test the value of cognitive therapy in the absence of such exposure. This presents a challenge for cognitive therapists, but it is possible, in principle, to reduce fears without exposure to the feared situation (see Chapter 15). Clark and Salkovskis have made a useful start in addressing this question, and the progress of the work will be watched with great interest.

In addition to demonstrating the efficacy of cognitive therapy in the absence of exposure practice, it is necessary for Clark's theory to account for the broad and dependable value of exposure exercises. Presumably there is an interaction between repeated exposures and cognitive change, and the exposures can be regarded as a series of disconfirmations of catastrophic misinterpretations. They are usefully self-correcting exercises. Fearful cognitions may interact with the habituation of fear and serve to impede the process. It follows that any therapeutic procedure that removes the fearful cognitions should facilitate the habituation of fear. Given the success of cognitive therapy, it will be necessary to explain why cognitive therapy works without exposure and why cognitive therapy works *with* exposure—a pleasant challenge.

Slow progress of rational therapies

There is a hidden obstacle to the development of cognitive therapy. The weakness of rational methods for reducing psychological problems is evident in the slow progress of earlier versions of therapy that depends on cognitive means.

Most forms of rational psychotherapy rest on the assumption that affect is post-cognitive rather than pre-cognitive. It is also assumed that cognition and affect operate within the same system, at least part of the time.

Both of these assumptions—the post-cognitive nature of affect and the accessibility of affective reactions by cognitive operations—have been challenged by Zajonc.[40]

The central thrust of Zajonc's argument is that

affective judgements may be fairly independent of and precede in time the sorts of perceptual and cognitive operations commonly assumed to be the basis of these affective judgements. Affective reactions to stimuli are often the first reactions of the organism and for lower organisms they are the dominant reactions. Affective reactions can occur without extensive perceptual and cognitive encoding, are made with greater confidence than cognitive judgements and can be made sooner . . . it is concluded that affect and cognition are under the control of separate and partially independent systems.[41]

The cognitions occur after the fear response. Zajonc stresses the claim that affect is often, he might even say *usually*, pre-cognitive. "Feeling accompanies *all* cognitions," and the affective reactions often or usually are primary. Most decisions, he argues, take place without "*any* prior cognitive process whatsoever."[42] The features of a stimulus or set of stimuli that determine affective reactions "might be quite gross, vague, and global . . . thus they might be insufficient as a basis for cognitive judgements.[43] The affective and cognitive systems probably are separate and only partially interrelated—this view is similar to some aspects of Lang's three-system analysis, but Zajonc uses the idea for different reasons and with different conclusions.

His collection of challenging assertions can be summarized. "In contrast with cold cognitions, affective responses are effortless, inescapable, irrevocable, holistic, more difficult to verbalize, yet easy to communicate and to understand."[45] One might have thought this list of assertive adjectives, each one of which is presented and defended in turn by Zajonc, would be sufficient for any provocateur. However, this summary list is not complete. Affective responses also have the following characteristics: they are instantaneous, dominant, partly independent of cognition, primary, precognitive, basic, and automatic.

There are weaknesses in his argument,[46] but if he is even partly correct, it implies that cognitive therapists face a formidable task. Changing the cognitions amounts to closing the stable door after the horse has bolted. Fortunately the early signs are that cognitive therapy can be effective, and perhaps the primacy of affect will only present a problem in dealing with certain types of fear (for example, snakes). In time it may be necessary to supplement the cognitive tactics with methods that directly change affect.

CONCLUSION AND OUTLOOK

The debate about the nature and causes of panic will continue for some time. We can expect to see the proponents of the biological theory continue to trawl for a biological substrate, to explore the effects of new drugs, place increasing emphasis on individual vulnerability (as an answer and a question), and worry about the meaning and significance of spontaneous panic attacks and how they differ from other atacks. They are likely to make increasing concessions to the psychological theories of panic. The proponents of the cognitive explanation will also investigate the nature of vulnerability, produce more (both senses) persuasive evidence of the value of cognitive therapy, focus on increasingly precise connections between cognitions and panic, and explore the extent to which the cognitive approach can be applied to other types of fear. The difficulty of proving a causal connection between the cognitions and the panic will continue to be a challenge and an irritant, and complaints will be made about the unfalsifiability of the theory. Vociferous complaints are likely to come from proponents of a conditioning explanation as their examples of non-cognitive episodes of fear are turned away and as their claims of the successful behavioral treatment of panic fail to convince the critics that it was all done without cognitions. The possible role of cognitive changes is difficult to exclude. The cognitive and conditioning explanations share some features and are not mutually exclusive on all points of importance. A degree of interaction between the two explanations may emerge. On some aspects of panic, the explanations mesh and the treatment plans are similar, despite their differing rationales.

CHAPTER 10

THE BIOLOGICAL SIGNIFICANCE OF FEAR

According to Martin Seligman, "the great majority of phobias are about objects of natural importance to the survival of the species . . . (the theory) does not deny that other phobias are possible, it only claims that they should be less frequent, since they are less prepared."[1] Human phobias are "largely restricted to objects that have threatened survival, potential predators, unfamiliar places, and the dark."[2] Seligman postulates that certain kinds of fears are readily acquired because of an inherited biological preparedness. These phobias are "highly prepared to be learned by humans, and like other highly prepared relationships, they are selective and resistant to extinction, and probably non-cognitive."[3] The main features of prepared fears—and for present purposes, phobias can be regarded as intense fears—are as follows: They are very easily acquired, even by "degraded input" (that is, by watered down representations of the actual threat), and are selective, stable, biologically significant, and probably non-cognitive.

The contemporary significance of Seligman's ideas is best appreciated in relation to other attempts that have been made to explain the acquisition of fear. In common with most learning theories, the conditioning theory rests on the so-called equipotentiality premise. As Seligman and Hager observed, for a long time it was believed that

what an organism learned about is a matter of relative indifference. In classical conditioning the choice of the conditioned stimulus, unconditioned stimulus, and response matters little; that is, all conditioned stimuli and unconditioned stimuli can be associated more or less equally well, and general laws exist which describe the acquisition, extinction, inhibition, delay of reinforcement, and spontaneous recovery of all conditioned and unconditioned stimuli.[4]

Seligman quoted Pavlov's famous claim that "any natural phenomenon chosen at will may be converted into a conditioned stimulus . . . any visual stimulus, any desired sound, any odour and the stimulation of any part of the skin."[5] Learning theorists shared this view. For example, May wrote that "the general rule is that any stimulus may become a danger signal provided that it is immediately and repeatedly followed with an unpleasant, injurious, or painful experience."[6]

Seligman convincingly argued that this premise is untenable and proposed that it be replaced by the concept of preparedness.[7] In the following year, he developed this alternative idea and applied it to the explanation of phobias.[8]

The defining feature of a prepared phobia is the ease with which it is acquired, and phobias can be classified as prepared if they are learned even with "degraded input." In some parts of their exposition, Seligman and Hager interweave the two criteria. "A given contingency is specified by how degraded input can be before learning occurs . . . if the behavior which indicates learning occurs at the first exposure contingency, the animal is at the prepared end of the continuum with respect to this contingency . . . if the animal learns only after considerable exposure, he is unprepared."[9] The two criteria, "speed of acquisition" and "acquisition despite degraded input," deserve to be analyzed separately and then jointly. For example, it is possible to test how quickly someone acquires a fear of snakes, and then ascertain the degree of degraded stimulation that is capable of inducing the fear. How remote can the presentations of a live snake be and yet produce a fear? The two variables probably interact, and remote representations of the stimulus almost certainly require more exposure trials to elicit the fear than do non-degraded stimuli: a live, active, and proximal snake.

In keeping with the views of Pavlov, proponents of the conditioning theory implied that any stimulus can be transformed into a fear signal, and given comparable exposures, they all have a roughly equal chance of being transformed into such signals. Some reservations were noted, and Eysenck and Rachman argued that "neutral stimuli which are of relevance in a fear-producing situation and/or make an impact on the person in the situation are more likely to develop phobic qualities than weak or irrelevant stimuli."[10] Even when reservations of this sort were included, little attempt was made to specify the nature of these reservations or their implications.

Seligman's introduction of the preparedness concept, constructed within the framework of learning theory, provoked a good deal of interest, and the promising results of the pioneering experiments carried out by Ohman and his colleagues boosted this interest.[11] They were the first to demonstrate in the laboratory that people respond differently to presentations of prepared stimuli than to unprepared, neutral stimuli. For example, fear responses to photographs of snakes differed from those evoked by photographs of flowers or mushrooms. By this important step, they were able to promote Seligman's ideas, and provided a test-bed for further investigations.

In a series of experiments they demonstrated, not without difficulty, that certain types of conditioned responses are more readily established in response to prepared than to unprepared stimuli.[12] The early findings were encouraging, and consistent support appeared to be emerging, but some of the results were too fragile to reproduce.[13] Over the next few years there was a gradual accumulation of disappointing results,[14] and interest in the concept of prepared phobias waned. The phobias produced in the laboratory proved to be fragile; these are not deep fears. The effects tended to be weak, transient, and difficult to reproduce, and they usually were restricted to changes of skin conductance. It is difficult to interpret the significance of these changes. In most of the experiments, it was difficult to obtain evidence of prepared phobias with the most appropriate psychophysiological measure of fear, heart rate response. An exception to this general trend was reported by Cook and others, whose experimental subjects showed an increase in heart rate responding during the acquisition of fear, but even here the responses were no different than those of the control subjects during the extinction phase of the experiment.[15] In the same experiment the skin-conductance responses of the experimental and control groups were not significantly different.

Evidence that the prepared fears generated in the laboratory are easily extinguished by verbal instructions undermined one of the most appealing characteristics of the concept.[16,17] These laboratory fears fall far short of the main features of prepared phobias. They are not easily acquired, or stable, or non-cognitive. They do not provide a clear-cut manipulable paradigm of strong fears that evade rational control.

The most serious disappointment was the failure to obtain robust and reproducible evidence that prepared stimuli are easily and rapidly transformable into phobic stimuli. Unexpectedly, the most consistent effect was an increase in the resistance to the extinction of these laboratory fears, but even here the fear responses elicited tended to persist for only a few more trials than those elicited by non-prepared stimuli.

It is also a matter for regret that one aspect of the concept has failed to attract the attention of investigators. Seligman and Hager defined the *relative preparedness* of a stimulus by "how degraded the input can be before the output reliably occurs which means that learning has taken place."[18] Given that organisms can acquire fears of exact representations of the prepared stimulus, at what degree of abstraction does the prepared stimulus lose this power? A partial representation of the prepared stimulus appears to be sufficient in some cases, but out knowledge of this defining attribute of preparedness is limited. No doubt the reason for this state of affairs is that the test-bed produced only weak responses, even under the best conditions, and therefore attempts to produce prepared fear responses using increasingly remote representations would have been unsuccessful.

Richard McNally concluded from his full review of the current status of prepared phobias that the best supporting evidence is "the enhanced resistance of electrodermal responses established to fear-relevant stimuli." The remaining hypotheses, those dealing with ease of acquisition (the critical feature of the concept), belongingness, and irrationality, have "received only minimal or equivocal support."[19]

In light of these disappointments and difficulties encountered in the laboratory research, it is perhaps surprising to find continuing interest in the subject. The original concept retains its intellectual appeal because it is a bold and plausible idea, it appears to fit, and it is clearly stated and argued. The dismissal of the idea on grounds of the disappointing laboratory findings would be premature, and it may be the laboratory paradigm that is weak, not the theory. My own view is that the plausibility of the concept has been weakened but not seriously damaged. More powerful stimuli and more appropriate measures of fear responding are needed before the theory can be subjected to rigorous testing. The prepared phobias which are the subject of the theory are intense, vivid, resistant, and persisting fears, and it is on such fears that the theory must be assessed, and not on watery, fragile, and fleeting fluctuations of skin conductance.

A fresh start can be made and the investigation of prepared fears placed on a new basis. The provision of an experimental basis for this theory was received with understandable enthusiasm, but the weaknesses of the testing method led the theory into a cul-de-sac.

A VICARIOUS METHOD

The adoption of a vicarious method is one way in which the subject can be revived and put to sterner tests. As an inducement and inspiration, Mineka's outstanding research on the origins of fears in monkeys can be taken as a model.[20] The fears induced in monkeys under tight laboratory conditions are intense, vivid, and lasting and leave no doubt whatever about whether one is or is not observing true fear.

Adopting Mineka's method, children who demonstrate no fear in the presence of a possibly prepared stimulus, such as a spider, could be shown videotapes of comparable children displaying fear when presented with a spider. If the observer children develop a fear of spiders, as expected, the *degree* of preparedness can be calculated by presenting videos that display "degraded stimuli," that show varying degrees of resemblance to a spider. Checks can be carried out by showing observer children videos of comparable models displaying fear when presented with non-prepared stimuli, such as flowers. The strong prediction is that the observers will develop a strong fear of spiders but not of flowers; they will quickly learn to fear prepared stimuli, but will not learn to fear the unprepared stimuli. For ethical reasons, only mild fears can be generated, and of course they must be eliminated promptly. There are other ways of approaching the problem, but a vicarious model of this type is worth considering.

EVOLUTION

Ohman, Dimberg, and Ost[21] made an evolutionary analysis of prepared fears, with special reference to fears of animals and social fears, and expressed the hope that it could be extended to other phobias, including agoraphobia, but at present it has little new to offer on the subject of agoraphobia.[22] Social fears originate from failures to assert or defend oneself in competitions for dominance, and are most obvious in "situations of uncertain dominance" and in "the context of social evaluation."[23] They are enhanced in social conflicts and encounters with strangers. Submissiveness is induced by angry faces, perhaps because they signal impending attack. In support of this argument, Ohman and his colleagues completed an interesting series of experiments on social fear, and determined that fears are more easily established to angry faces than to happy faces, especially when the angry face appears to be staring at the subject. They interpret the rise in social fears in teenagers as part of the person's struggle to establish his or her independent identity.

The slow progress in integrating agoraphobia may be attributable to their use of the conventional model of agoraphobia. As described earlier, there is good reason to re-view agoraphobia as a secondary consequence of panic disorders in a majority of cases. If the central fear in agoraphobia is not a fear of public places, but rather a fear that a catastrophic event might take place (in a public place), steps toward integration become possible. I think it likely that we are predisposed, or prepared, to respond fearfully to the perception of unexpected, novel, or inappropriate changes in our bodily sensations. No doubt most people experience several such events before they acquire a significant fear of bodily threat, but even a single, very unpleasant experience can initiate such a fear—it is highly prepared in terms of ease of acquisition and probably can be initiated even with "degraded input," in the sense of bodily sensations that are only a remote representation of a real threat. In certain circumstances, a sudden slowing or speeding of the heart can be misinterpreted as an impending heart attack and provoke almost as much fear as a genuine threat.

LOCK AND KEY

Despite the disappointments of the laboratory work on prepared fears, the results nevertheless provide some slight support for the notion of belongingness, the idea that prepared fears will emerge when there is an appropriate match between the pertinent stimulus and the associated response. In retrospect, we can now see that the equipotentiality premise began posing difficulties years ago. For example, English[24] was only partly successful in his attempt to replicate Watson's famous demonstration, in which he conditioned a young boy to fear a white rat.[25] English found that fear reactions could be conditioned only to selected stimuli. Similarly, Bregman failed in her thorough attempts to condition a group of infants to fear a range of simple but biologically insignificant objects.[26] The repeated presentation of geometrically shaped wooden objects and of cloth curtains, in conjunction with a disagreeably loud and startling sound, did not produce conditioned fear reactions to these biologically insignificant stimuli. She concluded that changes in emotional behavior are difficult to promote by joint stimulation in early life and therefore that conditioning cannot provide a satisfactory explanation of the acquisition of emotional responses in infancy. An engaging account of some weaknesses of the equipotentiality premise can be found in the writings of Valentine, a prominent child psychologist of his time. In his analysis of Watson's demonstration, Valentine considered whether the fear of the rat was perhaps "readily established partly because there was an existing innate tendency, though as yet unawakened, to fear the rat."[27] He then went on to describe some of his own tests, including an unsuccessful attempt to condition fear to an unfamiliar object that "could not be supposed to have any innate fear attached to it, namely, an old pair of opera glasses."[28] An earnest colleague once asked if Valentine might not have had a better result if he had used a new pair of opera glasses, but we can let that pass. Overcoming his resistance, Valentine performed further tests on his own child, despite causing "momentary discomfort to one's little ones." But the child was "an exceptionally healthy, strong and jovial youngster, and I hardened my heart sufficiently to try one or two simple tests with her."[29]

His demonstration followed the lines used by Watson, and when Valentine's child, aged 1 year, stretched out to touch the opera glasses, he loudly blew a whistle behind her. The child "quietly turned around as if to see where the noise came from." This procedure was repeated several times, but the child never showed any fear of the opera glasses. Later in the afternoon, the same experiment was repeated using a caterpillar as the stimulus. At the first loud noise, the child gave a scream and turned away from the caterpillar. This procedure was repeated four times and the effect was the same on each occasion. The tests were continued for the next few days and the child showed evidence of an unstable fear of the caterpillar. Although the fear showed signs of spontaneous fading, it was readily restored after only slight provocation. "Here we have again the *rousing of the lurking fear* by the added disturbance of the whistle" (italics added).[30] Using the analogy of a lock and a key, Valentine stressed that the noise itself became aversive when associated with the caterpillar, but not with the opera glasses.

Valentine's case for the selective quality of fear acquisition was supported by observations on other young children. He quoted the example of a 2-year-old girl who readily acquired a fear of dogs with only slight provocation, and this was contrasted with the absence of fear "even when real pain was suffered under circumstances in which no object stimulating an innate tendency to fear is present."[31]

Demonstrations of this type and the experimental information assembled by Seligman and Hager are a serious challenge to the equipotentiality premise and to theories that rely on the premise. The corollary for fears, that all stimuli have an equal chance of being transformed into fear signals, is not confirmed by surveys of the distribution of fears in the general population or in psychiatric samples. Subject only to their prominence in the environment, many objects and situations should have an equal probability of becoming fear-provoking. Instead, what we find is that some fears are exceedingly common—far too common for conditioning theory to explain. Other fears are far too rare. A fear of the dark is common among children but a fear of pyjamas is unknown. For animal fears, one might expect that within a city population a fear of lambs would be about as prevalent as a fear of snakes. In fact, the fear of snakes is common and that of lambs rare. Furthermore, a genuine fear of snakes often is reported by people who have little or no contact with them. The acquisition of the fear of snakes in the absence of direct contact opens three possibilities. The fear of snakes might be innate, might be transmitted indirectly, or might be "lurking" and will appear with only slight provocation. The last two possibilities are compatible.

UNPREPARED PHOBIAS

As opposed to prepared associations, unprepared connections should be more difficult to acquire and transient. The following three cases of patients who developed unprepared phobias are presented because of their inherent interest and because they led to some surprising conclusions.[32]

The first patient, Mrs. V., was admitted to the hospital with a severe and chronic neurotic disorder in which the main features were compulsive rituals centered on a strong fear of chocolate—scarcely the basis for a prepared fear of biological significance. It is difficult to imagine our pre-technological ancestors fleeing into the bushes at the sight of a well-made chocolate truffle. The patient complained of and demonstrated extreme fear when confronted with chocolate or any object or place associated with it. She avoided most brown objects and as a result would never agree to sit on any furniture that had brown in it. On one occasion, she walked up eight flights of stairs rather than push the elevator button because she saw a brown stain close to the button. The patient took great care to avoid any shops that might stock chocolate or any public places where chocolate might be eaten. In the course of several years, the fear grew until she was forced to cease working and became increasingly confined. Before admission to the hospital she was practically house-bound. There was no denying the authenticity of her distress when she was presented with a chocolate, nor was there any doubt about the vigor of the avoidance behavior evoked by such confrontation. Because of the rarity of this complaint and because a fear of chocolate is unrelated to natural dangers and has no biological significance, it meets the defining characteristics of an *unprepared* connection.

According to the patient and the independent account given by her husband, her problems began shortly after the death of her mother, to whom she was inordinately attached. After the death, she was depressed for a protracted period and became conscious of a strong aversion toward —and probably a fear of—cemeteries and funeral parlors. She first became aware of a slight distaste for chocolate several months after the death of her mother, but it was nearly four years after this event that she realized that she was actively avoiding chocolate and indeed had become extremely frightened of it. Before her mother's death, she had eaten chocolate with enjoyment, but this pleasure waned in the period immediately after her mother's death. In the course of her otherwise largely unsuccessful treatment, the patient regained the ability to eat small pieces of chocolate, but the pleasurable taste never returned.

The most relevant characteristics of this patient's intense fear of chocolate were its rarity, its gradual onset, its intensity, the accompanying avoidance behavior, the generalization from chocolate to a wide variety of brown objects, and its resistance to modification. The rarity, gradual acquisition, and biological insignificance mark it as different from the commonly recognized prepared phobias. It is an example of an unprepared fear.

The second illustration was provided by a psychiatric patient who complained of an intense and disabling fear of fiery colors, particularly red and orange. Like the previous patient, she experienced considerable distress when confronted with any of these colors, and as a result developed extensive and persistent patterns of avoidance. She too had become virtually house-bound because of her fear. Given its rarity, gradual onset, intensity, wide generalization, associated avoidance behavior, and resistance to treatment, this fear too can be classed as unprepared. Apart from the association of red and orange with the idea of fire, a fear of these colors cannot be said to have any biological significance. As it turned out, this fear was more closely associated with subjective feelings of distress, particularly with symptoms of feeling hot and flushed, than it was with fires or fire hazards.

The third unusual phobia was that of a young woman who was virtually blind from early infancy and complained of an excessive fear of vegetables and plants, particularly their leaves. The phobia had its origin in early childhood, and, like the other two patients, this person expressed and displayed intense fear and engaged in extensive and active avoidance. She attributed the genesis of the fear to a series of extremely unpleasant experiences that she had undergone as a child, claiming that other children had taunted and teased her by rubbing vegetables and plants on her face in order to irritate her. In her view, these experiences had produced an intense dislike of vegetables and plants that later turned into fear. Her phobia handicapped her in a number of ways and prevented her from engaging in ordinary social activities. She was unable to eat in public places or in unfamiliar homes in which vegetables or salads might be served. She took care to avoid certain areas where she knew there might be shops that stocked vegetables or plants. Each week she had two or more vivid or terrifying dreams in which vegetables or plants featured prominently. These dreams seemed to increase the severity of the fear. Like the other two patients, she made little progress in therapy despite receiving concentrated help.

These extraordinary examples present us with a conflict. On the one hand, the fears can be regarded as unprepared because they are rare, unrelated to natural dangers, and of no apparent biological significance. On the other hand, Seligman postulates that prepared learning, *not* unprepared learning, is unusually resistant to extinction, is non-cognitive, and generalizes widely. So these phobias have the defining features of unpreparedness but the empirical properties that are said to cohere with preparedness: resistance to extinction, irrationality, and wide generalization.

Among the possible resolutions considered by Rachman and Seligman it was suggested that the analysis of preparedness in phobias might retain its value but that some of the hypothesized consequences of having an unprepared phobia may need revision. "In particular, it need not follow that comparatively unprepared phobias will necessarily show easy extinction and narrow generalization."[33] They also considered the symbolic significance in each of these cases and the possibility that these rare instances may reflect a peculiar sampling problem.

These possibilities were taken up in a retrospective study carried out by de Silva, Rachman and Seligman.[34] Sixty-nine phobic and 82 obsessional patients treated at the Maudsley Hospital in London were rated for the preparedness of their fears, that is, for the evolutionary significance of the content and behavior of the disorder. A satisfactory and reliable rating system was developed, but it was found that the degree of preparedness was not correlated with any significant feature of the fear or of the patients' clinical condition and progress. They were unable to find support for the clinical predictions that flow from the theory, but the authors were careful to point out that their study did not disprove the theory.

It is entirely possible for the essentials of the theory to be in order even if the clinical implications that are drawn from it are found to be incorrect. So for example, the argument that the distribution of human fears is non-random and therefore indicative of evolutionary pressure on learning to be afraid of specific objects or situations is not weakened. And it is this non-randomness that forms the core of the preparedness concept.[35]

In this clinical sample, they found that the great majority of phobias and obsessions were prepared. Unprepared phobias were rare, but unprepared obsessions were not uncommon. Only 3 of the 69 phobic patients had unprepared phobias, but as has been pointed out, these clinically observed unprepared phobias do not conform to the pattern predicted by the theory. The absence of a connection between degree of preparedness and such clinically relevant variables as severity, duration, onset, or response to treatment was confirmed in a study of 49 patients with specific phobias.[36] Additional evidence of preparedness in a clinical sample was collected by de Silva, who found a "very high preponderance of prepared phobias" in 88 phobic patients. All 14 of the patients who said they had had their phobias "always" obtained high ratings of preparedness.[37]

On the other hand, Merckelbach and others found less evidence of preparedness in the fears of 50 obsessional and 13 phobic patients. The significance of this finding is unclear because the four raters of preparedness had disagreements.[38] The inter-rater correlations ranged from a low of 0.43 to 0.76. The inter-rater reliability in de Silva's study was 0.79, and 0.78 to 0.90 in the original report.[39] It is possible that the apparent conflict between theory and clinical material arises precisely from the fact that the material is clinical. Those rare instances when unprepared fears persist and lead the affected person to seek professional help, may be distinctive. A more appropriate test of the preparedness theory of fears will have to be based on an examination of the fears of a large random sample of people.

There are difficulties in attempting to evaluate any biological-evolutionary arguments applied to human behavior, but the major parts of Seligman's theory are open to examination. Among its other merits, the theory emphasizes the biological nature of fear, has a broad sweep, and helps to impose some order on the disparate information on human fears. It is my belief that supporting evidence in abundance will be uncovered when a suitable method for analyzing deep and strong fears is established. However, even if the theory fails to attract this support in the future, it has exposed the untenability of the equipotentiality premise applied to human fears and opened the way to a number of interesting alternatives.

PART

THE
ACQUISITION
OF FEAR

CHAPTER

THE CONDITIONING THEORY OF FEAR ACQUISITION —AND WHY IT FAILED

The first modern theory of the causes of fear, founded on the concept of conditioning, had a central role in the development of behavior therapy. By the middle of the 1970s it became apparent that conditioning theory was limited, and psychologists lost interest in the idea, turning instead to cognitive explanations. New findings on conditioning processes have now renewed interest in the subject and a radical revision of the concept of conditioning is underway. These changing ideas have direct implications for theories of how fears are acquired, and they may presage the formulation of a fully revised and expanded conditioning theory. Although that time has not arrived, the reasons for the radical revision are of consequence and will be described immediately after the premature funeral of the traditional theory is completed, on page 179.

Animals readily acquire fears under laboratory conditions. Evidence accumulated in numerous such experiments, expecially those on the induction of neurotic behavior, supplemented by naturalistic and clinical observations, led to the formulation of a theory to explain the genesis and spread of fears.[1] It was assumed that fears are acquired and that the process of acquisition is one of conditioning.[2]

CONDITIONING THEORY

The conditioning theory of fear acquisition was influential and for many years was accepted tacitly, even though there was relatively little debate about its merits. The theory constituted a major advance; it was useful in its own right, and it incorporated other theories, especially those which attempt to explain avoidance behavior. One version of the theory originated in the important work of Mowrer. "The position here taken is that anxiety is a learned response, occurring to signals (conditioned stimuli) that are premonitory of (i.e., have in the past been followed by) situations of injury of pain (unconditioned stimuli)."[3] He went on to argue that fear "may effectively motivate human beings" and that the reduction of fear "may serve powerfully to reinforce behavior that brings about such a state of relief or security."[4] Mowrer's thinking owed most to the writings of Pavlov, Freud, James, and Watson, and the developments of Mowrer's theory follow in the same tradition, amply encouraged by the results of research on the experimental induction of fears in animals. As it illustrates the main features, and flaws, of conditioning theories, this discussion will deal mainly with a version of the theory with which I have been associated.

Basing their theory on a combination of research findings, including the original experiments of Wolpe, clinical observations, and the writings of Mowrer, Watson and Rayner,[5] Wolpe and Rachman put forward this proposal. "Any neutral stimulus, simple or complex, that happens to make an impact on an individual at about the time that a fear reaction is evoked, acquires the ability to evoke fear subsequently . . . there will be generalization of fear reactions to stimuli resembling the conditioned stimulus."[6] This theory was elaborated by Rachman and Costello, who summarized the essentials of the theory in six statements.[7] After re-stating the elements of the original proposal, they added three new features. It was argued that neutral stimuli which are of relevance in the particular context are more likely to become fear signals, that the repetition of these associations between fear and the new phobic stimuli will strengthen the fear, and that associations of high-intensity fear situations and neutral stimuli are most likely to produce conditioned fear reactions. In 1965, three more elements were added and further consideration was given to the determinants of the strength of the fear. Eysenck and Rachman proposed that fear reactions are more likely to occur under conditions of excessive confinement.[8] They also incorporated the motivating qualities of the fear reaction in a manner originally proposed by Mowrer. Shortly after this extension was published, some of the difficulties, which are now acknowledged, began to appear. These led to a revision that for the first time incorporated the possibility, indeed the certainty, that emotional reactions, including fear, can be acquired vicariously.[9] The revision, which allowed that fears may be acquired directly *or* vicariously, led to a critical scrutiny of the whole theory.

Before drawing attention to the limitations of the theory, it is as well to give a concise account of some of the arguments and evidence in its favor.

Major features

The major features of the theory are as follows. It is assumed that fears are acquired, by a process of conditioning. Neutral stimuli that are associated with a pain-producing or fear-producing state of affairs acquire fearful qualities; they become conditioned fear stimuli. The strength of the fear is determined by the number of repetitions of the association between the pain or fear experienced and the stimuli, and by the intensity of the fear or pain experienced in the presence of the stimuli. Stimuli resembling the fear-evoking ones also acquire fearful properties, that is, they become secondary conditioned stimuli. The likelihood of fear developing is increased by confinement, by exposure to high-intensity pain or fear situations, and by frequent repetition of the association between the new conditioned stimulus and the pain or fear. It was proposed further that once objects or situations acquire fear-provoking qualities, they develop motivating properties. A secondary fear-drive emerges. Behavior that successfully reduces fear will increase in strength.

Supporting evidence was drawn from six sources: research on the induction of fear in animals, the development of anxiety states in combat soldiers, experiments on the induction of fear in a small number of children, clinical observations (for example, dental phobias), incidental findings from the use of aversion therapy, and a few experiments on the effects of traumatic stimulation. Reference will also be made to evidence that has accumulated since the theory was formulated.

Evidence

The strongest and most systematic evidence was drawn from a multitude of experiments on laboratory animals. Evidently, it is easy to generate fear reactions in animals by exposing them to a conjunction of neutral and aversive stimuli, usually electric shock. The acquired fear reactions (usually inferred from the emergence of avoidance behavior, physiological disturbances, and disruptive behavior or from some combination of these three indexes) can be produced readily by employing conventional conditioning procedures. There is little doubt about the facility with which fear reactions can be conditioned, at least in animals that are tested under laboratory constraints. (As we shall see, there are grounds for doubting whether the laboratory induction of fear in animals provides an adequate foundation for theorizing about fear acquisition by animals outside the laboratory and in human subjects, in or out of the laboratory. Also, the demonstration that fears can be generated by conditioning does not mean that they are ordinarily acquired in this way.)

Observations of people under combat conditions show that intense fear can result from traumatic stimulation. Flanagan reported that the overwhelming majority of combat air crew experienced fear during their missions and although these reactions were relatively transient, they sometimes presaged the development of combat fatigue that included strong elements of fear.[10] A minority of air crew developed significant and lasting fears. The form and content of these fears, their tendency to generalize, and the conditions under which they arose are consistent with conditioning theory.

In clinical practice, it is not uncommon for patients to give an account of the development of their fears that can be construed in terms of conditioning theory. Sometimes they can date the onset of the fear to a specific conditioning experience. From a study of 34 cases of dental phobia, we learn that every subject reported having had a traumatic dental experience, such as fearing suffocation from an anaesthetic mask, on at least one occasion in childhood.[11] However, these 34 people were found to be generally neurotic, and 10 comparison subjects who had experienced comparable traumatic incidents with dentists during their childhood showed little sign of dental fear.

In a study of people who are frightened of dogs, Di Nardo and others found that nearly two-thirds had experienced a conditioning event in which a dog featured, and in over half of these instances the animal had inflicted pain.[12] However, two-thirds of a comparable group of subjects who were not frightened of dogs reported that they too had experienced a conditioning event and that in half of the instances the animal had inflicted pain. These reports provide some support for the theory, but also illustrate the fact that conditioning experiences, even those of a painful nature, do not necessarily give rise to fear. Here as in other instances, there was less fear than an unqualified conditioning theory would lead us to predict. Presumably those people who experienced conditioning events, even painful ones, but failed to acquire a fear, placed a different interpretation on the event than did those who became frightened. Di Nardo and his colleagues note that all of their fearful subjects "believed that fear and physical harm were likely consequences of an encounter with a dog, while very few nonfearful subjects had such expectations . . . an exaggerated expectation of harm appears to be a factor in the maintenance of the fear."[13]

The role that subjects or phobic patients attribute to direct and indirect experiences in generating their fears differs with the content of the fear. In their analysis of 183 patients with clinically significant phobias, classified into six different groups of fear, Ost and Hugdahl found a range of attributions.[14] For example, 88 percent of the agoraphobic patients attributed the onset of their phobia to a conditioning experience, but only 50 percent of the patients who were frightened of animals attributed the onset of their fear to such an experience. Among those who feared animals, 40 percent traced the origin to indirect experiences, but this attribution was uncommon among the agoraphobics. The percentages of patients who attributed greatest importance to direct experiences, which in this analysis coincides with conditioning onset, were as follows, in ascending order: blood phobics, animal phobics, social phobics, dental phobics, claustrophobics, and agoraphobics.

Across all groups, there was a strong tendency to attribute the onset of the phobia to direct conditioning experiences, and three times as many patients made this attribution rather than one involving indirect acquisition. Interesting as they are, these figures cannot be taken at face value, because they are compiled from the patients' recollection of the onset of their phobia and their interpretation of those events. Information of this kind is open to some distortion as the result of forgetting and the operation of biases in interpreting past events. Ost's finding that the overwhelming majority of agoraphobic patients ascribe the onset of their fears to conditioning experiences has to be reconciled with contrary evidence reported by Mathews, Gelder, and Johnston,[15] who found little evidence of conditioning onsets in their patients. They criticized the conditioning theory and stated that the agoraphobics whom they studied "cannot as a rule recall either any event that provoked intense fear or any repeated fearful event that occurred in the circumstances they subsequently came to avoid."[16] Ost and Hugdahl argue that the *first* (original emphasis) episode of anxiety can be identified in only a minority of cases. However, they go on to point out that "after the first occurrence the anxiety attack reappears in the situations that are avoided, and this certainly serves as a repeated fearful event . . . nearly half (46%) of the patients described a rapid onset" and early development of the phobia so that "within two weeks from the first anxiety attack, they had a fully developed agoraphobia."[17] It emerges from this apparent conflict of evidence[18] that a good deal depends on the definition of the conditioning event, and these discrepancies are unlikely to be resolved until a standard criterion is applied in deciding whether or not an event is regarded as a conditioning experience.

The classical demonstration by Watson and Rayner of the deliberate genesis of fear in a young child had a considerable influence on the early theorists, but attempts to reproduce the phenomenon had little success.[19] The most systematic collection of information on the induction of conditioned fear in humans was compiled by Ohman and his colleagues in Sweden.[20] Stimulated by Seligman's introduction of the concept of prepared fears, they attempted to discover whether people are "prepared" to acquire fears to particular stimuli.[21] As described earlier, they were able to produce conditioned fear in humans under laboratory conditions, but the responses tended to be weak, transient, and incomplete. They are incomplete in the sense that the evidence for conditioning is confined largely to changes in electrical activity of the skin, and it has not been possible to obtain dependable consistent evidence of conditioned heart rate responses (electrical activity of the skin is a poor index of fear, and elevated heart rate is a preferable measure). The conditioned responses were of small magnitude and not readily evoked, and with few exceptions, the electrodermal responses were extinguished within a few trials. The conditioned responses were easily altered or abolished by instructions.

Incidental observations arising out of the use of aversion therapy, a technique explicitly based on the classical conditioning theory, provided some early support for the theory,[22] and in recent years has been supplemented by work carried out at Wisconsin University.[23] After undergoing repeated associations between alcohol and chemically induced nausea, many patients experience nausea when they taste or even smell alcohol. In a famous case reported by Hammersley, a successfully treated patient subsequently changed his mind and decided that abstinence was not the lesser of two evils. He embarked on a "deconditioning" program and repeatedly drank himself through many episodes of intense nausea until his conditioned reaction to alcohol subsided and finally disappeared.[24]

Hallam and Rachman described yet another reaction. An alcoholic patient "who had been given whiskey to drink during (electrical) aversion therapy accused the therapist of adding a chemical to the whiskey to give it a bad taste."[25] (This is not an uncommon report even when no chemicals are used.) The same patient "went into a bar against advice during treatment, but on trying to raise a glass of whiskey to his mouth had a panic attack and returned to hospital in an anxious state".

Bancroft observed the development of intense anxiety reactions among some of his patients, but pointed out that the large majority showed no signs of conditioned fear reactions, regardless of the success or failure of the treatment program.[26] These incidental findings indicate that what appear to be conditioned fear responses can develop during aversion therapy, but it does not follow that they are causally relevant to the outcome of therapy.

Recent evidence on the effects of aversion therapy convincingly demonstrates that "aversion therapy does indeed result in a conditioned response to the target stimulus."[27] This conclusion is drawn from investigations in which varying types of aversive stimulus, chemical or electrical, were used. After therapy, the subjects responded differently to the conditioned stimulus than they did to the neutral stimulus, supporting the view that there is an "associative process in aversion therapy."[28] Evidence of conditioning was provided by the psychophysiological responses to the target stimulus, negative evaluations of the stimulus, sometimes plain dislike for the stimulus, and indirectly by the decreased use of the addictive substance. It is of particular interest that the heart rate responses emerged as an "especially sensitive index of aversive conditioning effects"[29] and that no other variable predicted the outcome of therapy.

The research by Baker and his colleagues demonstrates that it is possible to develop methods for conditioning psychophysiological, cognitive, and behavioral reactions to aversive stimuli, but as they point out, the results defy a "simple conditioning hypothesis."[30] In any event the question that is presently at issue centers on the feasibility of conditioning *fear* reactions. Here it should be remembered that Hallam and others found comparable psychophysiological, cognitive, and behavioral changes in patients who had been treated by *non-conditioning* methods.[31] Nevertheless, these demonstrations that people can acquire conditioned responses to stimuli after aversive procedures make it possible to determine whether or not *fears* can be conditioned in this way. As before, it is necessary to bear in mind that even if successful, such a demonstration would not imply that naturally-acquired fears necessarily follow the same, conditioning, path.

Another source of support for a conditioning theory of fear acquisition comes from experiments in which subjects were given injections of scoline, which produces a temporary suspension of breathing.[32] Not surprisingly, most of the subjects who underwent this harrowing experience developed intense fears of the stimulus encountered in or connected with the experimental setting. In fact, the intensity of their fears tended to increase even in the absence of further unpleasant experiences (providing one of the few examples of fear incubation, see page 252).

The conditioning theory of fear acquisition does not require single trial or traumatic onsets, but fears that arise in an acute manner are more readily accommodated than those of uncertain onset. Even though acute onset fears are more easily accommodated, partly I suspect because our conception of conditioned fear is based largely on laboratory experiments in which the aversive stimulus often is traumatic, we also have to account for fears that are produced by experiences of a sub-traumatic or even of a non-traumatic nature.

Fears that emerge in the absence of any identifiable learning experience present difficulties for the theory. Hence, fears that develop gradually (for example, social fears) and cannot be traced to specific occurrences are a potential embarrassment. Even more troublesome are fears that arise even in the absence of any direct contact with the fear stimulus.

Although the importance of the phenomenon of acquired food aversions was not made evident until 1966, it sometimes is used to buttress the traditional conditioning theory. More fittingly, the findings on food aversions served as a prompt for critical thinking that led to a radical revision of the concept of conditioning. Garcia and his colleagues were the first to demonstrate that strong and lasting aversive reactions can be acquired with ease when the appropriate food stimulus is associated with illness,[33] even if the illness occurs many hours after eating. The phenomenon was given the catchphrase "the sauce Bearnaise" effect by Seligman, who elucidated the theoretical significance of the research.[34] Given that the genesis of food aversions is a form of conditioning, and if we also agree to an equation between the acquisition of a taste aversion and the acquisition of a fear, this phenomenon may provide a valuable means of collecting information about the conditioning theory of fear acquisition. In Seligman's use of these findings, phobias are seen as instances of highly prepared learning, and as we have seen, this prepared learning is "selective, highly resistant to extinction, probably non-cognitive, and can be acquired in one trial."[35]

The idea that food aversions and fear might be related receives some indirect support from the elevated incidence of food aversions in neurotic subjects. Wallen compared 240 normal adults with 95 people of comparable age who had been rejected from the U.S. Navy on the grounds of neurotic disturbance.[36] The neurotic men reported four times as many food aversions as did the other subjects. As neurotics have more fears than non-neurotic people, it seems possible that they have a sensitivity of some type that predisposes them to acquire fears and aversions more easily than do other people. If the acquisition of food aversions is used to support the conditioning theory of fear, it will have to take into account the unexpected temporal stretch of the taste aversion phenomenon, that is, the delay that supervenes between tasting the food and the onset of nausea. (The question of whether or not fear can be influenced by events that are temporally separated is discussed in Chapter 16.) Classical conditioning is expedited by temporal proximity between stimuli; although there are convincing examples of conditioned responses being established even when there are prolonged delays, these tend to be exceptional. Experimentally induced food aversions are easily, powerfully, and rapidly established, even when there are long delays between the events. Therefore, if the food-aversion phenomenon helps to provide support for a new or revised conditioning theory of fear, the temporal qualities of classical conditioning processes will have to be de-emphasized.

Weighing the evidence

There appears to be strong evidence to support the idea that fears can be acquired by a conditioning process. This conclusion is justified even though some of the evidence is subject to contrary interpretations or is inherently weak. The strongest evidence, in terms of replicability and completeness, comes from the genesis of fear in laboratory animals. This voluminous and convincing evidence is supported by some limited findings on the induction of fear reactions in adults, but the stimuli were traumatic. The work on the induction of fear in children is inconsistent and based on very small numbers, and all of the experiments have been criticized for errors of contamination and confounding. Clinical observations provide interesting supporting evidence, but unfortunately the quality of the information is unsatisfactory, comprising as it almost always does a selected set of observations rarely supported by external confirmatory evidence. It also suffers from the fact that the subject or patient's account of the genesis of the fear relies on the assumption of an accurate memory and powers of recall. This is an unsatisfactory basis for building a theory. Because it has greater immediacy and the possibility of at least some external confirmation, the evidence on combat fears and combat neuroses has something to recommend it. Very little of this information was collected in a systematic manner, and it too suffers from selection bias, incompleteness, and the interpretive gloss placed on the accounts by the reporting psychologist or psychiatrist. Nevertheless, it is rich in interest and authentic in quality. Fortunately, military combat is an exceptional experience and for purposes of psychological theorizing, it is unwise to overemphasize the significance of fears that are acquired in these unnatural circumstances. The intriguing findings on the speedy development of food aversions may have opened a door for the establishment of a more satisfactory theory of non-rational fears.

Given that fears can be produced by conditioning events, these events may be implicated to a greater or lesser extent in different types of phobias. They appear to play an important role in the development of dental fears and fears of dogs, but are less significant in the acquisition of a fear of snakes or of tarantulas. Murray and Foote found little evidence of the role of "direct conditioning experiences" in the acquisition of a fear of snakes in their 60 subjects, and added that most of them reported that they had had very little personal experience with snakes.[37] Kleinknecht found that slightly more than a quarter of his sample of tarantula-phobic subjects attributed the onset of the fear to direct experiences.[38] The idea that conditioning experiences are more significant in the genesis of certain types of fear than in others also receives support from Ost and Hugdahl's analysis of the way in which six subgroups of phobic patients acquired their fears.[39] A large majority of agoraphobic patients attributed the onset of their problems to a conditioning event, but only half of the animal phobics gave such reports.

Even in its strongest form, the conditioning theory of fear acquisition cannot encompass all of the observed fears. There is more than one pathway to fear.

In reviewing the types and sources of evidence in support of the conditioning theory, an attempt has been made to convey the impression that there is a good deal to be said in its favor. Why then is it necessary to revise the theory? It has merits, and some experimental and clinical support, but its applicability is limited. Whatever its value, the theory is not a satisfactorily comprehensive account of the genesis or maintenance of human fears.

WHY IT FAILED

There are eight arguments against acceptance of the conditioning theory of fear acquisition as a comprehensive explanation. People fail to acquire fears in what should be fear-conditioning situations, such as air raids. It is difficult to produce stable conditioned fear reactions in human subjects, even under controlled laboratory conditions. The conditioning theory rests on the untenable equipotentiality premise. The distribution of fears in normal and neurotic populations is difficult to reconcile with the conditioning theory. A significant number of people with phobias recount histories that cannot be accommodated by the theory. Fears can be acquired vicariously. Fears can be acquired by the reception of threatening information. Fears can be acquired even when the causal events are temporally separated.

The arguments

1. Failures to acquire fear.   It would seem that few experiences could be more frightening than undergoing an air raid, but as described earlier, the great majority of people endured air raids extraordinarily well during World War II, contrary to the universal expectation of mass panic. Exposure to repeated bombing did not produce significant increases in psychiatric disorders. Short-lived fear reactions were common, but surprisingly few persistent phobic reactions developed. Few of the civilians who were injured or wounded developed a fear of the situation in which they received the injury.

The observations of comparative fearlessness—despite repeated exposures to intense trauma, uncontrollability, uncertainty, and even injury—

are contrary to the conditioning theory of fear acquisition. People subjected to repeated air raids should acquire multiple intense conditioned fear reactions, and these should be strengthened by repeated exposures. Recent evidence of civilian reactions to the warlike conditions of the Middle East and Northern Ireland are consistent with the findings from World War II. These findings run contrary to prediction.

Lesser examples of the failure to acquire fear include people who fail to develop a fear of dogs despite having unpleasant experiences with them, and even having been bitten.[40] Dental fears are fairly common, but large numbers of people fail to develop a fear of dental treatment even though they have undergone uncomfortable and even painful experiences while confined in the dentist's chair.[41]

The apparent absence of a direct relationship between injury and subsequent fear runs contrary to conditioning theory. There should be a direct, easily demonstrable connection between injury and fear, but there is not.

2. The conditioning of human fears. Bregman's thorough attempt to condition fear in 15 normal infants was a failure.[42] Evidence from a different source and of a different nature is consistent with this failure and with the wartime observations that people failed to acquire fears in circumstances where the theory predicts that they should develop. Many writers on the subject of electrical aversion therapy appeared to "assume that the successful administration of treatment would result in the development of a mini-phobia—repeated associations of the conditioned stimulus with an unpleasant electrical shock would result" in a conditioned fear response to the presentation of the stimulus.[43] To the contrary, Marks and Gelder found that most of their patients reported indifference to the conditioned stimuli employed in electrical aversion therapy, and it was rare to find anyone who complained of fear after undergoing the course of treatment.[44] The same result was described by Bancroft, and by Hallam, Rachman, and Falkowski.[45]

Because the expected conditioned fear reactions did not emerge and for some related reasons, Hallam and Rachman carried out two studies that were intended to provide a laboratory analogue of electrical aversion therapy. The results failed to confirm the prediction that conditioned fear reactions would develop, and instead "the 'conditioned response' did not resemble either in magnitude or direction the cardiac responses of phobic patients who are presented with their phobic stimulus, and nor did the subjects report anxiety or discomfort in the presence of the conditioned stimulus."[46] We were equally unsuccessful in our search for evidence of conditioned fear reactions developing in alcoholic patients who undertook aversion therapy. "In effect, the results show that when alcoholics who have undergone aversion therapy are compared with alcoholics who have been treated in other ways, there is no difference in their subjective anxiety responses to alcoholic stimuli or in the peripheral autonomic responses that usually accompany states of fear or anxiety. Subjective distaste for alcohol seems to be the only specific consequence of aversion therapy."[47]

As described in the previous chapter, Ohman[48] and his colleagues had only limited success in generating conditioned fear reactions in the laboratory; the absence of expected conditioned responses and the instability, incompleteness, and weakness of those that were produced do not provide significant support for the conditioning theory.

3. The equipotentiality premise. The theory assumes that any stimulus can be transformed into a fear signal; the choice of stimulus is a matter of indifference. As discussed in Chapter 10, Seligman[49] has convincingly argued that this premise is untenable, and hence its incorporation in the theory is a serious weakness.

4. The distribution of fears. The corollary of the equipotentiality premise is that all stimuli have an equal chance of being transformed into fear signals. However, this is not borne out by surveys of the distribution of fears, either in a general population or in psychiatric samples. To take one example, the epidemiological study of common fears carried out in Burlington by Agras and others[50] showed that the prevalence of a fear of snakes was 390 per 1000 people, and the fear of dental treatment was only 198 per 1000—despite the fact that contact with a dentist was almost certainly much more frequent, and much more likely to be painful. To take another example from their survey, the prevalence of snake fears among the 30-year-old respondents was more than five times as great as their fear of injections.

Hallowell's observations of people living in an isolated Indian community in Canada are consistent with the view that the distribution of fears is not random. They were fearless of certain dangerous animals such as wolves and bears but were considerably frightened by some harmless creatures such as frogs and toads.[51]

Subject only to their prominence in the environment, many objects and situations should have an equal probability of provoking fear. What we find instead is that some fears are exceedingly common, and certainly much too common for the theory. Other fears are far too rare. The fear of snakes is common and the fear of lambs is rare; moreover, a genuine fear of snakes often is reported by people who have had not contact with the reptiles. Consequently, one is forced to conclude that the fear of snakes can be acquired even in the absence of direct contact, and this significant concession opens three possibilities. The fear of snakes is innate, it can be transmitted indirectly, or it is "lurking" and will appear with only slight provocation. The last two of these three possibilities are compatible.

5. *Patients' reports of fear onset.* Whatever its value, the conditioning theory is not a satisfactorily comprehensive account of the genesis of fear. It can be difficult to determine the origin of a patient's phobia, and there are phobias in which there was "no apparent trauma to initiate the phobia."[52] Goorney and O'Connor encountered this problem of identifying a plausible precipitant in their analysis of the excessive fears of RAF crews during peacetime. In a study of 97 cases, they were able to attribute the fear to specific precipitants such as accidents or frightening incidents in a quarter of the cases. In one-third there was no discernible cause, and in the remainder, the precipitants, such as a return to flying after a long abstention, were not of a traumatic or conditioning type.[53]

The absence of a plausible conditioning precipitant in a significant number of phobic patients was demonstrated in the analysis by Ost[54] referred to earlier. Twenty-one percent of 183 phobic patients reportedly acquired their phobia indirectly, and the remaining 14 percent were unable to recall the onset. In an expansion of this study, Ost found an association between the manner in which the phobia was acquired and the age of onset. The indirectly acquired phobias developed at an earlier age than the phobias with a conditioning origin.[55]

6. *The vicarious acquisition of fear.* The significant advances made in our understanding of the processes of observational learning and modeling made it plain that we acquire much of our behavior, including emotional responses, by vicarious experiences.[56] By 1978, it began to seem probable that "fears can be acquired either directly or vicariously, and that stimuli are likely to develop fearful qualities if they are associated, directly or vicariously, with painful or frightening experiences."[57] It was conceded at the time that the evidence in support of vicarious acquisition of fear in humans was indirect and largely anecdotal, but progress has been made and is described in the following chapter. The case for accepting that fears can be acquired vicariously is now very strong.

7. *The informational acquisition of fear.* It was suggested at the same time that fears might be acquired by the absorption of information, especially information that conveys a threat.[58] The accumulation of evidence on this proposition has been slower but is no less plausible.

8. *Acquisition by remote events.* At present there is not sufficient information to include the acquisition of fear by a temporally remote event as an additional argument against acceptance of the theory, but convincing proof that fears can be acquired even when the stimulus and response events are separated in time would oppose the original conditioning theory.

In conclusion, the weaknesses of the conditioning theory are serious but not necessarily fatal. One can either search for an entirely new theory to replace it or adopt a reformist view and formulate modifications and extensions of the theory. At its best, the theory can provide a partial explanation for the genesis of some fears. However, it cannot explain how the common fears are acquired, nor can it explain the observed distribution of fears, the uncertain point of onset of many phobias, the indirect transmission of fears, the ready acquisition of prepared phobias, and the failure of fears to arise in circumstances predicted by the theory. Fears acquired without direct contact with a fearful stimulus are an added problem for the theory, and the acquisition of fears when the causal events are temporally separated is yet one more burden.

A satisfactorily comprehensive theory of fear acquisition must accommodate all of that information plus the facts that fears can emerge gradually as well as suddenly, that there are individual differences in susceptibility, and the probable acquisition of fears of objects or situations that the person has never encountered. It is also necessary to account for the acquisition of fears by events that are temporally separated.

HOW THE THEORY WAS REVIVED

By 1977, the conditioning theory of fear acquisition appeared to be played out.[59] The theory had been used with skill by Eysenck, Wolpe, and others[60] in formulating a behavioral account of neurotic behavior, and provided the basis on which behavior therapy was constructed. It retained considerable explanatory power, but as described above, it was found to be incomplete: many people are unable to recount a conditioning onset of their fears, and fears can be acquired even when the stimulus (CS) and the aversive event (US) are separated in time (so-called non-contiguous acquisitions of fear). None of the eight objections to the original theory is fatal to the revised view of conditioning, but it is also true that certain phenomena, such as vicarious acquisition, are not deducible from the revision.

It turns out that the traditional insistence on the contiguity of the conditioned stimulus (CS) and the unconditioned stimulus (US) as a necessary condition for the establishment of a conditioned response is mistaken. Conditioned responses can develop even when the conditioned stimulus and the unconditioned event are separated in time. The most convincing examples of non-contiguous conditioning come from the literature on food aversions. If animals eat a novel food and are made ill (say, by injection of an emetic), minutes or even hours later, they form a strong aversion to the food. A single experience is sufficient to establish a lasting conditioned aversion. Rescorla observes that "although conditioning can sometimes be slow, in fact most modern conditioning preparations routinely show rapid learning. One trial learning is not confined to flavor-aversion."[61] Apparently the associative span of animals "is capable of bridging long temporal intervals."[62] However, the learning must be selective, otherwise the animals would collect a "useless clutter of irrelevant associations."[63] According to Mackintosh, the "function of conditioning is to enable organisms to discover probable causes of events of significance."[64]

Additional evidence that contradicts the contiguity theory of conditioning comes from research on the *blocking* effect and on the consequences of *random control*. A stimulus will not become a conditioned signal (CS) even if it is repeatedly presented immediately before a US event, unless it is of some value. If the US event is already well predicted by another stimulus, the addition of a second stimulus is of no value, and hence no conditioning occurs. If the delivery of the electric shock is already well-predicted by a tone (CS), then introducing a visual stimulus in addition to the tone will be of no predictive value and will not develop into a conditioned signal. The second stimulus is redundant and conditioning will not develop even if the conditioned stimulus is repeatedly presented in contiguity with the electric shock (US). The existing conditioned response is sufficient and blocks the development of the redundant new signal.

The random control effect also demonstrates that mere contiguity is not sufficient to produce conditioning. If a stimulus, say a bell, regularly precedes an electric shock, then conditioning will occur; however, if the electric shock also is delivered repeatedly in the *absence* of the bell stimulus, little conditioning will develop. "Temporal contiguity, then, between a CS (or response) and a reinforcer is neither necessary nor sufficient to ensure conditioning."[65] The stimulus will not turn into a conditioned stimulus unless it predicts the reinforcer better than other stimuli. The new stimulus is uninformative, and "conditioning occurs selectively to good predictors of reinforcement at the expense of worse predictors."[66]

The new view of conditioning is not merely an exercise in discrediting the traditional explanation. Interesting new phenomena have been discovered, precise predictions are now possible, and fresh explanations of associative learning have been put forward. If simple contiguity is insufficient, it begins to seems that it is information that is important; the modern view is that conditioning involves learning about relationships between events. Rescorla argues that "Pavlovian conditioning is not a stupid process by which the organism willy-nilly forms associations between any two stimuli that happen to co-occur."[67] Rather, the organism is better seen as "an information seeker, using logical and perceptual relations among events . . . to form a sophisticated representation of its world."[68] Conditioning is not merely a transfer of power from one stimulus to another.

Contrary to an assumption of the traditional theory, stimuli are not equally likely to develop conditioning properties; some are more easily used as conditioned signals than others. Pain is more readily associated with auditory and visual stimuli than with gustatory stimuli, and gastric distress is more easily associated with taste than with vision. People, certainly adults, do not come fresh to new stimuli; they already have a history of associations with the available stimuli. These previous associations influence the occurrence or non-occurrence of conditioning. So for example, we all have a history of (benign) associations with dog collars. No one, not even people who have had distressing experiences with dogs, ever learn to fear collars, despite the contiguous presence of the dog collar during the unpleasant events. Dog collars do not predict distress, and they do not become conditioned elicitors of fear. Although many people who have had distressing experiences with dogs learn to fear them, Di Nardo and others[69] found that comparable numbers of people who have had such experiences fail to acquire the fear. Presumably, a previous history of pleasant and friendly experiences with dogs produces strong conditioned predictions of harmless exchanges, and these predictions are not overturned by one or several unpleasant events. The history of the stimulus influences the conditioning process.[70] Food aversions develop most readily to novel foods. Familiar and especially well liked familiar foods are relatively immune to conditioned food aversions. Presumably, familiar and well-liked people, places, and animals are also relatively immune to conditioned fears. A relative fear-immunity to familiar and favored stimuli and situations may underlie the success of Neal Miller's[71] "toughening up" exercises as a way of preventing the development of fear.

The new research proves that animals can be conditioned not only to discrete stimuli but also to the relationships between stimuli, thereby reinforcing Rescorla's claim that "conditioning involves the learning of relations among events that are complexly represented."[72]

We have come a long way from classical Pavlovian conditioning, and the flexibility and range of conditioning is far greater than was previously supposed. Conditioning can occur even when the stimuli are separated in time, and in space, and it can occur not only to discrete stimuli but also to abstract relationships between two or more stimuli. Conditioning is a highly flexible and functional process.

This refreshing revival of interest in conditioning has widened our knowledge and clarified some puzzles, but it is not free of problems. Phenomena that were disallowed by the traditional theory, such as the emergence of learned associations between non-contiguous events, are now acceptable as forms of conditioning. This enriched view of conditioning enables one to incorporate some of the phenomena of fear and can shore up the heavily criticized traditional theory, but at its present stage the new view is still too liberal. It lacks limits, and there is little that it disallows. Fear can be acquired even when the signal (CS) and the aversive event (US) are separated in time. In theory, almost any stimulus or past stimulus or event can become a signal for fear, but in practice, people are found to have comparatively few fears. The fears that we do acquire are confined to a handful of stimuli; fears are not normally distributed. We no more have a clutter of irrelevant fears than we do a "useless clutter of irrelevant associations."[73]

Evidently, there are strict limits to the acquisition of fears by non-contiguous events, but the revived view of conditioning has not yet progressed to the identification of these limits. Seligman's[74] theory of prepared phobias, an earlier attempt to find such limits, is compatible with the new view of conditioning, but it was not set out within that perspective. At present, there are no laws of conditioning, or guidelines, to provide a basis for limiting the possibilities of fear. Pending further progress, it is preferable to pursue Seligman's theory of preparedness and also to retain the "three pathways to fear" construal of how fears are acquired (see Chapter 12). Given that the three pathways model and the revised model of conditioning both deal with the way in which (fear) information is processed, it is possible that the two models of fear acquisition will begin to merge. It is also worth drawing attention to an emerging connection between the new view of conditioning and cognitive explanations of the acquisition of fear. In the most refined cognitive theory, Clark's[75] explanation of panic, it is said that the affected person's misinterpretation of his or her bodily sensations (for example, trembling, palpitations) as signs of an impending catastrophe causes the panic. The sensations predict an extremely aversive event. A strong relationship between the sensations and an intense fear of catastrophe can be established rapidly and lastingly. If this (conditioned?) relationship can be disconfirmed, however, the appearance of the sensations ceases to predict catastrophe and the fear disappears. In Mackintosh's description, "the function of conditioning is to enable organisms to discover probable causes of events of significance,"[76] and in the case of panic disorder, the affected person makes an erroneous attribution of the probable causes of an event of significance.

Several forms of abnormal behavior can be thought of as examples of "probable causes" that are incorrectly interpreted, as in the case of panic disorder. Even more interesting are cases in which people recognize that their irrational fears are indeed irrational—but the fear persists nevertheless. Perhaps the "probable cause" here consists of the correct expectation that contact with the feared object, say, snake or spider, will indeed be followed by an unpleasant fearful reaction. This expectation is correct, as is the person's recognition that the spider or snake is harmless.

SOME CONCLUSIONS

This revised view of conditioning makes it possible, once more, to account for much of our knowledge about how fears are acquired. The deletion of the requirement that the conditioned stimulus and the aversive event must occur in temporal contiguity removes a major objection to the conditioning theory of fear. In addition, much of the new information about fear (especially the summation of fear, and over-predictions of fear) is pleasantly compatible with the revised view.

Some problems remain, and even a liberalized theory of conditioning cannot account for fears that arise without *any* contact between the fear stimulus and the aversive event. This informational acquisition of fear is considered in the following chapter on pathways to fear.

The liberalized theory does not help to explain why fears fail to arise in circumstances in which the conditioning theory would lead us to expect them (for example, aerial bombing). Recourse to newly described conditioning phenomena, such as blocking, are unlikely to succeed. What type of experience would block the development of a fear of bombs? The liberalized view greatly expands the explanatory value of conditioning but does not provide the basis for a comprehensive account of how fears are acquired. Fears can be acquired by conditioning and by other processes.

Acceptance of the view that the conditioning theory cannot account for the acquisition of a significant number of fears inevitably raises the question of what other processes might be involved. In 1977, it was proposed that there are at least three major processes of fear acquisition — the three pathways to fear.[77]

CHAPTER 12

THREE
PATHWAYS
TO FEAR

By 1977, it had become clear that conditioning theory was incomplete and that there was a need to identify other forms of fear acquisition. Accordingly, it was proposed that fear can be acquired by conditioning or by vicarious experiences or by the absorption of information that conveys a threat.[1]

Prompted by the growing success of therapeutic techniques for reducing fear, and by Bandura's persuasive writings on the ubiquity and power of vicarious processes of learning,[2] consideration was given to the possibility that fears can be acquired vicariously. Presumably, these vicarious processes can modify fear in either direction—up or down. The information available at the time was meager, but it is now possible to add new evidence. The sources of evidence that can be drawn upon in support of the proposition that fears are acquired vicariously include reports given by phobic patients, wartime observations, correlations between the fears displayed by parents and children, laboratory demonstrations of conditioned fear, and animal research.

THE VICARIOUS ACQUISITION OF FEAR

During World War II, it was reported that the fears or lack of fears displayed by mothers in the course of air raids was a determinant of whether or not their children developed similar fears.[3] If the children observed adults exhibiting overt signs of fears or other emotional upset, this increased the likelihood of the children becoming frightened. John commented on the social facilitation and inhibition of children's fears during air raids and obtained a correlation of 0.59 between the fears of the mother and her child.[4] In normal conditions, too, there is some correspondence between the fears of children in the same family, with correlations ranging from between 0.65 and 0.74.[5] However, the common occurrence of a fear being present in one sibling and absent in another requires an explanation. Hagman found a correlation of 0.67 between the total number of fears exhibited by children and their mothers,[6] and Grinker and Spiegel gave clear examples of combat airmen acquiring fears after observing a crewmate expressing intense fear.[7] Among 1700 infantry troops in the Italian theater of war, Stouffer and his colleagues found that 70 percent of the respondents had a negative reaction to seeing a comrade "crack up". Half of the total sample said that it made them feel anxious or like cracking up themselves.[8]

Murray and Foote found little support for the idea that a fear of snakes is acquired by conditioning, and most of their subjects said that they had had little experience with the reptile. Their results suggest that "fear may be acquired through a variety of observational and instructional experiences that communicate negative information about snakes."[9] In support, they quote examples of people who were directly influenced by observing fear in others, such as a man who reported that during childhood he had become frightened of snakes when his friends manifested fear and fled at the sight of a snake. The subjects also gave evidence of fears being transmitted by observation of parental fears of snakes, even if the parents themselves had had few or no experiences with the snake. Murray and

Foote go so far as to suggest that "the more experience people have with snakes, the less they fear them."[10]

Kleinknecht found similar results among a group of people who were or had been frightened of tarantulas.[11] Of the total sample, 35 percent felt that their fear had been acquired vicariously, and 61 percent attributed the origin of their fear to information received through the media. Additionally, 70 percent of those who had overcome their fear attributed the reduction to knowledge about tarantulas and spiders obtained through the media or by other observations. In his study of 56 animal phobics, Hekmat found that movies (30 percent) and television (52 percent) were the main sources of vicarious transmission of fear.[12]

These reports of the influential part played by vicarious factors in generating a fear of snakes or of tarantulas have to be considered against a background of other fears in which direct contact with the fear-evoking stimulus is the rule rather than the exception. For example, Rimm and others found that approximately half of their 45 subjects who had various types of phobia were able to recall relevant learning experiences "with direct experiences far more common than vicarious experiences."[13] The role that frightened people or phobic patients attribute to direct and indirect experiences in generating their fears differs from fear to fear.

In their analysis of 183 patients with clinically significant phobias, Ost and Hugdahl found that 40 percent of those who were frightened of animals traced the origin of the fear to indirect experiences such as modeling or informational sources, but these attributions were uncommon among the agoraphobics. None of them traced the onset of their problem to instruction or information, and only 5 percent attached any significance to vicarious experiences. The patients who attributed the greatest importance to indirect experiences, among which vicarious experiences were by far the most prominent, were the blood phobics, animal phobics, and social phobics.[14] Across all the groups there was a strong tendency to attribute the onset of the phobia to direct conditioning experiences, and three times as many patients made this attribution than one involving indirect acquisition. It should also be mentioned that 14 percent of the patients were unable to recall how the fear was acquired. (In virtually all of the reports on ths subject, between 5 percent and 25 percent of subjects or patients are unable to recall how they acquired the pertinent fear. These figures may be a result of loss of recall, but it is not impossible that they indicate the operation of a fourth process.)

In their first study of the acquisition of phobias, Ost and Hugdahl found that 17 percent of 106 patients with mixed phobias attributed their onset to vicarious experiences.[15] Contrary to an earlier suggestion,[16] there was no relationship between the components of the fear and the manner in which it was acquired, but information analyzed some years later was consistent with the prediction.[17] The authors found no difference in the severity of the phobias that had been acquired directly or indirectly, but left unanswered the prediction that fears that are acquired informationally will be milder than other types of fear.[18] Although their findings are not conclusive, the trends from Di Nardo's study suggest that animal phobics who report that their fears arose after a conditioning experience show stronger psysiological responses to phobic stimuli than do other phobics,[19] and patients who attribute the onset to an indirect experience show stronger cognitive than physiological responses.

Later, Ost discovered that the different pathways of acquisition had different ages of onset. "Phobias acquired through instruction/transmission of information or modelling started earlier than those acquired through conditioning processes."[20] He confirmed the prediction that a higher proportion of the commonly encountered fears are acquired indirectly than are clinically significant phobias. His results also support the prediction that in fears acquired by a conditioning process, the psychophysiological and behavioral components are the most prominent. Among the 100 agoraphobic patients, 81 percent attributed the onset of their fears to conditioning experiences, and they also had the highest heart rate responsiveness of all the groups.[21] However, the relationship between the mode of fear-acquisition and the component structure of the fear is not yet clear.

In Ost and Hugdahl's study of 80 agoraphobic patients, only 9 percent attributed their problem to vicarious learning, but the authors point out that their evidence of a strong predominance of conditioning in the onset of agoraphobia is consistent with some reports but at variance with the findings of Mathews and others and of Friedman.[22] One suspects that differences in definition of a "conditioning event" are responsible for the variations in the number of agoraphobics who are said to attribute the onset of their problems to conditioning or nonconditioning events.

The laboratory investigations carried out by Ohman and his colleagues demonstrated that conditioned fear reactions can be established directly, by conditioning procedures, and indirectly, by vicarious experiences or by instructions. "All these (three) pathways have been corroborated in laboratory studies of human autonomic responses to predator-relevant stimuli."[23] However, the fear responses tended to be weak (see previous Chapter).

Animal research

Miller, Murphy, and Mirsky described three experiments on the transmission of fear in animals.[24] They found that fear can be transmitted from a fearful model to an observer monkey and that the fear can be transmitted even by pictorial representations of fearful monkeys. In all of the experiments, the observers had at some time in the past been subjected to the fearful situation, and the transmission of fear was deduced from the occurrence of avoidance behavior. Interestingly, they noted that the monkeys did not respond fearfully when exposed to fearful models of other species.

The proposition that fears can be acquired by vicarious experiences was enlivened and strengthened by the outstanding research carried out by Dr. Susan Mineka and her colleagues at the University of Wisconsin in Madison. Their methodical program of research on rhesus monkeys showed that the animals can and do acquire an "intense and persistent fear of snakes as a result of observing their wild-reared parents behave fearfully in the presence of real, toy, and model snakes for a short period of time. The fear was context-specific, and showed no significant signs of diminution at three-month follow up."[25]

The fear was acquired with ease, and rapidly rose in intensity so that within minutes of observing the fearful model, the observing monkeys displayed fears that were almost as intense as those shown by the models.[26] After a 3-month interval, the observer monkeys were still showing intense fear which could be evoked in situations additional to the chamber in which the observational learning originally took place. There was a close association between the degree of fear displayed by the model and that subsequently displayed by the observer. The fear of snakes was as readily modeled from the behavior of unrelated and unfamiliar monkeys as from parental behavior. In one series, 4 of the 16 observer monkeys acquired comparatively weak fears, and Mineka attributes this to the fact that they had been exposed to models who displayed the lowest average levels of fear.

Familial transmission

Given the high correlation between the amount of fear displayed by the model and the fear picked up by the observer, Mineka and coworkers concluded that "parents who have strong fears or phobias should avoid confronting their phobic object as much as possible in the presence of their children.''[27] This caution is relevant principally for parents of young children.

Despite this evidence, and the modest correlations observed between parental and child fears, it should not be thought that observation of a fearful parent or other model necessarily generates fear. Striking examples of the absence of abnormal fears in the children of patients suffering from obsessional-compulsive disorders, in which abnormal fears are prominent, were encountered by Rachman and Hodgson.[28] Many of these parents instruct their children on the need for meticulous hygiene and promote and even demand that their children imitate their own compulsive cleaning behavior. It was surprising to find, therefore, that so few of the children of these patients display abnormal behavior similar to that of the affected parent. Typically, these children comply with their obsessional parent's insistence on compulsive cleaning, but quickly resume normal behavior when the insistence — or the parent — is no longer present.

Ost and Hugdahl found a low incidence of agoraphobia in the relations of people who have this disorder,[29] and it is not common for the growing children of agoraphobic parents to model fearful behavior in public places or transport. The spouses of agoraphobic patients appear not to acquire their husband's or wife's agoraphobic fears vicariously, and it is rare to find family contagion of agoraphobic fear. Incidentally, the rarity of family contagion of agoraphobia is compatible with cognitive explanations of this disorder.

The absence of similar fears in the children of phobic or obsessional patients, and the lack of a closer correspondence between the fears of parents and their children, can be accounted for by a combination of factors. First, the children are exposed to a wide range of fearless models, and these are likely to have the dominant effect on the child's behavior. Second, they are provided with a great deal of safety information that serves to inhibit fear. The exposure to other models and the acquisition of safety information and skill increase with age, and therefore one might expect to find evidence of corresponding fears, if any, between parents and *young* children. There are more fearless adults and peers than frightened mothers or fathers.

In the case of abnormal fears the affected person generally takes care to explain to the child that the fear is "silly" and has no rational basis. This information is reinforced by peers and other adults. The children of an obsessional parent receive reassuring safety information from virtually all of the adults and peers whom they meet, and are repeatedly exposed to non-fearful behavior at school and elsewhere. These multiple sources of vicarious, informational, and direct learning come to dominate and hence suppress the vicarious learning of the affected parent's abnormal fears. On this analysis, we may suppose that the transmission of significant and intense fears from parent to child is especially likely to occur if the family lives in an isolated style, or if the relationship between the fearful child and the patient is particularly close and exclusive. Vicariously acquired fears should be more evident in young than in older children.

In an excellent extension of her research, Mineka obtained evidence to show that monkeys are predisposed to acquire a fear of snakes.[30] Observer monkeys readily acquired a fear of snakes if they were exposed to videotapes of monkey models displaying fear in the presence of the reptile, but they failed to acquire a fear of flowers even when the videotapes were doctored in a way that showed monkey models displaying fear in the presence of flowers. This is a convincing demonstration of the monkeys' predisposition to acquire fears of a "prepared" stimulus. This work should serve as a model for testing the validity of Seligman's theory of prepared phobias.

In 1960, Neal Miller suggested that animals develop a degree of resistance to the acquisition of fear if they are exposed to a process of "toughening up."[31] In keeping with this idea, Mineka, Gunnar, and Shampoux showed that when infant monkeys were reared in an environment in which they were given extensive experience of control and mastery over a variety of reinforcers, they displayed lower levels of fear than did monkeys who were reared without comparable experiences of mastery and control.[32] "Thus, early experience with control and mastery appears to affect the level of fear that a traumatic event elicits."[33] She also draws attention to the fact that fears can be modified, even inflated, by seemingly unrelated events of an intense kind that occur after the original acquisition of the fear.

This work is of great interest and is consistent with the idea that there are at least three "pathways to fear." However, the fear-acquisition processes that operate in rhesus monkeys are not directly applicable to the acquisition of human fears. Having said that, it would be unwise to close one's eyes to this information and its implications, simply for that reason. There are obstacles to determining the extent to which Mineka's findings are applicable to human fears, not least the ethical objection to giving people intense and significant fears in order to satisfy our scientific curiosity. If it were possible to carry out a replication of Mineka's research on human subjects, especially children, there is little doubt that the main results would be highly similar to those described by Mineka.

In summary, it can now be said that some fearful people attribute the onset of their fears to vicarious experiences, and the frequency of such reports varies with the type of fear. Anecdotal evidence derived from wartime observations and some correlational studies of the fears of parents and children are consistent with the claim that fears can be acquired vicariously. The laboratory evidence on the vicarious acquisition of human fears is consistent with the trend of the evidence, but is limited by the weakness of the laboratory-conditioned fears. Notwithstanding the caution necessary in extrapolating from animal to human behavior, Mineka's research on vicarious acquisition of fear by rhesus monkey's is consistent with the proposition.

Contrary to original expectation[34] there is little evidence to support the idea that vicariously acquired fears are less intense than those acquired directly. The evidence on the component structure of vicariously acquired fears is mixed, and there is weak support for the prediction that the cognitive component is stronger in vicarious fears than in directly conditioned fears, and for the prediction that the psychophysiological component is stronger in directly acquired than in vicarious fears. If the evidence collected by Mineka is to be taken as a guide, and on this point there is little reason to hesitate, it appears that intense fears can be acquired vicariously with ease and rapidity. They persist with little evidence of weakening. Her findings strengthen the hypothesis that the fear of snakes is "prepared."

THE INFORMATIONAL ACQUISITION
OF FEARS

Information can generate a fear. Presumably, the information must contain a potential threat or be open to being misinterpreted as threatening. Clinical evidence, especially the evidence accumulating on the nature of panic disorders, suggests that fears can be generated by information that is slightly or not at all threatening but which is misinterpreted by the recipient as being threatening. For example, if a kind friend tells a vulnerable person that his complaints about recurrent palpitations indicate the presence of a cardiac problem, the information may lead him to misinterpret the next occurrence of palpitations as a sign of an impending heart attack. If a person makes a catastrophic misinterpretation of this type of information, it may end in fears.

The fear and avoidance experienced after the tragic fire in the London subway system, described on page 95, is an example of the informational acquisition of fear. People who lived some distance away from the underground station, and even those who rarely used the system, and had no direct experience of the tragedy, reported significant fear. Given the extensive descriptions provided on television, it is reasonable to assume that much of the subsequent fear was transmitted by this indirect pathway, but even people who simply read about the fire or heard about it on the radio appear to have been affected. The evidence of fear reported at the time was incomplete and not verified by scientific methods, and can do no more than illustrate how an informational acquisition of fear can take place.

When the notion of an informational pathway to fear was introduced, it was remarked that it had been strangely overlooked, despite the fact that it was obvious, or perhaps because it was too obvious.[35] The lack of bags of conventionally acceptable evidence that fear can be acquired through the transmission of information is regrettable, but the occurrence of the phenomenon seems to be undeniable.

The provision of information is an inherent part of child rearing and is carried on continuously by parents and peers during the child's earliest years. They learn which situations to fear (for example, busy roads, aggressive dogs), which situations are safe, and to distinguish between the two. (Hekmat's animal-phobic subjects "identified their mothers as a prime source" of the fear-inducing information.[36]) The information and instructions passed on during this period probably exert a strong influence on the acquisition and on the reduction of fears. We assume, and act, as if other people can be instructed to fear and avoid danger. Fears that are acquired informationally may be mild rather than severe and can be contrasted to the "prepared" fears that are lurking, easily triggered, intense and resistant to change. The idea that fears can be acquired by provision of information is compatible with the fact that people display fears of objects and situations that they have never encountered.

Adaptation to one's environment requires that we learn what is irrelevant as well as what is relevant. Moreover, we are taught to cope with dangers and to endure unavoidable discomfort or pain. The fire at King's Cross is illustrative, but the information collected by Ost and his colleagues is ordered and was collected specifically for the purpose. Ost analyzed the three pathways said by six types of phobic patients to have been responsible for the onset of their fears.[37] The figures for informational acquisition are as follows. Among the animal phobics, 14 percent said that they had acquired their phobia through information, 12.5 percent of the blood phobics made the same report, as did 11 percent of the claustrophobics. None of the agoraphobic patients attributed their fear to this mode of onset, and only 5 percent of the dental phobics and 4 percent of the social phobics made this attribution. These results are consistent with the earlier observation that the different types of phobia show different paths of acquisition. These retrospective clinical reports, illustrative examples of disasters, and anecdotes about child rearing need to be supplemented.

In theory, it is a simple matter to demonstrate that people who begin with no fear of object X will display signs of such a fear shortly after being informed that X is dangerous, but there are practical constraints. The following two examples are chosen from many possibilities in the hope that they are convincing. In the first of our hypothetical experiments, a group of trainee laboratory workers are introduced to specimens and animals in a pathology laboratory. After confirming the absence of significant fear, half of the subjects are informed (correctly) that direct contact with specified contaminated animals and specimens is dangerous and may lead to a fatal disease. Fear will be transmitted in this way, even in the absence of contact with the specimens or of exposure to a fearful model. The exposure-free transmission of information would be a sufficient cause of fear. In the second hypothetical experiment, the same general procedure is used to transmit appropriate fear to soldiers who are being trained to defuse bombs. This time they are warned that certain noises or sights indicate that the bomb is about to explode. This information unaccompanied by direct or even indirect exposures should be sufficient to induce significant and long-lasting fears of the cues that signify danger, and the fear will become manifest when the noises are heard or sights seen as the unexploded bomb is approached.

THE MISINTERPRETATION OF INFORMATION

Examples of intense fears arising from catastrophic misinterpretations of information are available in the rapidly accumulating literature on the psychology of panic. Clark's theory incorporates the assumption that information, especially if it is seriously misinterpreted, can produce intense fear.[38] He argues that panics are caused by catastrophic misinterpretations of bodily sensations, but there is no reason to exclude other types of information, in addition to information about one's bodily sensations.

The provision of identical information will generate fear in some people but not in others, and much will depend on how the information is interpreted. Even comparatively harmless information can be exaggerated or misinterpreted, and then generate fear. The introduction of this cognitive perspective on the informational transmission of fear offers three advantages. It provides a starting point for explaining the individual differences in fear responsiveness to information, it can accommodate a wider range of data on fear *reduction* than was possible, and it may help to explain why certain fears (such as agoraphobia) are apparently resistant to informational induction.

If agoraphobia is regarded in the conventional manner, as a fear of public places and transport, then information about the danger of department stores or buses should be capable of generating or at least intensifying agoraphobic problems. But patients rarely report such a connection, other than the significance of information about escape routes. However, if agoraphobia is re-viewed as a consequence of panic (in most cases), then we should look elsewhere for the critical information that might trigger the fear.

The information that contributes directly to an episode of panic is information from and about one's bodily sensations and health and well-being, and not information about the dangers of public places. For example, after hearing that a close and apparently healthy friend had died from a sudden heart attack, a healthy 40-year-old man began to experience repeated panics whenever he became aware of increases in his heart rate. The information about the death of his friend was misinterpreted to mean that his own health was in danger. No doubt other friends of the deceased person did not make this misinterpretation and were not troubled by panic episodes. Regardless of whether the source of the information is internal (bodily sensations) or external, if the information is interpreted as constituting a threat, especially if it is a catastrophic threat, a panic is likely to ensue.

The revised view of agoraphobia as commonly occurring as a consequence of panic episodes implies that information plays a part in the chain of events leading to the observed agoraphobic fear and avoidance. People with agoraphobia are said to ascribe etiological importance to information about their bodily sensations and well-being, and will attach little or no importance to information about the dangers of public transport. Information about the potentially harmful effects of excessive exertion will contribute to the fear, but information about the poor quality of buses will not.

The re-analysis of agoraphobia as a product of panic episodes makes intelligible the low significance that agoraphobic patients attach to vicarious experiences; only 8 percent of Ost's agoraphobic sample attributed their fear to this pathway.[39] The observation of other people displaying fearful avoidance behavior of public places is of little relevance if one's own avoidance behavior is a consequence of panics that occur when one experiences intense fear of an imminent threat to one's well-being.

UNKNOWN CAUSES

In all of the reports on the retrospective attributions made by patients, a proportion of the respondents were unable to recall how their fear began. The percentages of patients in Ost's review who were unable to recall the onset of their phobia ranged from 11 percent among the agoraphobics to 17 percent of the claustrophobics and 24 percent of the social phobics.[40] Does this mean that there is a fourth, unidentified, pathway to fear? The absence of information is not a sound basis for introducing an expansion of the concept of three pathways to fear, but if a significant proportion of subjects continue to say that they can recall no cause of the onset of their fear, even after close examination and after the formulation of specific questions, then the case for a fourth pathway will require consideration. There are at least four possible explanations: the determination of fear by unconscious processes,[41] symbolic transformations, the presence of innate fears, or the acquisition of fear by temporally remote events (see Chapter 11). A simpler explanation would be that the respondents have forgotten the events or misinterpreted them. Given the important role now ascribed to even fleeting cognitions and images in the genesis of panic and other fears,[42] it is perhaps not surprising that so many people are unable to recall the cause. If the causal role of catastrophic misinterpretations and irrational automatic thoughts is confirmed, then we will have to ask a different question. If the responsible cognitions are as fleeting, subtle, and elusive as is often suggested, why are the great majority of people nevertheless able to identify the way in which their fear arose?

In summary, we now have sufficient evidence to support the idea that fears are acquired by a conditioning process or by vicarious experiences. Support for the operation of the third pathway, an informational process, is patchy, and at present the main reason for its retention is its plausibility.

CHAPTER

PSYCHOANALYTIC
EXPLANATIONS
OF FEAR

Psychoanalytic writers and academic psychologists do not merely give different accounts of fear; on critical points they are in direct conflict. A clear example of one such disagreement, and its practical consequences, is the way in which they view the fear of animals and insects.

Over 100 experiments on the desensitization of fear have now been published, and with very few exceptions the method successfully reduced fear. Almost as large a number of experiments have been carried out on the derivatives of desensitization, including participant modeling, and here the results have been even more impressive, and more quickly achieved.[1] In many of these experiments, the target was a fear of spiders or a fear of snakes, and consequently a great deal of information about these fears is now available.

Psychoanalytic writers regard fears of this type as manifestations of a more profound underlying problem, usually of a sexual nature. The reduction or elimination of the fear is said to require deep analysis, spread over months or years. The complexity of the sexual symbolism, of such fears which is a critical feature of psychoanalytic theorizing on the subject, can be illustrated by the following contributions.

Melitta Sperling, writing in the *Journal of the American Psychoanalytic Association* in 1971, stated that "most investigators seem to agree that the spider is a representative of the dangerous (orally devouring and anally castrating) mother, and that the main problem of these patients seems to center around (sic) their sexual identification and bi-sexuality."[2] Developing these ideas, she wrote, "It is my contention that the choice of the spider symbol indicates a fixation to the pregenital and in particular to the anal-sadistic phase in a very ambivalent and predominantly hostile relationship to the mother, with an inability to separate from the hated mother."[3] The depth and seriousness of a fear of spiders is plain.

The spider symbolism as well as the symptoms most frequently found associated with it, such as severe sleep disturbances and phobias, are also an indication of unresolved separation conflict and a high degree of ambivalence which intensifies bisexuality and the problem of sexual identification. The mechanisms of defense employed in spider symbolism and in phobias are denial, externalization, projection, splitting, and displacement. They indicate the primitive, ambivalent, narcissistic ego organization of this phase. The personalities of these patients, and in the others in cases where it was possible to study them, showed marked paranoid trends. They also used psychosomatic symptoms in stress situations, either epidosically or more persistently for the immediate (somatic) discharge of threatening impulses. The spider symbolism in most cases remained latent and became manifest in traumatic life situations and in analysis when the phobic and psychosomatic defenses were invalidated. In the analytic situation the spider symbolism was indicative of a specific mother transference.[4]

The only comfort that can be offered in the face of such a demoralizing array of problems—bisexuality, anally castrating mothers, primitive egos, paranoid trends, psychosomatic symptoms, and the rest—is that a fear of spiders generally can be desensitized within five sessions, or reduced by participant modeling in one session. The "marked paranoid trends" of these hostile mother-hating spider-phobics are no barrier to the speedy removal of the fear.

According to Sperling, the development of a fear of spiders, like other fears, is a form of psychological defense against some more threatening problems or impulses. In most cases the spider symbolism is latent and becomes manifest when the phobic and psychosomatic defenses are invalidated. If the reduction or elimination of a spider fear during modeling or desensitization is taken to be "an invalidation" of a "phobic defense", then presumably the spider symbolism should be made manifest by this change. In the experimental treatment of such fears, dramatic changes are rarely observed. On the contrary, the process of desensitizing the fear of spiders and other creatures is bland and unsurprising.

Sperling was much influenced in her approach to spider fears by the views of one of Freud's closest associates, Karl Abraham, who wrote a classic paper on the subject in 1922.[5] He maintained that the fear of spiders is symbolic of an unconscious fear of bisexual genitalia: "the penis embedded in the female genitals." The second meaning Abraham attributed to the spider is that of a phallic, wicked mother. In their contribution to the *Journal of the American Psychoanalytic Association* in 1969, Newman and Stoller supported Abraham's view and illustrated it with the description of a patient who was psychotic, physically deformed, and had hermaphroditic genitalia.[6] Perforce this was not a group study.

Most of the psychoanalytic writing on the subject is speculation prompted by observation of one patient, or at most a small selection of patients with a common problem. The difficulties one faces in attempting to evaluate this work will be gone into presently. Meanwhile, even if Abraham and his successors are entirely correct in their assumption that a fear of spiders is symbolic of a fear of bisexual genitalia or of a phallic, wicked mother, there is room for optimism. Fears of bisexual genitalia and wicked mothers appear to be amenable to change — spider fears are easily modified. The fear of snakes has challenged the imagination of many theorists and been found to be decidedly symbolic, but it too responds easily to direct modification.

THE CLASSIC CASE OF LITTLE HANS

In 1905, Freud laid the foundations for a psychoanalytic theory of fears with the publication of the analysis of a phobia in a 5-year-old boy, commonly referred to as the case of little Hans, the boy who feared horses.[7] The importance of this contribution is explained by Ernest Jones, Glover, Abraham, and other authorities on psychoanalysis. According to Jones, "the brilliant success of child analysis" was "inaugurated by the study of this very case."[8] Glover said that it supported the concepts of castration anxiety, the Oedipus complex, repression, and others.[9]

In this famous paper, Freud described and discussed in great detail (over 140 pages) the events of a few months. The case material on which the analysis was based was collected by the father of little Hans, and he kept Freud informed of developments by regular written reports. The father had several consultations with Freud concerning the boy's fear (both parents were lay adherents of psychoanalysis). During the analysis, Freud saw the little boy only once.

The essence of the case is that at the age of 4 Hans began to complain of a fear of horses. Shortly afterwards he began to fear other large animals, such as giraffes, and objects that resembled a horse's muzzle. During a 2-week illness the fear waned but then returned in a slightly more intense form, only to show a gradual decline in the course of the succeeding 6 months. During the period when he complained of the fear, Hans was engaged by his father in repeated conversations and interrogations, and the father then communicated his interpretations to Freud. The material on which Freud's extended account is based, and which provided the raw material for a theory of fear, was almost entirely thirdhand, and the reporter was a central figure emotionally involved in the case.

Naturally the theory has undergone some revisions, but the major propositions set out by Freud are still accepted by numbers of psychoanalytic writers. It is assumed that the observed or reported fear, the *manifest* fear, is symbolic of a deeper but more threatening or unacceptable fear; with rare exceptions, the underlying, or *latent,* fear is presumed to be sexual. The latent fear is so threatening or unacceptable that it is unconsciously transformed into a more acceptable fear, such as a fear of spiders or snakes or horses. It is a means of defending one's self against more serious psychological disturbance, and the mechanisms employed are those of denial, reaction formation, displacement, and repression, among others. The fear is generally precipitated by an increase in *id* impulses.

Little Han's fear of horses was interpreted as being a symbol of a more serious latent fear—in him, as in so many others, it was a fear of his father, engendered by anticipation of punishment (probably castration) for having experienced sexual desires for his mother. It can be seen that the fear of horses was interpreted as a manifestation of the child's Oedipus complex: Hans experienced a sexual desire for his mother, followed by a fear of retribution from his father. These thoughts were unacceptable and the fear of the father was transformed into a more acceptable manifest fear, that of horses.

The full report has been discussed at length by Wolpe and Rachman, who conducted a critical examination of the evidence on which Freud relied. They concluded that much of the testimony was unreliable. The child misled everyone on several occasions and gave conflicting reports. Most important of all, what purport to be Hans's views and feelings are simply the father speaking.[10] Freud conceded,

> It is true that during the analysis Hans had to be told many things which he could not say himself, that he had to be presented with thoughts which he had so far showed no signs of possessing and that his attention had to be turned in the direction from which his father was expecting something to come. This detracts from the evidential value of the analysis, but the procedure is the same in every case.[11]

The critics quote several examples in which the child's reports were distorted, misinterpreted, and even constructed for him. They dispute the six major points put forward by Freud in the construction of his theory and regard as unsupported the following contentions. The child had a sexual desire for his mother, he hated and feared his father and wished to kill him, his sexual excitement and desire for his mother were transformed into anxiety, his fear of horses was symbolic of his fear of his father, the purpose of the illness was to keep him near his mother, and finally, his phobia disappeared because he resolved his Oedipus complex.

Some idea of the quality of the evidence can be conveyed by the following brief extracts, but the full impact of the father's introduction and interpretations can be appreciated only by reading the entire case record. In conformity with Freud's belief in the sexual basis of all phobias, the father, encouraged by Freud, repeatedly told little Hans that his fear of horses was really a fear of their penises. The child said that he was afraid of being bitten by a horse, and when Hans said, "widdler [penis] doesn't bite," his father replied, "Perhaps it does, though".

After further interpretations along the same lines, Freud remarks: "Doctor and patient, father and son, were therefore at one in ascribing the chief share in the pathogenesis of Hans' present condition to his habit of onanism."[12] When the phobia persisted despite this insight, the father proposed to little Hans that he should sleep in a sack to prevent him from wanting to touch his penis. Later, while they were visiting the zoo, the father reminded the child that he was afraid of large animals because they have "big widdlers and you're really afraid of big widdlers." This was denied by the boy, without any effect on the father's views.

In his monograph, Freud emphasizes the child's supposed hostility towards his younger sister. The father was talking to little Hans about the birth of the younger child, Hanna. Father: "What did Hanna look like?" Hans: "All white and lovely. So pretty." Those are the words reported, but in Freud's account this is how it comes out: "Hans (hypocritically): 'All white and lovely. So pretty.'"[13]

Incidentally, the little boy's explanation of the origin of his phobia was straightforward. He claimed that it started when he witnessed a street accident in which a horse collapsed, and his father added that "all of this was confirmed by my wife as well as the fact that the anxiety broke out immediately afterwards."[14] By any standards, the monograph on little Hans is a poor product and an unsuitable foundation for constructing a theory of fear.

SOME WEAKNESSES

The crucial reliance placed on the verbal testimony given by non-representative people, many of them psychiatric patients, and gathered over a large number of sessions in the course of a treatment lasting several years is misplaced.[15] The interpretation and selection of the material that appears in the report finally given by the psychoanalyst should also be regarded with caution. The absence of public demonstration, repetition, and accountability undermine one's confidence in the evidence. Many of the fundamental propositions of psychoanalysis are indefensible.[16] There is no good reason to accept the view that observed and reported fears are merely manifestations of a more fundamental, latent fear. Furthermore, it is difficult to see why one should accept the assumption that virtually all fears are manifestations, direct or indirect, of sexual problems and conflicts.

Freud asserted that phobias never occur if the person has a normal sexual adjustment. "The main point in the problem of phobias seems to me that *phobias do not occur at all when the vita sexualis is normal*"[17] (original emphasis). He made no attempt to substantiate this claim of a necessary connection between phobias and sexual life, and it remains unproven. It is almost certainly incorrect.

I know of no reliable statistics on the subject, but it is highly probable that the large majority of people with phobias have a satisfactory sexual life. They establish and maintain satisfying sexual relationships. Proponents of the Freudian theory may well object that a normal "vita sexualis" is something other than, or more than, satisfactory sexual relationships. If so, three steps must be taken: the nature of the normal vita sexualis must be specified, the nature of the necessary connection with phobias needs to be explained, and Freud's misleading generalization should be qualified or quietly interred.

The development of dependable methods for reducing fear has raised formidable problems for psychoanalytic theorists. Manifest or latent, fears can be reduced or eliminated readily. Following the psychoanalytic view, the elimination of what is presumably a manifest fear (of spiders, for example) should leave the latent fear unaltered. But if it is assumed, and it is, that the appearance of a manifest fear is part of psychological defense reaction, then it is only reasonable to expect that the elimination of the defensive reaction should be followed by some other attempt at defense. The elimination of one manifest fear should be followed by the substitution of a new one or, failing that, by the occurrence of some other, perhaps worse, psychological disturbance. These two possibilities have been discounted by experimental research (Chapter 14).

After the successful reduction of a circumscribed fear, such as that of snakes, the appearance of a new fear is rare. The appearance of some general disturbance, perhaps diffuse anxiety or depression, is also rare. The evidence is straightforward. In the overwhelming number of cases the reduction or elimination of a circumscribed fear is not followed by untoward effects.[18]

Another important consequence of the research findings on reducing fear is the conclusion that it is possible to bring about substantial reductions in fear without undertaking a major analysis of the fear itself or of the subject's personality, childhood, sexual life, or other topics that are so important in psychoanalytic theory. It is perfectly possible to approach the fear directly, describe and measure it directly, and modify it directly.[19] One can proceed on the assumption that the fear is manifest and need not have latent roots.

Does this mean that there are no "psychoanalytic" fears? Not necessarily, for it remains possible that some fears are partly or largely symbolic,[20] and it is of course true that some fears are implicitly or explicitly sexual in content. The frequency with which "psychoanalytic" fears occur is not known, but the indications are that only a small percentage of human fears belong in this category. Psychoanalytic theory cannot succeed as a comprehensive account of human fears, but it may help us to understand some of the more unusual fears.

It is regrettable that psychoanalytic writers have not yet attempted to apply the three-system conception of fear to aspects of their theories. Is it possible in some way to link discordances between subjective and autonomic indexes of fear to analytic ideas of unconscious fears? Is autonomic disturbance without subjective fear-recognition an example of unconscious fear? These questions raise interesting possibilities.

The past few years have not been kind to psychoanalysis. A major attempt to evaluate the effects of psychoanalysis was initiated at the Menninger Clinic in 1954, but numerous difficulties interfered with progress and the Final Report appeared 18 years later. It produced no evidence to support the claims of analysts, and the Editor, Dr. Kernberg, felt that the project suffered from the "lack of formal experimental design."[21] With commendable candour, Kernberg and his colleagues admitted that it had not been possible "(i) to list the variables needed to test the theory; (ii) to have methods of quantification for the variables, preferably existing scales which would have adequate reliability and validity; (iii) to be able to choose and provide control conditions which could rule out alternative explanations for the results . . . (iv) to state the hypotheses to be tested; or finally (v) to conduct the research according to the design."[22]

The philosophical basis for the theory has been subjected to detailed and severe criticism by Grunbaum,[23] and after a century of study there still is no acceptable evidence that psychoanalysis is an effective treatment.[24]

In 1985, Eysenck turned his critical power on psychoanalysis again and undermined two well-established beliefs about the origins of the theory.[25] It appears that Anna O, one of the most famous and important cases in the history of psychoanalysis, continued to suffer from serious psychological problems after her supposedly successful treatment. Despite the strong implication from her therapist, Breuer, that Anna had improved, it appears that she was later admitted to the Bellevue Sanitorium because she was disturbed and made several suicidal attempts.[26] She was heavily medicated there and remained a patient for several months.[27] Ellenberger concluded from his discovery of new documents about the case that "the patient had not been cured. Indeed the famed 'prototype of a cathartic cure' was neither a cure nor a catharsis."[28] Freud's biographer and colleague, Ernest Jones, said that Breuer "confided to Freud" a year after discontinuing the treatment that she was "quite unhinged and that she wished she would die and so be released from her suffering."[29] For a few years, she continued to experience disturbed states as evening drew on. In his autobiography, first published in 1927, Freud wrote that Breuer had "succeeded . . . in relieving his patient of all her symptoms"[30] He said that "the patient had recovered and had remained well."[31]

Contrary to general belief, prompted in part no doubt by Freud's account in his autobiography, the initial reception of his ideas was not hostile, but attentive and partly favorable.[32] Freud complained that he had been shunned and isolated and that his book on dreams was "scarcely reviewed."[33] This book and his essay on dreams received between them at least 30 reviews.[34]

It is customary for critics of psychoanalysis to put to boot in and then compliment Freud on his acute clinical observations. The current interest in the psychology of panic provides an opportunity to follow this custom, for Freud's observations on the subject were indeed perceptive and prescient.

The psychoanalytic theory of fear is stagnant. There is no sign here of new discoveries, refinements of methodology, improved treatment, or growth. Instead of intellectual bustle there is lethargy, and the theory has been passed by.

Psychoanalysis cannot provide a satisfactory general theory of fear, but the literature on sexual fears and on symbolism is not without interest. Extravagant claims about the generality, not to say universality, of these ideas, and a weakness for the bizarre, have turned people away from a scientific analysis of fear symbolism: all fears of spiders are symbolic of bisexual genitalia, all snakes are phallic symbols, and so on. The implausibility of these claims prompts a total rejection of symbolism, but fears are not always exactly as they seem. Contrary to psychoanalytic beliefs, however, it is unwise to assume that fears are *never* as they seem.

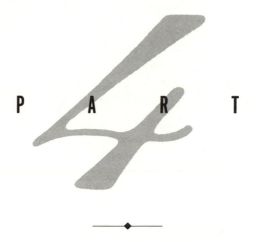

P A R T 4

THE MODIFICATION OF FEAR

CHAPTER 14

THE REDUCTION
OF FEAR

With some exceptions, it is now possible to reduce substantially or even eliminate circumscribed fears within a single training session. The basic method is straightforward and simple. The trainer or therapist assists the fearful person gradually to approach the fear-evoking object, initially in a safe and reassuring setting and then in more demanding conditions.[1] The provision of a therapist model, whom the fearful person can imitate, expedites the process. The reduction of very intense or complex fears, such as agoraphobia, is more demanding and requires a greater expenditure of effort and time. The methods are similar to those used in dealing with circumscribed fears, and significant reductions of fear are achieved in the majority of cases.[2] These advances were part of a wider scientific movement in which the methods and findings of experimental psychology were applied successfully to various aspects of abnormal behavior and which gave rise to new forms of psychological treatment, collectively described as behavior therapy.[3] The term refers to a group of techniques for treating a variety of psychological deficits and disorders and also to a theory of the nature of these problems and how they can be modified. Many of the underlying ideas and some of the methods of behavior therapy are exemplified in the way that the reduction of fear was tackled.

The roots of the new methods for reducing fear can be traced to the work of Pavlov and Watson,[4] both of whom emphasized the role of learning in the acquisition and modification of emotional responses, including fear. Inspired by Watson's[5] work, in 1924. Mary Cover Jones applied a conditioning method in an attempt to help a 3-year-old boy overcome his fears.[6] The child displayed a fear of white rats, rabbits, fur, cotton wool, and similar objects. The fear of rabbits was tackled first because it appeared to be the focus of the boy's other fears. He was gradually introduced to contacts with a rabbit during his daily play period and was placed in a play group with three fearless children. Each day the rabbit was brought into the room for short periods, and the child's tolerance gradually improved. The rabbit was shown in a cage 12 feet away, then 4 feet away, then close by but still in the cage. Eventually the rabbit was set free in the room. Jones also used feeding as a means of inhibiting the fear; the boy, Peter, was given desired food whenever the rabbit was shown and this helped to replace the fear with a positive response. Using these techniques, Jones succeeded in overcoming Peter's fear of rabbits and related objects. The boy was kept under observation for some time and showed no resurgence of the fear of rabbits or the other objects. It would be difficult to better her success in a similar case today.

The significance of this work passed unnoticed for a long period and was recovered only when the ideas that gave rise to behavior therapy began to circulate. The direct influence of Jones' work can be illustrated by a case history that was published 40 years after her description of Peter.[7] The 7-year-old boy with a phobia of bees was referred for treatment. The fear had emerged 3 years earlier, was intense, and interfered with many of his activities. The child could not remember having received a bee sting, but knew of several people who had been stung or who had displayed excessive fear of bees. The nature of the fear was elicited and a list of fear-evoking situations was compiled. The techniques chosen to overcome his fear were drawn from Jones' work and included feeding responses, social approval, and exposure to visual stimuli that were made progressively more realistic. At first he was shown small photographs of bees, then large photographs, coloured photographs, dead bees in a bottle at the far end of the room, a dead bee in a bottle brought gradually closer, a dead bee out of the bottle, gradually increasing manipulations of the dead bee, the introduction of several dead bees, playing imaginative games with the dead bees, and so on. As the boy made gradual and systematic progress, he was exposed to a range of situations in which live bees are encountered. After eight sessions, his avoidance behavior had diminished significantly and he and his mother reported a considerable improvement. His progress was reviewed over a 2-year period and there was no sign of a return of the fear. This case study, reported 25 years ago, illustrates a bridge between the explorations carried out by Mary Cover Jones and current methods, which are fundamentally unchanged but faster and more refined. Nowadays the same result could be achieved in less than half the time.

The prescience of Mary Cover Jones is evident from the fact that all five of the methods that she recommended are in use today. She concluded that neither verbal reassurance nor disapproval are effective methods for reducing fear in children, and she recommended instead that the following alternatives be considered: social imitation, feeding responses, systematic distraction, affectionate responses, or direct conditioning.

SYSTEMATIC DESENSITIZATION

Early in the 1950s a major advance was made by Joseph Wolpe, who translated the results of his laboratory research into clinical practice.[8] Working in comparative isolation, he developed a fear-reduction technique that he called systematic desensitization. It consists of two elements: the fearful person is given training in muscle relaxation and is then asked to imagine increasingly fearful scenes while remaining in a state of calm relaxation. With repeated practice of the imaginal experience of the fearful scenes, the subject or patient gradually acquires the ability to tolerate the fearful ideas or scenes in his imagination, and this improvement usually transfers to some extent to the real situation. In his original work, Wolpe exposed his fearful patients to the very objects which provoked their fears, but for practical reasons he shifted the emphasis to imaginary representations of these fearful stimuli. In an amusing cycle, most therapists have now re-adopted the earlier method of exposing fearful subjects to the real stimuli rather than to imaginal representations of them. The return to using real objects rather than imaginal representations, although cumbersome and time-consuming in the short term, is justified because in most instances substantially greater reductions in fear can be achieved. In addition, the use of real objects reduces the number of misses and expands the range of effectiveness of the procedures. The use of imaginal representations has the advantages of flexibility and speed and retains a useful place among the fear-reducing procedures.

In addition to its clinical value, desensitization prepared the way for a significant increase in our understanding of fear and its modification. The success of desensitization confirmed the value of applying ideas drawn from experimental psychology to clinical problems, indirectly contributed to the abandonment of needlessly complicated explanations of fear, and demonstrated that fear can be unlearned. There was no doubt, and there is no doubt, that fears can be acquired by a learning process, and Wolpe and Eysenck were convinced that they can also be unlearned. The second part of Wolpe's program of research was devoted to a search for methods that could "unlearn" these acquired fears.

Prompted by Wolpe's experimental reports and clinical descriptions, Lang and Lazovik[9] conducted an experiment that became the model for a stream of similar studies of the modification of fear. Their pioneer experiment, carefully designed and executed, was carried out on 24 snake-phobic students at the University of Pittsburgh. The subjects were chosen from a large pool of fearful students, who in turn had been chosen from a larger group of randomly selected students. Those subjects whose verbal reports of significant fear of snakes were confirmed in a behavioral avoidance test, during which they were exposed to a live but harmless snake, were included in the study. This use of a behavioral test was an important innovation and reflected the growing application of empirical and behavioral methods to clinical problems. These tests are now a standard procedure in most experimental studies and evaluations of the effects of psychological therapy. "The best measure of behavior is behavior, not reports about it."[10] Lang's experiments showed that direct behavioral methods can be applied to the study of abnormal behavior, and what started as an innovation soon turned into a requirement. The results from the behavioral tests contributed significantly to Lang's radically new interpretation of fear.[11] Fear behavior was recognized to be one of three loosely coupled components that comprise the construct of fear.

Having verified that their subjects were intensely fearful, Lang and Lazovik desensitized half of the subjects and used the remainder as an untreated control group. Each experimental subject was given up to 11 sessions of desensitization during which they were asked to imagine increasingly fearful situations involving snakes while they remained relaxed. The control subjects were given training in relaxation and participated in the construction of a graded list of fearful snake images, but they were not desensitized. At the termination of the experimental treatment period, the desensitized subjects were significantly less fearful of snakes than the control subjects. The reductions of fear were evident in their subjective reports, psychometric ratings, and behavioral avoidance tests. The changes were maintained for at least 6 months, and were not followed by the emergence of new problems.

In a subsequent study, Lang, Lazovik, and Reynolds[12] found that desensitization produces a specific change, over and above any modification that might result from the general therapeutic preliminaries or other non-specific influences. The control subjects, who were given a cleverly designed form of pseudotherapy, showed little change. The development of a sympathetic relationship between the therapist and subject was not sufficient to change the fear, and the therapist had no need to delve into the presumed causes of the subject's fear. The successful desensitization of the specific fear of snakes generalized to other fears, and modest all-round reductions in fear took place.[13]

Virtually all of the conclusions reached by Lang and his colleagues in these pioneering experiments have been confirmed, with the same and different techniques, the same and different types of subjects, the same and different assessment procedures. The extent of the investigations, the degree of agreement in their outcomes, and their overall significance are remarkable. The rehearsal of fearful scenes in imagination, or in reality, while the subject is relaxing proved to be a robust technique for reducing fear. Many variations have been tested—shortening the rehearsal time, abbreviating the number of training sessions, not grading the fearful scenes, and so on, and in virtually all of them at least a moderate degree of fear reduction was obtained. In addition to providing support for Wolpe's main claim, research workers have also explored the nature of the desensitization process itself. Attempts were made to isolate the effective elements in the procedure, and it appears that the fear-reducing effects are potentiated by the combined action of relaxation, instructions, and the graduated presentation of fearful images. However, the role and action of muscle relaxation training has been re-appraised. Muscle relaxation appears to facilitate desensitization, but it is not a prerequisite for the reduction of fear. The degree of fear reduction is not related to the suggestibility of the frightened subject, and relaxation, whether alone or accompanied by pseudotherapeutic interviews, does not reduce the fear. The establishment of a sympathetic relationship does not of itself reduce fear but might facilitate the process, especially in complex fears. Interpretive methods combined with relaxation reduce fears slightly or not at all.

Presentations of fearful scenes in imagination confer some practical advantages and flexibility, but exposures to real objects and situations are more powerful. Automated desensitization procedures can be effective, and although their practical value should not be underestimated, the theoretical significance of their effectiveness is greater. There is no need to discount the contribution that a sympathetic experimenter or therapist can make toward reducing a person's fear, but a satisfactory explanation of the effects of desensitization must take into account the expendability of a therapist. Any attempt to account for the fear-reducing effects of desensitization that relies on the personality, or even the presence of a therapist, is unlikely to succeed.

Over the years, the emphasis has shifted from imaginary representations to so-called *in vivo* presentations of the real object or situation. Nowadays, repeated exposure to the real object of the person's fear is the central feature of the most effective of the behavioral techniques.

FLOODING

Some ten years after the introduction of desensitization, two new procedures for reducing fear, flooding and modeling, were added. As soon as their value had been confirmed, attempts were made to discover whether there might be a common underlying mechanism or process responsible for the effects of all three methods. Desensitization and flooding always, and modeling often, share the evident common feature of repeated exposures to the fear-evoking stimulus. Attempts to find a common explanation therefore focused on the nature and effects of these repeated exposures. The impetus for the development of *flooding*, a method in which the fearful subject is exposed to stimulation that provokes intense fear for a protracted period, came from experimental investigations of small animals. Interest in the possible value of flooding was reinforced by the clinical work of Stampfl,[14] who introduced the technique of "implosive therapy," in which patients were required to imagine scenes of great unpleasantness that were derived from psychodynamic explorations of their experiments. Disturbing psychodynamic material was introduced into the treatment sessions, and the patient was asked to recall and relive in his imagination distressing experiences, especially those that had occurred during childhood. The theoretical explanation put forward by Stampfl was unconvincing, but some of the clinical effects aroused considerable interest and contributed to the development of the flooding technique. Regrettably, it also contributed to an unfortunate and unnecessary confusion between the terms and methods of flooding and implosion.

The provocative material was used to stimulate the patient's imagination, but as occurred in the use of desensitization, therapists increasingly began to substitute *in vivo* exposures to the anxiety-evoking objects or situations. These applications sometimes took bizarre forms, such as locking claustrophobic patients up for several hours at a time, but the trend of the results obtained in controlled investigations was consistent. Flooding often is followed by a substantial reduction in fear, and this within surprisingly few sessions, even though the overall duration of exposure might add up to several hours. However, despite some early hopes for improved efficacy, it turns out that flooding has no advantages to offer over the gradual and less demanding methods of *in vivo* desensitization or therapeutic modeling.

Contrary to some expectations, there have been remarkably few reports of flooding producing adverse effects, but I suspect that flooding increases the number of people who refuse or defect from treatment. Flooding might also inflate the size of the return-of-fear effect (see p. 253). This method does not appear to be the first choice of many therapists, nor should it be. In practice, the clear divisions between *in vivo* desensitization, flooding, and participant modeling are blurred, and the treatment is focused on ensuring that the fearful subject or patient is exposed to the fearful stimulus for a sufficient length of time and in an acceptable fashion. In most theoretical analyses flooding is now classed with the other fear-reducing techniques.

Flooding was sometimes confused with a method called response prevention, which refers to the blocking of an escape from a frightening stimulus. In a well-planned and systematic series of experiments on animals, Baum convincingly demonstrated that prevention of the escape response can lead to rapid reduction of fear.[15] The method of response prevention was adopted by clinicians and applied in the treatment of previously resistant neurotic disorders. Then the methods of exposure and response prevention were welded together to produce a robust technique for reducing fear. This combination proved to be particularly useful in the treatment of severe obsessional-compulsive problems, and typically took the form of exposing the patient to the many stimuli felt to be contaminating or otherwise disturbing, and then preventing the unadaptive compulsive response, which usually takes the form of compulsive cleaning.[16] It remains the treatment of choice in most cases of obsessional-compulsive and other anxiety disorders.

THERAPEUTIC MODELING

In view of the extensive evidence that desensitization is capable of reducing fear, any method that claimed to produce results superior to those of desensitization demanded close inspection. The first such claim was made by Bandura, Blachard, and Ritter, who reported that the technique of live imitation, in which the fearful subject observed and then copied the approach behavior of the model, produced a significantly larger reduction of fear than did desensitization.[17] This experimental report was also remarkable for the magnitude of change reported by what is now known as the method of participant modeling. In 92 percent of the subjects their excessive fear of snakes was virtually eliminated.

Like the other two major techniques of fear reduction, participant modeling is simplicity itself. To begin, the fearful subject has merely to observe the trainer-therapist model engaging the fearful stimulus on a number of occasions. After this period of passive observation, the observer's fear generally begins to diminish. When it reaches a suitably reduced level, and the fearful subject is willing and able to proceed to the next step, the model encourages the frightened person to begin imitating the coping behavior. The fearful observer is gradually integrated into the coping behavior, and he or she is encouraged to participate ever more fully. A point is reached at which the fearful observer, whose fear by now has been substantially reduced, engages the fearful object or situation with the therapist observing. Finally, the therapist fades from the situation, and the formerly fearful person is encouraged to practice the fearless coping behavior many times.

The successful application of therapeutic modeling is interesting for four reasons. First, large reductions in fear can be achieved comfortably and in large segments, with few exceptions. Second, it was one of the two principal methods recommended by Mary Cover Jones in 1924. "Social imitation (in which) we allow the subjects to share under controlled conditions the social activity of a group of children especially chosen with a view to prestige effect."[18] Third in addition to its therapeutic value, the concept of learning by modeling was important in the construction of an expanded explanation of the genesis of fear; the idea that fears can be acquired vicariously was introduced as one of the three pathways of fear and was derived, in part, from demonstrations that fear can be *reduced* by vicarious experiences. Fourth, the fact that fear can be reduced even by passive modeling procedures, in which the fearful person merely observes someone else engaging the fearful object, led to a reconsideration of the nature of the exposure element in fear reduction procedures.[19]

What is the nature of the information conveyed? Can passive modeling of the fear-coping behavior of another person be conveyed by auditory material rather than visually? At what point is a remote contact with the fearful stimulus no longer regarded as exposure? How do we define "exposure"?

The fundamental work on therapeutic modeling was conducted by Bandura and his colleagues in an impressively successful program of research.[20] Bandura argued that modeling transmits new patterns of coping behavior, prevents or interrupts unnecessary responses, and facilitates the expression of previously learned adaptive behavior.[21] The results of his research enabled him to develop a simple and effective method for reducing fear.

He recommends that the fearful person be given repeated modeling experiences, that multiple models should be used, and that progressively increasing demands should be made of the fearful subject. He also recommends that the modeling should be supplemented by repeated practice in naturally occurring situations and that attempts should be made to ensure the regular reinforcement of the newly acquired fearless behavior. All of these efforts are aimed at achieving an increase in the person's "perceived self-efficacy," which Bandura proposes as the main basis for all behavioral change.[22] Are these recommendations justifiable?

The research into the fear-reducing power of modeling was conducted along similar lines to the work carried out on desensitization, and the results, too, are similar. Modeling produces significant reductions of fear under specifiable conditions. The reduction in fear is enduring and generalizes to fear-evoking situations that bear a resemblance to the one in which the modeling took place. As Bandura claimed, therapeutic modeling is facilitated by repeated practice, prolonged exposure times, and the use of multiple models and multiple fear stimuli.

There appear to be two major determinants of the fear-reducing effects of modeling: the number of successful exposures to the model and the total time of the successful exposures. It is not argued that modeling is a necessary condition for the reduction of fear, but rather that it can usefully facilitate such reductions.

The introduction of this powerful method of reducing fear was most welcome, but the implementation of therapeutic modeling raises some theoretical questions. If the method is so successful, why do fearful people fail to model fearless conduct in their natural environments? Why does exposure to a model in a clinical setting produce changes that have not been achieved elsewhere? There are several possible replies to these questions, and all of them may contribute to a final answer.

First, large numbers of people do in fact lose many of their fears in their natural environment. The great majority of children's fears decline in middle to late childhood despite the absence of deliberate modeling.[23] Presumably, a significant part of the explanation for the natural decline in fears can be attributed to the uncontrived occurrence of repeated exposures to fearless models. Some fears fail to decline spontaneously, because the people concerned are repeatedly exposed to *fearful* models, and children probably learn some fears by modeling the behavior of their parents. If a person has been exposed repeatedly to a fearful mother or other person, he or she may continue to experience and manifest fear in a wider variety of situations than will his peers. Children who are brought up under conditions of isolation, and therefore have fewer opportunities to model fearless behavior from a variety of models, will fail to acquire the fearless behavior that is displayed by their peers. Some intense fears are not easy to reduce, by modeling or any other deliberate procedure. Some people and some fears appear to be resistant to change and fail to respond to therapeutic modeling or flooding or desensitization. Such failures can occur among people who are deeply depressed or who retain extremely abnormal ideas about the objects of their fear.[24]

Participant modeling has considerable appeal because the method is so easy to use. However, there are some limitations. In some studies, therapeutic modeling had little impact, and the treatment of patients with severe obsessional problems can be unusually difficult.[25] Some of these patients are unable to approach their dreaded situations despite intensive modeling treatment, and this type of failure was thought to be the result of depression or extraordinarily high levels of fear.

Three obstacles to the successful use of therapeutic modeling are encountered but are not insuperable. As mentioned earlier, some people simply do not experience a reduction in fear. Others learn the necessary skill during the sessions of modeling, but fail to translate the learning into performance outside of the clinical setting. Others acquire the skills and even transfer them to the natural environment, but for one reason or another fail to maintain their improvements. These are not new clinical problems, but therapeutic modeling confers no immunity to them.

Therapeutic modeling has many advantages. It is capable of producing changes rapidly and can transmit large and complex units of behavior. It is readily accepted by most people and the few problems of non-cooperation arise out of skepticism rather than reluctance or distaste. Fearful subjects and patients express disbelief when the modeling method is explained to them. They cannot believe that watching another person engaging the phobic stimulus will reduce their own fear. Observing their polite disbelief change into surprise and delight can be gratifying. The fact that passive modeling, in which the fearful person merely observes a therapeutic model, *does* produce a measure of fear reduction is somewhat surprising, and of theoretical interest. However, it is *participant modeling* that produces the largest and most impressive changes. Lastly, it is easier to provide advice, and practical advice at that, about how to reduce and prevent fears. It has been applied with considerable success in the prevention of fear among children admitted to hospital for surgery.[26]

COGNITIVE METHODS

The powerful fear-reducing effect of repeated exposures is a large fact that has to be taken into account by any theory. However, the reduction of fear in the *absence* of exposures to the fearful stimulus makes the resort to cognitive influences understandable, perhaps unavoidable. The effects of these influences is now evident and is the starting point for most of the recent research on panic. Do a person's cognitions, especially those relating to the feared object, influence the reduction of fear?

There is plentiful evidence of fearful cognitions during episodes of intense fear, such as panic, and it has been argued that they play a causal role.[27] And there is new evidence that cognitive changes can reduce fear, especially in the treatment of panic.[28] Cognitive factors can influence habituation in humans,[29] and recent findings on claustrophobics indicate that such factors may influence the habituation of fear.[30] It is possible that fearful cognitions impede habituation.[31] Interesting differences were found between claustrophobic subjects whose fear was reduced following repeated exposures (habituation?) and those whose fear remained unchanged despite the exposures. Those who failed to show habituation of fear endorsed more fearful cognitions at the beginning of the habituation training than did those subjects who showed habituation of fear. For example, 86 percent of the non-habituators initially endorsed the cognitive items stating, "I am going to pass out" and "I am going to suffocate." The comparable figures for the subjects who did habituate to the fear situation were 23 percent and 31 percent. One interpretation of these findings is that certain cognitions impede the habituation of claustrophobic fears. In this experiment no attempt was made to influence the process of habituation by tinkering with the fearful cognitions, and it remains to be demonstrated that the removal or weakening of the critical cognitions will facilitate habituation to being enclosed in a small space. The argument that fearful cognitions influence fear-reduction is well supported.

Fear reduction may be the product of a combination of habituation and cognitive change, but each of these two may separately reduce fear. Each may be more or less effective in reducing particular fears. Habituation probably plays an essential part in reducing irrational, intense fears of a circumscribed nature, and the modification of cognitions may be of particular value in dealing with panic disorders and diffuse fears such as generalized anxiety. The interesting possibility is that in most instances the reduction of fear is mediated by an interaction of cognitions and habituation.

Beck's approach

The views of Beck, a leading exponent of cognitive therapy, fresh from his successful work on depression, provide a useful introduction to the clinical evidence relating cognitions and fear reduction. As in the treatment of depression, so in the management of anxiety disorders, Beck and Emery combine cognitive modification with behavioral exercises that involve exposure.[32] Beck introduced the useful metaphor of anxiety disorders as "hypersensitive alarm systems," and he proposed that anxiety is precipitated by specific thoughts or images that the person feels are a signal of danger.[33] "The crucial element in anxiety states, thus, is a cognitive process that may take the form of an automatic thought or image that appears rapidly, as if by reflex, after the initial stimulus (e.g., shortness of breath) that seems plausible, and that is followed by a wave of anxiety."[34] Anxious patients are unduly sensitive to any signals that indicate the possibility of potential harm, and they tend to discount contrary evidence.[35] It follows that the introduction of a dependable safety signal should reduce the pervasiveness of anxiety, make it more specific, and limit it in time and space.[36]

In therapy it is necessary first to identify the faulty cognitions. These are scrutinized, their validity is undermined by the collection of contrary evidence, and the possible consequences of the person's fearful thoughts or images are examined. Attempts are then made to correct the faulty cognitions.

These cognitive explorations and changes are supplemented by specific behavioral exercises, without which the cognitive work may not bite. "An over-riding strategy is for the patient to approach what he fears."[37] It is "generally agreed that exposure" is a "crucial element in the treatment of agoraphobia," and the provision of *in vivo* homework in which the "individual confronts the situation" is included as a "crucial element in the treatment of anxiety."[38] The implication is that cognitive changes and habituation training are interactive, at the very least in the treatment of agoraphobia.

The treatment recommended for dealing with anxiety closely resembles that used in the treatment of depression, and the similarities outweigh the differences. The value of this expansion remains to be evaluated, but an integration of Beck's views on anxiety with his theory of depression would help matters along. It should be mentioned that cognitive therapy as described and advocated by Beck and Emery is not a minor skill that can be learned quickly and simply.[39] It is a complex method that can be acquired only by systematic instruction and supervised clinical experience.

The Oxford approach

The approach of the Oxford group,[40] described in the discussion of panic, owes a great deal to Beck's work and shares the basic assumption about the crucial role of cognitions in fear. Given the progress already made in tackling the modification of panic disorders, it is surely a matter of time before Clark, Salkovskis, and their colleagues in

Oxford turn their energies to dueling with other types of fear. Presumably, many types of fear will be construed as mainly the product of misinterpretations of internal or external events. The affected person interprets the information as evidence of a significant threat, and this provokes a fearful response. Anxious people are particularly prone to detect potentially harmful information and are particularly prone to make unduly threatening interpretations of such information. Episodes of fear are the product of threatening cognitions, and it follows that if the cognitions are changed or blocked, less fear will be experienced. Given the powerful fear-reducing effects of repeated exposure to the fear stimulus, special importance must rest with the behavioral exercises that presumably are a vehicle for changing the fearful cognitions and for confirming the validity of the more satisfactory cognitions. It was suggested earlier that circumscribed, irrational fears, such as snake and spider phobias, present a stiff test for cognitive explanations, and the test will not be long in coming.

The concept of self-efficacy

The combination of cognitive modification and behavioral exercises has attracted much support,[41] but critics have drawn attention to some disappointing results of cognitive therapy applied to the reduction of fear or anxiety.[42] Behavioral exercises involving exposure are demonstrably effective, cognitive therapy on its own produces discouragingly weak results, and therefore there is nothing to be gained by adding cognitive therapy to behavior therapy. This observation leads to the complaint that although it is the behavioral methods that are most effective, many people are drawn to cognitive rather than behavioral explanations. Bandura was among the first to draw attention to the gap between cognitive theory and cognitive therapy, and his attempt to solve the problem requires careful consideration.[43]

Performance-based treatments, such as exposure, produce the best results, but the explanations proposed to account for the changes are increasingly cognitive.[44] Bandura argued that psychological changes, "regardless of the method used to achieve them," derive from a common mechanism. The apparent divergence of theory and practice is reconciled by recognizing that "change is mediated through cognitive processes, but the cognitive processes are induced and altered most readily by experiences of mastery arising from successful performance."[45] All of the procedures for achieving changes in fearful and avoidant behavior alter the level and strength of self-efficacy: "the conviction that one can successfully execute the behavior required to produce (the desired) outcomes."[46] Increases in self-efficacy produce corresponding reductions in defensive behavior. The expectations of personal efficacy determine how the person will attempt to cope, how long he will continue to cope, and how much effort he will expend "in the face of obstacles and aversive experiences."[47] The expectations are derived from successful performances, verbal persuasion, vicarious experience, and physiological states.

He argues that psychological treatment, including the methods for reducing fear, is successful to the extent that it produces increases in self-efficacy. The theory accounts for the fact that people differ in their responses to the same form of treatment, and it provides a rationale for using estimates of self-efficacy as a means of predicting the success or failure of an intervention. So, for example, in an experiment on the reduction of fear by means of participant modeling, it was found that self-efficacy predicted the reduction of fear correctly in 92 percent of the total assessment tasks.[48] The estimates provided an 84 percent level of accuracy in predicting how the subjects would perform on highly threatening tasks that they had never encountered before. This complex and closely argued theory has been the subject of considerable discussion, and critics have complained that self-efficacy may be a reflection of the mechanisms responsible for change, rather than the mediator of the change.[49] Eysenck argued that this cognitive theory, in common with others, is off target, and deals with epiphenomena, while "leaving out the truly causal elements in the chain of events which mediates changes in behavior."[50] It has also been objected that the theory is circular and that "there is no firm experimental evidence to support the contention that all psychological procedures serve as a means of strengthening expectations of personal efficacy".[51] Notwithstanding these reservations, the theory has attracted support,[52] and most writers agree that estimates of self-efficacy provide a useful basis for predicting the outcome of interventions of therapy.

The gap between cognitive theory and cognitive therapy might be explained in other ways. One possibility is that the weak results are the outcome of poor and hastily devised methods of therapy. Some of the early attempts at cognitive therapy were indeed ill conceived and shabby, and consisted of little more than trying to persuade the frightened person to see the irrationality of his ways and make a fresh start. The first few attempts to treat agoraphobia by cognitive methods produced discouragingly weak results, and are sharply different from the recent reports of successes in treating panic disorder, mostly associated with agoraphobia. As mentioned, Beck's[53] preliminary findings suggest that the method is powerful, and equally promising preliminary results have been reported by the Oxford group[54] and others. If these and other claims are confirmed, it certainly would strengthen the argument that highly developed and well-practiced versions of cognitive therapy can reduce fear, and that we should not be discouraged by the early failures. The gap between the explanatory powers of cognitive theories and the weakness of cognitive therapy may close.

It remains possible that the cognitive theories are mistaken and that the gap emerged because the theories were out of touch with the facts. Worse still, the theories might be mistaken even if the results of therapy are improved.

The combination of cognitive and behavioral techniques will continue and will be refined. It is likely that different types of fear will require different proportions of the mixture. Intense, irrational and circumscribed fears, such as the fear of snakes and of spiders, call for habituation training; cognitive modification will play a small part and might well be dispensed with. On present information, cognitive therapy seems likely to prove particularly effective in dealing with panic disorders. In time, the more diffuse clinical problems of social and generalized anxiety might yield. Tackling diffuse fears by habituation training is clumsy but produces some improvement; however, it is common for the person to be left with residual fears.

The addition of cognitive methods to behavioral ones was foreshadowed by Wolpe in 1958.

It is often important to remove a patient's misconceptions, whether they relate to simple items of misinformation, such as the idea that masturbation weakens the body and the mind, or to complex mistaken attitudes to society, to other people, or to the patient himself . . . but although the correcting of misconceptions is not in itself psychotherapeutic in our sense, it is often an essential precondition to psychotherapeutic success.

In parts, his early writings have the ring of recent work by Beck and by Clark.

It amounts . . . to [correcting] the connotation of certain stimulus configurations; the patient has reacted unpleasantly to X because he has wrongly believed it to imply Y and now the therapist convinces him that X does not imply Y.[56]

Twenty years later he continued to press the argument and said that therapeutic requirements differ for different patients. The three basic types of patients are those who are fearful of something which they feel to be harmless and whose "anxiety is a conditioned response to the perception" of the object; those who are afraid because they erroneously *believe* that a harmless object is harmful; and those who simultaneously have erroneous beliefs and conditioned responses. Phobias of the first type require "emotional deconditioning," those of the second type require "cognitive correction," and the third type requires both.[57] Wolpe may have been on the correct path.

If the present analysis and interpretation has merit, research will have to be directed toward unraveling the mechanisms involved in these cognitive changes and how they impede or facilitate habituation. How do cognitions gear in with habituation? These are complex and inviting questions.

CHAPTER

IN SEARCH
OF AN
EXPLANATION
FOR FEAR
REDUCTION

Important progress has been made in developing effective methods for reducing fear. We now have several successful techniques, the range of their efficacy is being expanded yearly, and progressive refinements have led to the development of some remarkably speedy methods of reducing fear. Despite all of this progress there is some uneasiness in the air. The practical progress has advanced faster than our understanding of the processes involved. The addition of new techniques is welcome, but it is unclear whether such additions are based on new processes or are simply new variations of the same theme.

Can a single explanation accommodate the effects of the current methods of reducing fear? As mentioned earlier, the addition of modeling and flooding methods to the desensitization procedure raised the question of whether we are dealing with three different processes or whether all three of these behavioral methods achieve their effects in the same manner.

RECIPROCAL INHIBITION

At least two processes appear to be involved, habituation and cognitive changes, but it may be possible to encompass both under the umbrella of "emotional processing." Wolpe's explanation for the fear-reducing effects of his technique of desensitization is based on the concept of reciprocal inhibition, an idea borrowed from physiology.[1] He argues that the therapeutic benefit is derived from the repeated evocation of small amounts of fear and their immediate suppression by relaxation. The relaxation response inhibits the fear. In the course of desensitization, whenever the formation of the image produces a small amount of fear, it is then suppressed by the incompatible relaxation response; this is reciprocal inhibition. Each instance of this suppression, the reciprocal inhibition of fear, contributes to the growth of a lasting inhibition of the fear, known as conditioned inhibition. And each step in the treatment program adds one more block toward the construction of fearlessness. In order to produce a lasting conditioned inhibition of the fear, the therapist gradually moves up a hierarchy of fear-producing images, starting with minimally disturbing ones and proceeding up to the most frightening images at the top of the hierarchy. Wolpe argued that other types of inhibitory processes also are capable of reducing fear, by repeated evocations of the fear without counter-conditioning, but in his concentration on the theory of reciprocal inhibition, he did not develop the idea.

Much of the evidence is consistent with Wolpe's theory, and in some studies desensitization was found to produce substantial reductions in fear only if the repeated presentations of the fearful stimuli were accompanied by deep relaxation (reciprocally inhibited?).[2] Results of this type are consistent with Wolpe's idea of the necessary interaction between the experience of fear and its suppression by an incompatible response. It has also been found that fearful subjects who relax well and obtain evocative images on instruction show the greatest improvement during desensitization. On the other hand, some findings are not consistent with the theory. The omission of relaxation training does not prevent the reduction of fear. In the absence of relaxation or any other evident suppressant of fear, what is responsible for producing a *reciprocal* inhibition? In addition, fear and relaxation are incompatible in many circumstances but are not always so, and sheer muscle relaxation does not preclude the experience of subjective fear. It has also been observed that Wolpe's theory is not sufficiently explicit on certain points, and his attempt to draw an analogy between the physiological process of inhibition and a psychological process has been criticized.

It is difficult to accommodate the evidence of the fear-reducing effects of flooding within the theory, and the success of this method certainly is not predictable from Wolpe's theory of reciprocal inhibition. So the theory has to be modified, or it could be argued that flooding involves a different process and requires a separate explanation. The fear-reducing effects of modeling procedures raise few complications. There are obvious similarities between modeling and desensitization, especially when these methods are carried out *in vivo*. They both involve repeated exposures to attenuated fear stimuli. Given that fear reduction can occur even in the absence of an identified reciprocal inhibitor and given the prominence of repeated exposures in most of the successful fear-reduction techniques, it has been suggested that desensitization should be classed with the other two methods, both of which are assumed to achieve their effects by extinction or by habituation.

HABITUATION

A recent interpretation of the process of habituation contains an echo of Wolpe's theory, sometimes described as a counter-conditioning theory because it posits the super-imposition of an incompatible response over the fear. Mackintosh argues that the best explanation of long-term habituation to biologically significant or potent stimuli, but not other instances of habituation, is that it "involves the conditioning to contextual stimuli of an opponent process or compensatory reaction which counteracts the initial responses elicited by the stimulus."[3] There may be common ground between habituation as interpreted by Mackintosh and the reciprocal inhibition of fear as construed by Wolpe, but

Mackintosh's emphasis on the importance of contextual cues in long-term habituation seems not to fit the evidence of durable and generalized reductions in fear observed after desensitization treatment.

Mackintosh emphasized that habituation is "probably the most widespread form of learning" and is a very simple procedure, requiring no more than the repeated presentation of the stimulus. And "the results are no more complex: typically the subject's initial response to the stimulus declines."[4] Despite its simplicity, there is no generally accepted psychological theory to account for habituation.

Habituation occurs most easily to mild stimuli, but the fact that it also occurs after intense stimulation necessitates its inclusion in discussions of the reduction of fear. The adaptation to air raids is a telling example of what appears to be habituation to intense and unpredictable stimulation, and Klorman has provided a clinical example of this phenomenon.[5] Habituation has also been cited as a partial explanation for the decline of childhood fears, combat fears, fears of enclosed spaces, and so on. However, we have also to take into account the exceptions that are encountered; some fears do persist unaltered for long periods, and yet others appear to *increase* in strength with repeated exposures to the fearful stimulus. Nevertheless, the prominence in the major fear-reduction methods of repeated exposures to the fearful stimulus marks an obvious similarity to habituation training, and it may be advantageous to cast these fear-reduction methods within an habituation model.

Groves and Thompson suggested that habituation comprises two independent processes.[6] The first is the commonly recognized one of declining responsiveness with repeated stimulation, and the second is a less obvious sensitizing process, which refers to increases in responsiveness as a result of stimulation. Habituation is determined largely by stimulus repetition, and sensitization by stimulus intensity. Habituation and sensitization develop independently but interact to yield a "final behavioral outcome." During habituation training, sensitization occurs early and then decays. The accounts given by Mackworth[7] and by Groves and Thompson suggest that there is common ground between habituation processes and fear reduction. The factors that facilitate habituation resemble those that facilitate the reduction of fear. Repeated stimulation is the major facilitator of habituation and fear reduction. The use of depressant drugs facilitates habituation and fear reduction, as does a lowering of the subject's level of arousal. Other factors that facilitate habituation, and probably fear-reduction as well, include an increase in the rate of stimulation, attenuation of the stimuli, regularity of presentations, and reduced complexity of the stimulation. If we used our knowledge of habituation to design a technique for reducing fear, what would that technique look like?

First, we would attempt to reduce the level of the subject's arousal. Next, we would present the fearful stimulus in an attenuated form, repetitively, regularly, and frequently. This hypothetical treatment, deduced from habituation, is remarkably similar to Wolpe's desensitization technique.

However, the two concepts developed independently, and it was not until 1966 that Lader and Wing first proposed that desensitization might profitably be conceived of as a form of habituation.[8] They viewed desensitization as a form of habituation training since it consists of the repetitive presentation of attenuated (fearful) stimuli. Relaxation lowers the level of the subject's arousal and therefore facilitates quicker habituation. Desensitization can be "more simply regarded as straightforward habituation carried out when the habituation rate is maximal, i.e., with the patient at as low a level of activity as possible."[9] Their neat argument was supported by experimental evidence of a significant correlation between habituation rate under laboratory test conditions and the response to treatment of various types of phobic patients. Those patients who were slow to habituate to an auditory stimulus responded less well to desensitization than did the patients who habituated easily.

Lang, Melamed, and Hart obtained corroborative evidence from subjects with various types of fears.[10] Those who were frightened of speaking in public were the slowest to habituate to auditory stimulation, as was the case with Lader's socially phobic patients. Lang's spider-phobic patients habituated as readily as did Lader's patients with circumscribed phobias. Among snake-phobic subjects there was a correlation between habituation to short films of snakes and to auditory tones.

The habituation hypothesis has an appealing simplicity and can be used to generate specific and clear predictions, but is not without difficulties. It has not always been possible to replicate the initial correlation that led Lader and Wing to construe desensitization as a process of habituation. Failures to confirm the correlation between habituation rate to auditory tones and to phobic stimuli were reported by Gillan and Rachman, and by Klorman.[11] Another objection to the model is that although the fear-reduction techniques generally produce enduring decrements, habituation training characteristically produces transient changes. It has also been objected that habituation describes a decremental process that affects non-learned rather than learned behavior.

The effects of habituation training do show less persistence than other types of decremental change, but under given conditions, habituation can persist. The evidence and arguments on this matter were considered by Kimmel, who concluded that habituation is not "an entirely temporary state of affairs which dissipates completely when the stimulus is withheld."[12] The durability of habituation effects has not been determined in human subjects, and the significance of the transience of the effects of habituation training remains to be determined.

The habituation hypothesis included an assumption that each person has a general rate of habituation and that this can be measured accurately, but the extent of the generality may have been exaggerated. It can be argued, however, that support for this assumption is not essential for the success of the model; no critical changes would be needed if the assumption failed to gather support. But the model does encounter difficulty in explaining the persistence of some circumscribed fears. It is difficult to see why naturally occurring habituation does not eliminate these fears, some of which persist for decades.[13] The technical problems of specifying in advance what is a satisfactorily low level of physiological activity, or indeed an unsatisfactorily high level, may undermine the predictive value of the hypothesis. We also need to know why so many people have a single intense and persisting fear—are they high- or low-level responders?

It is unlikely that the habituation hypothesis would have provided a satisfactory basis for predicting the successful effects of flooding, but it is fair to point out that it was introduced originally as an attempt to explain the effects of desensitization, some time in advance of the introduction of flooding methods. The habituation hypothesis might satisfactorily account for desensitization and leave the effects of flooding unexplained, thereby indicating the need for multiple processes rather than a unitary explanation.

The habituation model is appealing because of its simplicity, because of the pervasiveness of the phenomenon of habituation, and because it meshes so well with many findings on fear reduction, especially the beneficial effects of repeated exposures to the feared object. Regrettably, there is no explanation of habituation itself,[14] and there is a major obstacle to progress in evaluating the hypothesis that habituation is the process responsible for fear-reduction. Clark[15] has pointed out that we do not have a means for independently testing this hypothesis. The reduction of fear (especially by repeated exposures) is taken to indicate that habituation has occurred, but at present we have no way of separating the two—we have no independent index of habituation. Using the observed reduction of fear as an index of habituation renders the hypothesis untestable. Unless and until we possess an independent index, one that allows the possibility of concluding, say, that the fear was reduced but the index of habituation was unchanged, the critical questions cannot be tested. The undoubted descriptive value of viewing fear reduction as a form of habituation should not be allowed to obscure this obstacle to using habituation as an explanatory construct.

EXTINCTION

A third explanation for the effects of fear-reduction techniques is based on the phenomenon of extinction. The idea is that learned responses that are not followed by reinforcement tend to weaken; repeated but unreinforced evocations of a fear response should lead to its extinction. An explanation based on the extinction process appears to offer an initial advantage because it can accommodate the effects of flooding as well as desensitization. In flooding, the repeated evocations of the fearful response are not followed by reinforcement. However, the fact that flooding treatment produces extinction, if that is what it is, in fewer trials than those required for achieving extinction by desensitization may present a problem. It is also difficult to explain the fear-reducing effects accomplished by automated desensitization because no explicit reinforcement is involved, and there is no explicit connection between the practice trials and the withholding of reinforcement. In this example, as in many clinical demonstrations, the identity of the putative reinforcing conditions remains elusive.

The proponents of conditioning theory also attribute fear reduction to a process of extinction. In common with explanations that are based on reinforcement or on habituation, this view draws support from the large and important changes that follow repeated exposures to the fearful stimulus. However, fear reduction can occur even in the absence of exposure, and techniques in which exposure is the prominent feature are not always successful. Failures can occur even with repeated and systematic exposures to the fearful stimulus.[16] These failures, clinical and experimental, cannot all be attributed to insufficient practice, for there are instances in which hundreds of trials, extended over many months, failed to produce significant reductions in fear. High levels of arousal certainly can interfere with the progress of exposure training or treatment, but failures occur even when the patient or the subject's level or arousal is successfully reduced.[17]

Some clues point to the possibility that cognitive factors play an important part in these failures. For example, Foa reported that patients who had fixed abnormal ideas about their problem tended to experience reductions of fear within the training session, only to have them return by the following session.[18] The reductions of fear achieved within the session were followed by a return of fear between sessions.

One of the main reasons for the lack of progress in reaching a conclusion about the value of explanations based on a process of extinction is the confusion that arose between extinction and habituation. Progress was hampered by doubts about whether or how the two processes could be distinguished. Both are decremental processes and the repeated presentation of the fearful stimulus is the central operation in both. They share some parametric properties, such as the duration of the simulus presentations and the intervals between stimuli. The differences between them include the following. Habituation is often taken to refer to decrements in the strength of unlearned responses, whereas extinction necessarily refers to decrements in learned responses. Habituation is said to be a temporary decrement, whereas extinction tends to be stable. Only one condition is required for habituation to occur, namely the repeated presentation of the relevant stimulus. But for extinction, two conditions are necessary: the repeated presentation of the relevant stimulus and an absence of reinforcement. In extinction, one has to break a (learned) link.

The first distinction, that between learned and unlearned responses is difficult to maintain, partly because of our ignorance about the origin of many types of behavior. In the case of fear reduction, we are unable to specify whether some of the important fears, such as a fear of the dark, are learned or not, and therefore an insistence on this distinction between habituation and extinction is unworkable and unprofitable.

The second distinction between habituation and extinction is based on the temporary nature of the decrements resulting from habituation training. If the training seldom or never produces enduring decrements, then habituation obviously fails as a unifying explanation of fear-reduction techniques because they do produce enduring changes. Habituation training generally produces transitory decrements in responding, but as mentioned above, lasting changes can occur; however, the ease with which an extinction model can accommodate permanent reductions in fear is an advantage.

The third distinction between habituation and extinction, based on the role of reinforcement, offers a useful way of differentiating between the two. In theory we can separate them by manipulating the occurrence of reinforcement. As mentioned earlier, the effects of flooding present a problem for the habituation hypothesis, unless we assume that habituation can take place to intense and/or prolonged stimulation. It had been assumed that habituation only takes place with repeated presentations of attenuated stimuli while the person is in a low level of arousal, and hence the effects of flooding appeared to rule out an explanation based on habituation. It turns out that the presumption that habituation cannot take place if intense stimuli are used might have been mistaken. Klorman demonstrated similar patterns of rapid habituation to highly provoking and mildly fear-evoking film material.[19] This result makes a habituation explanation more plausible, and perhaps we were misled by the fact that habituation is most effective when stimuli are attenuated and the subject's level of arousal is low. However, we no longer have a reason for rejecting a habituation explanation on the grounds that it excludes decrements in responding to intense stimuli, even under conditions of high arousal.[20]

It appears that much of the information on fear reduction can be viewed as a form of habituation. The extinction model is able to accommodate some of the information about fear reduction, but may more usefully be applied to explaining changes in the behavioral component of fear rather than the subjective or psychophysiological components of fear.

THREE SYSTEMS

Up to this point, the examination of competing explanations has been based on the assumption that fear reduction involves the modification of a single, composite component. However, if we apply a three-systems analysis, we can consider the possibility that the three components are subject to different decremental processes. The physiological component may be particularly susceptible to habituation, and the behavioral component to extinction. The subjective component appears to be modifiable by both processes.

If we allow the possibility that at least two decremental processes play a part in fear reduction and that these two processes do not always produce synchronous changes, is there any way of disentangling the two? As proposed earlier, habituation and extinction can be teased out by controlling the introduction of reinforcement. Habituation should proceed regardless of the exclusion or inclusion of reinforcement; therefore, if changes in the physiological component are subject mainly to habituation, this component should decrease in strength with repeated stimulation regardless of the provision or exclusion of reinforcement. The behavioral component, on the other hand, should be more responsive to reinforcement contingencies. If the contingencies are re-arranged so that avoidance behavior is followed by non-reinforcement and approach behavior is followed by positive reinforcement, then the avoidance behavior should decline in strength.

Returning to the original question about whether or not we require multiple explanations of fear reduction, the answer appears to be that a single explanation is not likely to be sufficient. Previously it was argued that no single theory can account for the effects of the three methods,[21] and it is now suggested that there is an additional reason for that conclusion: it is unlikely that a single explanation can account for changes in all three components of fear. The need to include more than one process in the explanation derives from variations of the effects of the three methods and also from the nature of fear itself, when it is construed as a set of loosely coupled components. These can change desynchronously, and may be differentially susceptible to reciprocal inhibition, habituation, and extinction.

In addition to the general schema of emotional processing, discussed in Chapter 19, fear-reduction can be viewed in other ways. There is now a fresh possibility that advances in cognitive-behavioral therapy will lead to a unitary explanation based on cognitive processes. Bandura made the first attempt, and argued that self-efficacy is the main basis for all behavioral change.[22] The need for a cognitive explanation is strengthened by recognition of the significance of those reductions in fear that occur in the absence of exposure to the fear stimulus. Neither habituation nor extinction processes can be said to occur in the absence of such exposures, so we need to look elsewhere for an explanation.

IS EXPOSURE A NECESSARY CONDITION FOR FEAR REDUCTION?

The fear-reducing techniques of desensitization, modeling, and flooding have in common the prominent and facilitating feature described as "exposure." Presumably because of its prominence, it was assumed that exposure to the fear-provoking stimulus is a necessary condition for the successful reduction of fear. This assumption is mistaken. It is correct that in many circumstances exposure is a sufficient condition for the promotion of fear reduction, but there is no reason to suppose that exposure is a necessary condition for success. Fear reduction can take place in the absence of such exposure.

In considering the processes involved in fear reduction, "exposure" is taken to mean "planned, sustained and repeated evocations" of the fear-evoking stimulus or representations of that stimulus and to exclude mere thoughts or fleeting images.[23] A distinction is also made between passive exposure and engaged exposure because the passive observation of feared objects is less effective than engagement.[24]

It must be admitted that each of the following examples of fear reduction without exposure is open to criticism of one sort or another, but the trend is strongly in support of the idea that fear can be reduced in this manner.[25] As argued earlier, fears can be acquired by three pathways, including the transmission of information. It is now suggested that fear can be reduced by any of the three processes involved in fear acquisition, and that the transmission of information can induce or *reduce* fear. A person's fear reactions can be weakened or eliminated by giving him the information that the fear stimulus and circumstances are not dangerous. Informing a person who is fearful of spiders that the insect in front of him is dead can terminate his immediate fear reaction. By extension, it is probable that providing reassuring information about a stimulus or set of circumstances that was thought to be dangerous, can have lasting fear-reducing effects. Fear can be reduced by the provision of reassuring information, even in the absence of contact with the fear stimulus.

Bandura has argued that dependable sources of information, regardless of form and regardless of direct exposure to the fear stimulus, can lead to a reduction in fear,[26] and Lang's bio-informational theory also "allows" the reduction of fear without exposure.[27] Recognition of the power of information to reduce fear should not be misinterpreted to mean that fears, especially intense fears, are easily modified in this way—most are resistant to the provision of corrective or reassuring information.

Anxiety is a central element in a large proportion of neurotic disorders, and hence one can draw on clinical reports of the fluctuations of neuroses while bearing in mind that the information often is indirect and incomplete. The widespread occurrence of spontaneous remissions, said to be in the region of two-thirds within the first two years of onset[28] indicates that many fears wane or remit without professional therapy. It can be objected, correctly, that in many cases of spontaneous remission, exposure of one sort or another probably has taken place. However, it seems to be stretching the point too far to assume that all spontaneous remissions of all neuroses, including those in which fear plays an important part, are a consequence of repeated exposures to the fear stimulus. It is plausible that at least a proportion of the spontaneously remitting disorders diminish in intensity even in the absence of exposures. Such remissions probably are facilitated by the occurrence of fortunate life events or by the reduction of depression. It is not uncommon to see a patient's fears diminish after the dissipation of his or her depression.

The reductions in fear are too broad, occur too quickly, and in circumstances too confined, to explain the improvement as a result of repeated exposures to the fearful stimuli.

Reductions in fear can occur after the administration of placebos. Here again it would be stretching matters too far to assume that all of these improvements are the result of repeated, inadvertent exposures to the fearful stimuli.

A related set of examples comes from controlled studies of various techniques for reducing fear.[29] Many patients show decrements of fear even after having received treatment that does not involve exposure to the fear stimulus. Five studies can be cited to illustrate this phenomenon. In the second of his pioneering studies of desensitization, Lang found that the reduction of a fear of snakes generalized to some "un-treated" fears and modest all-round reductions in fear took place.[30] This result has been confirmed many times. In a comparison of the effects of desensitization and psychotherapy in the treatment of outpatients suffering from mixed phobias, Gelder and coworkers found that 5 of the 26 patients who received psychotherapy without exposure were rated as "much improved."[31] Marks and coworkers compared the effects of desensitization and hypnosis in a group of phobic patients, and reported that 3 of those who received hypnosis were much improved, and 4 were improved.[32] The hypnotic treatment did not include exposure to the fear stimulus. It is worth noticing that in both of these clinical studies, improvement was obtained in fears additional to the main or treated phobia, thereby reinforcing the idea that fears can be reduced even in the absence of exposure.

Jannoun and others found that problem-solving therapy was equally effective as exposure in the treatment of agoraphobic patients.[33] Mavissakalian and Michelson compared three types of exposure treatment with anti-depressant medication in the treatment of agoraphobic patients, and found that the patients receiving drugs improved to the same extent as those who had systematic exposure.[34] Moreover, the patients who improved most and those who improved least did not differ in the amount of self-directed exposure which had been practiced between sessions.[35]

Fearful subjects have been successfully treated with cognitive therapy that did not include contact with the fear stimulus.[36] In a study by Wein and others, snake-phobic subjects treated by cognitive restructuring showed marked reductions in subjective fear and behavioral gains that were equal to those seen in the subjects who received desensitization. Evidence of the fear-reducing effects of cognitive therapy is accumulating,[37] and although the combination of these methods with behavioral treatment is particularly effective, significant changes have been reported in the absence of exposure.

Reductions of fear can of course be achieved by the administration of anxiolytic drugs, and the addition of exposure exercises usually is facilitative but not essential.[38]

In summary, there are several examples of fear reduction that take place in the absence of exposure to the fearful stimulus. The provision of information about the harmlessness of the stimulus can lead to a reduction in fear. Fear can be reduced by anxiolytic drugs, and by the administration of placebos. The results of controlled trials show improvements in some phobic patients after therapy that does not include exposure. Reductions in fear are observed after cognitive therapy, even without supplementary exposure. Anxious neurotic behavior remits spontaneously in a proportion of patients. Patients experience reductions in fears in addition to the one that has been the subject of the treatment.

In all of this we should not lose sight of the fact that most methods of treatment, whether predominantly cognitive or directly behavioral, include exercises that involve exposure to the stimuli which provoke the relevant fear. Methods that incorporate planned and systematic exposures usually have considerable therapeutic power. My intention is not to devalue these methods, but rather to identify and argue against the assumption that exposure is essential if fear reduction is to be achieved. The jump from the proposition that in many circumstances exposure is a sufficient condition for reducing fear to the assumption that it is a *necessary* condition is unwarranted.[39]

Recognition of the occurrence of fear reduction even in the absence of exposure introduces some fresh questions and expands the scope of the existing problem of identifying the process or processes responsible for the reduction of fear. Broadening the inquiry in this way reduces the chance of reaching a partial explanation prematurely, but it also increases the difficulty of producing a comprehensive explanation.

In view of our failure to formulate a unitary theory to account for the fear-reducing effects of the three major techniques, the addition of non-exposure methods of fear reduction might seem to be an unwelcome complication. However, if we broaden the search for an explanation for the fear-reduction processes to include the effects of procedures that do not include exposure, it might facilitate the search for a unitary explanation.

The first need is to delineate the conditions under which fear reduction will take place without exposure and to identify the critical factors that bring about this effect. Given some progress on these lines, one can profitably ask whether exposure and non-exposure techniques for reducing fear share some common explanatory factor. Experimental[40] and theoretical[41] attempts have been made to accommodate the evidence of fear reduction within a broader model of emotional processing.

The key questions that require an answer include the following. Is a single process responsible for the reduction of fear by the three behavioral methods? Even more challenging, is a single process responsible for the reduction of fear by cognitive and by behavioral methods? And the most difficult challenge is to find an explanation that will include the reduction of fear without exposure to the fear object. Candidly, the prospects of producing a single explanation seem bleak at present. A modest set of goals, consisting of separate explanations for one or more of the methods, is perhaps more realistic, and given some success here, we can begin to re-consider the lofty aim of finding a single explanation.

CHAPTER **16**

DO FEARS
RETURN?

The reduction of fear is not always a permanent change. In many instances, fear reduction, whether contrived or not, is followed by the return of some or all of the original fear. Fears can be squashed, but they do not always stay squashed.

An early example of the return of fear was encountered by Grey, Sartory, and Rachman in the course of carrying out a laboratory investigation into the speed of fear reduction.[1] Twenty-seven subjects with intense and circumscribed fears showed large and rapid reductions in fear during the course of the experimental treatment (training), but in some subjects the fear reappeared after an interval of a week. It turned out that there was a tendency for fear to return in those subjects who had completed a highly demanding form of fear-reduction training. By contrast, the subjects who received an undemanding form of training showed regular and progressive reductions in fear, with little or no recurrences.

In a subsequent experiment, the same research workers found that those 4 of their 28 subjects who had conspicuously high heart rates, with a mean level of 120 beats per minute, showed a significant return of fear after an interval of 1 week, even though they had originally shown the same amount of improvement as the remaining 24 subjects.[2] At the termination of the treatment the two groups of subjects were indistinguishable, both having shown rapid and large reductions in fear. This result suggested that a person's state during fear-reduction training may have a delayed effect on the fate of the fear. A high level of arousal, as indexed by heart rate, predicted a return of fear 1 week later.

A clinical example of the return of fear was described by Barlow and others in their account of the outcome of an evaluation of a psychological treatment for agoraphobia.[3] One of the patients who showed particularly rapid and large progress reported that by the end of the seventh session, she was free of anxiety. This was confirmed by her husband and by direct observation. However, her heart rate was exceedingly high before, during, and after the completion of the treatment. Four weeks after completing treatment, the patient "tearfully reported that she had relapsed completely, and was once again unable to leave her house."[4]

In view of the emphasis placed on the importance of acquiring skills in achieving mastery of fears,[5] a study was made of 63 anxious musical performers.[6] Once more it was found that the strongest predictor of the return of fear was a high heart rate. Regardless of the level of their perceived skill, performers who had a high heart rate showed significant returns of fear after a three-month interval. The performers who showed a return of fear had given fewer musical performances during the three-month interval than had those performers who did not experience a return of fear.

Prompted by these findings and a desire to develop methods of preventing the recurrence of clinically significant fears, the phenomenon has been subjected to serial laboratory investigations. Some useful progress has been made, but many questions remain unanswered and a satisfactory explanation of the return of fear remains elusive. The available knowledge on the subject can be summarized.[7]

The return of fear is a robust and common occurrence. The best predictor of the return of fear is the presence of an elevated heart rate response at the start of a fear-reduction program.[8] The initial level of fear reported by the subjects at the start of these programs sometimes is a predictor of a return of fear. These returns of fear can occur regardless of the speed at which the fear is originally reduced. Surprisingly, the return of fear is not simply a reflection of incomplete fear-reduction. The return of fear is as likely to occur after a treatment or training program in which the fear is eliminated as it is after a treatment program that comes to an end after the level of fear is reduced to half of its original level. It is probable that highly demanding training or treatment sessions contribute to the return of fear, and there is some evidence and good reason to predict that the return of fear is more likely to occur in the early stages of mastering a task in which fear can occur (for example, skiing). Furthermore, the probability of a return of fear is increased if tasks of this kind are not practiced regularly.

That is to say, the return of fear can be blocked by carrying out the fear-reducing exercises in intervals between completing the treatment and the point at which a test is carried out to determine whether or not the fear has returned. It is probable that a return of fear can be inhibited by repeated training sessions, and there is a slight possibility that it can be prevented by a period of over-learning during the course of the initial training or therapy.

Before considering the factors that might contribute to the return of fear, it is necessary to ask *when* the determining events occur. Where in the process of returning fear should the search be concentrated? The fearful person's state of arousal immediately before the treatment session is relevant, and the method of training (demanding versus undemanding) also exerts an influence. In addition, the events that take place immediately after the treatment session can increase or decrease the likelihood that fear will return. The fact that the return of fear can be influenced by events that occur before, during, or after a treatment session certainly complicates matters, and the likelihood that these influences might act in opposing directions on occasions is a complexity that justifies the admission of at least a moderate amount of dismay.

Evidence from research on the induction of fear in animals gives rise to yet one more possibility. Existing fears can be inflated after "chance encounters with a traumatic event, even of a different sort than that involved in the original conditioning."[9] In addition to the inflation of fear, the reinstatement of a previously extinguished fear has been reported. The evidence on this subject, derived from animal research, has been well considered by Jacobs and Nadel.[10] The reinstatement of fear refers to the reappearance of an extinguished fear after the interpolation of a non-relevant stimulus which is usually aversive, but presumably the interpolated stimulus or event need *not* be aversive.

At present we lack evidence of the operation of fear-inflation processes in humans, but clinical accounts, especially of cases of posttraumatic stress disorder, make it highly probably that human fears can be inflated by the occurrence of unrelated traumatic events. Clinically, this means that a patient may experience a return of fear as a result of having an aversive or fearful experience of an unrelated kind, well after the completion of the treatment. In pursuit of some clinical evidence of fear inflation, enquiries were made of a number of clinicians who customarily treat patients troubled by excessive fear. The clinicians were asked to retrieve information from patients who had experienced a significant motor accident after completing treatment and to find out, if possible, whether any return of fear had become manifest. Several suggestive examples were gathered, but the best supported was the case of a patient suffering from a driving phobia.[11] As fortune would have it, her fear had been assessed in the middle of a program of treatment, one week before she was involved in a significant motor accident, and then again one week after the accident had taken place. Her specific phobia of driving showed a slight increase after the accident, but the interest lies in the fact that she reported increases in a range of *unrelated* fears that included fire, crowds, sirens, and strange shapes.

The return of fear can be promoted by events at three points—before, during, or after the reduction of fear—and probably, by events that are unrelated to the fear itself!

The relationship between fearful cognitions and the return of fear is bound to be significant and has yet to be investigated. Given the connection between inappropriately alarming cognitions and the occurrence of episodes of panic, it is only to be expected that if the disturbing cognition returns after an initially successful course of treatment, then the person will be at risk for a recurrence of fear or panic. In the course of her research into the treatment of obsessional disorders, Foa uncovered a phenomenon that may have a bearing on the return of fear.[12] Searching for an explanation of failures in treatment, she found that the presence of severe depression or of fixed abnormal thinking about the problem often was associated with failure. Although they made satisfactory progress within a therapy session, patients who expressed abnormal beliefs about their obsessional problems tended to show a return of fear in subsequent sessions. The fact that obsessions and fears can recur during or after a period of depression[13] raises the possibility of a general connection between mood state and the return of fear.[14]

The two specific explanations that were proposed to account for the return of fear failed to gain convincing support,[15] and a recent attempt to apply Bandura's concept of self-efficacy to the return of fear also was unsuccessful.[16] As there are some similarities between the return of fear and two other psychological processes in which previously weakened responses reappear, the links between the return of fear and *spontaneous recovery* and *dishabituation* were considered.

On the basis of this comparison, it was decided to test the idea that the return of fear might be a form of spontaneous recovery, regarded as evidence of incomplete extinction.[17] However, the notion that the return of fear might reflect incomplete fear reduction failed to receive support. We are left in the unsatisfactory position of having a robust and common facet of fear that is unexplained but bears some similarity (and differences) to two well-established psychological phenomena—spontaneous recovery and dishabituation. In order to head off any premature optimism, not in abundance so far, we must concede that the nature of spontaneous recovery is unclear and that even so simple a phenomenon as habituation has defied psychological explanation. In his thorough analysis of habituation, Mackintosh concluded with an admission that applies equally well to the return of fear. The fact that habituation is such a simple phenomenon "makes it all the more humiliating that we should remain in total ignorance of the nature of the processes responsible for the effects."[18]

CLINICAL IMPLICATIONS

The return of fear comes closest to the clinical phenomenon of relapse. The two concepts are not synonymous, for there are many types and causes of clinical relapse, and the return of fear is relevant only in clinical problems in which fear plays a prominent part. Furthermore, the return of fear can occur in many circumstances and conditions, and only a minority of these are of clinical significance. Setting aside these reservations, it is not unreasonable to expect that the accumulation of more and better information about the return of fear will assist clinicians and educators. In time, it should be possible to predict and therefore prevent the return of certain kinds of fears. Fortunately, it is relatively easy to deal with fears that do return; they are easily reduced or removed

by additional practice. On the evidence so far, it appears that a return of
fear can be impeded by arranging for practice sessions in which the
training or treatment occurs under conditions of low arousal and low
demand, and by then ensuring the regular practice of the new skills. On
the cautionary side, excessively demanding treatments or training may
provoke a return of fear, especially among highly aroused patients or
subjects. People who experience elevated heart rate immediately before
or during treatment are at greatest risk for a return of fear.

ARE FEARS INFLUENCED BY REMOTE EVENTS?

The idea that unrelated aversive events — even if separated
in time from the fear experience — can promote a return of fear leads to a
wider question. Can unrelated, remote aversive events generate a new
fear? Is it possible that some fears have a (temporally) remote onset? In
most instances these fears would have the appearance of delayed onset
fears. Before the emergence of the revived and liberalized view of conditioning, which de-throned the assumption that only contiguous events
can be linked by conditioning, these questions would have seemed very
farfetched.

Remote events can affect fears in three ways. They can inflate existing
fears, a phenomenon sometimes described as fear enhancement, renew or
"reinstate," former fears, and probably generate new fears. It is likely that
the inflation and renewal of fear will turn out to be closely related, but
the generation of new fears by remote events may have particular
properties.

Discussions about the onset of fears, including the notion that there are
three pathways to fear, have been confined to the *proximal* causes of fear,
the conditions prevailing at the time of the initial appearance of the fear.
One searches for events or stimuli that were occurring or present *when the
fear first appeared*. For example, the onset of a fear of dogs is explained by
reference to the aversive event (barking and biting) that took place
immediately before the fear appeared. One attempts to identify the immediate cause of the fear. The assumption that all fears have a proximal
cause may be unsound. Perhaps some fears have causes that are temporally
separated from the observed emergence of the fear?

Attempts to connect the causal conditions to the first emergence of the
fear is not a necessary part of the concept of the three pathways, and other

explanations should not confine themselves exclusively to the first emergence. In passing, it should be noted that this type of enquiry, this search for proximal causes, concentrates on fears that have a sudden onset, to the relative neglect of fears that have a gradual onset. It is far easier to recall or to re-construe events with a single cause than to re-construe the gradual emergence of a fear over a period of many years (for example, social fears, or a fear of enclosed spaces). This methodological limitation probably was responsible for the emphasis that has been placed on fears of sudden onset.

We have two challenging questions. Are there distal causes of fear? If so, how do they produce their effects?

Once we set aside that assumption that the causes of fear are necessarily contiguous with the first emergence of the fear, the path is opened for temporally separated causes of fear. Estes observed that "nothing in psychology is more certain, however, than that orderly changes in response tendencies (e.g., spontaneous recovery, forgetting) do occur during intervals when the organism and the situation are well separated."[19] He went on to ask how these "spontaneous" changes can be accounted for, and the same question can be raised in respect of fear. Significant changes in fear certainly do occur during intervals when the person and the fear-provoking stimulus are "well separated." Rescorla demonstrated that animals manifest an inflation in existing fear after exposure to an unrelated aversive event,[20] and we have anecdotal evidence of similar occurrences in human beings. We also know that remote events can provide a return of fear.

Some people report a delayed onset of fear and say that at the time of the critical event they had not been frightened (for example, posttraumatic fears that arise years after the event). In these instances, it seems that the fear process is initiated at the time of the critical event but the "changes in response tendency" occur over a prolonged interval in which the "organism and the situation are well separated." The fear appears months or years after the initiating cause.

The content of these delayed fears can be directly connected to the traumatic event. A successful and confident 50-year-old patient sought help for an intense and disabling but inexplicable fear of medical investigative procedures. His fear was extremely intense, out of all proportion to the discomfort of the procedures, and totally unexpected by him. In the course of successfully completed psychological therapy, it became evident to the patient that his intense, current fear was directly related to the painful torture that he had undergone while a prisoner during World War II. He was certain that he had not been frightened of the medical investigations which he had undergone shortly after being liberated, within six months of having been tortured. He was equally confident in attributing his current fear of the specific medical procedures (urogenital) to the torture that he had undergone more than 25 years earlier. The thoughts and images that his current medical treatment evoked were unquestionably similar in content and feeling to his memory of what he had endured in prison.

A second example of an unexplained delay in the emergence of fear was provided by a military bomb-disposal operator who participated in one of the studies described in Chapters 20 and 21. Recalling his tour of operational duty, he described an incident in which he had (totally uncharacteristically) neglected the normal operating procedures and professional caution when called out to investigate a brown package that had been spotted in the back of a stolen vehicle. He began by making the normal protected approach to the suspect parcel, but then decided, inexplicably, that it had been put there as a hoax. He opened the door of the car and stretched out toward the parcel. Fortunately, he restrained himself just in time and decided to revert to standard procedures. The package contained a live bomb, and he had come literally within an inch of killing himself. At the time, he was surprised but not upset or fearful. In the following week, however, he had two nightmares, and three months after the completion of his tour he began to experience frightening ruminations about the experience. During the course of recalling it for the purposes of the study, he displayed physical signs of fear, and his dry mouth prevented him from speaking comfortably. He found the recollection to be frightening.

The patient with a driving phobia, who reported an increase in her main phobia (p. 244) and, most interestingly, an increase in a range of unrelated fears after she had been involved in an accident, is another example of remote influence. The unrelated fears were increased by the temporally remote accident. This example of fear inflation bears a resemblance to Rescorla's report that animals manifest fear enhancement after an unrelated aversive event.[21] The inflation of fear was produced by exposing the animal to an aversive stimulus well after the establishment of the conditioned response, and the size of the effect can be exaggerated if there is a long interval between the conditioning and the aversive experience.[22] This may help to account for fears that return after a long period of non-exposure or non-practice,[23] but it leaves unanswered the question of quite what happens in those long intervals, and why indeed they are long.

TIME AND THE GENESIS OF FEAR

It is possible that the genesis of fear, like the *return* of fear, can be influenced at any of four stages. The return of fear can be modified by the person's state before exposure to a fear-evoking stimulus and by the nature of the contact with the fearful stimulus (that is, the temporally associated events). However, it also can be affected by events that take place after the original association and by the person's state immediately before being re-exposed to the fear stimulus by temporally remote events.

Might the genesis of fear be open to mediation or modification at these four stages? The first two stages are familiar, and it is the third possibility that holds most interest: the events that take place after the original association. So far the evidence points to *aversive* events, even of an unrelated nature.

Given that fears can be enhanced by unrelated aversive events, one can speculate about whether enhancement is capable of raising a sub-threshold fear to a level at which it becomes manifest. If an established fear can be enhanced by the occurrence of an unrelated aversive event, presumably a sub-threshold fear can be raised above the threshold by such an event, or perhaps by a significant increase in arousal. In addition, it seems that a non-fearful association can be changed into a fearful one after the occurrence of an unrelated aversive event (or an increase in arousal?), as in the two case examples described here.

If such changes into fear can be confirmed, they might help to explain the delayed onset of fears and the emergence of fears in which no precipitating event can be identified. The manner in which an unrelated aversive event enhances or generates a fear is likely to become the subject of keen investigation.

UNRELATED EVENTS

Sixty-two percent of the 963 people who participated in a national survey of agoraphobia reported that their problems had emerged after what permissibly can be described as an apparently unrelated aversive event.[24] For example, 23 percent reported that their agoraphobia had started after a bereavement, and another 17 percent attributed the onset to an illness. Five percent were unable to recall any precipitating event.[25] It is conceivable that in some of these cases, the responses associated with public places became frightening as a result of fear enhancement caused by an unrelated aversive event, such as bereavement, or by a significant increase in arousal. An explanation in terms of fear enhancement assumes the prior existence of a sub-threshold fear, but one cannot rule out the possibility that these aversive events might have induced a new fear.

Numerous patients with panic disorder report that their first panic came "out of the blue." They describe having felt normal and unconcerned while in a familiar place, before suddenly feeling overwhelmed by panic. It is possible, of course, that such intense fears can arise, fullblown, in a single incident, but others might be the product of a delayed onset fear. The learned connection, between, say, public places and feelings of loss of control, is already present, but not fearful. The person then experiences an unrelated aversive event or an unusual elevation of arousal, and the connection between the feelings of loss of control and public places becomes frightening. Applied to Clark's cognitive theory of panic, one might say that the event that triggers the (delayed) onset of the fear is a catastrophic misinterpretation of bodily sensations.[26] These sensations are exaggerated during an aversive event or during high arousal, and therefore provide the opportunity for a catastrophic misinterpretation. The association between the unpleasant changes in bodily sensations, such as dizziness and palpitations, and the loss of control is established in the person well before the panic episode, but is triggered into a panic by the misinterpretation of the bodily sensations that are caused by the aversive event or elevated arousal.

PREPARED CONNECTIONS

Fears with delayed onset must be of limited range, otherwise any learned connection might provide the basis for a later fear. People would be as pervasively frightened as our earlier theories wrongly implied. However, the distribution of human fears is skewed: some objects are feared by large numbers of people and others are rarely the object of fear (snakes versus sheep). Presumably the selective factors that give rise to this skewed distribution apply equally well to fears of delayed and immediate onset. Delayed onset fears of snakes and spiders are to be expected, but delayed onset fears of sheep are not.

It is probable that there is a connection between delayed onset fears and prepared phobias, in that an association between a prepared stimulus and a fear response is far more likely to be ignited by an unrelated aversive event than the connection between a non-prepared stimulus and fear. In fact, it can be said that this pre-existing connection between the stimulus (snake) and the response (fear) is the very essence of the concept of prepared phobias — the connection is *prepared*, and it can perhaps be triggered by a temporally remote event or an aversive event. It is well to remember that the early demonstrations of the genesis of intense taste aversions, which can emerge even after long delays and in which unrelated aversive events play a prominent part, were critical elements in Seligman's[27] construction of the concept of prepared phobias.

Whatever the plausibility of the notion that fear can be enhanced or even induced by an unrelated aversive event that is separated from the response, it leaves unexplained the stability of the fear reductions that regularly are accomplished in therapy. All subjects or patients with unadaptive intense fears who benefit from a course of training or treatment experience unrelated aversive events at some time, but the return of disabling fear, or clinical relapse, is not common. Furthermore, as argued throughout this work, people have fewer fears than we might expect, and certainly fewer fears than we would expect if the fears were continually subject to inflation by aversive experiences. Plainly then, the inflation, revival, or induction of fear by an unrelated aversive event must be uncommon, and therefore it is necessary to ask what specific conditions are likely to promote the enhancement or the induction of fear by events that are temporally remote.

If a significant elevation of arousal turns out to one of the mediators of these increments of fear, then aversive events are pertinent to the extent that they elevate the person's level of arousal. A small piece of supporting evidence for this possibility was recently collected in a preliminary study designed to investigate the effect of an unrelated aversive event on the return of fear.[28]

INCUBATION

It will not pass unnoticed that some features of delayed onset fears resemble Eysenck's concept of incubation; both concepts refer to a growth of fear.[29] Incubation refers to increments in an existing fear, which resembles fear inflation, but the present interest includes the delayed onset of a new fear, one that arises in the absence of recent contact with the relevant stimulus.

Eysenck defined incubation as "the increase in (fear) responses due to CS-only exposure."[30] The conditions that are said to favor the emergence of incubation of fear responses are short presentations, strong unconditioned stimuli, and high introversion and high neuroticism. The concept has not been fully exploited, and the strengths[31] and the weaknesses[32] are the subject of continuing debate. It is an interesting concept because it describes the apparent reversal of a common phenomenon and is used in order to explain the growth and persistence of unadaptive neurotic behavior. It addresses the question of why fear sometimes increases rather than decreases, as generally occurs, when a fear stimulus is presented repeatedly.

Incubation deals with increments in an existing fear and is said to be promoted by brief exposures to the fear stimulus, and therefore it is not relevant to the fears that emerge after a long interval has elapsed between the original learning and the appearance of a fresh fear, as in post-traumatic stress disorders. Nor does the concept fit the bill for the sudden emergence of agoraphobia in a person who has used the same public transport and public facilities hundreds of times without experiencing significant fears.

If it can be confirmed that incubation is indeed influenced by unrelated aversive events, it might help to explain why it has been so difficult for experimenters to reproduce the incubation effect. In most experiments the subjects or animals under study would, correctly, be shielded from exposure to unrelated aversive events. Hence, the control exerted over experimental subjects might have ensured that the incubation effect could not be captured in a laboratory setting. The unrelated aversive events that might promote incubation are specifically excluded from the experiments.

DELAYED ONSETS AND SENSITIZATION

The two types of events thought to be capable of generating a delayed onset of fear, aversive events and elevations in arousal, probably produce their effects by a process of sensitization. Given that the effects of sensitizing events are broad and non-specific,[33] delayed onset fears should be accompanied by broad psychological changes, including changes in affect, and also by the enhancement of existing fears. As the effects of other sensitizing events tend to be of limited duration, delayed onset fears might be less persistent than other fears.

Specifically, then, it is predicted that delayed onset fears are accompanied by (i) broad psychological changes and by (ii) the enhancement of existing fears. (iii) Additionally, delayed onset fears should be less persistent than fears of immediate onset (unless the aversive arousal persists).

The generation of delayed onset fears by aversive or arousing events does not exhaust the possibilities. They might also be generated by cognitive changes. A highly significant or arousing event may acquire frightening properties after a lapse of time if the person's knowledge about or interpretation of the event is changed. "I was not frightened at the time, but knowing what I now know, I am too frightened to do it again." A person can acquire a retrospective fear of particular social events or people if he learns some time after the event that he had been the subject of critical scrutiny and disapproval. A person who is excessively concerned about his health can acquire a retrospective fear of strenuous physical exertion if he comes to believe that he had been risking a heart attack by over-exerting himself.

This line of reasoning is the other side of the coin to cognitive therapy, in which it is assumed that changes in knowledge about or the interpretation of past fearful events can render them non-fearful. The events lose the power to evoke fear *now*. There is no certainty that cognitive changes can operate equally well in both directions—rendering past events non-fearful or fearful—but it would be surprising to find that they have the power to reduce but not induce fears. Delayed onset fears can arise after aversive events, during or after periods of elevated arousal, or after changes in significant cognitions.

If the ethical and technical difficulties can be dealt with in a manner that makes the demonstration of the delayed onset of fear permissible, it may help to make some aspects of fear more intelligible. For example, it might help us to understand the appearance of a significant fear after an unrelated aversive event, such as bereavement-onset agoraphobia. It might also help to account for that minority of instances in which people with a phobia are unable to recall a (proximal) cause of their fear. It might help to appreciate the sudden and sometimes bewildering onset of intense fear in an unfamiliar setting, such as the panics that "come out of the blue." And it may help us to understand the emergence of fears a long time after the occurrence of a traumatic event.

To conclude, it is suggested that fears certainly can be influenced by temporally remote events. They can be inflated, renewed, and possibly induced by such events. Aversive events appear to have the properties that can exert a remote influence on fears, and these events need not be directly related to the fear in question. It is suggested that prepared connections are more easily generated into fear by remote influences (especially aversive events) than are un-prepared connections.

THE OVER-PREDICTION OF FEAR

Fearful people have a strong tendency to overestimate how frightened they will be when they encounter a fear-provoking object or situation.[1] The over-prediction of fear is common among people who are disturbed by excessive fear, including claustrophobic people and patients suffering from panic disorder.

Recently gathered evidence suggests that the tendency to over-predict fear might be part of a more general psychological phenomenon in which we are inclined to overestimate the subjective impact of aversive events of many types, including pain.[2] It begins to seem likely that the over-prediction of fear, pain, and other aversive events is strongly linked to avoidance behavior; we are likely to avoid those events which we predict will be aversive or frightening. If the postulated link between prediction of an aversive event and the generation or maintenance of avoidance behavior is confirmed, it may follow that people who tend to over-predict their fears are more likely than people who make accurate predictions to engage in excessive avoidance behavior.

A commonly encountered clinical phenomenon, the extensive avoidance behavior displayed by agoraphobic patients, bcomes more intelligible if cast in these terms. Given that patients show the same tendency as people with other types of fear to over-predict, their avoidance behavior, which is a primary feature of the problem, might be a product of their over-predictions. It is not unusual for agoraphobic patients to describe severe and extensive avoidance and then to be somewhat surprised to find that when it is put to the test, they can move about more widely and with less fear than they anticipated; they discover that they have been over-predicting their fear.

In laboratory research into the nature of fear, many potential subjects who report on questionnaires that they have intense fears discover that they can complete the behavioral test preceding most experiments with comparatively little fear or difficulty. As many as 30 percent of the people who endorse the highest fear item on a screening inventory are subsequently found to demonstrate negligible fear in the laboratory, and for most experimental purposes are excluded for that reason.

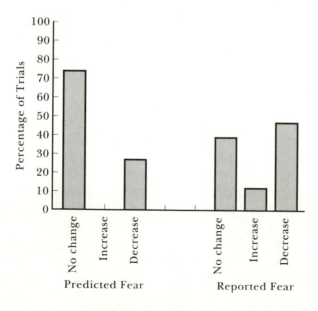

Figure 2 *Following a correct match, predicted fear showed few changes, and reported fear tended to decrease or remain unchanged (Rachman and Lopatka, 1986b, p. 399. Reprinted with permission of Pergamon Press.)*

When people over-predict their fears, there is a strong tendency for certain consequences to follow. If their predictions of fear are repeatedly disconfirmed, they tend to make corrections in their predictions of future experiences; they begin to predict that they will have less and less fear. Sequences of repeated disconfirmations of expected fear tend to be accompanied by steadily decreasing *reports* of fear.[3] In the analysis of over-predictions of fear, it is necessary to make place for two other types of prediction. On some occasions, people under-predict their fear, that is, the reported fear exceeds their expectation. And of course it is possible for people to make correct predictions of their fear; the prediction and the report of fear coincide.

The method for calculating whether a person has made a correct prediction or an over- or under-prediction is simple. The person makes a prediction on a 0–100 scale before entering the situation that is expected to provoke some fear, and then at the completion of the encounter, he or she *reports* how much fear was actually experienced, using a similar scale of 0–100. The difference between the prediction and the report is used to determine the type and extent of the erroneous or correct prediction. This matching procedure has been used in investigations of fear, panic, and pain.[4] For example, a snake-phobic person might be asked to predict how much fear he expects to experience when he is exposed to a live harmless snake in a cage placed 2 feet away. He then meets the snake and gives a report of the actual fear experienced. In the investigation of episodes of panic, the person is asked to predict the probability that he or she will experience a panic when exposed to the threatening situation, and then reports whether a panic did or did not occur. A distinction must be made between over-predicting the amount of fear that one expects to experience and predictions about the probability that an aversive or fearful event, such as panic, will occur within a defined period.

A military example of the over-prediction of fear was encountered in a preliminary study of the fear experienced by trainees undergoing a course in parachuting.[5] They were asked to predict how much fear they anticipated during the most difficult, final jump of the training course, and their average score was 48 on the 100 scale. After the event, they reported having experienced the significantly lower score of 40. It is of interest that their fear scores declined during the series of jumps, even though their estimates of the dangerousness of jumping remained unchanged. These findings were replicated in a larger study of 105 recruits to the Parachute Regiment in the British Army.[6] Once again it was found that the trainees over-predicted how much fear they would experience during the most difficult jump. They predicted a fear score of 52 percent, but

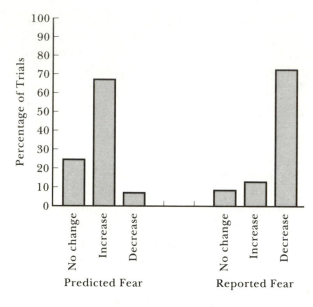

Figure 3 *Following an underprediction, predicted fear increased but reported fear decreased (Rachman and Lopatka, 1986b, p. 399. Reprinted with permission of Pergamon Press.)*

after the jump, they reported having experienced the significantly lower score of 41 percent. Clinical examples of the over-prediction of aversive events have been reported by Butler and Mathews[7] on a sample of anxious patients and by Chambless[8] on an agoraphobic sample.

The effects of underestimating one's fear tend to be immediate and large; under-predictions are more disruptive than over-predictions. The effects of overestimating one's fear are slower to emerge, and it appears that repeated disconfirmations of one's predictions of fear are needed before large and stable corrections are made in subsequent predictions. There is an asymmetry in the effect of over-predictions and under-predictions.

The currently available evidence on the over-prediction of fear can be summarized. Fearful subjects tend to over-predict how much fear they will experience. Their predictions of fear tend to decrease after they have made an over-prediction, and to increase if they under-predict their fear. After a correct prediction has been made, subsequent predictions remain unaltered. The *reports* of fear tend to decrease with repeated exposures to the fearful stimulus, regardless of the accuracy of earlier predictions. And it appears that with practice, people can learn to predict their fear with increasing accuracy.

Most of this new information is comfortably compatible with the radically new view of conditioning; the emphases on the importance of the predictive role of fear stimuli and the tendency for responses to become increasingly precise are common to both phenomena.

THE PREDICTION OF PANIC

These patterns of prediction, and their consequences, have also been observed in research on panic.[9] Predictions of panic tend to decrease after an overestimation and tend to increase after an under-prediction. Predictions of panic tend to remain unchanged after the person has made a correct prediction of panic or a correct prediction of no-panic. It is the erroneous predictions of panic, whether they are overestimations or underestimations, that are followed by changes.

The under-prediction of panic, equivalent to an unexpected panic, is particularly disruptive. These laboratory findings suggest that people who experience many panics probably develop some degree of tolerance for these experiences, particularly if they learn to predict with accuracy when a panic is likely to occur.[10] Expected panics may well be distressing but are not likely to be unduly disruptive or to produce major changes. It is partly for this reason no doubt that the first one or two panics appear to be the most damaging.[11]

It is probable that there are individual differences in the tendency to over-predict fear, and possibly there are differences in the tendency to over-predict other types of aversive events as well. A dispositional tendency to be pessimistic features in Beck's theory of depression, according to which people who have a depressive self-schema persistently over-predict the probability that they will experience aversive events.[12] An example of this tendency to over-predict was reported by Kent, who found that highly anxious patients expected more pain than they experienced in dental treatment.[13] The dental patients who had little anxiety predicted accurately the amount of pain that they would experience.

CONSEQUENCES OF ERRORS

The most common consequences of over-predictions are reductions in reported fear and reductions in predicted fear. However, the most common consequences of *under*-predictions are reductions in fear, but *increases* in predicted fear. Divergences of this type, in which serial over-predictions of fear diverge from reported fear, are interesting and may reflect the strong tendency for fears to habituate to repeated stimulation. But the interest here lies in the fact that for a time the predictions of fear continue to be overestimates, despite the decline in reported fear. This seeming irrationality can be explained in part by the effects of under-predictions. After an under-prediction, there is a strong tendency

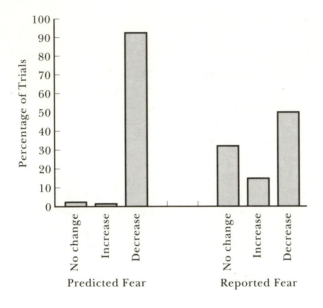

Figure 4 *Following an overprediction, predicted and reported fear decreased (Rachman and Lopatka, 1986b, p. 400. Reprinted with permission of Pergamon Press.)*

for people to adjust their subsequent prediction upwards. So even if the reported fear declines, the person over-predicts the next experience of fear because, relatively speaking, he has made an error and therefore adjusts his next prediction upward to avoid a repetition of the error.

The strong tendency to over-predict fear appears to be subject to change, even among people with excessive fears. After a sequence of repeated disconfirmations of over-predicted fear, patients and subjects tend to make increasingly accurate predictions of their fear and of the probability of experiencing a panic. It seems likely that the strong tendency to over-predict fear remains relatively unchanged unless and until the person experiences disconfirmations. In most clinically significant fears that are accompanied or followed by a strong avoidance behavior, the possibilities of experiencing such disconfirmations are limited. In this way, the over-predictions of fear are preserved from disconfirmation, and therefore continue relatively unchanged.

CHANGING PREDICTIONS

The pervasiveness of over-predictions of fear raises a problem. Given that repeated over-predictions tend to be followed by reductions in predicted and reported fear, they should show a natural decay.

There are three overlapping answers to the questions of why they are nevertheless pervasive.

First, most over-predictions probably do undergo a natural decay; over-predictions are neither rigid nor universal. Second, it requires only a single under-predicted fear experience, as in unexpected panics, to steeply increase the likelihood and the degree of subsequent overpredictions. Third, the initial decline in predicted fear that follows a single occurrence of over-prediction tends to be slight. Large decreases in over-prediction are seen after *repeated* disconfirmations of the over-prediction.

It is also possible that intensely fearful experiences are especially memorable. People are inclined to have good recall of vivid experiences of pain,[14] and our judgments under conditions of uncertainty are strongly influenced by vivid and salient events.[15] In addition, people show a tendency to "attend only to occurrences when making inferences, seriously disregarding . . . non-occurrences of behaviors or events."[16] Fearful people may overpredict fear, and panic, because they vividly recall a first experience of intense fear and fail to recall or attend to all of the earlier and subsequent occasions on which they experienced little or no fear in that same situation. A person who develops agoraphobia at the age of 28 is most strongly influenced by three episodes of panic in a department store, and attaches little weight to the many dozens of occasions on which trips to the same department store were free of fear.

In sum, over-predictions of fear persist as long as people continue to attach excessive weight to the occurrences of fear and to disregard the non-occurrences. Over-predictions of fear can be quickly established but are slow to decline. Several disconfirmations appear to be required before the over-prediction of fear declines. But a single unpredicted fear (or panic) may be all that is needed to produce a large increment in prediction of subsequent fear. This asymmetry may be one more example of our tendency to overlook experiences that were uneventful (that is, produced little or no fear) and to give excessive weight to episodes of intense emotion.

TIMOROUSNESS

Is the over-prediction of fear also promoted by our view of timorous man? Many psychological theories imply that people are more easily and enduringly frightened than is the case, and this view may well be shared by laymen. So, when a person is asked to predict how frightening he or she (or other people) will find a comparatively novel situation, the tendency is to overpredict. We expect people to be easily upset by frightening creatures, places, or events.

The overpredictions made prior to World War II are illustrative. As described in Chapter 2, the widespread expectations of panic and hysteria were disconfirmed. More recently in Israel, the expectation that children and adults who are subjected to repeated shelling will become increasingly anxious was not confirmed,[17] and Lebanese students reported no increase in anxiety during or after the bombardment and siege of Beirut.[18] These examples are not instances of over-prediction as such, but in both cases the non-appearance of increments in anxiety caused some surprise.

There is of course a distinction to be made between over-predicting one's own fears and overpredicting how frightened other people will be in given circumstances. So far we have collected experimental evidence for the first type and anecdotal evidence for the second type. If it can be shown that we share a tendency to over-predict the fears of populations of people, if we share a view of timorous man, then the tendency to over-predict one's own fears is conforming. People who do not subscribe to the model of timorous man may be less inclined to over-predict their own fears.

MATCH-MISMATCH AS A COMPARATOR

This research on match-mismatch predictions of human fear may have a bearing on theories of habituation. The original theory of habituation and its derivatives are based on the phenomenon of matching. Broadly, "comparator" theories state that if an incoming stimulus matches one in the organism's memory, then there will be no response. But if the incoming stimulus is not matched, a response occurs.

If we accept that the steady decline in reported fear responses, trial by trial, reflects a process of habituation, we have an interesting divergence —in some instances the habituation of fear proceeds even when mismatches occur. Specifically, reported fear continues to decline even when the person's *predictions* of fear increase. This pattern occurred after overpredictions and after under-predictions of fear (that is, mismatches). After making an under-prediction, the subject on the next trial typically predicts an increased level of fear — but in the event the fear declines on that trial. Habituation, if that is the process involved, proceeds even after a mismatch.[19] Following a correct match, the fear response on the next trial showed no change in 39 percent of the occasions, but decreased in 47 percent of occasions. This pattern is consistent with a habituation explanation of the changes in fear.

This application of the results from fear-matching experiments to an analysis of habituation is itself not an exact match because the experiments do not involve the comparison of two stimuli, the incoming stimulus and the existing stimulus representation. Rather, it is a match between the person's expectation of his likely response to the stimulus (for example, snake) and his actual response to it. If the fear experiments *are* interpreted as a matching procedure, then the continuation of habituation despite incorrect matching is inconsistent with a comparator model. If not, not. On the basis of the results from matching experiments of this type,[20] it was also suggested that Gray's[21] theory of anxiety might benefit from the introduction of a distinction between the effects on the behavioral inhibition system of two types of mismatch: over-predictions and under-predictions. The effects of under-predictions fit comfortably into the theory, but those of over-predictions are less easily accommodated.[22]

AVOIDANCE BEHAVIOR

It has yet to be put to a direct test, but it seems probable that there is a strong link between the prediction of fear and the genesis and maintenance of avoidance behavior. Given a choice, most people prefer to avoid situations in which they expect to experience fear. The strength of the avoidance behavior is likely to be most influenced by the expectation of fear and the degree of certainty in the prediction. The expected aversiveness and other factors make secondary contributions.

This hypothesis, linking the prediction of fear with avoidance, is consistent with Bandura's assertion that "most human behavior is maintained by anticipated rather than by immediate consequences,"[23] and the results of a study of the cognitions reported by patients with panic disorder provide some encouragement for this point of view. Telch, Brouliard, and Telch studied the cognitions of 75 patients with panic disorder and concluded that "anticipated panic emerged as the most potent predictor of agoraphobic avoidance."[24]

The possibility that people frequently over-predict how much pain they will experience was mentioned earlier. Dental patients in particular appear to predict that their treatment sessions will be more painful than turns out to be the case. Kleinknecht and Bernstein[25] found that their 128 dental patients expected more pain than they experienced, and Kent's 76 patients expected more pain than they experienced when they underwent unpleasant procedures.[26] However, the discrepancy between prediction and experience was slight when they merely had a check-up. Wardle obtained similar results and concluded that "fearless patients had accurate expectations about dental pain but fearful patients had inaccurate and negative expectations."[27]

FEAR AND PAIN

The idea that over-predictions of fear and over-predictions of pain might be similar was investigated in a group of 29 arthritic patients.[28] They were asked to predict the amount of pain they expected to experience on each of a repeated set of therapeutic exercises. Overall, their predictions were more accurate (62 percent) than those made by the fearful subjects, but when over- or under-predictions occurred, they were followed by the same pattern of changes observed in the fearful patients. There was a strong tendency for under-predictions of pain to be followed by increases in subsequent predictions. A great majority (87 percent) of the over-predictions of pain were followed by reductions in predicted and reported pain on subsequent trials. The relatively accurate predictions of these patients might be the result of their prolonged and repeated experiences of pain, which enable them to learn to predict accurately. In their novel experiment, Arntz and van den Hout deliberately provoked an under-prediction of pain in 19 normal subjects.[29] These experimentally induced under-predictions were followed by the same pattern of consequences as those recorded under the relatively uncontrived conditions that prevailed during the testing of the arthritic patients. The under-predictions were followed by increases in predicted pain, and over-predictions were followed by decreases in predicted pain. They were unable to confirm the operation of an asymmetric pattern between the two types of mismatch, but they uncovered a strong recency effect. The subjects' predictions of pain were most strongly influenced by the immediately preceding trial. In a subsequent experiment, they obtained support for their hypothesis that under-predictions that occur late in a sequence of trials are more disruptive than under-predictions that are made early in the sequence.[30] Under-predictions that occur after a sequence of relatively stable and uniform responses are perhaps more "surprising," and therefore more disruptive.

Despite the similarities in the patterns of prediction and report observed in fear and in pain, it is premature to conclude that we are dealing with the same underlying process. It is not out of the question, however, that the over-prediction of aversive events is a common occurrence. The predictive process detected in fear may well be common to aversive experiences in general. It is also possible that the tendency to over-predict aversive events, including fear and pain, is partly dispositional.

FUNCTIONS

The over-prediction of fear, and other aversive experiences may be functional. It may serve to prevent distress, insofar as over-predictions promote avoidance of the fear-evoking situations. If this is so, the prevention of fear may be achieved at some cost because avoidance behavior can become excessive and impose limitations on mobility. It may then preserve the fear. If the over-prediction of fear promotes avoidance behavior, it serves to reduce the opportunities for learning trials and for disconfirmations. In other words, over-predictions might be functional in the short-term, but dysfunctional in the long term.

The same reasoning can be applied to chronic pain. Avoidance behavior is a common response of many sufferers, and in the long run avoidance may serve to exacerbate rather than ameliorate the pain problem.[31] Reduced activity can lead to increased physical distress (for example, muscle atrophy) and to increased psychological distress, such as depressed mood. As with fear, if overpredictions of pain are common and if they show the same postulated connection with avoidance behavior, then they too may be functional in the short term but dysfunctional in the long term. The fact that people can learn to predict fear with increasing accuracy is a safeguard against the persistence of serious over-predictions of fear. We have preliminary evidence that sufferers from chronic pain can learn to predict their pain more accurately,[32] and this has obvious practical advantages.

LEARNING TO PREDICT

The tendency to become increasingly accurate in predicting pain or fear suggests that people might have a preference for accurate prediction, and there is evidence that in aversive situations, animals and humans prefer predictability.[33] "A large body of literature now shows that animals and humans prefer predictable to unpredictable aversive events."[34] The preference for predictability may be related to the preference for controllability. No doubt, increases in the accuracy of prediction serve to increase the opportunities for control. Accurate predictions can also serve a safety function; the conditions that are used to predict accurately can take on the properties of a safety signal.

What goes into making the predictions? The information provided by earlier trials appears to have an influence on subsequent predictions, but it is not clear if this is because the person perceives some similarity between the conditions prevailing on separate occasions of exposure to the fearful stimulus. In the case of a correct match, and no change in the prevailing condition, the prediction is simply repeated on the next occasion. However, if the conditions are changed or if the person makes an error of prediction, the new information will be incorporated into the process of making the subsequent prediction. In this way, the matching procedure can be analyzed as a form of information processing and should take into account the apparent asymmetry in the effects of an over-prediction and the effects of an under-prediction.

Does a fearful person need to be aware of the discrepancy between his or her prediction and report in order to change subsequent predictions, reports of fear, and even avoidance behavior? This awareness may not be necessary, but the question has yet to be tackled in a direct test. If a person is made aware of the discrepancy, does this influence his or her judgments? In cases of over-prediction, if the person is given evidence of the error, will this lead to a more rapid decline in the rate of over-prediction? If so, then deliberately drawing attention to the discrepancies between expectation and experience might be a useful strategy to introduce into the treatment of fear and chronic pain. Clark and Salkovskis's use of "behavioral experiments" to help panic-disorder patients correct their crucial misinterpretations is an apt example.[35] The imposition of the matching procedure on these "experiments" may yield some fruitful results.

Research into the nature of over-predictions of fear and of other aversive events has the attractions of a simple methodology and the hope of useful rewards. In particular, if the postulated link between over-predictions and avoidance behavior can be confirmed, important implications will follow.

WHAT IS THE CONNECTION BETWEEN FEAR AND AVOIDANCE?

Excessive and injudicious avoidance behavior is a common consequence of fear, and as described earlier, recent investigations of panic disorders provide fresh examples of an apparently causal connection between episodes of intense fear (panic) and the emergence of (agoraphobic) avoidance behavior. Panic and avoidance are correlated, most patients attribute their avoidance to the episodes of panic, and the temporal relations between panic and avoidance are all indicative of a strong connection. Even so, exceptions do occur and panics are not necessarily followed by avoidance. On the other side, avoidance behavior is not always a product of fear. Furthermore, there are significant examples of fear apparently giving rise to approach rather than avoidance behavior. What then is the connection between fear and avoidance?

A mountain of laboratory evidence demonstrates a direct connection between fear and avoidance in animals. If they are shocked in an experimental chamber that physically permits them to avoid further shocks or to avoid exposure to stimuli that predict such shock, then strong and persisting avoidance is quickly established. The evidence is so clear and reproducible that it became the starting point for what was the most influential explanation of the relation between fear and avoidance.

"Fear is a decisive causal factor in avoidance behavior," according to Mowrer.[1] Ever since its introduction in 1939, Mowrer's two-stage theory of fear and avoidance has had a major influence on the way in which psychologists view fear. In the original statement of the theory, Mowrer critically examined the contrasting theories of Freud, Pavlov, and Watson and concluded that anxiety is best construed as a conditioned pain reaction. He argued that fear is not merely a reaction to painful stimuli or associations, but can also energize behavior. This motivating quality of fear is of central importance, and Mowrer added that behavior which leads to a reduction of fear is stamped in: the reduction of fear acts as a reinforcement. The final part of the theory is the proposition that behavior motivated by fear is avoidant and that when it is successful, it leads to a reduction of fear and thereby to the strengthening of the avoidance behavior itself. "Fear . . . motivates and reinforces behavior that tends to avoid or prevent the recurrence of the pain-producing (unconditioned) stimulus."[2] In an elaboration, Mowrer shifted the emphasis from the cause of fear to its motivating qualities. He claimed that "two causal steps are necessary . . . fear in the case of both active and passive avoidance behavior is an essential intermediate 'cause' or 'variable.'"[3]

Abundant empirical support for these ideas was obtained, and for a period the findings were conveniently incorporated into the two-stage theory. Difficulties began to arise in the early 1950s. The first problem is the remarkable persistence of the acquired avoidance patterns. In a number of experiments, laboratory animals continued to engage in avoidance behavior for hundreds of trials, even after the unpleasant stimulus had been withdrawn. This presents a problem for the theory because in the absence of further unpleasant experiences, active avoidance behavior should be extinguished.

The second problem is that the theory incorporates two assumptions that are no longer defensible. It assumes that all fears are acquired by conditioning and that neutral stimuli are all equally prone to be turned into fear signals. As discussed earlier, the conditioning theory of fear suffers from major weaknesses, and the presumption that all stimuli are potential fear signals is dubious. The two-stage theory was correctly criticized by Harlow on the grounds that it exaggerates the motivating role of fear in human behavior. "The greater part of our energies are motivated by positive goals, not escape from fear and threat."[4]

Most important of all, the claim that fear is a necessary causal stage in the development of avoidance behavior is mistaken. A wide range of avoidance responses arise, wax and wane, even in the absence of fear. Curiously, this obvious fact was overlooked for a long time, but there is no doubt about its validity. Without difficulty, one can engender, maintain, or modify complex patterns of avoidance behavior without evoking fear at any stage. Teasdale used the commonplace example of a man who takes his umbrella with him when he leaves the house on a cloudy day; he is engaging in active avoidance behavior in order to save himself from discomfort later in the day.[5] Going to the station to get an early train is a way of avoiding the discomfort of congested travel. Passively avoiding sauce Bearnaise is for some psychologists an effective way of avoiding digestive problems. Actively avoiding a muddy field is effort-reducing, not fear-reducing, behavior.

There are important examples of significant fears that are not followed by consistent avoidance behavior. Reference has been made to the wounded fighter pilots who were as willing as other pilots to return to combat. Telling clinical examples of fear without avoidance are also encountered, even among patients who experience panics.[6] Chambless[7] found that agoraphobic avoidance behavior correlated significantly with depression (0.40) in 378 outpatients, but not with panic frequency (0.14). Craske, Sanderson, and Barlow analyzed interview data from 57 patients with panic disorder and also found that "panic frequency is not the major determinant of avoidance behavior."[8] Furthermore, a long history of repeated panics was "frequently unaccompanied by a pattern of extensive avoidance."[9] Telch reported that anticipated panic emerged as the "strongest predictor of agoraphobic avoidance" and argued that cognitive factors play an important role in the genesis of phobic avoidance in this type of patient.[10] Additional difficulties encountered by Mowrer's theory are carefully analyzed by Seligman and Johnston, and for our purposes, it is unnecessary to state more than three of the problems.[11] In their view, persuasively argued, the theory does not explain the undue persistence of avoidance responses, the concomitant absence of fear, and what they refer to as the "elusiveness" of the conditioned stimulus. Often it is difficult to specify precisely which stimulus the person or animal is supposed to be avoiding.

Acting on the basis of the two-stage theory, clinicians took care to advise and encourage patients to refrain from avoiding fearful situations, especially during treatment. It was customary to warn patients that they risked increasing both fear and avoidance if they fled from the fear-provoking scene; they were told that although temporary relief might be obtained, it would be purchased at the cost of greater difficulties later. The reduction of anxiety that is accomplished by fleeing serves to increase that avoidance behavior. For a long period many therapists, including the writer, urged patients to remain in the fearful situation until the fear begins to subside. The golden rule is "to try never to leave a situation until the fear is going *down*."[12]

There are good reasons for agreeing that the reduction of fear can increase avoidance behavior, but it is most unlikely that this behavior is generated or maintained solely by escape from fear. Adoption of the three-system conception of fear allows and even demands that avoidance behavior can wax or wane independently of reports of subjective fear.

CLINICAL EVIDENCE

In an attempt to demonstrate that the connection between fear and avoidance is not inflexible and unvarying, de Silva and Rachman carried out a study with eight agoraphobic patients.[13] They were divided into two groups, and each patient received individually administered *in vivo* exposure treatment, but the instructions regarding avoidance behavior were varied. The patients in one group were given conventional instructions and were told that it was highly desirable for them to remain in the fear-revoking situations, despite their subjective fears, and that if they left the situation while still frightened, it might promote increased fear. They were encouraged to remain in the situation until their fear subsided, that is, to refrain from escaping or avoiding. The patients in the other group were told to leave the situation as soon as their subjective fear reached a "fear thermometer" reading of 25 — a low amount of fear. They were told to escape.

Fear and avoidance were assessed by the patients' verbal reports and by behavioral testing, before, during, and after treatment sessions. The patients in both groups made slight progress, and despite our encouragement of an escape strategy for the members of one group, neither their fears nor their agoraphobic avoidance behavior increased significantly—contrary to predictions drawn from the two-stage theory.

This study was replicated on two fresh groups of agoraphobic patients who were given eight individual sessions of exposure treatment. The patients in the no-escape group were exposed progressively to selected fearful situations in the standard manner. The patients in the escape group were also exposed progressively, but they were instructed to escape when their fear reached a preset level of 70 on a scale of 0 to 100. Both groups of patients showed significant and equivalent improvements on all measures of agoraphobia, and these changes were still evident three months later. Escapes were not followed by increases in either fear or estimates of danger, and it was concluded that "escape behavior does not necessarily strengthen agoraphobic avoidance."[14] It is of interest that the patients in the escape condition reported that they felt that they had greater control and, overall, reported less fear than did the patients who followed the no-escape instruction.

Another observation from this study was that among the patients in the no-escape group there was no relationship between the reductions in their fear and their estimations of the dangerousness of the excursion tasks. Their estimations of danger remained moderately high despite the fact that their fear decreased significantly. This dissociation between estimations of dangerousness and fear also has been observed in military samples.

The patients tended to overestimate the dangerousness and the uncontrollability of the treatment sessions, especially in the early stages of the program, and it is possible that this was an expression of the tendency of fearful subjects to over-predict the degree of expected fear, especially after they have experienced a panic. It is striking, however, that fear and avoidance declined regardless of the occurrence or non-occurrence of escape behavior.

FRESH POSSIBILITIES

If it is agreed the two-stage theory of fear and avoidance, despite its remaining explanatory value, is insufficient, then a number of new possibilities are opened. On the theoretical side, it becomes possible to explain some previously incomprehensible phenomena, and on the clinical side it opens the way for the development of new or refined techniques of managing fear.

From a practical point of view, the immediate implications of the relative failure of the two-stage theory include the following. Clinicians dealing with patients whose problems include a significant element of fear need no longer assume that there is a tight connection between the subjective complaint of fear and the manifestation of avoidance behavior. Patients who complain of excessive fear but refrain from carrying out what might seem to be appropriate patterns of avoidance are not necessarily dissimulating. Similarly, patients who engage in extensive avoidance behavior but deny that it is accompanied by subjective fear may well be reporting accurately. A revised view of the relationships between fear and avoidance — one that recognizes that they are only loosely coupled — corresponds to clinical observations showing that the evocation of fear during such treatment as flooding is not necessary. It might be facilitative in some cases, but the deliberate enhancement of fear is not necessary and where possible should be avoided. One of the unforeseen and unfortunate consequences of an uncritical acceptance of the lump theory of fear (Chapter 1) is that when the technique of flooding was introduced, many clinicians mistakenly assumed that in order to reduce fear it is necessary first to evoke it. As a result of this understandable but mistaken belief, fear was sometimes provoked unnecessarily in already distressed patients.

IS AVOIDANCE BEHAVIOR A PRODUCT OF PREDICTION?

If one expects that a situation will be very frightening, and there is a choice, it makes sense to avoid it. The more aversive the expected fear, the greater the likelihood of avoidance. Hence, people who significantly over-predict their fears should display greater avoidance behavior.[15] Other factors (such as motivation, the expected level of aversiveness, the availability of safety, earlier conditioning) play a part in determining avoidance behavior, but the probability of a person engaging in fearful avoidance is determined by his or her expectation that contact with the situation will evoke fear. Fearful avoidance behavior is mainly the product of predicted fear. (As argued earlier, avoidance behavior can be prompted not only by fear but by a range of expected or experienced discomforts.)

Maladaptive avoidance behavior of potentially fearful situations arises when people over-predict how much fear they will experience in those situations. The gradual correction of these overproductions will be followed by a decline in the avoidance behavior. These hypotheses, drawn from the assumption that avoidance behavior is mainly determined by prediction, remain to be tested directly, but some indirect evidence is encouraging. For example, Telch and others compared 35 panic patients who displayed minimal avoidance with another 40 who showed severe agoraphobic avoidance.[16] The two groups were similar on measures of panic symptoms, panic frequency, and severity. They did, however, differ in their *anticipations* of panic and in the perceived consequences of these panics. As mentioned earlier, Telch concluded that anticipated panic is the most potent predictor of agoraphobic avoidance. Similarly, the report by Craske and others is consistent in showing that panic frequency is not the major determinant of avoidance behavior. Instead, they concluded that elevations of *anticipatory* fear "provide a strong motivation for avoidance of some situations that have in some way been associated with panic."[17] They also found that concordance between the levels of fear and avoidance was increasingly evident as fear intensified. "At milder levels of fear, avoidance levels varied considerably."[18]

Even if fearful avoidance behavior is a product of overpredictions of fear, it does not follow that all predictions of fear lead to avoidance behavior—remember courage. Moreover, there are different types of non-fearful avoidance behavior, including the avoidance of discomfort, noise, pain, boredom. Given that fearful avoidance behavior varies in relation to predicted fear, information about the nature of the prediction should help to change the course of such avoidance behavior.

Safety signals also play a part in the determination of avoidance behavior, and their influence must be included. The essence of a safety signal is that it indicates a period of freedom from fear, pain, or aversive threat. In the presence of such a signal the person feels safer and therefore can act with greater freedom. In cases of agoraphobic avoidance the introduction of a safety signal (for example, a trusted companion) enables the affected person to travel more widely. No doubt the anticipated presence of a safety signal modifies a person's prediction of fear. It should lower the prediction of fear and thereby weaken the fearful avoidance behavior. However, the withdrawal of an anticipated safety signal will be followed by a prediction of increased fear, and hence by stronger avoidance.

Safety signals can be integrated into the present interpretation of the connections between predicted fear and avoidance behavior by emphasizing the essentially predictive nature of such signals. The anticipated or actual presence of a safety signals ensures a period of protection and of relief from an aversive event and therefore gives rise to a prediction of a lower level of fear, or a lower probability of experiencing fear. Predictions of low fear serve to weaken the avoidance behavior.

STRIVING FOR SAFETY

Although it was implicit in his original theorizing, Mowrer did not pursue the role of the search for safety in the genesis and maintenance of avoidance behavior.[19] The addition of a "safety perspective" may help to address some continuing problems of avoidance behavior.[20] For example, if agoraphobic avoidance is regarded as a balance between avoidance and safety signals, it is possible to re-examine the question of why avoidance behavior shows such remarkable persistence.

Clinicians and researchers have remarked that a striving for safety appears to play a prominent part in fearful behavior, notably agoraphobic avoidance. "The cardinal feature of the agoraphobic symptoms can be described *either* as staying at home behavior or avoidance of venturing out. The latter is consistent with the idea of agoraphobia as fear of discrete cues, such as streets . . . whereas the former view implies that the fear or anxiety arises in the absence of familiarity and safety."[21] Discussing the varieties of agoraphobia, Wolpe remarked that "what is common to all cases of agoraphobia is that the patient responds with anxiety to physical distance from a place of safety or the relative accessibility of a safe person—in some instances to both."[22]

A safety perspective has been used in an attempt to tackle some problems of agoraphobia, such as the disproportionate sex ratio and the age of onset. It is also helpful in trying to explain why the presence of a trusted companion exerts such a strong influence on an agoraphobic person's ability to travel. Agoraphobic people tend to become attached to talismans (symbols of safety?) without which they are reluctant to venture out. The daily fluctuations in the intensity of agoraphobic problems and in the person's reported ability to travel might result at least in part from changes in feelings of safety. The danger threatening the person is balanced against the prevailing safety precautions and the accessibility of assistance. As the danger point is approached, the fear increases and is likely to rise if it is discovered that access to safety procedures is blocked. Hence the need to sit on the aisle and near an exit. In a simple example, agoraphobic patients report steep increases in fear if they unexpectedly lose sight of their trusted companion during an excursion. They can also get distressed if they find that their automobile has been blocked in a parking position.

The nature of the safety signal depends on the content of the fear. If the fundamental fear is that of falling seriously ill when alone, then the presence of a trusted companion is a satisfactory safety signal. However, if the greatest fear is that of being trapped, then sitting near the exit in a bus or theater offers access to safety. Standing at the far end of a crowded bus blocks access to safety. People who are troubled by excessive fear learn to develop a pattern of safety signals. They learn which people they can rely on, and they establish new and often narrow paths of safety. They learn how to avoid such threatening places as crowded stores or the busiest times in the store or the times and places when public transport is congested. Consequently they time their excursions and ensure that they have access to escape. We all have established paths of safety, but those of agoraphobic patients are abnormally constricted and unadaptive.

FEAR AND APPROACH

The connection between fear and avoidance was so widely accepted, and so seldom questioned, that the many other causes of avoidance behavior were overlooked. Even more curious, we failed to notice that fear often gives rise to the opposite behavior — approach behavior, especially social approach.

Some socially anxious people avoid company and others seek company. The probability of approach behavior is of course increased if there is an over-riding need for the affected person to mix with other people. In the face of nonsocial threats, people usually find some safety and comfort from the presence of a companion. The fears that arise or multiply when a person is in solitude are a reverse example of the social buffering of fear, described below.

Fear can give rise to imitation, to conformity, and to vigorous approaches to the fear-reducing presence of familiar people.

DOES FEAR PRODUCE IMITATION?

It was argued earlier that fear can be reduced or increased by observational learning. Interestingly, the reverse sequence — fear producing an increase in imitative behavior — can also occur. A simple and common illustration of this sequence can be seen in the behavior of children as they enter a new social group for the first time. Many children display overt signs of fear, tensely watching the other children, and take particular care to do as the other children do. During their first few days of attendance at nursery school, many children are subdued and imitative.

In view of the preceding critique of the claim that fear "is an essential intermediate cause" of avoidance behavior, it is worth noticing that this is an example in which fear generates behavior other than avoidance. Avoidance and escape behavior implicitly admit defeat. The generation of imitative behavior in fearful situations is an attempt to achieve a degree of control over a potentially threatening situation.

We can interpret this imitative behavior as an attempt to acquire control through observational learning, using models as a guide. In these circumstances, exposure to a coping model can be expected to have at least three distinct effects: it produces a direct reduction in fear, transmits a good deal of information (and this in turn can reduce the unpredictability of the situation and increase the possibilities of control), and facilitates the vicarious acquisition of coping behavior. If the period of observing the model coping adequately is then followed by the translation of the newly acquired skills into appropriate actions, the value of the modeling experience is powerfully increased.

In many circumstances the display of excessive and inappropriate imitative behavior might be an indication that the person is fearful. From that possibility one can move on to contemplate the relationship between excessive imitative behavior and social conformity. Is it possible that unduly conforming people are more fearful than their less conforming companions? And are certain kinds of nonconforming behavior indicative of comparative fearlessness?

FEAR, IMITATION, AND CONFORMITY

Conduct that is strongly modeled on the behavior of the majority of the members of the group in which one finds oneself is taken as a clear instance of conformity. By extrapolating from the example of fearful children showing increased imitative behavior in a novel situation, it is not unreasonable to predict that fear facilitates conformist behavior. If our definition of conformity includes the imitation of normative group behavior, in a novel and potentially threatening situation conformist behavior may well be an effective method of coping. Observation of the behavior of established members of the groups is an important source of information for a newcomer. He or she can learn the relationships between behavior and its consequences in that setting and reduce the unpredictability and expedite the learning of coping skills. It need hardly be said that excessive conformity or inappropriate conformity may be much less adaptive than independent behavior—as well as being morally indefensible, as in the commission of war crimes based on the justification of obedience to higher authority.

If we pursue this line a little further, it is possible to deduce that timid people are more likely to display conformist behavior and, conversely, that fearless and courageous people will display more independent behavior. Courageous behavior derives at least in part from perceived competence; to pursue the present argument, people with high levels of perceived competence should display more nonconforming behavior than those with low levels of perceived competence. Although none of these deductions is particularly novel, it is nevertheless interesting that each can be reached from a novel starting point—the three-system analysis of fear.

Inspired by the pioneering work of Asch,[23] social psychologists devoted a good deal of attention to the phenomenon of conformity. Aronson summarized the subject in this way: among the variables that increase or decrease our strong inclinations to conformity, the unanimity of the majority opinion is particularly influential. "If the subject is present with only one ally, his tendency to conform to an erroneous judgement by the majority is reduced sharply."[24] Prior success in dealing with the task of situation also helps to reduce the tendency to conformity (thus, if fear has been reduced on earlier occasions, the tendency to model the behavior of others decreases). Aronson points out that the tendency of the observer to conform is strongly influenced by the constitution of the group: he is more likely to conform if the members are experts, if they are important to him, and if they share important characteristics with him. All three of these variables have been shown, in research on other aspects of behavior, to be important determinants of modeling: we are more likely to model the behavior of experts, of people who are significant to us, and of people who share attributes similar to ours. I am not here suggesting that the presence of fear is the sole or even the major determinant of conformist behavior. Rather, the presence of fear increases the probability that a person will model the behavior of others when he enters a threatening or novel situation, and this tendency will be strengthened if the members of the group are perceived as being competent and as having characteristics that are important to the observer and similar to his own. Since we have noted that excessive or inappropriate conformity can be seriously maladaptive, it should also be said that successfully modeling the behavior of competent people is a powerful way of acquiring skilled and adaptive behavior—especially when one begins by being fearful.

THE SOCIAL BUFFERING OF FEAR RESPONSES

It was suggested earlier that exposure to a coping model can produce a direct reduction of fear. The company of many people can have a similar effect.

Civilians under air attack and soldiers in combat claimed that they were better able to control their fear when they were in the company of familiar people. Vernon concluded from his review of the effects of air raids that "the majority of people were helped by the company of other people and that those who live alone tend to find raids much more trying."[25] Agoraphobic patients tend to be at their worst when they are alone, and the great majority report that their fear is reduced and their mobility increased when they are accompanied by a trusted companion.[26] The fear-reducing effect of the presence of one or more companions, sometimes referred to as a form of "social buffering,"[27] has also been observed in animals.

It has been described in baboons living in their natural environment[28] and in monkeys studied in the laboratory.[29] "Life on the ground exposes baboons to predation . . . when (they) are away from trees foraging in open country, the vulnerable members (mothers with infants, and young juveniles) cluster in the group center, around the most dominant and protective males."[30] A comparable phenomenon was observed under laboratory conditions by Coe and others[31] who tested the behavioral and psychophysiological responses of monkeys when exposed to novelty or to fear-producing snakes. When the monkeys were accompanied by a partner, they appeared to be less disturbed. Furthermore, monkeys showed a strong preference for close proximity to their partners when stress was introduced. Interestingly, signs of behavioral disturbance were suppressed by the presence of a partner even when the hormonal activity of the test animals showed the usual signs of reactivity to stress. According to Coe, social buffering is most evident in large groups and in familiar circumstances. The effect of social buffering is less evident in the presence of severe stress or unfamiliar surroundings. In addition, as Epley[32] has pointed out, the buffering effects occur only when the companion is calm—fear can increase steeply in the presence of a frightened or disturbed companion.[33] Coe and his colleagues concluded that social support is biologically valuable in reducing human vulnerability to life stresses, and Schradle's[34] review tends to support their claim.

The probability that human fears can be buffered by social influences fits well with Bandura's social learning theory, in which emphasis is placed on the social transmission of emotional learning.[35] Group therapy and therapy derived from social learning theory, such as therapeutic modeling, can be effective, and buffering may play a part here.

The social buffering of fear probably exerts an influence on the way in which a trusted companion modifies agoraphobic fear and avoidance behavior,[36] and Chambless and her colleagues incorporated the "presence of a companion" in their construction of an inventory for measuring restrictions on mobility.[37] The two parts of the inventory are divided by the distinction between a person's ability to travel alone and his or her ability to travel when accompanied. With very few exceptions, people are less avoidant when they are accompanied, and this difference is particularly marked among people with agoraphobic disorders. In a sample of people with this disorder, the ratings of their avoidance when alone always exceeded the avoidance-when-accompanied ratings.[38] This difference may be attributable in part to the effects of social buffering.

It has also been suggested that companions can act as safety signals and that their presence is capable of reducing fear and increasing mobility. The removal of safe figures, especially at times of threat, can precipitate disabling fears, such as those that occur shortly after a bereavement. Clear examples of the fear-reducing or fear-preventing effects of social buffering are found in the literature on military psychology and include such demanding tasks as bomb-disposal duties.[39] The abrupt loss of this social support, or buffering, can have disturbing consequences, especially in combat conditions.

Social support can serve as a buffer against stress in general,[40] and the stress-reducing effects of companions may contribute to the value of therapy that is provided in groups. On the other hand, group therapy in which the patients are exposed to fear-evoking situations may be hampered if a member displays uncontrollable fear or reacts excessively in novel situations. Maintaining a therapeutic balance between the social buffering of fear and the eruption of fear contagion requires considerable skill.

CHAPTER

EMOTIONAL PROCESSING

Do recurrent nightmares, the pressure to talk repeatedly about an unpleasant event, obsessional ideas and images, flashback experiences of terror, and the return of fear have anything in common? Possibly. If a fear keeps returning, even though no relevant aversive events have occurred, can we evade the conclusion that a fragment or partial representation of that fear remains, unabsorbed? If one repeatedly has nightmares about a disturbing experience, say an accident or painful rejection, that too suggests the persistence of an unabsorbed fragment. This notion of the persistence of an unabsorbed emotional experience is supported by the fact that when the aversive material is reduced, related nightmares, obsessions, or fears decline in frequency. For example, when snake-phobic subjects overcome their fear, they report a steep decline in the number of unpleasant snake-related dreams. Patients who are successfully treated for their fear of contamination experience a significant decline in the number of their unwanted and intrusive ideas and images about threats to their health and well-being. War veterans who overcome their combat fears cease to experience horrific flashbacks. Attempts have been made to find connections between these phenomena.

Some apparently disconnected findings and observations on the nature of fear can be herded into the same framework by using the concept of emotional processing, the process whereby emotional disturbances are absorbed and decline to the extent that other behavior can proceed without disruption.[1] If an emotional disturbance is *not* absorbed satisfactorily, some signs become evident. These are likely to recur intermittently, and may be direct and obvious, or indirect and subtle. The central indispensable index of unsatisfactory emotional processing is the persistence or return of intrusive signs of emotional activity (such as fear, obsessions, nightmares, pressure of talk phobias, or inappropriate expressions of emotion that are out of proportion or simply out of time). Indirect signs may include an inability to concentrate on the task at hand, excessive restlessness, and irritability. As all this suggests, it is far easier to come to grips with *failures* of emotional processing than with successes. Broadly speaking, successful processing can be gauged from the person's ability to talk about, see, listen to, or be reminded of emotional events without experiencing distress or disruptions.

Using emotional processing as a framework, we can connect apparently unrelated sets of events: the return of fear, incubation of fear, abnormal grief reactions, failures to respond to fear-reducing procedures, obsessions, and nightmares. Whatever their dissimilarities, and there are many, all of these phenomena can be regarded as indices of incomplete emotional processing.

Some of the impetus for the concept of emotional processing comes from the need to integrate the findings on fear reduction, and a more immediate prompt was provided by Lang's stimulating analysis of fear imagery.[2] He found that subjects who had minimal heart rate responses showed little improvement with desensitization. He concluded from these results, which contrasted with the concordance observed in the successfully treated subjects, that psychophysiological reactions to imagined scenes "may be a key to the emotional processing which the therapy is designed to accomplish."[3] Lang asserts that "the critical requirement . . . is that at least partial response components of the affective state must be present if an emotional image is to be modified."[4]

An account of his complex elaborations of the original theory would take us too far afield, but the expressed purpose of the work is to define and analyze the structures in long-term memory that form the basis for fearful behavior and to identify the conditions under which this structure is accessed and processed. "Phobic expression is produced when a sufficient number of input concepts match those in the network . . . The network activation is most likely when the phobic is confronted by the actual phobic object, which presumes a near perfect stimulus match. However, phobic emotions may also be elicited by degraded input — pictures, verbal descriptions" and the like.[5] Phobic reactions to circumscribed stimuli are coherent and stable prototypes. Activation spreads across the network rapidly and can be instigated by limited stimulus input. The more diffuse reactions characteristic of generalized anxiety states are far less coherent, less stable, and less closely tied to specific stimulus activators. People with circumscribed phobias have more stable and coherent structures than people with social anxiety.

Foa and Kozak's[6] attempt to link Lang's concept of deep fear structures to the schema of emotional processing appears at its most successful when applied to the analysis of simple phobias and to posttraumatic stress disorders. Their analysis of other types of problem is less successful, in part because of their insistence that fear *must* be evoked before it can be modified and their assumption that evocation requires some sort of exposure.[7] The analysis also leaves unexplained the successful reduction of fear, or even its facilitation, when the fearful person is distracted during presentations of his or her fear stimulus. In addition, as discussed earlier, there are plausible examples of fear changing, indeed reducing, without evocation.[8] "Fear can be evoked without exposure; threatening information will do it, and so will the withdrawal of safety signals."[9] The proposals of Foa and Kozak would benefit from greater specificity.

The idea that fear-reduction techniques proceed more satisfactorily if the stimulus material provokes at least some sign of reaction has received partial support from a study of speech-anxious subjects conducted by Borkovec and Sides.[10] On the other hand, an indirect attempt by Grey and others to confirm Lang's observation of a relationship between heart rate responsiveness and the outcome of a fear-reduction technique, was not successful.[11] Nevertheless, the interest attached to Lang's work is not thereby diminished (Grey used an *in vivo* method of presentation, and Lang was referring to the processing of *imagery*).

FAILURES OF PROCESSING

Three aspects of abnormal fear are worth considering in terms of unsatisfactory emotional processing: the undue persistence of a fear, the unprovoked return of fear, and the incubation of fear. This is perhaps the point at which to recall that the overwhelming number of fear-provoking experiences are satisfactorily processed.

What if anything is to be gained by regarding those minority instances of persisting, excessive fear as failures of emotional processing? First, it offers a possible connection with related emotional phenomena. Second, it can be linked with the processes of habituation and extinction, and for purposes of analyzing fear-reduction, it incorporates both of them under one concept. Third, it opens a door for the development of new methods of reducing fears—the main therapeutic aim now being redefined as one of facilitating the desired emotional processing.

The undue persistence of fear can be accounted for in several ways (for example, insufficient extinction trials, preservation of avoidance behavior), but the unprovoked return of fear presents some problems for traditional theories. The return of fear points to the need for a concept such as emotional processing. These returns, after an interval during which the new learning of fear is unlikely to have taken place, imply that at least some of the fear-reduction originally accomplished must have been transient and, in that sense, incompletely processed. So the return of fear can be used as a test-bed for analyzing the degree and duration of emotional processing. Under experimental conditions, we should be able to *predict* the recurrence of fear from our knowledge of the type and degree of emotional processing accomplished during the experimental treatment periods. If the return of fear is to be regarded as an index of incomplete processing, it is essential to avoid circularity of argument, and this can be done by making precise predictions and by using independent test-probes.[12] At present, the emotional processing viewpoint does nothing to advance our understanding of the incubation of fear, because incubation can be taken not merely as evidence of uncompleted emotional processing, but also as signifying the influence of as yet unidentified sensitizing factors.[13]

A WORKING DEFINITION

In order to satisfy the working definition of emotional processing, a return to ongoing behavior after an emotional disturbance has waned, three conditions must be met. We need evidence of a return to routine behavior. If the first condition is met (that is, an emotional disturbance occurs) but conditions two or three (declining disturbance, and a return of routine behavior) are not met, then the emotional processing is incomplete.

This definition presents some problems. For example, a person may suffer from reminiscences; signs of incomplete processing may be delayed, and so on. How and when can we be confident that the emotional processing is complete? How long a period of tranquil, routine behavior is required before we can be confident of our judgment? As it is unlikely that a suitable time scale can be developed for this purpose, one turns instead to use of test *probes*. After an emotional disturbance has subsided, the extent of emotional processing can be estimated by presenting relevant stimulus material in an attempt to re-evoke the emotional reaction. The degree to which the test probes are successful in provoking the reaction provides a measure of emotional processing. For example, 6 months after successfully completing a fear-reducing training course, a subject is re-represented with the phobic stimulus and experiences moderate fear. Or, a former griever may be asked to speak about the dead person some time after he has ceased to show overt signs of grief. Test probes offer the most direct and best ways of ascertaining the progress of emotional processing, but there are other signs that can be used alone or in combination. The signs that index the satisfactory completion of emotional processing are listed in Table 1.[14]

There are many more signs of *unsatisfactory* or incomplete emotional processing (see Table 2). Running through all of these indices is the time factor. Emotional processing may reach completion but take an inordinate length of time, and hence be regarded as unsatisfactory. All of the

Table 1 *Indices of satisfactory emotional processing*

Test probes fail to elicit disturbances
Decline of subjective distress
Decline of disturbed behavior
Return of "routine" behavior (e.g., concentration)

Table 2 *Indices of unsatisfactory emotional processing*

Direct signs
    Test probes elicit disturbances
    Obsessions
    Disturbing dreams
    Unpleasant intrusive thoughts
    Inappropriate expressions of emotion (as to time or place)
    Behavioral disruptions or distress
    Pressure of talk
    Hallucinations (e.g., after bereavement)
    Return of fear

Indirect signs
    Subjective distress
    Fatigue
    Insomnia
    Anorexia
    Inability to direct constructive thoughts
    Preoccupations
    Restlessness
    Irritability
    Resistance to distraction

signs listed in Table 2 can be regarded as falling within normal limits if they occur shortly after the emotional disturbance takes place. Their failure to subside, their undue persistence, would signal unsatisfactory emotional processing. Some of the indices, especially if intense, may provide sufficient evidence in themselves of unsatisfactory emotional processing (for example, terrors, repetitive nightmares, severe obsessions), but the indirect signs (such as restlessness) are insufficient.

FACILITATION

There are five groups of factors that facilitate emotional processing: state factors, personality factors, cognitions, stimulus factors and concurrent activity. Most people successfully process the overwhelming majority of the disturbing events that occur in their lives. Among the state factors, it seems likely that a state of relaxation helps to ensure that future difficulties are avoided. On the personality side, it is to be expected that people who have broad competence and a high level of self-efficacy should successfully process most emotional experiences. The early signs are that changes in specific fearful cognitions can promote processing. The stimulus qualities that are least likely to give rise to processing difficulties include signaled events, mild events, signals of safety, prepared and controllable events, predictable events, stimuli in small chunks, and progressive increments. The activity factors that are likely to facilitate emotional processing are those that give one a sense of increased controllability.

It has to be said that at the present time we appear to have more clues about the factors that initiate difficulties in processing. The personality factors that are likely to be associated with difficulties in processing include a sense of incompetence, high levels of neuroticism, and introversion. The state factors that are probably associated with difficulties in emotional processing are high arousal, dysphoria, illness, fatigue, disturbing dreams, sleeplessness, and immaturity. The inclusion of disturbing dreams, itself an index of incomplete processing, is merited because there appear to be occasions on which fears of obsessions are triggered by aversive dream material.

The stimulus factors that are likely to give rise to difficulties in processing include sudden stimuli, intense stimulation, signals of danger, prepared stimuli, uncontrollable stimuli, unpredictable stimuli, irregularity of presentation and large chunks of stimulation. The associated activities that might impede satisfactory processing include the presence of concurrent stressors (hence giving rise to an overload), intense concentration on a separate task, heat and noise, and possibly the need to suppress the appropriate emotional expression. The persistence of an unchanging and serious misinterpretation of potentially threatening events may be a major impediment to successful processing.

PROMOTING PROCESSING

Given that experiences, or certain kinds of material, are proving difficult to process, how might one set about overcoming the difficulty? In Table 3 a division has been made between factors that are likely to promote and factors that are likely to impede the process. The factors that are thought to promote satisfactory emotional processing are familiar to therapists, and most of them are drawn directly or indirectly from current methods. In sum, it is expected that the following factors will facilitate processing: engaged exposure to the disturbing material, habituation training, extinction trials, calm rehearsals (especially of coping behavior), long presentations, repeated practice, proceeding from

Table 3 *Factors that promote or impede emotional processing*

Promote	Impede
Engaged exposures	Avoidance behavior
Calm rehearsals (especially of coping)	Agitated rehearsals
Talk	Silence
Habituation Training	Distractions
Extinction	Poorly presented material
No distractions	Excessively brief presentations
Catharsis	Inadequate practice
Vivid presentations	Excessively large "chunks"
Long presentations	Immobility
Repeated practice	Fatigue
Descending (?) presentations	Irregularity of stimulation
Relaxation	Unresponsive autonomic reactions
Autonomic reactivity (?)	Persisting misinterpretations of threat
Correction of critical misinterpretations of threat	

high to low provoking stimuli, the use of relaxation, vivid presentations of stimuli, the evocation of controlled autonomic reactions, a sense of perceived control, relevant conversation, and correction of critical misinterpretations of potential threats.

PROCESSING INFORMATION ABOUT FEAR

The answer to a question posed a few years ago can now be answered affirmatively. It *is* "possible to change fear by the mere provision of corrective information" and by other non-exposure methods.[15] However, the provision of information can be a "relatively weak reducer of fear."[16] Previously, it was thought that corrective information is a weak means of change because the fear structures are too firm and coherent "to be affected significantly by a change in one element of the network,"[17] but this argument ignores the fact that the prototype of a stable and coherent fear (for example, those of a circumscribed nature) can be changed readily and speedily by repeated exposure. The coherence of these fears is no barrier to their modification. For similar reasons, it is improbable that the explanation for the weak fear-reducing effects of information can be explained by the intensity of the fears. Even extremely intense circumscribed fears respond readily to exposure. For reasons that are unclear, the informational channel, or in Lang's terms, the informational part of the network, is not easily modified. Interestingly, the weakness of informational fear-reducing effects can be contrasted to the ease and speed with which fears can be *induced* by the provision of information. This asymmetry has yet to be explained.

The induction and reduction of fear by the provision of information presents no problem for Lang's bio-informational theory, according to which various forms of information should be capable of changing fear structures. There seems to be no fundamental reason for insisting that the fear must be evoked in order for the fear structure to be changed. The argument that fear structures can be changed without the evocation of fear is strengthened by drawing attention to increases of fear as well as to decreases of fear. The incorporation of informational changes within the bio-informational theory may prove to be a useful expansion, but does not appear to offer any simple solution for the twin problems of the weakness of information as a fear-reducer, and the asymmetry in the relations between information and fear induction or reduction. There is little to be gained by insisting that fear must be evoked in order to be changed. A simplified version is preferable — various forms of information, including that transmitted by exposure to a stimulus, can change fear, and fear evocation may powerfully facilitate change, but it is not a pre-condition for such change. If the current research on the power of cognitive changes to reduce intense fears, such as panic, succeeds, it will have major implications for the concept of emotional processing.

To conclude, the factors that appear to impede emotional processing include the avoidance of situations in which the fear or other emotions are evoked, a refusal or inability to talk about them, repeated exposures to disturbing material under uncontrolled conditions, poorly presented material, excessively brief presentations, few practice sessions, presentations that evoke no autonomic reactions, immobility, fatigue, irregularity of stimulation, absence of perceived control, and serious misinterpretations of potential threat.

This schema setting out the factors that facilitate or impede emotional processing is the menu, not the meal.

P A R T

COURAGE

CHAPTER 20

TELL ME,
IF YOU CAN,
WHAT IS
COURAGE?

Socrates: Then, Laches, suppose we set about determining the nature of courage and in the second place, proceed to enquire how the young men may attain this quality by the help of study and pursuits. Tell me, if you can, what is courage?[1]

Most people acquire remarkably few fears. Before World War II the population and the authorities greatly over-predicted how much fear would be provoked, especially during air-raids on civilian populations. As described earlier, the expected panic and fear did not occur.

As a clinician working with people who are distressed and disabled by intense fear, I was struck by the apparent contrast between the patient's uncontrollable fear and the fearlessness of people who were the victims of repeated air attack. My curiosity about this fearlessness was then enhanced by observing a remarkable paradox that arose out of the introduction of behavioral methods for the treatment of abnormal fears.

THE COURAGEOUS ACTS OF FRIGHTENED PEOPLE

The paradox is that we request and require patients to carry out acts of considerable courage, we ask them to do what frightens them most, and to do it frequently and for protracted periods. We expect them to perform courageously—and they generally do. Examples of fearful people displaying courageous behavior are everyday clinical experiences made more prominent by the common use of methods in which the person is exposed to the very situations that provoke the fear. A middle-aged woman who was deeply troubled by intense, irrational fears of disease, germs, and dirt was given a course of such treatment. These chronic fears had distorted and damaged all aspects of her life. She was extremely frightened of touching "unsafe" objects, eating foods that she believed were dangerous, or even touching people whom she felt were diseased. She avoided physical contact with other people, including members of her own family, and spent most of the day sitting in the only chair that remained safe. Even her safe chair had to be scrubbed down with powerful antiseptics each day.

The treatment was described to her, and it was explained that she would have to come into direct contact with the objects and people whom she felt were diseased and dangerous. After a difficult struggle, in which her fear was extremely high, she bravely chose to carry out the treatment. She made good progress during the 15 sessions even though the first 3 were exceedingly difficult for her. She felt extremely frightened and at times terrified, and had unpleasant physical reactions, which included profuse sweating and strong palpitations. After completing each of these early sessions, she felt exhausted and limp for a couple of hours. Even so, she persevered, displaying commendable courage. After 2 months of treatment she was greatly improved, her fears had subsided, and she was once again able to touch all the people and objects she had learned to avoid. Unfortunately, her courage eroded when she returned home and she refused further help.

A severely anxious and totally housebound agoraphobic woman provides a second clinical example of courageous perseverance. When her elderly mother fell ill and was confined to bed for 6 weeks, the patient forced herself to go out repeatedly to obtain food and medicine for her parent. She dreaded each excursion and experienced intense fear, but she persisted nevertheless.

Patients with panic disorder who fear that the palpitations they experience during excursions are a sign of an imminent heart attack, perhaps death, display courage in carrying out their therapeutic excursions. Given appropriate support and advice, agoraphobic and other extremely frightened people can be helped to endure and then overcome their fears. These patients display courage every time they carry out one of their exercises while experiencing extreme fear. Frightened people perform courageous acts.

SOLDIERS AND PHILOSOPHERS

Psychologists display a strong interest in fear and comparative indifference to courage, but the concept of courage has not been neglected. Soldiers and philosophers have had a long and lively interest in courage, as illustrated in the quotation from Socrates at the opening of this chapter. The Platonic exchange between Socrates and the two generals, Laches and Nikias, is disappointingly inconclusive, and they fail to reach the second part of the question of how people may attain "this noble quality." We are now in a position to tackle both questions freshly and to bring to bear some new scientific information.

Our main sources of information are wartime surveys of the type described earlier, which testify to the resilience of people subjected to raids; direct observations of combatants and civilians; and experimental analyses of training programs designed to teach people how to carry out dangerous tasks such as dealing with explosive devices or jumping from an airplane. A start has been made in attempting to answer the question of whether or not people can acquire courage "by the help of study and pursuits."

Most of the information is reassuring, and it appears that people *can* learn to persevere in the face of fear and stress. Although fear reactions during or immediately after stress are common, we apparently have the capacity to recover very quickly.[2] We also have good powers of adaptation to repeated stresses and dangers.[3]

In a comparison of combat soldiers and air crews, Stouffer and others found that the airmen displayed significantly more courageous behavior.[4] They had higher morale than the combat soldiers, expressed more courageous attitudes, and won four times as many medals as their comrades on the ground. Stouffer attributed the difference to motivation and confidence. The airmen were volunteers and said that they benefited from the high morale engendered in the small groups that constituted an aircrew. They also expressed considerable self-confidence in their flying and combat skills. Both airborne and ground combatants said that their desire to avoid letting down their comrades played an important part in helping them to control their fear.

The influence of self-confidence on courageous, or fearless, behavior is borne out by observations of combat troops in the Pacific arena during World War II. Fearlessness in battle and precombat ratings of self-confidence were clearly related. Fifty-six percent of the soldiers who expressed high self-confidence before combat reported little or no fear during battle, and 62 percent of the soldiers who expressed little self-confidence reported a high degree of battle fear. Confidence and low fear were related, but as these figures indicate, there were exceptions. Some of the confident soldiers did experience considerable fear, and some who were lacking in confidence experienced little or no fear.[5] In research on military subjects, Rachman, Hallam, and Cox confirmed the existence of a positive relationship between self-efficacy and low fear, and also encountered some notable exceptions.[6]

Parachute training has been a fertile source of information about acquired courage. Walk asked trainee parachutists to rate their subjective fear before and after jumping from a 34-foot practice tower. Each trainee was required to jump from an exit door and drop nearly 8 feet before his fall was arrested by the straps of the parachute harness. The comprehensive training program was difficult and potentially dangerous, but the large majority of trainees passed satisfactorily.[7]

At the start of the program, most of the trainees reported at least a moderate amount of fear, but this tended to subside within five jumps. Successful execution of the required jump despite the presence of fear (i.e., courageous performance) was usually followed by a reduction of fear. The successful jumpers started the program with slightly less fear than those who failed, but there were few differences between the groups on measures of physiological disturbance, such as sweating and tremor. The successful jumpers persevered satisfactorily in the face of moderate fear and physiological disturbances. The main difference between the successful jumpers and the failures was in the degree of self-confidence.

A positive relationship between self-confidence and successful parachute performance was also reported in a study of 21 members of the

Parachute Regiment.[8] The trainees who expressed low self-confidence reported significantly greater fear than the others when they had to carry out the jumps from an aircraft. Interestingly, there was no correlation between their estimates of the dangerousness of the task and their reports of experienced fear. The successful performance of this small group of trainees was matched in a larger study by MacMillan and Rachman.[9] All 105 recruits to the same Unit successfully completed their parachute training, unless it was interrupted by an injury incurred during training. In both studies, the recruits reported significant decreases in fearfulness as they passed through the training program. These declines in fearfulness were accompanied by increased levels of self-confidence.

FEARLESSNESS

For most of us, fear is a familiar emotion, and it is difficult to imagine life in which it plays no part. However, there is a small number of people who are relatively impervious to fear. Henry Cooper, former heavy-weight champion of Europe, who had a long and punishing career, said that he could not remember ever fearing anyone.[10] He described mild fears of flying or driving fast, but was unable to think of any person or situation that had frightened or could frighten him. He had not experienced fear before or during any of his professional fights, despite having faced the hardest men in boxing. It seems extraordinary that repeated exposures to the punishments of boxing failed to generate any significant fear in Cooper. Moreover, he experienced none of the usual physical accompaniments of fear, such as palpitations or sweating. Henry Cooper seems to be one of those unusual people whom we can describe as being literally fearless. Like many writers before him, Mowrer linked fearlessness with courage. "May it not be," he asked, "that courage is simply the absence of fear in situations where it might be expected to be present?"[11]

Fearlessness is often regarded as synonymous with courage, but there is some value in distinguishing it from another view of courage. As well as fearlessness, or the absence of fear, we can recognize the occurrence of perseverance despite fear. One could argue that such perseverance is the purest form of courage. It certainly requires greater effort and endurance.[12]

World War II soldiers discriminated between fear that is endured and fear that is not tolerated. They made a distinction between comrades who were cowards and those who were ill, even though both showed the same symptoms of fear.[13] The difference depended on whether the soldier had or had not made a genuine effort to resist fleeing when experiencing fear. Soldiers who were visibly upset by danger were not regarded as cowards "unless they made no apparent effort to stick out their job." If a soldier tried hard but could not perform adequately, he was regarded as a legitimate casualty. On the other hand, a soldier who exhibited the same symptoms of fear could be labeled a coward if he made no apparent effort to overcome his reactions and carry on with his duties. "Thus men were not blamed for being afraid . . . but they were expected to try and put up a struggle to carry on despite their fear."[14] In many cases the "distinction between anxiety neuroses and cowardice" was painfully difficult to determine. Soldiers whose symptoms persisted long after the danger had subsided were generally regarded as being ill.

Soldiers who displayed the most courageous behavior received the greatest admiration from their comrades. When veteran troops were asked to characterize the best combat soldiers they had ever known, fearless behavior was rated as by far the most important characteristic on which to make a judgment. As Birley noted, the admiration of courage appears to be universal. "Courage, from whatever angle we approach it, whatever origin or purpose we assign to it, no matter what form it assumes, not even what motives underlie it, will always be a quality beloved of man."[15] This admiration extends to courage shown by one's opponents. Samuel Johnson observed that "courage is a quality so necessary for maintaining virtue, that it is always respected, even when it is associated with vice."[16] Without exploring the reasons for this admiration, we can turn instead to examples of fearless or courageous acts and the factors that contribute to their commission.

The wartime observations and surveys, coupled with recent investigations and studies, suggest that several factors contribute to courageous behavior. Self-confidence is an important factor. Possession of the appropriate skill required to deal with the dangerous situation also serves to increase courage. A high level of motivation to succeed and a set of conditions conveniently summarized under the term "situational demand" also play a part in determining courageous behavior. These demands include the person's sense of responsibility to himself and to others, the powerful effects of group membership and group morale, and the need to avoid disapproval. A modern example of the powerful influence of situational demands is provided in the description of Israeli soldiers who received decorations for gallantry.[17]

Courageous behavior is promoted by a courageous model. The wartime observation that children who were exposed to air raids model the courageous or fearful conduct of their parents has been echoed in recent years by research on therapeutic modeling for phobic patients. We are also open to the acquisition of fears by a process of modeling. In their study of combat troops, Stouffer found that 40 percent of the troops reported significantly increased fear after observing a fellow soldier panic in battle. Fearful and courageous performance can be modeled. For many soldiers, a courageous leader was the most critical determinant of their own perseverance and ability to cope in combat conditions.[18] The contagiousness of courage is "caught as men take diseases one after another and may rapidly infect the whole army."[19] As with panic, so with courage — both are contagious.

COURAGEOUS ACTS OR COURAGEOUS ACTORS?

Recognition of the fact that fearful people are capable of performing courageous acts does not rule out the existence of courageous actors. Before addressing the second part of Socrates' challenge to Nikias and Laches, about whether people can acquire the "very noble quality" of courage, it is necessary to clarify the concept of a courageous actor and its relation to the distinction between courage and fearlessness.

Courageous actors are people who perform courageously more than once and in a variety of circumstances. If a person behaves courageously in one situation, does it imply that he will behave courageously in other circumstances? A single act of courage or one that is carried out under exceptional demands is not sufficient to describe someone as a courageous actor. In addition, courageous people are allowed only a few non-significant fears.

In common use, the concept of courageous actors does not include a distinction between people who experience no fear when carrying out dangerous acts (fearlessness) and people who persevere despite their fear (courage). The case for introducing this distinction is an elaboration of the general argument that the concept of courageous actors is valid and that such actors are identifiable.

The "contagion of courage" described by military observers and the therapeutic modeling of courageous behavior kindled by clinicians are instances of the situational determination of courage. In specifiable circumstances, courage can be promoted by clinicians, research workers, firemen, nurses, and soldiers. Courage can also be instigated by insistent demands in dangerous situations, without the influence of another person.

Furthermore, acts of courage can be promoted in people who are regarded by themselves and by others as timid, even excessively timid. Under the appropriate conditions, phobic patients can be helped to face and endure the objects, people, or places that elicit their worst fears. It is not necessary to be a courageous actor in order to carry out a courageous act.

ASTRONAUTS

Although it is not necessary to be reliably courageous, it certainly helps. Slowly accumulating evidence points to the possibility that there is a small group of people for whom courageous or fearless behavior presents few problems.

The Mercury astronauts were required to carry out extremely difficult and dangerous tasks in conditions of great uncertainty. The seven original astronauts, all of whom were experienced jet pilots selected from the military services, were the subject of study by Ruff and Korchin.[20] They were all married men in their early thirties who had grown up in middle-class families in small towns or on farms. They were Protestant, enjoyed outdoor living, had university degrees in engineering, were of superior intelligence (mean IQ, 135), and were inclined to action. The astronauts were aware of the dangers involved in the Mercury project but regarded them as similar to those tasks they had already accomplished in test flying. According to the authors, the astronauts had no special wish to face danger but were willing to accept the risks demanded by their work.

In the event, they performed their tasks with exemplary skill and success. The astronauts experienced positive and negative emotions but exerted excellent control. They had faced situations in which fear was appropriate and found that they were able to function despite its effects. The astronauts benefited from these mastery experiences and were confident that they had the skills and knowledge necessary to overcome realistic threats. They were not given to dwelling on unrealistic ones. In describing their reactions to combat, they readily admitted fear but pointed out that they were skilled pilots. These people had particular psychological competence and the resources for coping effectively with danger.[21]

During their journeys into space, they experienced remarkably little fear. Before the flights there was little evidence of significant anxiety, and instead, "the launch of a space vehicle and the flight itself often induced a feeling of exhilaration. . . . Anxiety levels had not been extraordinarily high (and) even in the instances where a possibility of death has been encountered, emotional reactions have remained within normal limits."[22] The astronauts felt that as a result of their intensive training and past experience, they were prepared to handle any emergency. In addition to their training and successful experiences, this small group of remarkable performers may have had the benefit of some constitutional resistance to vulnerability. Their performance on all of the tests — psychomotor, intellectual, and emotional — was well above average and their reactions under the stress of preliminary training were adaptive. It is of interest that although they had experienced fears during combat flying, by the time they had completed the training they were able to complete the space journey with minimal fear. They had undergone a transition from courage to fearlessness.

The possibility of some constitutional invulnerability in these people must be allowed for, but their actual and perceived psychological competence seems to have been the factor of dominating importance. Ruff and Korchin sum up their findings in this way: "The capacity to control emotions seems to be gained through past experience in the mastery of stress, and through confidence in training and technical readiness."[23] This reflects the views of the astronauts themselves, who placed greatest importance on competence, and foreshadowed the concept of "perceived self-efficacy," formulated by Bandura in his explanation of behavioral changes.[24] Apparently, the astronauts felt convinced that their past experience and intensive training had prepared them to handle any emergency.[25] The importance of training and self-confidence in promoting courageous behavior is evident in a number of military duties, but some of these duties are so exceptional and demanding that one wonders whether they can be carried out only by people with special endowments. Rendering safe an improvised explosive device appears to be one such exceptional task, and the qualities of bomb-disposal operators are therefore of special interest. Are bomb-disposal operators courageous actors?

A PERILOUS TASK

In an attempt to extend our understanding of courageous performance and the conditions that facilitate it, we carried out several studies of military bomb-disposal operators.[26] These soldiers are required to carry out skilled technical acts under conditions of extreme danger, in which a single error can be fatal. Bomb-disposal duty was described by Churchill as a "task of the utmost peril."[27] The circumstances and manner in which operators fulfill their dangerous duties, which require reasoning and technical skill, provide a particularly apt testing ground for some emerging ideas on courage.

Initially, a retrospective analysis was carried out on the records of over 200 Royal Army Ordnance Corps (RAOC) bomb-disposal operators who had seen service in Northern Ireland.[28] The major finding was that virtually all of them performed extremely well. During a 10-year period, they dealt with 31,273 incidents. The hazardous nature of the work is illustrated by the fact that 17 operators were killed between 1969 and 1981, and roughly one-quarter of the operators received decorations for gallantry. During the period from 1970 to 1981, 73 awards were made to operators of the RAOC. They faced the greatest danger early in the bombing campaign, but with experience and the introduction of improved equipment, the hazards have now been reduced. It will be appreciated, however, that in spite of these advances, rendering safe an improvised explosive device inevitably involves danger. In light of the astonishingly large number of "incidents" that have been successfully dealt with, the performance of the operators must be judged as a remarkable success. This success is all the more noteworthy for being carried out by operators who did not undergo positive selection. The major selection procedure used by the RAOC was one of negative exclusion. Ordnance personnel were expected to carry out bomb-disposal duties after completing an additional course of specialized training. Most of them (54 percent) were not aware at the time of joining the service that bomb-disposal work might be involved.

DEALING WITH EXPLOSIVE DEVICES

The psychological significance of bomb-disposal duties is best appreciated by keeping in mind the nature of the tasks that the operators are called upon to perform. The psychological demands of these duties are illustrated by excerpts from the specially designed daily diaries in which the operators recorded their thoughts and feelings.[29]

Operator A dealt with one explosive device in the first week of his four-month tour and said that he felt very lively and active, on duty and off. He had a busy second week during which he dealt with three explosive devices and reported that he had been "slightly frightened when dealing with one of them", but remained lively and alert throughout the week. In order to render safe one of the devices, he had to spend a lot of time exploring the area to rule out a range of possible dangers, and as a result had worked through most of the night. On the following day he reported a slight disturbance of sleep and a confusing and disturbing dream involving bombs and violence. Having successfully completed a difficult job, he reported a large and significant increase in confidence.

During the fourth week, he had to deal with two devices and one false alarm. He remained lively, alert and interested, and was starting to relax when off duty. Towards the end of the fourth week, he reported that, "we were faced with a new type of device (a funny) but I was flexible enough to deal with it". The fifth week was very busy and he had to deal with several devices, including a number that were hidden in various parts of a large and poorly lit warehouse. "I was involved for something like 24 hours, and towards the end I was truly shattered as were the rest of the team. I had a constant worry that there was a booby-trap somewhere. However, by a gradual process of elimination, this proved not to be so.

"During the reconnaissance phase of the operation, the cab of a suspect vehicle exploded quite violently. The fact that precisely one minute before I was on a house roof looking down on it did not scare me at the time or during the task. However, knowing now what happened, the cab bomb inspires me to think that these trucks should be marked with a Government Health Warning!" By the end of a busy tour, his confidence was very high and he had reported minimal fear at any time. The only negative aspect of his tour was a number of disagreements with soldiers from a supporting regiment.

Operator B was posted to a relatively quiet area and by the sixth week he was complaining of inactivity and the lack of opportunity for exercise. Suddenly he was called out to deal with five separate explosive devices over the course of a few days. His level of alertness and confidence increased rapidly, but when the area quietened down again, he complained of his "great disappointment at not doing more work".

This operator's experience illustrates a phenomenon that we encountered early in our association with the bomb-disposal service. To our surprise, the operators told us that they looked forward to the ringing of the alarm telephone so that they could go out on a task. The notion that someone can look forward to being called out to such a dangerous task, in which one's life might be at risk, can only be comprehended against a background of prolonged inactivity, restriction, and boredom. One should never underestimate the power of boredom that can be so great as to induce people to prefer exposure to great danger rather than sitting in cramped quarters watching dreary and repetitious television programs. This is an unasked for, but by no means surprising, example of the power of television. It should not be thought that the desire to carry out their duties was simply an attempt to avoid the boredom of cramped barracks. Virtually all of the operators took pride in their skills and the responsibility entrusted to them.

Operator C had an unhappy tour, but performed courageously despite the fact that at times he felt extremely frightened. His mood fluctuated and he experienced periods of anger and irritability. His confidence in his ability to perform competently also fluctuated. As the tour continued, he became increasingly unhappy and lethargic, but despite all these difficulties, he successfully dealt with 23 explosive devices and 23 hoaxes. Curiously, his end-of-tour report did not reflect his unhappiness, and he said that the tour had gone reasonably well, and that his performance and mood had been stable throughout the tour. He stated that he had not felt fearful before or during the execution of his bomb disposal duties, in clear contrast to his daily diary reports.

PERSONALITY OR PROFICIENCY?

Before being called upon to carry out these duties, each operator was required to complete a set of psychometric tests, undergo a psychiatric interview, pass a series of military interviews and training tasks, and complete a comprehensive and thorough course of specialized training. Less than 10 percent of the more than 200 operators who completed these tests and training in the period 1972–1980 were rejected. Of these, fewer than 5 percent were rejected on psychiatric grounds. The bold assumption underlying the selection process used by the RAOC was that virtually all of their officers and non-commissioned officers are capable of carrying out this difficult and dangerous work, providing that they are given specialized training in addition to their normal training. This apparently optimistic expectation has been borne out by events in a remarkable manner.

The psychometric information shows that the operators were an unusually well-adjusted group of people. On most of the psychometric tests, they scored above the civilian population norms on all of those characteristics that we regard as indicating psychological well-being and healthy adjustment. They did not score above the mean on any tests or sub-tests indicative of abnormalities or anti-social tendencies or behavior. There were very few exceptions.[30]

The attributes of operators who received ratings of "average" were compared with those who were rated as "below average," or "above average" by their commanding officers at the end of their tour of duty. There were few differences between the operators in these three categories but there was a tendency for the "above average" operators to be a little more calm, confident, and psychologically fit than the others. It is necessary to remember the the total sample consisted of people who were unusually competent and well adjusted.

Continuing the search for markers that might indicate the existence of a select few who are capable of carrying out acts of exceptional courage that distinguish them from their fellow operators, we carried out separate analyses of decorated operators, and of equally experienced and competent operators who were not decorated. To our surprise, we came across a feature that distinguished the operators who had received decorations for gallantry.

The decorated operators were found to be slightly but significantly superior in all-round psychological health and bodily fitness. They said that they felt well in their bodies and were mentally fit and alert, even to a greater degree than their colleagues who had also scored above civilian norms. The characteristic opposite to that reported by the decorated soldiers is described as "hypochondriasis" (a subscale of a widely used personality test, the Cattell 16PF test), and on this scale most of the decorated operators returned zero scores. They had no bodily or mental complaints at all. It should be emphasized that all of this psychometric information had been collected well before the operators went on operations and well before the decorations were awarded.

Most of the evidence that we gathered points to the overwhelming importance of training, group cohesion, and situational determinants,[31] but the findings on the decorated group of operators began to suggest that individual characteristics may make some contribution to the execution of acts of bravery. There are perhaps courageous actors as well as courageous acts.

THE TRAINING AND PERFORMANCE OF BOMB-DISPOSAL OPERATORS

In a study of the effects of training we found clear evidence of a substantial increase in skill and confidence after completion of the specialized course.[32] The value of the training course is emphasized by the finding that after completing it, the novices (that is, those who had not yet carried out a tour of duty as a bomb-disposal operator) expressed approximately 80 percent of the confidence of the experienced operators. To put it another way, the training course succeeded in taking them 80 percent of the way to that combination of confidence and competence that makes a successful operator. The specific value of the training is evident from the fact that before entering the course, soldiers with previous military experience in Northern Ireland unrelated to bomb-disposal duties had as little confidence in their ability to deal with explosive devices as soldiers who had never served in Northern Ireland.

Our next investigation dealt with the adjustment and performance of the operators during a tour of duty in Northern Ireland. The most important fact is that almost all of them performed their duties successfully and without problems. They quickly adapted to the dangers of the work, despite that fact that most of them had to live and work under confined and cramped, improvised conditions.[33]

The process of adaptation was accelerated once the operator successfully carried out his first operation on a genuine device. Experience of dealing with false alarms or hoaxes made no contribution to either their confidence or their competence, but once the inexperienced operators successfully dealt with a genuine explosive device, their confidence and competence quickly rose to a level close to that of the experienced operators. Most of the operators reported feeling calm for much of the 4-month tour. Seven of the 20 operators reported no fear at any time; the fearless ones. Four of the 20 had a great deal of fear and can be described as courageous performers. In general, there was a close correspondence between the ratings of self-efficacy and reported fear, but exceptions were encountered. A few operators maintained high self-efficacy ratings during the tour, but nevertheless reported very large fluctuations in the level of their fear.

The percentage of fearless operators is higher than that reported by the U.S. airmen who participated in a study of combat fears; only 1 percent experienced no fear during combat.[34] In a comparable study by Hastings[35] and his colleagues, 6 percent of the airmen were fearless. Reports from infantry soldiers indicate similarly low proportions of fearless people, but 26 percent of 105 paratroop trainees were classified as fearless.[36] Having experienced some fear while flying aircraft, the Mercury astronauts were almost free of fear during their trips in space, even in the most uncertain and dangerous parts of their adventure. There was no evidence of fear before the space flights. The evidence of fearless performances accumulates. Do some people display fearless behavior consistently?

CHAPTER

THE GENERALITY OF FEARLESSNESS AND COURAGE

Having discovered that the decorated bomb-disposal operators rated their mental and physical health even more favorably than their equally competent and stable but non-decorated colleagues rated their own health, we decided to test the generality of this finding. In particular, we wished to determine whether operators who had been decorated for acts of gallantry would perform and react differently to their non-decorated colleagues when given a stressful laboratory task. The operators were required to make increasingly difficult auditory discriminations while under threat of shock for making errors. By correctly moving a lever to the left or right in response to an auditory signal, they were able to avoid the shock; during the final two phases of the test the auditory discrimination task was insoluble.

The comparison between the decorated and the non-decorated operators was the core of the study, but we also used the opportunity to test a few civilians and recently trained young soldiers. The subjective and psychophysiological reactions of the seven decorated operators were compared to those of seven equally experienced and successful but non-decorated bomb-disposal operators. The decorated subjects maintained a lower heart rate when making difficult discriminations under threat of shock. There were no differences between the groups on their subjective reactions or on their behavioral responses.[1] Both of these groups of operators showed significantly less fear and physiological reactivity than the civilians, and less fear than the young soldiers. The idea of a link between courage/fear and the heart is expressed in everyday terms, such as "lion-hearted" and "faint-hearted," and the word "courage" is derived from *cor*, Latin for "heart."

It remains to be determined whether the stable physiological pattern identified in this experiment is attributable to military training or to constitutional factors or both. The psychophysiological difference between the decorated and non-decorated operators is unlikely to be the result solely of military training, as they shared the same training. On the other hand, the non-decorated operators and the recently trained young soldiers showed less cardiac acceleration than the civilians, and this may point to a contribution of (military) training for coping with stress. As in the psychometric study of the distinction between courageous actors and courageous acts, the experimental investigation showed that the decorated and non-decorated operators have a great deal in common, but a difference can be found.

As the observed difference was so particular and had not been specifically predicted, a replication was necessary. Twenty-four operators were asked to participate in a very close copy of the original experiment. All soldiers who had taken part in the previous study were excluded. The fresh group of eight decorated operators had all received the George Medal or the Queen's Medal for Gallantry. A matched group of eight non-decorated operators was drawn at random from the same pool, and a third group of eight young RAOC technicians who had no operational experience was included for a second comparison. The results of the original experiment, showing lower cardiac reactivity under stress among the decorated operators, was replicated.[2] With minor exceptions, no group differences in subjective reactions or behavioral performance were

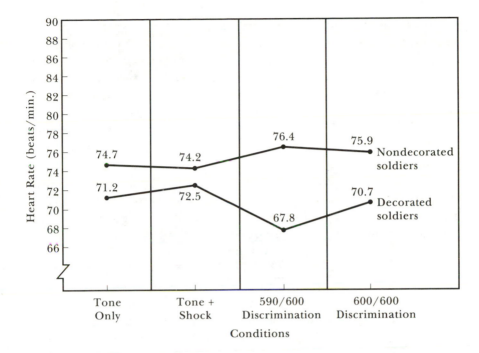

Figure 5 *The heart rate of decorated and non-decorated bomb-disposal operators during a laboratory stress test (Cox et al., 1983. Reprinted with permission of British Journal of Psychology.)*

found. These results strengthen the view that it may indeed be possible to identify psychophysiological indices of fearlessness/courage.

FALKLANDS VETERANS

Is this low responsiveness to stress confined to decorated bomb-disposal operators? In an attempt to find out whether this psychophysiological pattern can be identified in other groups, the study was replicated on 34 members of the Parachute Regiment who were veterans of the Falklands War. Sixteen had received decorations, either for a particular act of bravery or for generally outstanding behavior while on active service in the Falklands. The 18 non-decorated veterans were matched in terms of age and experience, and had all performed well on active service.

This time, we could find no difference between decorated and non-decorated soldiers. We therefore combined the two groups and compared their data to that obtained from the bomb-disposal operators. The heart rate under stress of the Falklands veterans was initially similar to that of the non-decorated bomb-disposal operators, but as the stress was increased, their cardiac reactivity resembled that of the decorated operators. Overall, the psychophysiological reactivity of the decorated and non-decorated members of the Parachute Regiment approximated that of the *decorated* bomb-disposal operators. Furthermore, the paratroops reported significantly less subjective anxiety before and during the stress test than had the bomb-disposal operators. The difference between these veteran paratroopers and the bomb-disposal operators may be a product of selection and training.[3] The training of bomb-disposal operators emphasizes technical skill,[4] and the men are trained to carry out defensive duties, whereas the paratroopers are trained to be aggressive. They accept their role as an elite force and know that they may be called upon to conduct offensive operations in which the likelihood of casualities is high.

These laboratory investigations provide some evidence to support the argument that it is possible to identify a group of people who are capable of carrying out courageous/fearless acts and who also show a muted psychophysiological reaction when subjected to stress under controlled conditions. There is also evidence that they report an optimal level of functioning on self-report tests of mental and physical well-being. They appear to be unusually resilient. Evidence of cross-situational consistency in fearless/courageous behavior is beginning to emerge.

COURAGEOUS OR FEARLESS?

In order to pursue the viability of making a distinction between courage and fearlessness, we carried out a study of 105 recruits to the Parachute Regiment who were about to undergo parachute training.[5] Self-report measures were obtained prior to undertaking the training and again at the conclusion of the course, which they all completed successfully. A cluster analysis was carried out on 14 variables, and a three-part solution emerged. The first cluster encompassed two-thirds of the sample; the recruits in this group expressed moderate optimism and moderate fear but nevertheless performed successfully. They formed a group described as courageous performers, who persevere despite the presence of fear.

One-quarter of the sample fitted into the second cluster, described as the fearless performers. These soldiers were optimistic and confident, and they anticipated and reported very low levels of fear. The third cluster, comprising 7.5 percent of the paratroop recruits, was unexpected. The members of this group underpredicted how frightened they would be during the jumping and also underestimated how dangerous they would find the tasks. This small minority was described as "over-confident".

The fearless performers reported very little fear (14/100) during the jumping, compared with scores of 41 in the courageous group and 50 in the over-confident group. The fearless performers also had significantly lower scores on the hypochondriasis scale that distinguished the decorated from the non-decorated bomb-disposal operators. On this measure, the fearless paratroops scored 0.7, which was significantly lower than the already very low scores reported by the other two clusters of paratroops. Additionally, the soldiers in the fearless group were significantly more confident than the other two and rated the task as being less dangerous than did members of the other two groups. Their actual scores are worth recording—they were 96 percent confident of their ability to jump satisfactorily, and the dangerousness of jumping was rated at 20 on a 100 scale (versus 50 by the overconfident jumpers). The courageous operators predicted that they would be moderately fearful, and were; confidence in their ability to jump satisfactorily was 58 percent before the training and rose to 80 percent after completion of the jumping. They rated the training as being slightly more dangerous than expected. During the jumping, they reported a moderate amount of unpleasant bodily symptoms, at a level that was significantly higher than the fearless jumpers.

The results of this study, viewed in the light of the earlier research, encourage the idea that a distinction can be made between fearless and courageous performers and that classifications based on this distinction are associated with the quality of performance of a demanding and dangerous task. It remains to be seen whether this type of classification is predictive of future conduct, and that question is now under investigation.

CAN COURAGE BE ACQUIRED?

Before turning to the implications of these findings on courageous and fearless actors, we can attempt a reply to the second question put by Socrates. Yes, it is possible for people to attain the noble quality of courage by study and training. A particularly apt example is provided by the specialized training given to the members of the Royal Army Ordnance Corps, which enables the great majority of operators to perform a perilous task successfully. There is now some evidence of a constitutional contribution to courageous or fearless conduct, but this does not overshadow the findings that point to the great value of adequate training (for example, the experienced operators were less fearful and less responsive to stress than the untrained soldiers and considerably less frightened than the civilians). The most impressive piece of evidence of the value of training arises from the justified assumption that any member of the Ordnance Corps can carry out bomb-disposal duties once he has specialized training. As discussed in the previous chapter, several factors contribute to the performance of courageous or fearless acts. The appropriate skill required for dealing with a dangerous situation serves to increase courage, as does a general sense of self-confidence. Situational demands and support from a cohesive group also play their part. Specific training, the provision of coping models, and the support of a small and familiar cohesive group are conditions that can be relied upon to promote courageous behavior.

Young men, and not only young men, can be trained to attain the noble quality and perform courageously. The provision of graded realistic training designed to promote the required skills and to increase the person's self-confidence is a dependable way of promoting courageous behavior. The execution of courageous acts will be enhanced by the support of a tightly integrated, familiar, small group of people. We can also give a partial answer to a question that Socrates never asked. There is a small group of people who are particularly well suited to the performance of dangerous or difficult tasks by virtue of their relative fearlessness.

ARE BOMB-DISPOSAL OPERATORS PSYCHOPATHIC?

In passing, it is worth mentioning that contrary to speculation, there is no evidence to suggest that bomb-disposal operators are "psychopathic." To the contrary, their psychometric results show the 200+ RAOC operators were emotionally stable, and the overwhelming majority were classified as being free of any psychological abnormality by the interviewing psychiatrist. Moreover, many of them were engaged in socially responsible activities. As described earlier, the operators who received awards for courageous/fearless behavior were, like their fellow operators, free of psychological abnormalities or anti-social propensities. Most of them had lasting and satisfactory relationships with other people.

The Cleckley checklist[6] of the characteristics of psychopaths, which forms the basis for most descriptions of psychopathy, includes adjectives such as "irresponsible" and "impulsive," and these certainly do not describe the characteristics of the operators.[7] The criteria for diagnosing psychopathy on the DSM-IIIR system do not apply to the bomb-disposal operators who formed the sample for these studies. Lastly, the bomb-disposal operators showed only small to moderate responses when subjected to stress,[8] whereas psychopaths are responsive to stress and obtain high scores on measures of neurotic behavior.[9]

One should guard against assuming an identity between bomb-disposal operators and psychopaths on the specious grounds of a common characteristic of fearlessness. As a group, psychopaths are neurotic rather than fearless and are not hypo-responsive to stress. The hypo-responsive decorated operators included courageous as well as fearless performers. Finally, the large majority of operators were well adjusted, socially responsible, and capable of establishing satisfactory emotional relationships.

IS OPTIMISM A PRECONDITION FOR COURAGEOUS BEHAVIOR?

The apathy and docility displayed by many victims of air raids requires consideration. In 1941, Vernon noted a connection between lethargy and pessimism, and said that among the victims "there is widespread lethargy and lack of energy even after lost sleep has been made up, and pessimistic feelings of the future."[10] This and other descriptions of the "negative" behavior of the victims suggests that they might have been displaying depressive reactions, and therefore Seligman's revised theory of depression might be a useful tool for examining the matter.[11] Having argued that pessimism promotes depression, Seligman has now proposed that optimism promotes courage.[12] He goes further and postulates that optimism is a pre-condition for courage.

According to Seligman's theory, a pessimistic explanatory style predisposes a person to depression. The main proposition is that if a person habitually finds internal, stable, and global causes for adverse events, he or she will tend to become depressed when adverse events occur.[13] Some of the consequences of depression undermine courage. Depression, it is said, "reduces voluntary response initiation, and this vitiates a major precondition for courage."[14] The passivity that Seligman believes may undermine courage was a prominent feature of these victims.

The introduction of Seligman's revised theory to the study of fear and courage is refreshing, and some information can be enlisted to encourage this expansion. For example, the idea that an optimistic explanatory style predicts courage is supported indirectly by studies of courageous soldiers. The trainee paratroopers who were most optimistic about how they would perform during the training course expected to experience little or no fear. These optimistic expectations were reinforced because in the event they reported little fear. The second cluster of trainees, comprising two-thirds of the sample, expressed moderate optimism and experienced slight to moderate fear. Incidentally, the results of this study also point to the risks of being over-optimistic, for the 7.5 percent of the recruits who overestimated how well they would manage the training, the third cluster, showed the greatest fear and a significant decrease in confidence by the end of the training. Other examples of the positive relationship between optimism and fearlessness/courage were found in studies of bomb-disposal operators.

The application of Seligman's theory to information about the effects of air raids is less promising. It is difficult to reconcile the view that passivity undermines courage with the description of the (passive, lethargic) victims of air raids as "courageous." Certainly these people showed remarkably little fear despite being attacked repeatedly. Is it possible that they were both courageous *and* passive? If they were, how can this be reconciled with the claims that passivity undermines courage?

As the occurrence of passivity among victims is undisputed, we need to reconsider whether or not their behavior is correctly interpreted as courageous. The view promoted in this book is that courage is best construed as perseverance in the presence of a threat, despite one's fear. As most of the victims displayed relatively little fear, perhaps the best solution is to interpret their behavior as fearless—and lethargic, perhaps depressed. Might this be an example, writ large, of the idea that "sorrow casts out all fears"?

This idea is plausible, but it presumes that apathy and docility necessarily indicate the presence of depression. Depression often produces lethargy, but not all instances of lethargy are indicative of depression. So if we accept Seligman's argument that voluntary response initiation is a precondition for courage, we might end up by excluding the victims of air raids other than the active and remarkably fear-resistant air-raid workers, firemen, nurses, and so on.

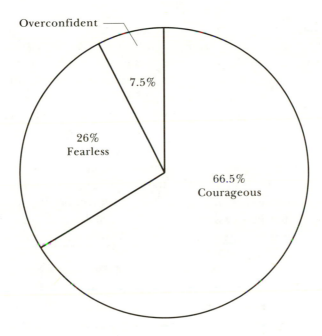

Figure 6 *The results from recruits undergoing parachute training formed three clusters: courageous, fearful, and overconfident performers (Macmillan and Rachman, 1988, p. 376. Reprinted with permission of Pergamon Press.)*

The victims of the air raids endured far more than they initiated. Are we correct in withholding the interpretation that they behaved courageously, or more accurately, fearlessly, because of their passivity? They showed little fear and they persisted. Other examples that would have to be excluded are instances of passive resistance, such as that used by exponents of Gandhian tactics and contemporary dissidents, some of whom have endured prolonged imprisonment and torture with little or no fear. Unyielding passive resistance can be courageous or fearless.

In recognition of the occurrence of "passive courage" and "passive fearlessness," it seems that voluntary response initiation may not be a precondition, but rather a facilitator, of courage. This interpretation leaves open the possibility that in instances of passive courage/fearlessness, we see the operation of optimism, but it is an optimism that is not or cannot be translated into voluntary response initiation. We should also avoid the mistake of restricting the term "voluntary response initiation" to observable physical acts. Dissidents such as Sharansky "passively" endured torture but nevertheless initiated and persisted in bold, defiant, and vigorous mental resistance and attack.[15] In a final act of resistance, shortly before his release, he defiantly rejected his captors' orders to walk in a direct straight line, by taking a zig-zag path to the waiting vehicle.

Optimism probably does promote courageous behavior but it need not take the form of voluntary response initiation in the sense of voluntary physical acts. There is passive courage and passive fearlessness, and we need to learn what part an optimistic explanatory style plays in the promotion of these acts, as well as in more obvious expressions of fearlessness and courage.

The fear-preventing effects of activity, especially those of a socially responsible character, can be understood in Seligman's terms. If passivity undermines courage, presumably activity can promote it. Activities that can be interpreted in a positive, internal, and stable fashion will help to promote an optimistic explanatory style. Optimistic people are "more likely to take bold action when stressed."[16]

In summary, the application of the revised theory to courage is consistent with some of our knowledge about courageous military behavior and gives rise to some new possibilities, for example, on the relationship on optimism and bold actions. However, the theory manages less well in dealing with behavior that we will now have to describe as "passive courage" and "passive fearlessness." These concepts require a more complex analysis. In reply to the opening question, it is not possible to confirm that optimism is a precondition for courage—but it probably helps.

CONCLUDING OBSERVATIONS

The research on bomb-disposal operators, attack troops, and trainee paratroops arose from an application of the three-systems concept of fear, according to which fear is best construed as a set of loosely coupled components. When the behavioral component of fear changes desynchronously in relation to the other two components, the result can be interpreted as courage. Persistence in dealing with a dangerous situation despite subjective and physical signs of fear is regarded as courageous; the person's behavior advances beyond his subjective behavior. People who continue to approach a dangerous situation without experiencing subjective fear or unpleasant bodily reactions are showing a concordance of the three components that defines fearless behavior. As described earlier, competence and confidence contribute to courageous performance, and both are strengthened by repeated and successful practice. In the early stages of training people to perform courageously, success is more likely if the person's motivation is raised. Raising someone's motivation helps him or her to persevere, even in the face of subjective apprehension. It follows that courageous behavior that is particularly subject to (changeable) motivational and situational influences is likely to be less consistent than fearless behavior.

In addition to competence and confidence, situational demands contribute to the execution of courageous acts, and these include the facilitative roles of courageous models and social cohesiveness. That minority of people who remain hypo-responsive under stress are less vulnerable and better equipped to carry out dangerous acts. They probably carry out a disproportionately large number of fearless acts.

We are not yet in a position to attach weights to each factor, but at present it seems that the factors of confidence, competence, and demand make the greatest contribution to courageous performance. Hyporesponsiveness to stress is postulated to play a major part in fearless acts but falls short of being a necessary condition. Situational demands and confidence are thought to be important determinants of fearless behavior.

The successful practice of courageous behavior leads to a decrease in subjective fear and finally to a state of fearlessness. Courage grows into fearlessness. People who are learning to parachute from an aircraft display courage when they persevere with their jumps despite subjective fear. Veteran parachutists, having successfully habituated to the situation, no longer experience fear when jumping; they have moved from courage to fearlessness.

The research on courage has some practice implications. The results emphasize the continuity of behavior: fear, and acts of courage are not confined to selected groups of people. Extreme fear is not necessarily a form of pathology, and all people are capable of courageous actions, including the most fearful of us. People are far more resilient than our theories have implied, and even fearful neurotic patients do not lack the potential for courageous behavior. Having several strong fears need not set a person apart from others, and it does not preclude the acquisition of skills to deal with fear. It does not preclude the performance of courageous acts.

CONCLUSION

———◆———

CHAPTER

THE VIEW
AHEAD

Significant advances were made in the past decade, and
now we are in a period of accelerated growth, characterized by ferment
rather than completeness. New information about fear and courage was
collected, some extremely promising new ideas were introduced, some
old ideas were revivified, and steady progress was made in refining and
extending the range of the methods for reducing fear. However, there is a
sense of incompleteness; we still have no strong theory to explain how
fears are reduced, and the prospect of formulating a unifying theory of
fear-reduction seems remote.

The influence of cognitive explanations has grown and now dominates
the subject of fear. Cognitive factors are thought to play a role in the

acquisition of fear, and in its reduction. The cognitive theory of panic is the best established and has generated a promising form of treatment. It is the dominant psychological alternative to the biological explanation of panic. The current debate between the psychological and biological explanations of panic is important in its own right and because it is the subject of a clash between two powerful paradigms of psychopathology. The resolution of this great debate, which should take place within the next few years, will have wide and lasting implications for our conception of abnormal behavior and experiences. It promises to be an exciting intellectual event.

The growth of cognitive explanations was stimulated by dissatisfaction with the limitations of conditioning theory, and the matter appeared to have been resolved. It was agreed that some, perhaps many, fears are acquired by a process of conditioning, but the explanation had to be stretched to accommodate the vicarious acquisition of fear, and it could not encompass fears that are acquired by the provision of information. The emergence of fears even in the absence of a close temporal association between the feared stimulus and an aversive event was an embarrassment. This obstacle and some others were eliminated when the revised view of conditioning was introduced. The new view is stimulating and has led to the discovery of interesting new phenomena. The full implications of the revision are not yet visible, but it is unlikely that a comprehensive theory of fear will emerge from the ashes. However, we are certain to benefit from an enlargement of research on the subject. It will add new and unexpected information and contribute to an improved understanding of fear phenomena. Oddly, at present the revision promises to explain too much, and the limits of the new concept of conditioning will need to be determined. Some effects must be forbidden.

The idea that there are three pathways to fear remains plausible and has gathered support in the past decade. The concept of a vicarious pathway has been strengthened by some clinical findings and by outstanding research on fear acquisition in monkeys. This research opens the door to a greatly improved method for studying the idea of prepared phobias. We can expect rapid progress as soon as the new approach is adopted, and my expectation is that the main hypothesis, that we are predisposed to acquire fears to particular stimuli, will be confirmed.

A subtle and important change has occurred in our analyses of certain human fears, such as agoraphobia. The earlier view, that people fear open spaces, or closed spaces, has been replaced by the idea that in these and other instances, the person is fearful of what might happen to him or her in these places. They are not frightened of supermarkets, but they *are* frightened of what might happen to them *in* a supermarket—and therefore avoid visiting it. This revised view is more accurate and has had important clinical and theoretical consequences. The shift away from regarding the physical stimulus or place as that which is feared toward regarding the person's appraisal and predictions of fear as the key features of fear, coincided with and was supported by the growing influence of cognitive explanations. Fresh interpretations will be made of the other objects of our fears, and the present analyses of claustrophobia and "blood phobia" are a move in that direction.

More precise analyses of what exactly it is that we fear are bound to make easier the task of finding an explanation for our success in reducing fears. For example, an explanation of therapeutic success in reducing agoraphobia that rests on the belief that the patients are fearful of supermarkets is bound to be off-target. At best, it might explain why they no longer fear the context in which they were frightened. The new analyses of fear are most compatible with cognitive explanations of fear reduction, and much progress can be expected. The cognitive theories also play a valuable role in generating methods of fear reduction that promise greater precision and success. The best example is the cognitive theory of panic, which virtually prescribes the content and format of a method for reducing panic. Its precision is as attractive as the prediction that the method deduced from the theory should produce a complete solution. At the end of a competently conducted course of therapy, the patient should be free of panic.

The apparently simple connection between fear and avoidance has turned out to be a little more complex than was originally believed. The idea that fear is the decisive causal factor in avoidance appeared to cover the ground, but then discordances between fear and avoidance were encountered, and it was shown that avoidance can persist long after the disappearance of the fear. At present, we tend to construe avoidance as the result of several factors, among which the person's prediction of fear is the dominant influence. A person is likely to continue avoiding a place or object as long as it is predictive of fear or other aversiveness. Signals that predict fear are avoided and signals that predict safety are approached. There are circumstances, such as an over-riding need, in which a person will persist in approaching a frightening place or object.

Persistence despite fear is the core definition of courage and is distinguished from fearlessness. Several studies of soldiers have been added to the existing information about civilian courage during wartime and the courage shown by fearful patients. The results confirm the view that people are considerably more resilient than was implied in all psychological theories. Given thorough training and close support, people can carry out perilous tasks with success. With repeated successes, courage turns into fearlessness. Experimental findings on decorated bomb-disposal operators raise the possibility that certain people are particularly well suited, by virtue of their low responsiveness to stress, to carry out hazardous tasks. The information about courage that has been gathered so far is consistent and reassuring but constitutes no more than a beginning. There is a need to balance our interest in fear with greater consideration of courage.

NOTES

CHAPTER 1 Human Fears

1. E.g., Rachman and Lopatka, 1986a,b; Ost, 1989.

2. E.g., Barlow, 1988; Marks, 1987a; Mathews, Gelder, and Johnston, 1981; Masters et al., 1987; Michelson, 1986, 1988; O'Leary and Wilson, 1987; Rachman and Wilson, 1980; Wilson, 1982, 1986.

3. The works of Gray (1971, 1982) and Mackintosh (1980, 1982) are admirable guides to this research.

4. Rachman, 1978.

5. Ibid.

6. Clark, 1985, 1988.

7. Bandura, 1977a, p. 78.

8. Paul, 1966, pp. 61–64.

9. Lang, in Levis (Ed.), 1970.

10. Lang, Melamed, and Hart, 1970.

11. Leitenberg et al., 1971.

12. Hepner and Cauthen, 1975.

13. McCutcheon and Adams, 1975; Suarez, Adams, and McCutcheon, 1976.

14. Examples of desynchrony, in which subjective fear failed to correlate with the other components, are given by Hersen et al. (1973). Patterns of concordance and of

synchrony–desynchrony in agoraphobia are lucidly discussed by Michelson; patterns of discordance are set out by Lader and Marks; and Borkovec, Werts, and Bernstein have provided a useful analysis of the methodological and measurement problems.

15. See also Barlow, 1988; Barlow et al., 1980, pp. 441–448; Craske and Craig, 1984, pp. 267–280; and Vermilyea et al., 1984, 1984, pp. 615–621.

16. Michelson, in Michelson and Ascher (Eds.), 1988. Lader and Marks, 1971; see also Hodgson and Rachman, and Rachman and Hodgson, 1974; Borkovec, Weerts, and Bernstein, in Ciminero et al. (Eds.), 1976.

17. Rachman and Hodgson, 1974.

18. Craske and Craig, 1984; Michelson and Mavissakalian, 1985; Sartory et al., 1977.

19. Ibid., p. 267.

20. See also, Sartory, Rachman, and Grey, 1977.

21. Matias and Turner, 1986.

22. Fenz and Epstein, 1967.

23. Hodgson and Rachman, 1974.

24. Sartory, Rachman, and Grey, 1977.

25. Barlow et al., 1980.

26. See the review by Ost, in Magnusson and Ohman (Eds.), 1987.

27. Ost, Jerremalm, and Johansson, 1981; Ost, Johansson, and Jerremalm, 1982.

28. Ost, Jerremalm, and Jannson, 1984.

29. Haug et al., 1987.

30. Mackay and Liddell, 1988.

31. Norton and Johnson, 1983.

32. Jerremalm et al., 1986.

33. Michelson, 1986.

34. Ibid., p. 273.

35. Ibid., p. 270.

36. Mathews, 1971; Lang, Melamed, and Hart, 1970; Sartory, Rachman, and Grey, 1977.

37. Rachman, 1978.

38. Hugdahl, 1981.

39. Barlow, 1988.

40. Seligman, 1975, p. 9. A revised, extended version of the learned helplessness theory was published by Abramson, Seligman, and Teasdale in 1978. In this complex

development, the person's attribution of the cause of the uncontrollability is given a central position. Comprehensive reviews were published in 1984 by Peterson and Seligman and in 1987 by Seligman and Nolen-Hoeksema.

41. Ibid., p. 16.

42. Ibid., p. 56.

43. Ibid., p. 99.

44. For exceptions, see Miller and Seligman, 1976.

45. See also Mineka and Kihlstrom, 1978; Mineka, in Overmier and Brush (Eds.), 1986; and Mineka, in Maser and Tuma (Eds.), 1985.

46. Rachman, in Rachman and Maser (Eds.), 1988; Rachman and Bichard, 1988.

47. Barlow, D. April, 1988.

48. These ideas have something in common with Bandura's theory in which he argues that perceived self-efficacy is the main basis for behavioral change. However, Bandura emphasizes the specificity of the person's estimation of efficacy (e.g., Can I deal with this particular threat in these specific circumstances?). The theory has been the subject of considerable discussion (see for example, Rachman [Ed.], 1978) and is described in Chapter 15.

CHAPTER 2   Fear Under Air Attack

1. Vernon, 1941.

2. Rickman, 1938.

3. Vernon, op. cit., p. 463.

4. Stengel, 1946.

5. Janis, 1951, p. 99.

6. Ibid., p. 83.

7. Selections from *London War Notes*, 1939–1945 by Mollie Panter-Downes. Copyright © 1939, 1940, 1941, 1942, 1943, 1944, 1945, 1971, by Mollie Panter-Downes. Copyright renewed 1967, 1968, 1969, 1970, 1971, 1972, 1973 by Mollie Panter-Downes. This material appeared originally in *The New Yorker*. Reprinted with the permission of Farrar, Strauss & Giroux, Inc.

8. Ibid.

9. Vernon, 1941, p. 459.

10. Ibid., p. 460.

11. Ibid., p. 474.

12. Wilson, 1942, p. 284.

13. Aubrey Lewis, 1942, p. 179.

14. Ibid., p. 179.

15. Ibid., p. 181.

16. Saigh, 1985, pp. 679–682; 1984, pp. 185–190. See also reports from Northern Ireland, e.g., Cairns and Wilson, 1984.

17. Saigh, 1988.

18. Milgram, in Goldberger and Breznitz (Eds.), 1982, p. 658.

19. Ibid., p. 662.

20. Janis, 1951, p. 87.

21. Ibid., p. 92.

22. Ibid., p. 93.

23. Solomon, 1942.

24. Janis, op. cit., p. 94.

25. Janis, op. cit., p. 65.

26. Ibid., p. 111. In this connection, it is of great interest that being wounded or injured did not increase fear (see also ibid., p. 124). The data on reactions to air attacks contain no direct and full comparison of the fears of injured versus uninjured victims, but the number of physical injuries greatly exceeds the number of psychological breakdowns. The case histories of bomb-phobic patients contain very few references to the occurrence of physical wounds or injuries, and RAF pilots who were wounded or injured were not more reluctant than their uninjured colleagues to return to combat; they did not display greater avoidance behavior. The apparent absence of a direct relationship between injury and fear is also contra the conditioning theory.

27. Ibid., p. 111.

28. Ibid., p. 113.

29. Janis, op. cit., p. 114.

30. Rachman and Levitt, 1988.

31. Janis, p. 114.

32. Ibid., p. 114.

33. MacCurdy, 1943.

34. Janis, op. cit., p. 120.

35. Gal and Lazarus, 1975. They argued persuasively that activity is adaptive in stressful situations. Activities that bear on the source of the stress may generate mastery or a sense of control, and activities that are not relevant to the stress may nevertheless be beneficial insofar as they are distracting.

36. Rakos and Schroeder, 1976.

37. Rachman, 1979.

38. Janis, op. cit., p. 124.

39. Rachman and Bichard, 1988.

40. M. Seligman, 1975; and Seligman and Nolen-Hoeksema, 1987.

41. Vernon, 1941, p. 467.

42. Janis, op. cit., p. 88.

43. Seligman, 1971.

CHAPTER 3 **Fear in Combat**

1. Shaffer, 1947, p. 143.

2. Flanagan, USAAF Aviation Psychology Research Report No. 1, 1948, p. 207. The 17 volumes of this series contain a large amount of important psychological information, ranging from fear and courage in combat to sophisticated analyses of psychomotor behavior. The psychologists recruited by Flanagan and his colleagues were unusually talented, and many of them went on to make distinguished contributions to civilian psychology. They included Bijou, Ghiselli, Irion, Jensen, Neal Miller, Rotter, and others. In Britain, a comparably distinguished group of psychologists contributed to the RAF and included Bartlett, Vernon, Mackworth, Craik, Russell Davis, Oldfield, and Drew. The information on fear, much of it gathered by questionnaire and interview methods, was subject to distortion by the pervasive social pressures that endorsed courageous behavior. On the other hand, most of the material was provided anonymously, and for the first time in military history, troops were given permission, and on occasion encouragement, to admit their fears and discuss them with their officers, and with inquisitive, jumped-up army psychologists. The collection of data on RAF crews, published by Dearnaley and Warr (1980) also contains much useful information.

3. Reid, in Dearnaley and Warr (Eds.), 1980.

4. Stafford Clark, 1949, p. 13.

5. Flanagan, 1948, p. 208.

6. Shaffer, op. cit.

7. There are several reports of the importance of knowing how long one will have to endure fear, discomfort, or danger. People apparently prefer to know how long they will have to endure such unpleasantness, and uncertainty probably inflates the aversiveness of potentially unpleasant experiences. The apparent value of knowing the duration of an aversive experience may be linked to the operation of safety signals, indicators of a period of freedom from aversive stimulation (see p. 273). The pacifying effects of prior knowledge about the duration of the aversive event might result from the anticipation of a safety signal. If so, the pacifying effects of known durations should show some of the characteristics of safety signals, for instance, they should have strong incentive value.

8. See Grinker and Spiegel, 1945.

9. Lidz, 1946.

10. Seligman, 1975; Seligman and Nolan-Hoeksema, 1987.

11. Shaffer, op. cit., p. 131.

12. Harold Macmillan, 1966.

13. Grinker and Spiegel, op. cit., p. 67.

14. Ibid., 1945, p. 54.

15. Seligman, op. cit., 1975.

16. Stouffer et al., 1949. This work, carried out on many thousands of U.S. troops during World War II, includes over 200 surveys and is published in four volumes. From this mass of data, I have attempted to extract the findings that are relevant to the subject of fear. In order to simplify the exposition, I have not maintained the authors' careful distinctions between army units, between officers and men, between theaters of campaign and so on, unless the distinctions are of importance for the point in question.

17. Hastings, Wright, and Glueck, 1944.

18. Ibid., p. 153.

19. Lepley, 1947, pp. 197–198.

20. Wickert, 1947, p. 121.

21. Hallam, in Rachman (Ed.), 1983. See also Davis's conclusion that among RAF aircrew, there was a "weighty . . . absence of association between the psychiatrists' grades of predisposition . . . and the occurrence of accidents," Davis, 1948, p. 30.

22. Wickert, 1947, p. 186.

23. Shaffer, 1947, p. 249.

24. Stouffer et al., op. cit.

25. Ibid., p. 173.

26. Flanagan, 1948.

27. Dollard, 1944.

28. Shaffer, op. cit., pp. 130–131.

29. See the analysis by Bandura, 1977a. See also Chapter 14.

30. Stouffer et al., op. cit.

31. *Social Learning Theory* (1977a), and Bandura (1977b).

32. Stouffer et al., op. cit., p. 22.

33. Cox and Rachman, in Rachman (Ed.), 1983.

34. Macmillan and Rachman, 1988.

35. Rachman (Ed.), 1983.

36. Shaffer, op. cit., p. 249.

37. Korchin and Ruff, in G. Grosser et al. (Eds.), 1964.

39. Shaffer, op. cit., p. 136.

CHAPTER 4   **Influences on Fear in Combat**

1. Stouffer et al., 1949, pp. 80–82.

2. Reid, in Dearnaley and Warr (Eds.), 1980, p. 3.

3. Stouffer, op. cit., p. 407.

4. Symonds and Williams, in Dearnaley and Warr (Eds.), 1980.

5. Stouffer et al., op. cit., 1949.

6. Shils and Janowitz, 1948.

7. Dollard, 1944. This short report proved to be influential and provided a basis for parts of the extensive research into fear that was carried out by teams of psychologists during World War II.

8. Stouffer et al., op. cit., p. 1107.

9. Wickert, Ed., 1947, p. 134.

10. Dollard, op. cit., p. 28.

11. Wickert, op. cit., p. 134.

12. Clark, in Rachman and Maser (Eds.).

13. George, 1967.

14. Wickert, op. cit., p. 134.

15. Flanagan, 1947, p. 17.

16. Hastings, Wright and Glueck, 1944; and L. Shaffer, 1947.

17. Rachman (Ed.), 1983.

18. Shils and Janowitz, 1948.

19. Marshall, 1963, p. 72.

20. MacMillan, 1966, pp. 89–90.

21. The fearless subgroup of bomb-disposal operators of the Royal Army Ordnance Corps, described in Chapter 21, could provide examples.

22. Symonds and Williams, op. cit., p. 20.

23. Stouffer et al., op. cit., 1949.

24. Dollard, 1944.

25. Bandura, 1969; 1977.

26. Stouffer et al., op. cit., p. 125.

27. Bandura, 1969; 1977.

28. Mineka and Kihlstrom, 1978; Seligman, 1975, 1984, 1987.

29. Stouffer et al., op. cit.

30. Stouffer et al., op. cit., p. 345.

31. Ibid., p. 408.

32. Ibid., p. 409. Also, relatively passive radar-observers reported more fear during dangerous flight activities, such as night landings on an aircraft carrier, than did the pilots of the aircraft (Ritter et al., 1970, p. 587). This well-chosen and interesting comparison of the fear reported by active and relatively passive fliers in the same two-seater aeroplane is consistent with the idea that control helps to inhibit fear.

33. Rachman (Ed.), 1983.

34. Flanagan, op. cit., p. 135. See also Gal and Lazarus, 1975.

35. Hastings et al., 1944.

36. Stouffer et al., op. cit., 1949, p. 83.

CHAPTER 5 **Varieties of Fear**

1. Agras, Sylvester, and Oliveau, 1969.

2. Ibid, p. 156. The results of a recent survey carried out on over 2000 people confirm the common occurrence of significant fears in the general population, leading the author to conclude that anxiety in the community is "poorly recognized and treated" (Wittchen, 1988, p. 15). See also Bourdon et al., 1988.

3. Costello, 1982. Thousands of people have been studied in recent population surveys designed to obtain estimates of mental health in the community (Bourdon et al., 1988; Wittchen, 1988).

4. Mathews, 1978.

5. Bandura, 1978; Borkovec and Rachman, 1979.

6. Costello, op. cit.

7. Kirkpatrick, 1984. The possibility of a selective migration to North Indiana by snake-phobic people is amusing but frivolous.

8. Ibid.

9. Seligman, 1971.

10. See Hallowell, 1938. Fearless familiarity, and on the other side, fear of the unfamiliar. The idea of *fearless familiarity* will take on greater significance as the revised view of conditioning (Chapter 11) permeates the literature on human fear.

11. Seligman, op. cit.

12. The present question addresses the dynamics of fear summation, not the statistical association between fears or the association between fears and other attributes of behavior. The statistical approach is well established, and it is known that many fears are correlated. For example, Kirkpatrick (1984) reported a correlation of 0.47 between a fear of snakes and of spiders, in a general population. Statistical associations between different kinds of fears are not necessarily related to the intensity of the fears (for example, Costello, 1982, p. 285).

13. Rachman and Lopatka, 1986c.

14. Rachman and Lopatka, 1987, unpublished report.

15. Rachman and Lopatka, 1986d.

16. Nisbett and Wilson, 1977.

17. The prediction that the removal of a fear will be followed by a substitute fear, the so-called substitution of symptoms, found little support (see *Fear and Courage*, First Edition). However, it is interesting to notice that the idea of fear substitution assumes a degree of connectedness between two fears.

18. Rachman and Lopatka, 1986d.

19. Agras, op. cit.

20. Costello, op. cit.

21. Marks and Mathews, 1979.

22. Connolly, Hallam and Marks, 1976.

23. Thyer et al., 1985, p. 452.

24. Ost, Sterner, and Lindahl, 1984. The mean heart rate of their subjects dropped from 77 beats per minute to 51 after 10 minutes of watching a gory film. The heart rate of the 4 blood phobics treated by Connolly et al. (1976) dropped as low as 40 beats per minute.

25. Kleinknecht, 1987, p. 175.

26. Ost, 1984; Thyer, 1985.

27. Recovery from a vasovagal faint usually is rapid and can be facilitated by placing the person in a supine position. According to Thyer and others (1985), these vasovagal faints are followed by a brief period of confusion, and weeping and perspiration sometimes occur. The faints are also followed in some instances by dizziness, stomach pain, or nausea, urinary urgency, and embarrassment. All of these provide a fertile basis for apprehension and avoidance behavior. The probability of fainting in response to the sight of blood or injuries can be reduced if the person assumes a recumbent

position, and the early signs of fainting can be reversed by lying down or placing the head between the knees. The relation between faintness and body position is readily demonstrated by showing the material to the person when he or she is on a tilt table. The faintness is promptly blocked by tilting the head of the table down.

28. Ost et al., 1984, 1985, 1986, 1987.

29. A similar physical reaction and sense of fainting can be provoked by auditory representations of blood or illness, but the strongest effects are produced by visual presentations.

30. Clark, 1986.

31. Rachman, Levitt, and Lopatka (1988).

32. Thyer et al., op. cit.

33. Ost, op. cit., p. 110.

34. Kleinknecht, 1987.

35. Thyer et al., op. cit., p. 451.

36. Torgersen, 1979.

37. Ollendick, 1983, p. 689. In Ost's (1987) study, 65 percent of the phobias of blood had emerged by the age of 9 years.

38. Ost and Hugdahl, 1985.

39. Rachman, 1978.

40. Ost, Sterner, Lindahl and Jerremalm, 1986. Ost, Sterner, and Lindahl (1984) confirmed the occurrence of a bi-phasic pattern in response to a film depicting blood and mutilation in a group of 18 subjects.

41. Ost, op. cit.

42. Teachers of biology, anatomy, physiology, surgery, and other subjects in which biological preparations are used reassure their "blood reactor" students that they will adapt to the material and feel decreasingly squeamish. This expectation, usually confirmed, is consistent with the idea that the effects of treatment or training can be construed as a process of habituation.

43. It will be objected, with justice, that this too is an awkward term. However, it avoids the error of describing the behavior as phobic, and "damage" can include injuries, deformities, and mutilations. Also, it is one word shorter . . .

CHAPTER 6 **Claustrophobia and the Fear of Suffocation**

1. Wolpe, 1958, p. 65. The exact relationship between a fear of closed places, physical restriction, and entrapment remains to be clarified. Interestingly, neurotic behavior is more quickly provoked in animals when they are confined (Chapter 11). Vulnerability increases under conditions of confinement.

2. Kirkpatrick, 1984; personal communication, 1987.

3. Rachman, in Rachman and Maser (Eds.), 1988.

4. Rachman, Levitt, and Lopatka, 1987, 1988.

5. See Erwin, 1963. (People who are greatly concerned about the integrity of their ears display avoidance behavior of barbers who allow their dogs to position themselves beside the chair and stare upwards.)

6. Rachman, Levitt, and Lopatka, 1987.

7. Ibid.

8. Clark, 1986, 1988.

9. Chambless, 1985.

10. Miller and Bernstein carried out three experiments on 125 claustrophobic subjects in 1972 and were mainly interested in the effects of increasing the pressure on the subjects to remain in the test room.

11. Johansson and Ost, 1982, and in Miller and Bernstein, op. cit.

12. Rachman et al., 1988.

13. Ibid.

14. Thorpe and Burns, 1983, p. 13.

15. Barlow, 1988.

16. Neiger, Atkinson, and Quarrington, 1981.

17. In six samples of students, totaling 383 people, 22 (5.7 percent) of the claustrophobics said that their fear reached severe or terror levels, versus 137 (35.8 percent) of slight to moderate intensity (Rachman and Whittal, 1988). Ost and his colleagues report that 73 percent of the 36 claustrophobic patients whom they studied in 1982 said that they would have applied for treatment earlier had they known that non-pharmacological methods were available. Sixteen of the 28 claustrophobic students who took part in a study by Miller and Bernstein (1972) needed or had received professional help for their problem.

18. Buglass and others, 1977, Marks, 1969, 1987.

19. Costello, 1982, and personal communications, 1987.

20. Kirkpatrick, 1984, and personal communications, 1987.

21. Bourdon et al., 1988, pp. 227–241.

22. Kirkpatrick, op. cit.

23. Ost and Hugdahl, 1981; Ost, 1987.

24. Ost and Hugdahl, op. cit.

25. Ost, 1987.

26. Wolpe, 1958.

27. Ploeger, 1977, p. 25.

28. See Thompson, 1988, for a recent report on the psychological effects of the fire.

29. Wolpe, 1958, p. 99.

30. See Jung (1969) and Freud (1950), which includes the case of a 5-year-old boy whose fear of horses was interpreted to signify a fear of his father, discussed in Chapter 13; Wolpe, 1958; and Lang, in Tuma and Maser (Eds.), 1985. Additionally, Rachman and Seligman (1976) have suggested that some strange, seemingly unprepared fears, such as the chocolate phobia described on p. 159, may be symbolic transformations.

31. Rachman, 1988; Rachman, Levitt, and Lopatka, 1988.

32. Rachman and Levitt, 1988.

33. Ost, Johannson, and Jerremalm, 1982.

34. Leitenberg, Agras, Butz, and Wincze, 1971.

35. Ost et al., op. cit. p. 145.

36. Miller and Bernstein, 1972.

37. Ibid.

CHAPTER 7   Agoraphobia: Core or Context?

1. Barlow, 1988; Emmelkamp, 1982; Hallam, 1985; Marks, 1987a; Mathews et al., 1981; Thorpe and Burns, 1983.

2. Beck, Laude, and Bohnert, 1974; Chambless, 1988; Thorpe and Burns, 1983.

3. Marks, 1987, Mathews, Gelder, and Johnston, 1981; Thorpe and Burns, 1983; Weissman, 1984, 1985; Wittchen, 1986. The figures differ because surveyors do not always use the same methods or classifications and because some of the figures describe the number of people affected at a point in time (point prevalence) and others describe the numbers affected over 3, 6, and 12 months or more. In the United States the lifetime prevalence for agoraphobia was estimated to be 6.1 percent (Fyer, 1987). The most recent data, from the NIMH survey of 18,572 people (Bourdon et al., 1988), puts the lifetime prevalence at 7.7 percent for women and 2.9 percent for men; 75 percent of the respondents who endorsed the agoraphobic items were women. The lifetime prevalence in a recent German survey was 5.74 percent (Wittchen).

4. See, for example, Fisher and Wilson, 1985.

5. Rachman and Wilson, 1980.

6. See, for example, Emmelkamp, 1982; Kazdin and Wilson, 1978; Marks, 1987; Mathews et al., 1981; Rachman and Wilson, 1980; Wilson, 1982.

7. Eysenck, 1959; Eysenck and Rachman, 1965; Kazdin, 1978; Wolpe, 1954, 1958.

8. Pavlov, 1941.

9. For example, Gantt, 1944; Liddell, 1944; Masserman, 1943.

10. Wolpe, 1958, p. 76.

11. Eysenck, 1959, p. 61.

12. For example, Edward Glover, a leading psychoanalyst at the time, wrote that Wolpe's work "is no mean essay in supportive suggestion for faint-hearted psychiatrists and deserves to be accurately placed in a hierarchy of contra-psychological approaches" (Br. J. Med. Psych., 1959, p. 74). He found it "riddled with naive thinking" (p. 74), "superficial" (p. 71), and "confused" (p. 73) and criticized it for advocating a "nursemaid's view of habit" (p. 73).

13. Ost and Hugdahl, 1983.

14. Thorpe and Burns, op. cit., pp. 23–24.

15. Mathews, Gelder, and Johnston, 1981.

16. Agoraphobia is not the only disorder associated with bereavement. Bereaved people show a "decline in health . . . and an increase in morbidity and mortality" for reasons and "by mechanisms that we do not understand" (Weiner, 1987, p. 312).

17. Hallam, 1978, p. 317.

18. Ibid., p. 314; Hallam, 1985.

19. Arrindell, 1980; Hersen, 1973.

20. Hallam, 1985, p. 25.

21. Chambless and Goldstein, 1983; Clark, 1986, 1988. See Chapter 8.

22. Buglass et al., 1977; Hallam, 1985.

23. Fisher and Wilson, 1985.

24. Hallam, 1978, p. 317.

25. Lang, 1985, 1987, 1988.

26. Clark, 1985, 1988.

27. Hallam, 1985; Marks, 1987a; Thorpe and Burns, 1983; most recently, Bourdon et al., 1988.

28. Robins et al., 1984; Myers et al., 1984.

29. Rachman, 1984. See also Himadi, 1987; Marshall, 1988.

30. Chambless and Goldstein, 1983; Hallam, 1978; Wolpe, 1982.

31. Thorpe and Burns, op. cit.

32. Rachman, 1984.

33. Arrindell, 1980, p. 238; Roth et al., 1959.

34. Thorpe and Burns, op. cit., p. 5.

35. For example, Marks, 1987a; Mathews et al., 1981.

36. Rachman, 1978; Rachman and Philips, 1980.

27. Costello, 1982, p. 283.

38. Craske et al., 1986. The elderly tend to avoid subways and public garages.

39. Norton et al., 1985. Recent evidence collected by Margraf and Ehlers (1988) is consistent; panics are common in non-clinical groups. The view that panic is best construed as a spectrum rather than a category received additional support from the study by Norton et alia (1988).

40. Craske, op. cit.

41. Lang, 1985, 1987, 1988.

42. Hallam, 1985. Not much is gained by construing agoraphobia as an illness, and it may reduce the affected person's sense of control and responsibility. The stigma that still attaches to "mental" illnesses may have a detrimental effect on the person concerned. There is no evidence that agoraphobia is caused by an infection, injury, or systemic dysfunction, as is the case in most traditional illnesses. See Bandura's discussion of abnormal behavior and pathology, 1978.

CHAPTER 8 **Panic: Biological and Cognitive Explanations**

1. Klein, 1964, 1987, in Klein (Ed.), Klein and Klein, in Tyrer (Ed.), 1989. For a contrary view see Marks, 1987a,b.

2. The overlap between professional discipline and position in the debate is unfortunate. A majority of psychiatrists appear to support the biological theory and most of the advocates of the psychobiological theory are psychologists, but these professional loyalties are unlikely to influence the outcome of the debate.

3. Seligman, 1988.

4. Ibid., p. 321.

5. The *Diagnostic and Statistical Manual of Mental Disorders*, 1987, edited by Dr. R. Spitzer for the American Psychiatric Association is now in its Revised Third Edition (hence, DSM-IIIR). It contains descriptions of 257 mental disorders and sets of inclusion and exclusion criteria. The introduction of the DSM was a much-needed step and helped to bring order into the chaotic diagnostic practices that prevailed until 1952. It also acts as a valuable prompt for research. Despite these useful advances, the DSM has serious weaknesses, including an unaccountable overinclusiveness in which an extraordinarily wide range of problems are included as mental disorders (for example, stuttering, premature ejaculation, reading backwardness, and bedwetting). Also, there is a neglect of behavioral and psychophysiological data and indices, and despite the title of the Manual, a regrettable lack of statistical information to support and supplement the diagnostic groups and criteria. The introduction into

the DSM of a new diagnostic disorder or concept is a mark of respectability and usually promotes clinical attention and research. The introduction of "panic disorder" is an example of this process of acceptance and promotion. (Where the term "panic attacks" is used by the original author it will be retained, but as it carries the connotation of an illness, and is perhaps reminiscent of a *heart* attack, the term "panic episode" is preferred.) The DSM now dominates virtually all research on psychiatric matters.

6. Gelder, 1986.

7. Klein and Klein, 1989.

8. Ibid., p. 20, MS.

9. Klein, 1987, *Anxiety*, p. 4.

10. The secondary arguments include the claim that separation anxiety influences the vulnerability to panic disorder, but has little support (for example, Margraf et al., 1986; Fyer, 1987; Marks, 1987b) and would in any event be more compatible with a psychological theory. The suggestion of a genetic determination was supported by Torgersen's (1979) first study of twins but negated by the second study (1983). None of the monozygotic twins of five index cases of panic disorder was diagnosed as suffering from panic disorder, and none of the six dizygotic cases of panic disorder were concordant. None of the monozygotic twins of eight index cases of agoraphobia with panic were concordant, and none of the 10 dizygotics with this disorder were concordant (Torgensen, 1983, p. 1086). See also the reviews by Marks, 1987a,b. See also Crowe et al., 1983, 1987. Maier et al. (1988) interpreted the results of their family study as support for "the distinction between panic disorder and major depression" (p. 183), but the first-degree relatives of the 15 panic patients had similar percentages of panic and of *depression*, 15 percent versus 11 percent.

11. Klein and Klein, 1989, p. 37, Ms.

12. Ibid. For a contrary view see Telch, 1988, p. 186.

13. Klein and Klein, op. cit., p. 45, Ms.

14. Ibid.

15. Ehlers, Margraf, and Roth, in Hand and Wittchen (Eds.), 1986.

16. Gorman, 1987, p. 66.

17. Clark, personal communication, 1987.

18. Margraf and Ehlers, in Hand and Wittchen (Eds.), 1986. Consistent with this point, Gorman (1987) reports that, relative to those patients who did not panic in response to lactate, those who did panic were in a "basal state" of "autonomic hyper-arousal" (p. 63), indexed by elevated heart rate, and higher scores on a self-rated measure of panic. He also notes that all of the drugs which block natural panics also block lactate panics — the imipramine connection between the two pillars is not exclusive (p. 62).

19. Gorman, op. cit., p. 60. Buller et al. (1988) produced panics in only 31 percent of cases and suggest that their patients' low level of arousal may account for the low rate.

20. Tyrer, 1986.

21. The case for using drugs is given by Fyer (1987), Gorman (1987), Klein (1987), and others. The main arguments are that the disorder is biological, the drugs are effective, and relapses can be dealt with by renewed and prolonged use of the drugs. The drawbacks to drug therapy include a high relapse rate, unpleasant side effects, disturbing withdrawal effects of some drugs (see Fyer, 1988, on alprazolam for example), high refusal and drop-out rates. See also Michelson (1987) and Zitrin (below). According to Telch's (1983) calculations, 27–50 percent of agoraphobics treated with antidepressant drugs relapse. Disarmingly, the "mechanism of panic blockade remains largely obscure" (Gorman, p. 71).

22. "To summarize, in patients who have panic disorder, with or without avoidance behavior, there are three classes of medication that effectively stop the panic attacks: tricyclics, MAO inhibitors, and the new benzodiazepine, alprazolam" (Zitrin, 1986, p. 200). See also Tyrer (1989) and Gorman (1987). There is no specific, exclusive connection between imipramine and panics.

23. Klein, 1988; Marks, 1987b; Mavissakalian and Perel (1985) found a dose-response effect of imipramine on agoraphobic symptoms, but *not* on panic. Antidepressants reduce panics (Lydiard and Ballenger, 1988), but so do some benzodiazepines (Pollack and Rosenbaum, 1988).

24. Zitrin, 1986, p. 191. See also the high relapse rate recently reported in a large, multicenter trial of alprazolam (Pecknold et al., 1988), and by Fyer (1988). Fifteen of his 17 patients relapsed when alprazolam was discontinued.

25. Klein and Klein, op. cit.

26. Ibid., p. 17, Ms. among other problems it is only the very first panic attack that is truly "spontaneous" in his sense of wholly unexpected; the second pillar of evidence rests on deliberately provoked laboratory panics which are remote from the spontaneous, out-of-the-blue attacks to which he attaches crucial importance.

27. Barlow and Craske, 1988; Turner et al., 1988. However, new methods, described in Chapter 9, may be a help here.

28. Barlow, 1988; Turner et al., 1988. See also Tyrer's view that "panic is a common station along the track to other neurotic destinations" (1986, p. 103).

29. van den Hout, 1988.

30. Marks, 1987a,b.

31. Marks, 1987b, p. 1162.

32. Ibid., p. 1162.

33. Ibid., p. 1162.

34. Klein and Klein, 1989.

35. Klein's reply that "these drugs may not be ordinary benzodiazepines" (ibid., MS, p. 43) needs to be developed.

36. The three reports deal with the efficacy of alprazolam (Ballenger et al., 1988), adverse reactions (Noyes et al. 1988), and the prevention of relapses (Pecknold et al., 1988).

37. Clark, 1986, pp. 462–463; see also Clark, 1987 and 1988, p. 73. Clark's theory is the fullest psychological theory and was formulated specifically to explain panics; the other psychological theories, such as conditioning, are extensions from the general to the specific, panic.

38. Clark, 1986, p. 462.

39. The importance of internal cues is stressed by many writers, including Barlow (1986, 1988), Beck (1985), Michelson (1987), van den Hout (1988). Beck uses the image of a scanner (personal communication, 1988). In addition to scanning the environment for external threats, we also scan our internal environment for threats to our body and health.

40. Salkovskis and Warwick, 1986.

41. Clark, 1986, 1988; Argyle, 1988; Chambless, 1988, Barlow, 1988; Hibbert, 1984.

42. Clark, 1987; Clark et al., 1987.

43. Rachman, 1988; Rachman, Levitt and Lopatka, 1987.

44. The list of cognitions used in the experiments was not exhaustive, and a full enquiry was not carried out after each non-cognitive panic. However, all of the patients who reported at least one non-cognitive panic also described at least one other panic in which a cognition *was* identified; it follows therefore that the occurrence of these non-cognitive panics cannot be attributed to the patient's inability to identify the relevant cognitions. Arntz (personal communication, 1987) has suggested that these panics might have been triggered by catastrophic images, and certainly such images are said by Beck (1985) to be of great importance in generating anxiety. Unfortunately they can be even more elusive than fleeting cognitions.

45. A view shared by biological theorists (for example, Klein and Klein, 1989) and by conditioning theorists (for example, Wolpe and Rowan, 1988).

46. Van den Hout and Griez, 1982; Clark, 1988; Rapee, Ancis, and Barlow, 1988.

47. Rachman, Lopatka, and Levitt, 1988.

48. Bonn, Harrison, and Rees, 1971. See also the apparent influence of the physician's knowledge of the person's status and the drug used in increasing the probability of inducing a panic by lactate infusions (p. 123).

49. Barlow, 1988.

50. The point of departure for Clark's theory of panic was his research on the effects of hyperventilation, and the influence of that research continues in his current theorizing. Additionally, in attempting to explain *spontaneous* panics, a resort to internal stimulation of some sort appears to be unavoidable.

51. Rachman, Levitt, and Lopatka, 1987.

52. Clark, 1988.

53. Clark, personal communication, 1987.

54. Griez and van den Hout, 1986; van den Hout, 1988.

55. Rachman and Levitt, 1985.

56. Heide and Borkovec, 1984, p. 1. See also Barlow, 1988.

57. Clark, 1988, p. 77. (The present discussion of vulnerability deals mainly with spontaneous panics.)

58. Rapee, Ancis, and Barlow (1988) found that panic-disorder patients experience more intense and frequent physiological sensations than other groups of people, and are much more likely to respond anxiously to their sensations. Reiss, Peterson, Gursky, and McNally (1986) have developed a measure to assess sensitivity to anxiety, and Holloway and McNally (1987), and others, have shown that people who score highly on this measure report more frequent and more intense sensations during hyperventilation, and a higher level of accompanying anxiety.

59. Beck, 1985, 1988; Seligman, 1975, 1984, 1987.

60. Alloy and Abramson, 1979.

61. Clark and others, 1988. The "thinking style" of panic patients, and the stressors that can precipitate a panic episode, are under investigation.

62. Clark and Hemsley, 1982; Salkovskis and Clark, 1986.

63. Barlow, 1988; Heide and Borkovec, 1984.

64. Rachman, Levitt, and Lopatka, 1987.

65. Barlow, 1988.

66. Seligman, 1988.

67. Ibid. After experiencing a heart attack, people commonly expect a repetition, and are inclined to be highly sensitive to their bodily sensations. With repeated disconfirmations of the expectations of another attack, the tendency to over-predict declines. The number of "false positive" predictions decreases and the person learns to predict accurately that he or she is no longer in imminent danger. Among those people who have intense and irrational fears of having a heart attack, as often occurs in panic disorder, the over-prediction of danger does not follow the usual pattern of decline despite repeated disconfirmations. In these cases, the affected person makes a double misinterpretation. They not only over-predict the probability of experiencing a heart attack, they also misinterpret the physical sensations that they falsely believe to be premonitory of a heart attack; true heart attacks usually are preceded by constriction and pain in the chest, whereas the most commonly reported sign of an impending heart attack, as described by patients with an anxiety disorder, is palpitations. It is worth mentioning that although many panic disorder patients irrationally fear that they may have a heart attack, few people who have actually experienced such an

attack develop *sustained* irrational or exaggerated fears of having further attacks (Byrne, 1987).

As far as the mystery raised by Seligman is concerned, perhaps the explanation is that the patients' expectations are *not* disconfirmed. After the initial episodes of panic, the fear is that they will panic again, not that they will have a heart attack: *that* expectation is disconfirmed and declines. The expectation that they will experience a panic is *confirmed* recurrently and hence persists; (see Rachman, 1989.)

68. Teasdale, 1988.

69. Barlow, 1988.

70. Rachman et al., 1987.

CHAPTER 9 **Panic II**

1. Wolpe and Rowan, 1988. See also van den Hout (1988) for the outline of a theory that combines features of conditioning and cognitions. These explanations are based on the classical theory of conditioning, now superceded by a revised view of conditioning (see Chapter 11).

2. Wolpe and Rowan, 1988, p. 445.

3. Ibid., p. 441 Barlow (1988) and van den Hout (1988) also emphasize the importance of interoceptive stimuli.

4. Wolpe & Rowan, p. 443.

5. See the reports by Doctor (1982) and Last, Barlow, and O'Brien (1984). Interestingly, Doctor found that 30 percent of the 404 agoraphobics in his study associated the first panic attack with a separation or loss. Kleiner and Marshall found that 22 percent associated it with loss or bereavement, and 23 percent of Thorpe and Burns's (1983) large sample of agoraphobics stated that the onset of their problem had been associated wth a bereavement. The onset of agoraphobia and/or panic disorder is not always associated with a frightening experience, and it has been suggested that loss or bereavement can be interpreted as a loss of important safety figures (Rachman, 1984), especially in dependent people. Loss and bereavement might also act by stimulating fearful thoughts about one's own health and future and thereby serve to increase the person's vulnerability; disturbing bodily sensations are more likely to be the subject of catastrophic misinterpretations which have been primed by the illness or death of a significant person.

6. Wolpe and Rowan, p 443.

7. Ibid., p. 446.

8. Levitt and Lopatka, personal communication, 1987.

9. Wolpe and Rowan, p. 445.

10. Ibid., p. 446.

11. Ibid., p. 447.

12. Seligman, 1988, pp. 324–325.

13. Rachman, 1988.

14. Uhde et al., 1985.

15. Craske et al., 1985; Norton et al., 1985.

16. Rachman, 1988. For a full account of the relation between panic probability and avoidance, and the counterintuitive ideas, see Rachman, 1989.

17. These unexpected, unpredicted panics resemble Klein's "spontaneous panics," and it has been suggested that the laboratory method of "matching" might usefully be applied to the analysis of spontaneous panics (Rachman and Lopatka, 1986d). See also Mavissakalian (1988).

18. Rescorla, 1988. For a detailed account of the consequences of panic, see Rachman, in Rachman and Maser (Eds.), 1988.

19. The success of the therapy may be open to more than one interpretation (Teasdale, 1988).

20. Even a critic of the theory has observed that "in most cases, it seems to produce total cure" (Seligman, 1988, p. 322).

21. Clark and Salkovskis, 1989, Barlow and Cerny (1988), and Beck (1988) describe forms of cognitive therapy that are similar, but less specific.

22. The research and testing is being carried out in the Department of Psychiatry of Oxford University, which is housed in the grounds of the Warneford Hospital. The Clark-Salkovskis method is a legitimate offspring of Beck's therapy (1985), but is specific to panic disorder and the details are deduced directly from the Clark theory.

23. Clark, 1988, p. 81.

24. For illustrative cognitive cases, and the results of the three treatment studies by Clarke and his colleagues, see Clark, Salkovskis, and Chalkley, 1985; Salkovskis, Jones, and Clark, 1986; Clark and Salkovskis, 1989.

25. Clark et al., 1985, p. 2.

26. Clark, 1988, p. 82.

27. Salkovskis and Clark, in Hand and Wittchen, 1986.

28. Clark, 1987.

29. Clark and Salkovskis, 1989.

30. Salkovskis and Clark, 1987, personal communication.

31. A sober analysis of progress so far was provided by Teasdale, whose verdict was, "Promising but not proven" (Teasdale, 1988, p. 200).

32. Clark, 1988.

33. Michelson et al., 1985; See also Michelson, 1988, and Jacobson et al., 1988.

34. For an example, Zitrin in collaboration with Klein and Woerner reported in 1980 that 40 percent of female agoraphobics who received group *in vivo* exposures and placebos showed marked improvement on a scale of spontaneous panics, and another 30 percent had a moderate improvement.

35. Zitrin, in Shaw et al. (Eds.), 1986 p. 200.

36. The supporting evidence from Kopp and his colleagues in Hungary is quoted by Clark, 1988.

37. Beck, 1988, p. 109. His method of treatment is an extension of his widely used method for treating depression, and is described in Beck and Emery (1985). The procedures used for treating the panic disorder patients include some of the techniques of Clark and Salkovskis—a fruitful example of cross-fertilization. See also Clark and Beck, 1988.

38. Barlow and Cerny, 1988. Klosko et al. (1988) report that "fully 85 percent of the (15 panic disorder) patients in this study receiving cognitive behavioral therapy were panic-free at the end of treatment," (p. 63). In the study by Shear et al (1988), "seventeen subjects, or 81 percent, reported zero spontaneous panic attacks post-treatment" (pp. 70–71). The positive evidence is mounting.

39. See Teasdale, 1988.

40. Zajonc, 1980.

41. Ibid., p. 151.

42. Ibid., p. 154, original emphasis.

43. Ibid., p. 159.

44. Lang, 1968, 1970, 1988.

45. Zajonc, 1980, p. 169.

46. Rachman, 1981.

CHAPTER 10   **The Biological Significance of Fear**

1. Seligman, in Seligman Hager (Eds.), 1972, p. 450.

2. Ibid., 1972, p. 465.

3. Ibid., p. 455.

4. Ibid., p. 2.

5. Ibid., 1972, p. 455.

6. May, 1944, p. 72.

7. Seligman, 1970.

8. Seligman, 1971.

9. Seligman and Hager, op. cit., p. 463.

10. Eysenck and Rachman, 1965, p. 81.

11. Ohman, Dimberg and Ost, 1985; Ohman, in Magnusson and Ohman (Eds.), 1985.

12. E.g., Ohman, Frederickson and Hugdahl, 1978. Thus far the research has dealt with two of the three fear components, subjective and physiological. Adoption of the vicarious method would easily allow for to inclusion of the third component, behavior.

13. Rachman, 1978.

14. See the reviews and extensive discussions provided by Ohman, 1987; Ohman, Dimberg, and Ost, 1985; Ohman, Frederickson, and Hugdahl, 1978; Cook, Hodes, and Lang, 1986; Maltzman and Boyd, 1984; McNally, 1987, and Rachman, 1978.

15. Cook, Hodes, and Lang, 1986, p. 200.

16. Cook, Hodes, and Lang (1986) concluded from their extensive review of their own experiments and those of Ohman and his colleagues, that "it is also clear that this effect is fragile; that is, it is small relative to the noise in the measurement system and thus depends for its demonstration on a substantial sample size. These experiments also reveal a related inconsistency in the measure of conductance that best represents the effect" (Ibid., p. 204). Additionally, the results obtained from female and male subjects tend to be inconsistent, much depends on the type of stimulus used, and as Cook et al. note, there is "some independence between the cardiac acquisition effects and electrodermal extinction, in for example, the independent variables that influence the two responses and their relative stability" (p. 205). That is, the results obtained from the two different measures, usually heart rate and electrodermal responding, do not coincide.

17. "Such instructions dramatically reduced the conditioned response, regardless of stimulus content" (Cook et al., op. cit., p. 206). The early indications that prepared fear responses are resistant to instructional changes, and are in that sense "non-cognitive" as postulated by Seligman, were not confirmed. A satisfactory test of this postulated property must await the experimental induction of substantial and robust prepared fears.

18. Seligman and Hager, op. cit., p. 4.

19. McNally, 1987, p. 253. Were Ohman's stimuli too remote, and might the fear responses have been clearer and more lasting if he had used real snakes, and angry people rather than photographic slides of angry faces?

20. Mineka, 1985, 1986.

21. Ohman, Dimberg and Ost, 1985.

22. Ibid.

23. Ohman, 1987, p. 150.

24. English, 1929.

25. Watson and Rayner, 1920.

26. Bregman, 1934.

27. Valentine, 1946, p. 216.

28. Ibid. p. 218.

29. Ibid., p. 214.

30. Ibid., p. 218 (emphasis added).

31. Ibid., p. 214. This recalls the surprising absence of fear among civilians injured in air raids, and the absence of fear in many victims of attacks by dogs (Di Nardo et al., 1988).

32. Rachman and Seligman, 1976.

33. Ibid., p. 338.

34. De Silva, Rachman, and Seligman, 1977.

35. Ibid., p. 76.

36. Zafiropoulou and McPherson, 1986.

37. De Silva, 1988, p. 97.

38. Merckelbach and others, 1988.

39. De Silva et al., 1977.

CHAPTER 11 **The Conditioning Theory of Fear**

1. "The causation of clinical neuroses is essentially similar to that of experimental neuroses," Wolpe, 1958, p. 76. And, "the production of human neuroses is analogous to that of animal neuroses," Ibid., p. 78. See also Eysenck (Ed.), 1972.

2. "Neurotic reactions, like all others, are *learned* reactions and must obey the laws of learning" (original emphasis), Eysenck, 1959, p. 5.

3. Mowrer, 1939, p. 565.

4. Ibid.

5. Watson and Rayner, 1920.

6. Wolpe and Rachman, 1960, p. 145.

7. Rachman and Costello, 1961.

8. Eysenck and Rachman, 1965.

9. Rachman, 1978; Rachman, 1968.

10. Flanagan, 1948.

11. Lautch, 1971.

12. Di Nardo et al., 1988.

13. Di Nardo et al. (1988), and Di Nardo, Guzy, and Bak (1988) who carried out an enterprising study in which they compared the physiological responses of dog-fearful and nonfearful subjects when exposed to a dog. The nonfearful subjects who had experienced a "conditioning event" involving a dog showed a higher level of arousal than those who had never had such an experience. Contrary to prediction (Rachman, 1978), the physiological responses of the fearful subjects who had or had not experienced a conditioning event did not differ. The problem of people who fail to develop fears after aversive dental events is analyzed by Davey, 1988.

14. Ost and Hugdahl, 1985.

15. Mathews, Gelder, and Johnston, 1981.

16. Ibid., p. 43.

17. Ost and Hugdahl, 1985, p. 629.

18. See also the estimates of Roth (1959), 83 percent versus Friedman (1966), only 10 percent. Thorpe and Burns (1983, p. 23) state that 70 percent of the 963 agoraphobics in their sample reported a precipitating event, but only 38 percent of the total can be classified as a *fearful* event.

19. Bregman, 1934; Valentine, 1946.

20. Ohman, 1978; Ohman, in Magnusson and Ohman (Eds.), 1987.

21. Seligman, 1971.

22. Rachman and Teasdale, 1969.

23. See the review by Cook, Hodes, and Lang (1986).

24. Hammersley, 1957.

25. Hallam and Rachman, 1976.

26. Bancroft, 1969.

27. Baker et al., 1984, p. 405.

28. Ibid. p. 405.

29. Ibid. p. 406.

30. Ibid. p. 408.

31. Hallam et al., 1972.

32. Sanderson et al., 1963.

33. Garcia and Koelling, 1966; Garcia, Ervin, and Koelling, 1966.

34. Seligman and Hager, 1972.

35. Ibid, p. 452.

36. Wallen, 1945.

37. Murray and Foote, 1979, p. 489.

38. Kleinknecht, 1982.

39. Ost and Hugdahl, 1985.

40. Di Nardo et al., 1987.

41. E.g., Lautch, 1971; Davey, 1988.

42. Bregman, 1934.

43. Hallam and Rachman, 1976.

44. Marks and Gelder, 1967.

45. Bancroft, 1971; Hallam, Rachman, and Falkowski, 1972.

46. Hallman and Rachman, 1976, p. 194.

47. Ibid., p. 195.

48. Ohman, 1987; See McNally, 1987.

49. Seligman, 1970; 1972.

50. Agras et al., 1969.

51. Hallowell, 1938.

52. Marks, 1969, p. 92.

53. Goorney and O'Connor 1971.

54. Ost, 1985.

55. Ost, 1987.

56. Bandura, 1969, 1977a.

57. Rachman, 1978.

58. Ibid., pp. 189–190.

59. Rachman, 1977; Rachman, 1978.

60. Eysenck and Rachman, 1965; Wolpe, 1958.

61. Rescorla, 1988, p. 154.

62. Mackintosh, 1983, p. 172.

63. Ibid., p. 172.

64. Ibid., p. 172.

65. Ibid., p. 173.

66. Ibid., p. 173.

67. Rescorla, op. cit., p. 153.

68. Ibid., p. 154. The implications of the revised view of conditioning are developed in detail in Rachman, *Implications of the Revised View of Conditioning for the Understanding of Human Fear* (to be published in 1990).

69. Di Nardo et al., 1987. An example of fearless familiarity.

70. The associative value of a conditioned stimulus is "determined not only by its current relationship to reinforcement, but also by the animals' past experience with that CS and its relationship to the reinforcer" (Mackintosh, p. 202), and it is evident that past experience plays a part in "determining the current rate of conditioning" (p. 202). Responses are conditioned to the stimulus that best predicts the outcome. Familiar stimuli that predict no aversive event are the basis for "fearless familiarity," e.g., of snakes or spiders. See also Rescorla (1980).

71. Miller, 1960.

72. Rescorla, 1988, p. 158. See also Mackintosh, 1983, p. 11, who states that animals learn "about the relationship between events in their environment, for example that the sound of the tuning fork signals an increase in the probability of food or that a particular action, pressing the lever, causes a pellet of food to appear," and he also points out that a CS may signal "no only the occurrence of food, but also of its absence" (p. 11).

73. Ibid.

74. Seligman, 1971.

75. Clark, 1988.

76. Mackintosh, op. cit., p. 172.

77. Rachman, 1977.

CHAPTER 12 **Three Pathways to Fear**

1. Rachman, 1977, 1978.

2. Bandura, 1969, 1977a.

3. Lewis, 1942.

4. John, 1941.

5. May, 1959.

6. Hagman, 1932.

7. Grinker and Spiegel, 1945.

8. Stouffer, 1949.

9. Murray and Foote, 1979, p. 492.

10. Ibid., p. 492. This information, and the suggestion that the more experience people have with snakes the less they fear them, is consistent with the idea put forward by Bolton (see Rachman, 1978). We start with a strong predisposition to fear snakes and learn through experience to overcome this fear; in some cases, direct or indirect experience of snakes will trigger the existing predisposition. Repeated non-aversive exposures to snakes will promote 'fearless familiarity.'

11. Kleinknecht, 1982.

12. Hekmat, 1987.

13. Rimm et al., 1977, p. 231.

14. Ost and Hugdahl, 1985.

15. Ost and Hugdahl, 1982. The possibility of an interaction between the content of fears and the manner in which they are acquired is consistent with an earlier suggestion (Rachman, 1977), and Ost (1987) recently found some evidence to support the prediction which flows from the original suggestion.

16. Rachman, 1976, 1978.

17. Ost, 1987.

18. Rachman, 1978.

19. Di Nardo et al., 1987.

20. Ost, 1987, p. 228.

21. Ibid., p. 220.

22. Mathews et al., 1981; Friedman, 1966.

23. Ohman, Dimberg, and Ost, 1985, p. 145. See also Hekmat's study, 1987.

24. Miller, Murphy, and Mirsky, 1959.

25. Mineka, Davidson, Cook, and Keir, 1984, p. 355. See also Cooke and Mineka, 1987.

26. Mineka, 1985.

27. Mineka et al., 1984, p. 374.

28. Rachman and Hodgson, 1980.

29. Ost and Hugdahl, 1985.

30. Mineka, in Eysenck and Martin (Eds.), 1988.

31. Miller, 1960. The new view of conditioning, which includes the importance of the organism's history with the to-be-conditioned stimulus, fits well with Miller's ideas of "toughening up."

32. Mineka, Gunnar, and Champoux, 1986.

33. Ibid.

34. Rachman, 1978.

35. Ibid.

36. Hekmat, 1987, p. 207. He found evidence that the animal phobias of his 56 subjects were acquired by one or other of the three pathways, and in keeping with the observations of Di Nardo and others (1987), his non-phobic comparison subjects reported at least as many fear-relevant aversive experiences as had the phobics.

37. Ost, 1987.

38. Clark, 1985, 1988.

39. Ost and Hugdahl, 1981.

40. Ibid.

41. Seligman, 1988.

42. Beck and Emery, 1985.

CHAPTER 13 **Psychoanalytic Explanations of Fear**

1. In volunteer subjects, the fear of snakes or spiders, even of long-standing, can be virtually eliminated in one session (e.g., Rachman and Lopatka, 1986a,b). For the fears of psychiatric patients, see the reviews by Masters et al., 1987; O'Leary and Wilson, 1987; Rachman and Wilson, 1980. Recently, Ost (1989) reported successes in treating the circumscribed fears of psychiatric patients within one session.

2. Sperling, 1971, p. 493.

3. Ibid., p. 493.

4. Ibid., p. 493.

5. See Abraham, 1927 edition.

6. Newman and Stoller, 1969.

7. Freud, 1905, reprinted 1950.

8. Jones, 1955, p. 289–292.

9. Glover, 1956, p. 76.

10. Wolpe and Rachman, 1960.

11. Freud, 1905, p. 246.

12. Ibid., p. 173.

13. Ibid., p. 216.

14. Ibid., p. 193.

15. See for example, the data collected by the Fact-gathering Committee of the American Psychoanalytic Association and reported in 1967 (D. Hamburg, Ed.). To quote only two of the many unrepresentative features of the analytic patients, 60 percent of them were *at least* college graduates, compared to 6 percent of the general population. Every 14th analysand was a psychiatrist, and so on. See also Rachman, 1971, for a discussion of the significance of these data.

16. For incisive, detailed analyses, see A. Grünbaum, in R. Stern et al., Eds., *Science and Psychotherapy,* 1977; and especially, *The Foundations of Psychoanalysis* (1984).

17. Freud, 1950, p. 120.

18. For example, see Sloane et al., *Psychotherapy Versus Behavior Therapy,* 1975, p. 100: "We have no evidence whatsoever of symptom substitution . . . on the contrary, assessors had the informal impression that when a patient's primary symptoms improved, he often spontaneously reported improvement of other minor difficulties." For general reviews, see O'Leary and Wilson, 1987; Rachman and Wilson, 1980; Masters and et al., 1987. For experimental findings see Lang et al., 1970, for example. The work of Sloane et al., and the general reviews deal with the question of whether new symptoms appear after treatment of various types of disorder, not only fear.

19. For example, Rachman, 1967; Lang et al., 1966; and reviews by O'Leary and Wilson (1987) and by Masters et al. (1987).

20. See the examples discussed on p. 95 (claustrophobia) and p. 159 (fear of chocolate), and p. 160 (fear of fiery colors).

21. Kernberg, 1972, p. 76.

22. Ibid., p. 75. In view of this gloomy conclusion, it is surprising to learn from Malan (1976, p. 21), a leading psychoanalytic researcher, that "when I met Dr. Kernberg at the meeting of the Society for Psychotherapy Research in Philadelphia in 1973, he said he regarded the problem of measuring outcome on psychodynamic criteria as essentially solved, and I could only agree with him."

23. Grünbaum, 1977; especially Grünbaum, 1984.

24. Rachman and Wilson, 1980, p. 72.

25. Eysenck, 1985.

26. Ellenberger, 1972, p. 276.

27. She was given high doses of chloral hydrate and morphine.

28. Ellenberger, 1972, p. 279.

29. Jones, 1955, p. 247.

30. Freud (Ed.), 1948, p. 35.

31. Ibid. p. 35.

32. Eysenck, op. cit.

33. Freud (Ed.), 1948, p. 87.

34. Eysenck, op. cit., p. 29.

CHAPTER 14   The Reduction of Fear

1. Rachman, 1988; Rachman and Lopatka, 1986a,b, among others. For the speedy reduction of clinically significant circumscribed fears, see Ost, 1988.

2. Emmelkamp, 1982; O'Leary and Wilson, 1987; Mathews et al., 1981; Michelson, 1987.

3. There is an impressively large literature on behavior therapy, including seven journals devoted to the subject. A full reading list is unwarranted and this selection provides an opening and an historical perspective. Wolpe (1958) is a seminal work by one of the leading contributors to the growth of behavior therapy. Bandura (1969) is a scholarly text that covers the most significant developments of the subject with critical understanding, combined with fresh and constructive ideas. Several texts that are well worth consulting include Kazdin and Wilson, 1978; Masters et al., 1987; O'Leary and Wilson, 1987; Eysenck and Martin, 1988.

4. Kazdin, 1978.

5. Watson and Rayner, 1920.

6. Jones, 1924. According to Eysenck (1959, p. 3), the work of Watson and Cover Jones "formed the springboard for a new advance in the scientific treatment of neurosis."

7. Eysenck and Rachman, 1965, p. 210.

8. Wolpe, 1958, 1985.

9. Lang and Lazowik, 1963.

10. Bandura, 1978, p. 244.

11. Lang, 1968.

12. Lang, Lazowik, and Reynolds, 1966.

13. Rachman, 1967; 1971.

14. Stampfl, in Levis (Ed.), 1970.

15. Baum, 1969.

16. Rachman and Hodgson, 1980.

17. Bandura, Blanchard, and Ritter, 1969.

18. Jones, 1924, p. 390.

19. Rachman, 1972; and in M. Feldman and A. Broadhurst (Eds.), 1976.

20. Bandura, 1969; 1977a; Rosenthal and Bandura, in Bergin and Garfield (eds.), 2nd Ed., 1971.

21. Bandura, 1969, 1977a,b.

22. Ibid.

23. Rachman, 1978.

24. Foa and Emmelkamp, 1983.

25. Roper, Rachman, and Marks, 1975.

26. Melamed and Siegel, 1980.

27. E.g., Hibbert, 1984; Chambless, 1988; see Clark's theory, 1985, 1988.

28. E.g., Beck, 1988; Clark, 1988.

29. The "influences of cognitive variables on the orienting response and its habituation are well documented," Thompson et al., 1979, p. 55. Habituation—the decline in responsiveness to repeated presentations of a stimulus, and its relevance for explanations of fear reduction—is discussed in the following chapter. Roughly, it refers to increasing adaptation to a fearful stimulus.

30. Rachman and Levitt, 1988.

31. Ibid. Note also the indication from Foa's (1979) clinical reports that "over-valued ideas" can *dis*-habituate fears that have been therapeutically reduced. Cognitions might both impede the process of habituation, and undermine it.

32. Beck and Emery, 1985.

33. Ibid., p. 31.

34. Ibid., p. 5.

35. Ibid.

36. Rachman, 1984.

37. Beck and Emery, op. cit., p. 193.

38. Ibid., p. 258.

39. Ibid.

40. Clark, Salkovskis, Gelder, Fennell, Hackmann, Anastasiades, Middleton, Jeavons and Jones, and others in the Department of Psychiatry, University of Oxford.

41. Beck and Emery, 1985; Clark and Salkovskis, 1986; Meichenbaum and Cameron, 1982; Wilson, 1982; and others.

42. Eysenck, 1978; Emmelkamp, 1982; Ledwidge, 1980; Marks, 1987; Marshall, 1988; Last, 1987.

43. Bandura, 1977a,b.

44. Bandura, 1977a, p. 70.

45. Ibid., p. 79.

46. Bandura, 1988, p. 141.

47. Ibid., p. 139.

48. Bandura, 1978.

49. Borkovec, 1978, p. 63.

50. Eysenck, 1978, p. 175.

51. Teasdale, 1978, p. 215.

52. Rosenthal, 1978; Wilson, 1978.

53. Beck, 1988, p. 109.

54. Clark, 1988, p. 82–83. Also, Barlow and Cerny, 1988; Klosko et al., 1988; Shear et al., 1988; Beck, 1988.

55. Wolpe, 1958, pp. 199–200.

56. Ibid., p. 106.

57. Wolpe, 1978, p. 234.

CHAPTER 15 **In Search of an Explanation**

1. Wolpe, 1954, 1958.

2. Rachman, 1978.

3. Mackintosh, 1987, p. 81.

4. Ibid., p. 81.

5. Klorman, 1974.

6. Groves and Thompson, 1970.

7. Mackworth, 1969.

8. Lader and Wing, 1966; see also Lader and Mathews, 1968; Watts, 1979.

9. Ibid., p. 145.

10. Lang, Melamed, and Hart, 1970.

11. Gillan and Rachman, 1947; Klorman, 1974.

12. Kimmel, 1973, p. 222.

13. Ost, 1987. See also Wittchen, 1988.

14. Mackintosh, 1987.

15. Clark, personal communication, 1988.

16. Foa, 1979.

17. Foa and Emmelkamp, 1983.

18. Foa, op. cit.

19. Klorman, op. cit.

20. See also Mackintosh, op. cit.

21. Rachman, 1978.

22. Bandura, 1977a,b.

23. de Silva and Rachman, 1980, p. 227.

24. Ibid. For examples, see Marshall et al., 1979; for the superiority of active modeling to passive observation, Bandura, 1969.

25. Ibid.

26. Bandura, 1977a.

27. Lang, 1985, 1988.

28. Eysenck, 1960; 1974; Rachman and Wilson, 1980. Recent evidence from population surveys suggests that some forms of anxiety are more stable (e.g., Wittchen, 1988), but there are no direct tests of Eysenck's hypothesis that many anxiety disorders remit spontaneously within two years of onset.

29. Barlow, 1988; Michelson, 1988.

30. Lang et al., 1966.

31. Gelder et al., 1967.

32. Marks et al., 1969.

33. Jannoun et al., 1980.

34. Mavissakalian and Michelson, 1983.

35. See also Hallam, 1985.

36. E.g., Meichenbaum et al., 1971; Wein et al., 1975; Weissberg, 1977. However, there have been many failures to reduce phobias by cognitive methods (Last, 1987).

37. Beck and Emery, 1985.

38. Mavissakalian and Barlow, 1981.

39. Foa and Kozak (1985) have suggested that two conditions are required for the reduction of fear. First, the person "must attend to fear-relevant information in a manner that will activate his/her own fear memory . . . indeed if the information remains unaccessed (i.e., the fear is not experienced), as would be the case for a successful avoider, the fear structure could not be modified" (p. 435). Second, the fear-evoking information "must contain elements that are incompatible with some of the elements that exist in the patient's fear structure" (p. 435).

This is an interesting proposal that would benefit from greater specification about the operations involved. What does "access" to the fear memory mean, and how can we decide if such access has taken place? Is it possible to test the hypothesis that fears cannot be modified if "the information remains unaccessed"? As it is highly probable that fears can be modified in the absence of a "fear experience" and can be modified even without exposure to the fear stimulus, the first of the two requirements may need to be reconsidered. Before the second requirement can be tested, clarity is needed on the nature of the "incompatibility" of fear elements. To avoid circularity, the incompatibility or compatibility of a new element with the existing elements must be determined before its effects on the fear structure are tested. (See also Foa and Kozak, 1986.) The idea of incompatability is central to Wolpe's theory, and Mackintosh (1987) attaches importance to its role in long-term habituation to biologically significant or potent stimuli.

40. Lang, 1985, 1988.

41. Rachman, 1980.

CHAPTER 16   Do Fears Return?

1. Grey, Sartory, and Rachman, 1979.

2. Grey, Rachman, and Sartory, 1981.

3. Barlow et al., 1980.

4. Barlow et al., op. cit., p. 445.

5. Rachman, 1979; 1988.

6. Craske and Rachman, 1987.

7. Rachman, 1988.

8. Interestingly, elevated heart rate is one of the few predictors of the success of aversion therapy (Hallam and Rachman, 1976), and low responsiveness of heart rate under conditions of stress is the distinctive property of soldiers who have received awards for gallantry (see Chapter 21). Heart rate is also the best physiological index of fear (Sartory, Rachman, and Grey, 1977).

9. Mineka, in Tuma and Maser (Eds.), 1985, p. 210.

10. Jacobs and Nadel, 1985.

11. Mary Mahon, personal communication, 1987.

12. Foa, 1979.

13. Rachman and Hodgson, 1980.

14. Samsom and Rachman, 1989.

15. Rachman, 1988.

16. Bandura, 1977a; Craske and Rachman, 1987a.

17. Following Skinner, 1938.

18. Mackintosh, 1983, p. 233.

19. Estes, 1955, p. 145.

20. Rescorla, 1974.

21. Rescorla, 1975.

22. Mineka, 1985.

23. Rachman, 1988.

24. Thorpe and Burns, 1983.

25. Ibid., p. 24.

26. Clark, 1988.

27. Seligman, 1971.

28. In a pilot study, a return of fear was detected in subjects who were shown an aversive film of motor accidents shortly before they were reexposed to the snakes/spiders that they feared. The subgroup of subjects who were agitated by the exposure to the motor film manifested a return of fear, but subjects who were not agitated by the film failed to do so.

29. Eysenck, 1976; 1985. The delayed onset of fear also resembles a phenomenon in which an increment in an existing fear takes place even in the absence of contact with relevant stimulation (see McAllister and McAllister, 1967).

30. Eysenck, 1976, p. 257.

31. Eysenck, 1976, 1978, 1985.

32. Bersh, 1980; Levis, 1985.

33. Groves and Thompson, 1970.

CHAPTER 17 The Over-Prediction of Fear

1. Rachman and Bichard, 1988. Persistently irrational overpredictors are fear-pessimists and perhaps general pessimists in Seligman's sense (1988).

2. Rachman and Lopatka, 1988. If the over- and underpredictions of pain (and other aversive experiences) and fear can be proven to share important features, as seems probable, the implications will be of considerable significance.

3. Rachman and Bichard, 1988; Rachman and Levitt, 1985.

4. Rachman and Levitt, 1985; Rachman and Lopatka 1986, 1988.

5. Rachman, 1983.

6. Macmillan and Rachman, 1988.

7. Butler and Mathews, 1983.

8. Chambless, 1988.

9. Rachman, 1988; Rachman and Levitt, 1985.

10. As agoraphobic patients "do not readily differentiate between 'spontaneous' and 'situational' panic attacks," Mavissakalian (1988) proposed the adoption of the matching procedure so that a distinction can be made between predicted and unpredicted panics. See also Rachman, 1988.

11. Rachman and Levitt, 1985.

12. Beck, 1976.

13. Kent, 1985.

14. Wardle, 1984.

15. Tversky and Kahnemann, 1974.

16. Alloy and Tabachnik, 1984, p. 118.

17. Milgram, 1982.

18. Saigh, 1984, 1985.

19. Rachman, 1988; Rachman and Levitt, 1985.

20. Rachman and Lopatka, 1985a,b.

21. Gray, 1985.

22. Rachman and Lopatka, 1985b.

23. Bandura, 1977a, p. 109.

24. Telch, Brouliard, and Telch, 1988.

25. Kleinknecht and Bernstein, 1978.

26. Kent, 1984.

27. Wardle, 1984, p. 553.

28. Rachman and Lopatka, 1988. Comparable results have now been obtained from people suffering headaches, and from people suffering menstrual pain.

29. Arntz and van den Hout, 1988.

30. Arntz, 1988, personal communication.

31. Philips, 1987; Slade et al., 1983.

32. Rachman and Lopatka, 1988.

33. Mineka and Kihlstrom, 1978; Miller, 1979; Seligman, 1975; Mineka, 1985.

34. Mineka and Kihlstrom, 1978, p. 258. See also Mineka, 1985, pp. 238–240.

35. Clark and Salkovskis, 1988.

CHAPTER 18 **What Is the Connection Between Fear and Avoidance?**

1. Mowrer, 1960, p. 97. See also his original statement of the theory in the *Psychological Review*, 46, 1939.

2. Mowrer, 1939, p. 554.

3. Mowrer, 1960, pp. 48–49.

4. Harlow, 1954, p. 37.

5. Teadsale, 1974.

6. Uhde et al., 1985.

7. Chambless, 1985, p. 308.

8. Craske, Sanderson and Barlow, 1987, p. 153.

9. Ibid., p. 153.

10. Telch, 1988.

11. Seligman and Johnston, 1973.

12. Mathews, Gelder, and Johnston, 1981, p. 182 (original emphasis).

13. de Silva and Rachman, 1984.

14. Rachman, Craske, Tallman, and Solyom, 1986, p. 366.

15. Rachman and Bichard, 1988.

16. Telch, op. cit.

17. Craske et al., 1987, p. 159.

18. Ibid., p. 158.

19. Mowrer, 1939, 1960.

20. Rachman, 1984.

21. Hallam, 1978, p. 314 (original emphasis).

22. Wolpe, 1982, p. 284.

23. Asch, 1956, 1962.

24. Aronson, 1976.

25. Vernon, 1941, p. 459.

26. Chambless et al., 1985.

27. Coe et al., 1982.

28. de Vore and Hall, 1965.

29. Coe et al., op. cit.

30. de Vore and Hall, op. cit., p. 49.

31. Coe et al., op. cit.

32. Epley, 1974.

33. Mineka, 1985

34. Schradle, 1985.

35. Bandura, 1977.

36. Rachman, 1984.

37. Chambless et al., 1985.

38. Ibid.

39. Rachman, 1983.

40. Cohen, in Spielberger and Sarason (Eds.), 1986.

CHAPTER 19 **Emotional Processing**

1. Rachman, 1978 and 1980.

2. Lang, 1977, 1983, 1985, 1987, 1988.

3. Lang, 1977, p. 863.

4. Ibid., p. 874. See also Foa and Kozak, 1985, 1986.

5. Lang, 1983, p. 43.

6. Foa and Kozak, 1985; Foa and Kozak, 1986.

7. Foa and Kozak, 1985, p. 435. In a later paper the insistence on exposure was dropped and replaced by the requirement that "fear-relevant information must be made available" (Foa and Kozak, 1986, p. 22).

8. de Silva and Rachman, 1981.

9. Rachman, 1985, p. 457.

10. Borkovec and Sides, 1979.

11. Grey et al., 1979.

12. Rachman, 1980.

13. Eysenck, 1979.

14. Rachman, 1980.

15. Rachman, 1985, p. 457.

16. Rachman, 1984, p. 291.

17. Ibid.

CHAPTER 20 **What Is Courage?**

1. *The Dialogues of Plato, Vol. 1: Laches.* Trans. B. Jowett, 1953, p. 85.

2. While treating obsessional patients, Raymond Hodgson and I were astonished by the speed with which these distressed people recovered their composure after disturbing sessions of exposure to the stimuli and circumstances that frightened them. Within minutes of the end of a session, most of them were sufficiently calm to enjoy a chat over a cup of tea, and we accepted this as one more confirmation of the healing properties of a well-made cup of tea.

We were so impressed that we planned a controlled evaluation study in which a comparison was to be made between the therapeutic effects of weak tea and strong mega-tannin tea, but could find no Ethics Committee willing to sanction the provision of weak tea to patients already in distress.

3. People are capable of speedily recovering their composure when a threat is removed. Another example of speedy recovery was observed in a study of the mothers of children who were about to undergo surgery (tonsilectomy). Prior to the operation they suffered from distressing, intrusive thoughts, anxiety, and sleep disturbances. Directly they were informed that the operation was over and that the child had regained consciousness, they experienced great relief, and the anxiety and intrusive thoughts quickly subsided (Parkinson and Rachman, 1980).

4. Stouffer et al., 1949.

5. Ibid.

6. Rachman (Ed.), 1983.

7. Walk, 1956.

8. Rachman, op. cit., 1983.

9. Macmillan and Rachman, 1988.

10. Rachman, 1976. pp. 271–273.

11. Mowrer, 1960, p. 435.

12. The use of the term "courage" and the conditions under which people describe behavior as courageous is the subject of a considered analysis by Evans and White (1981). With increasing age, people are more inclined to describe courage as approach behavior displayed by a fearful person. As evidence, the present author.

13. Stouffer, op. cit.

14. Symonds and Williams, 1979, p. 34.

15. Birley, 1923, p. 779.

16. Boswell's *Life of Johnson.*

17. Gal, 1983, 1984.

18. Stouffer, op. cit.

19. Birley, p. 784.

20. Ruff and Korchin, in Grosser (Ed.), 1964.

21. The choice of military pilots as the first astronauts was successful, but the particular skills needed for the space flights had little to do with aviation skills. A range of other people with "particular psychological competence" probably would have performed as successfully. Interestingly, the Russians also selected military aviators for astronautics, but appear to have placed greater emphasis on physical strength and youthfulness than did the U.S. authorities who selected older, and more experienced fliers.

22. Ruff and Korchin, op. cit., p. 216.

23. Ibid., p. 218. This account recalls Neal Miller's (1960) concept of "toughening up."

24. Bandura, 1977a.

25. Ruff and Korchin, op. cit.

26. Much of this work is collected in the monograph *Fear and Courage in Military Bomb-Disposal Operators* (Ed., S. Rachman), 1983. The research was made possible by the excellent cooperation and assistance provided by the commanders, officers, and men of the Royal Army Ordnance Corps, and is gratefully acknowledged.

27. Churchill, 1949.

28. Hallam, in Rachman (Ed.) 1983, op. cit., pp. 105–120.

29. Cox and Rachman, in Rachman, op. cit., pp. 127–152.

30. Hallam, op. cit.

31. Rachman, in Rachman (Ed.), op. cit., pp. 99–104, 163; and Flanagan, 1948, p. 208.

32. Hallam and Rachman, in Rachman (Ed.), op. cit., pp. 121–126.

33. Cox and Rachman, op. cit.

34. Flanagan, 1948; and Shaffer et al., 1947, Vol. 4.

35. Hastings et al., 1944.

36. Macmillan and Rachman, 1988. This larger proportion may simply reflect the limited duration, 2–4 weeks, and circumscribed nature of the parachute training.

CHAPTER 21 **Generality of Fearlessness and Courage**

1. Cox, Hallam, O'Connor, and Rachman, 1983.

2. O'Connor, Hallam, and Rachman, 1985.

3. Macmillan and Rachman, 1988.

4. The bomb-disposal operators tend to talk about their work in ordnance as "the trade." People learn the trade, are "in" the trade or not, join it or leave it, and so on.

5. Macmillan and Rachman, op. cit.

6. Cleckley, 1976.

7. Hallam, in Rachman (Ed.), 1983.

8. Cox et al., 1983; O'Connor et al., 1985.

9. Hare, Frazell, and Cox, 1978; Hare, 1982. See also Eysenck, 1967.

10. Vernon, 1941, p. 467.

11. Seligman, 1975; Seligman and Nolen-Hocksema, 1987; Abramson, Seligman, and Teasdale, 1978; Peterson and Seligman, 1984.

12. Seligman, personal communication, 1988.

13. Peterson and Seligman, 1984; Seligman and Nolen-Hoeksema, 1987.

14. Seligman, 1988.

15. Sharansky, A., 1988, *Fear No Evil.*

16. Seligman, 1988.

BIBLIOGRAPHY

Abraham, K. 1927. *Selected papers.* London: Hogarth Press.

Abramson, L., M. Seligman, and J. Teasdale. 1978. "Depression and learned helpless-ness: Critique and reformation." *Journal of Abnormal Psychology* 87:49–74.

Agras, S., D. Sylvester, and D. Oliveau. 1969. "The epidemiology of common fears and phobias." *Comprehensive Psychiatry* 10:151–156.

Alloy, L., and L. Abramson. 1979. "Learned helplessness, depression, and the illusion of control." *Journal of Personality and Social Psychology* 42:1114–1126.

Alloy, L., and Abramson, L. 1988. "Depressive realism: Four theoretical perspec-tives." In L. Alloy (Ed.), *Cognitive processes in depression.* New York: Guilford Press.

Alloy, L., and N. Tabachnik. 1984. "Assessment of covariation by humans and animals: The joint influence of prior expectations and current situational infor-mation." *Psychological Review* 91:112–149.

Argyle, N. 1988. "The nature of cognitions in panic disorder." *Behaviour Research and Therapy* 26:261–264.

Arrindell, W. A. 1980. "A factorial definition of agoraphobia." *Behaviour Research and Therapy* 18:229–242.

Arntz, A. 1987. Personal communication.

Arntz, A., and M. A. van den Hout. 1988. "Generalizability of the match/mismatch model of fear." *Behaviour Research and Therapy* 26:207–224.

Aronson, E. 1976. *The social animal.* San Francisco: W. H. Freeman and Company.

Asch, S. 1962. *Social psychology.* Englewood Cliffs, N.J.: Prentice Hall.

Asch, S. 1956. "Studies of independence and conformity." *Psychological Monographs* 70:9.

Baker, T. B., D. S. Cannon, S. T. Tiffany, and A. Gino. 1984. "Cardiac response as an index of the effect of aversion therapy." *Behaviour Research and Therapy* 22:403–411.

Ballenger, J., et al. 1988. "Alprazolam in panic disorder and agoraphobia: Results from a Multicenter trial. Efficacy in short-term treatment." *Archives of General Psychiatry* 45:413–422.

Bamber, J. 1979. *The fears of adolescents.* London: Academic Press.

Bancroft, J. 1969. "Aversion therapy of homosexuality." *British Journal of Psychiatry* 115:1417–1431.

Bandura, A. 1969. *The principles of behavior modification.* New York: Holt, Rinehart, and Winston.

Bandura, A. (Ed.) 1971. *Psychological modeling.* Chicago: Atherton Press.

Bandura, A. 1977a. *Social learning theory.* New York: Prentice Hall.

Bandura, A. 1977b. "Self-efficacy: Toward a unifying theory of behavioral change." *Psychological Review* 84:191–215.

Bandura, A. 1978. "On paradigms and recycled ideologies." *Cognitive Therapy Research* 2:79–103.

Bandura, A. 1986. *Social foundations of thought and action.* New York: Prentice Hall.

Bandura, A. In press, 1989. "Self-efficacy conception of anxiety." *Anxiety Research.*

Bandura, A., E. Blanchard, and B. Ritter. 1969. "The relative efficacy of desensitization and modeling approaches for inducing behavioral, affective and attitudinal changes." *Journal of Personality and Social Psychology* 13:173–199.

Barlow, D. H. 1986. "A psychological model of panic." In B. Shaw et al (Eds.), *Anxiety disorders.* New York: Plenum Press.

Barlow, D. 1988. "The influence of an illusion of control on panic attacks provoked by the inhalation of carbon dioxide." *Proc. British Psychological Assn.*, April.

Barlow, D. H. In press, 1988. *Panic, anxiety, and the anxiety disorders.* New York: Guilford Press.

Barlow, D. H., M. R. Mavissakalian, and L. D. Schofield. 1980. "Patterns of desynchrony in agoraphobia: A preliminary report." *Behaviour Research and Therapy* 18:441–448.

Barlow, D. H., and J. Cerny. 1988. *Psychological treatment of panic.* New York: Guilford Press.

Barlow, D. H., and M. Craske. 1988. "The phenomenology of panic." In S. Rachman and J. Maser (Eds.), *Panic: Psychological perspectives.* Hillsdale, N.J.: Erlbaum.

Baum, M. 1969. "Extinction of an avoidance response following response prevention: Some parametric investigations." *Canadian Journal of Psychology* 23:1–10.

Beck, A. T. 1976. *Cognitive therapy and the emotional disorders.* New York: International Universities Press.

Beck, A. 1988. "Cognitive approaches to panic disorder: Theory and therapy." In S. Rachman and J. Maser (Eds.), *Panic: Psychological perspectives.* Hillsdale, N.J.: Erlbaum.

Beck, A. T., and G. Emery (with R. Greenberg). 1985. *Anxiety disorders and phobias: A cognitive perspective.* New York: Basic Books.

Beck, A. T., R. Laude, and M. Bohnert. 1974. "Ideational components of anxiety neurosis." *Archives of General Psychiatry 31:*319–325.

Behnke, A. 1945. "Psychological and psychiatric reactions in diving and in submarine warfare." *American Journal of Psychiatry 101:*720–725.

Bersh, P. 1980. "Eysenck's theory of incubation: A critical analysis." *Behaviour Research and Therapy 18:*1–11.

Birley, J. L. 1923. "The psychology of courage." *The Lancet 1:*779–789.

Bolton, D. 1977. Personal communication.

Bond, D. 1952. *The love and fear of flying.* New York: International University Press.

Bonn, J. A., J. Harrison, and W. L. Rees. 1971. "Lactate induced anxiety: Therapeutic applications." *British Journal of Psychiatry 119:*468–471.

Borkovec, T. D. 1978. "Self-efficacy: Cause or reflection of behavioural change?" In S. Rachman (Ed.), *Perceived self-efficacy; Advances in Behaviour Research and Therapy,* 2.

Borkovec, T. D., and S. Rachman. 1979. "The utility of analogue research." *Behaviour Research and Therapy 17:*253–261.

Borkovec, T. D., T. Weerts, and D. Bernstein. 1976. "Behavioural assessment of anxiety." In A. Ciminero, K. Calhoun, and H. Adams (Eds.), *Handbook of behavioral assessment.* New York: Wiley.

Bourdon, K., et al. 1988. Gender differences in phobias: Results of the ECA Community Survey." *Journal of Anxiety Disorders 2:*227–241.

Bregman, E. 1934. "An attempt to modify the emotional attitudes of infants by the conditioned response technique." *Journal of Genetic Psychology 45:*169–196.

Breier, A., D. S. Charney, and G. R. Heninger. 1986. "Agoraphobia with panic attacks." *Archives of General Psychiatry 43:*1029–1036.

Buglass, D., J. Clarke, A. S. Henderson, N. Kreitman, and A. S. Presley. 1977. "A study of agoraphobic housewives." *Psychological Medicine 7:*73–86.

Buller, R., W. Maier, and O. Benkert. 1988. "Factors relevant to lactate response in panic disorder." In I. Hand and H. Wittchen (Eds.), *Panic and phobias,* Volume 2. Berlin: Springer.

Butler, G., and A. Mathews. 1983. "Cognitive processes in anxiety." *Advances in Behaviour Research and Therapy 5:*51–62.

Byrne, D. 1987. *The behavioral management of the cardiac patient.* New Jersey: Ablex Publishing.

Cairns, E., and R. Wilson. 1984. "The impact of political violence on mild psychiatric morbidity in Northern Ireland." *British Journal of Psychiatry 145*:631–635.

Chambless, D. L. 1988. "Cognitive mechanisms." In S. Rachman and J. Maser (Eds.), *Panic: Psychological perspectives.* Hillsdale, N.J.: Erlbaum.

Chambless, D. L., and A. J. Goldstein (Eds.) 1982. *Agoraphobia: Multiple perspectives on theory and treatment.* New York: Wiley.

Churchill, W. 1949. *History of the second world war, Vol. 2.* London: Cassells.

Clark, D. M. 1986. "A cognitive approach to panic." *Behaviour Research and Therapy 24*:461–470.

Clark, D. M. 1987. "A cognitive approach to panic: Theory and data." *Proceedings of the 140th Annual Meeting of the American Psychiatric Association*, Chicago.

Clark, D. M. 1988. "A cognitive model of panic attacks." In S. Rachman and J. Maser (Eds.), *Panic: Psychological perspectives.* Hillsdale, N.J.: Erlbaum.

Clark, D. M., and A. T. Beck. 1989. "Cognitive approaches." In C. Last and M. Hersen (Eds.), *Handbook of anxiety disorders.* New York: Pergamon Press.

Clark, D. M., and D. R. Hemsley. 1982. "The effects of hyperventilation: Individual variability and its relation to personality." *Journal of Behavior Therapy and Experimental Psychiatry 13*:41–47.

Clark, D., and P. Salkovskis. 1986. "A cognitive-behavioural treatment for panic attacks." In W. Huber (Ed.), *Proceedings of the SPR European conference on psychotherapy research.* Louvain: Louvain University Press.

Clark, D., and P. Salkovskis. 1989. *Cognitive therapy for panic attacks: Treatment manual.* Oxford: Pergamon Press, in press.

Clark, D. M., P. M. Salkovskis, and A. J. Chalkley. 1985. "Respiratory control as a treatment for panic attacks." *Journal of Behavior Therapy and Experimental Psychiatry 16*:23–30.

Clark, D. M., P. M. Salkovskis, M. Gelder, K. Koehler, M. Martin, P. Anastasiades, A. Hackmann, H. Middleton, and A. Jeavons. 1988. "Tests of a cognitive theory of panic," in *Panic and Phobias, II,* ed. I. hand and H. Wittchen. Berlin, Springer Verlag.

Cleckley, I. F. 1964. *The mask of sanity.* St. Louis: Mosby.

Coe, C., et al. 1982. "Hormonal responses accompanying fear and agitation in the squirrel monkey." *Physiology and Behaviour 29*:1051–1057.

Cohen, S. 1986. "Cognitive processes as determinants of environmental stress." In C. Spielberger and I. Sarason (Eds.), *Stress and anxiety*, Vol. 10. New York: McGraw-Hill.

Collett, L., and D. Lester. 1969. "The fear of death and the fear of dying." *Journal of Psychology* 72:179–181.

Connolly, J., R. S. Hallam, and I. M. Marks. 1976. "Selective association of fainting with blood-injury-illness fear." *Behavior Therapy* 7:8–13.

Cook, E. W., P. J. Lang, and R. L. Hodes. 1986. "Preparedness and phobia: Effects of stimulus content on human visceral conditioning." *Journal of Abnormal Psychology* 95:195–207.

Cook, M., and S. Mineka. 1987. "Second-order conditioning and overshadowing in the observational conditioning of fear in monkeys." *Behaviour Research and Therapy* 25:349–364.

Costello, C. G. 1982. "Fears and phobias in women: A community study." *Journal of Abnormal Psychology* 91:280–286.

Cox, D., R. Hallam, K. O'Connor, and S. Rachman. 1983: "An experimental analysis of fearlessness and courage." *British Journal of Psychology* 74:107–117.

Cox, D., and S. Rachman. 1983. "Performance under operational conditions." In S. Rachman (Ed.), *Fear and courage in military bomb-disposal operators.* Oxford: Pergamon Press.

Craske, M. G., and K. D. Craig. 1984. "Musical performance anxiety: The three-systems model and self-efficacy theory." *Behaviour Research and Therapy* 22:267–280.

Craske, M. G., and S. Rachman. 1987. "Return of fear: Perceived skill and heart-rate responsivity." *British Journal of Clinical Psychology* 26:187–199.

Craske, M. G., S. Rachman, and K. Tallman. 1986. "Mobility, cognitions, and panic." *Journal of Psychopathology and Behavioural Assessment* 8:199–210.

Craske, M. G., W. C. Sanderson, and D. H. Barlow. 1987. "The relationships among panic, fear and avoidance." *Journal of Anxiety Disorders* 1:153–160.

Crowe, R. R., R. Noyes, Jr., A. F. Wilson, R. C. Elston, L. J. Ward. 1987. "A linkage study of panic disorder." *Archives of General Psychiatry* 44:933–937.

Crowe, R. R., et al. 1983. "A family study of panic disorder." *Archives of General Psychiatry* 40:1065–1069.

Davey, G. 1989. "Dental phobias and anxieties." *Behaviour Research and Therapy* 27:51–58.

Dearnaley, E., and P. Warr (Eds.) 1979. *Aircrew stress in wartime operations.* New York: Academic Press.

De Silva, P., and S. Rachman. 1981. "Is exposure a necessary condition for fear-reduction?" *Behaviour Research and Therapy* 19:227–232.

De Silva, P., and S. Rachman. 1984. "Does escape behaviour strengthen agoraphobic avoidance? A preliminary study." *Behaviour Research and Therapy* 22:87–91.

De Silva, P., S. Rachman, and M. Seligman. 1977. "Prepared phobias and obsessions: Therapeutic outcome." *Behaviour Research and Therapy* 15:65–77.

De Vore and Hall, K. 1965. "Baboon ecology." In de Vore (Ed.), *Primate behavior.* New York: Holt, Rinehart and Winston.

Di Nardo, P. A., L. T. Guzy, and R. M. Bak. 1988. "Anxiety response patterns and etiological factors in dog-fearful and non-fearful subjects." *Behaviour Research and Therapy* 26:245–252.

Di Nardo, P. A., L. T. Guzy, J. A. Jenkins, R. M. Bak, S. F. Tomasi, and M. Copland. 1988. "Etiology and maintenance of dog fears." *Behaviour Research and Therapy* 26:241–245.

Doctor, R. M. 1982. "Major results of a pre-treatment survey of agoraphobics." In R. L. Dupont (Ed.), *Phobia: Comprehensive summary of modern treatments.* New York: Brunner/Mazel.

Dollard, J. 1944. "Fear in battle." *The Infantry Journal.* Washington, D.C.

Duff, I., and C. Shillin. 1947. "Psychiatric casualties in submarine warfare." *American Journal of Psychiatry* 103:607–613.

Ehlers, A., J. Margraf, and W. Roth. 1986. "Experimental induction of panic." In I. Hand and H. Wittchen (Eds.), *Panic and phobia.* Berlin: Springer.

Ellenberger, H. F. 1972. "The story of Anna O: A critical review with new data." *Journal of History of Behavioural Science* 8:267–280.

Emmelkamp, P. 1982. *Phobic and obsessive-compulsive disorders.* New York: Plenum Press.

English, H. 1929. "Three cases of conditioned fear response." *Journal of Abnormal and Social Psychology* 34:221–225.

Epley, S. 1974. "Reduction of the behaviour effects of aversive stimulation by the presence of companions." *Psychological Bulletin* 81:271–284.

Epstein, S., and W. Fenz. 1965. "Steepness of approach and avoidance gradient in humans as a function of experience." *Journal of Experimental Psychology* 70:1–12.

Erwin, W. 1963. "Confinement in the production of human neuroses." *Behaviour Research and Therapy* 1:175–184.

Estes, W. K. 1955. "Statistical theory of spontaneous recovery and regression." *The Psychological Review* 62:145–154.

Evans, P. D., and D. G. White. 1981. "Towards an empirical definition of courage." *Behaviour Research and Therapy* 19:419–424.

Eysenck, H. J. (Ed.) 1960. *Behaviour therapy and the neuroses.* Oxford: Pergamon Press.

Eysenck, H. J. 1967. *The biological basis of personality.* Springfield, Ill.: Thomas.

Eysenck, H. J. (Ed.) 1972. *The handbook of abnormal psychology,* Second Edition. London: Pitmans.

Eysenck, H. J. 1976. "The learning theory model of neurosis—a new approach." *Behaviour Research and Therapy* 14:251–267.

Eysenck, H. J. 1978. "Expectations as causal elements in behaviour change." In S. Rachman (Ed.), *Perceived self-efficacy*. Oxford: Pergamon Press.

Eysenck, H. J. 1985. *Decline and fall of the Freudian empire*. London: Penguin.

Eysenck, H. J., and I. Martin. (Eds.) 1988. *Theoretical foundations of behaviour therapy*. New York: Plenum Press.

Eysenck, H. J., and S. Rachman. 1965. *The causes and cures of neurosis*. London: Routledge and Kegan Paul.

Fenz, W., and S. Epstein. 1967. "Gradients of physiological arousal in parachutists." *Psychosomatic Medicine* 29:33–51.

Fisher, L. M., and G. T. Wilson. 1985. "A study of the psychology of agoraphobia." *Behaviour Research and Therapy* 23:97–107.

Fischer, M., et al. 1988. "Failures in exposure treatment in agoraphobia." In I. Hand and H. Wittchen (Eds.), *Panic and phobias, II*. Berlin: Springer Verlag.

Flanagan, J. (Ed.) 1948. The Aviation Psychology Program in the Army Air Forces. *USAAF aviation psychology research report no. 1*. Washington, D.C.: U.S. Government Printing Office.

Foa, E. 1979. "Failure in treating obsessive-compulsives." *Behaviour Research and Therapy* 17:169–179.

Foa, E., and P. Emmelkamp (Eds.) 1983. *Failures in behavior therapy*. New York: Wiley.

Foa, E. B., and M. J. Kozak. 1986. "Emotional processing of fear: Exposure to corrective information." *Psychological Bulletin* 99:20–35.

Foa, E., and M. Kozak. 1985. "Treatment of anxiety disorders: Implications for psychopathology." In A. Tuma and J. Maser (Eds.), *Anxiety and the anxiety disorders*. Hillsdale, N.J.: Erlbaum.

Fowlie, D. G., and M. O. Aveline. 1985. "The emotional consequences of ejection, rescue and rehabilitation in Royal Air Force aircrew." *British Journal of Psychiatry* 146:609–613.

Freud, S. (Ed.) 1948. *An autobiographical study*. London: Hogarth Press.

Freud, S. 1950. "The analysis of a phobia in a five-year-old boy." *Collected papers of Freud*. Vol. III. London: Hogarth Press.

Friedman, J. H. 1950. "Short-term psychotherapy of 'phobia of travel.'" *American Journal of Psychotherapy* 4:259–278.

Fyer, A. 1987. "Agoraphobia." In D. Klein (Ed.), *Anxiety*. Basel: Karger.

Fyer, A. 1988. "Effects of discontinuation of anti-panic medication." In I. Hand and H. Wittchen (Eds.), *Panic and phobias*, Vol. 2. Berlin: Springer.

Gal, R. 1983. "Courage under stress." In S. Breznitz (Ed.), *Stress in Israel.* New York: Van Nostrand.

Gal, R. 1984. Personal communication.

Gal, R., and R. S. Lazarus. 1975. "The role of activity in anticipating and confronting stressful situations." *Journal of Human Stress 1:*4–21.

Gantt, W. H. 1944. "Experimental basis for neurotic behaviour." *Psychosomatic Medicine Monographs 3:*82, 211.

Garcia, J., F. Ervin, and R. Koelling. 1966. "Learning with prolonged delay of reinforcement." *Psychonomic Science 5:*121–122.

Garcia, J., and D. Koelling. 1966. "Relation of cue to consequence in avoidance." *Psychonomic Science 4:*123–124.

Gelder, M. G. 1986. "Panic attacks: New approaches to an old problem." *British Journal of Psychiatry 149:*346–352.

George, A. 1967. *The Chinese Communist Army in Action.* New York: Columbia University Press.

Gillan, P., and S. Rachman. 1974. "An experimental investigation of desensitization in phobic patients." *British Journal of Psychiatry 124:*392–401.

Gillespie, R. D. 1945. "War neuroses after psychological trauma." *British Medical Journal 1:*653–656.

Glover, E. 1956. *On the early development of mind.* New York: International Press.

Glover, E. 1959. "Critical notice." *British Journal of Medical Psychology 32:*68–74.

Goorney, A. B., and P. J. O'Connor. 1971. "Anxiety associated with flying." *British Journal of Psychiatry 119:*159–166.

Gorman, J. 1987. "Panic disorders." In D. Klein (Ed.), *Anxiety.* Basel: Karger.

Graham, D., J. Kabler, and L. Lunsford. 1961. "Vasovagal fainting and diphasic response." *Psychosomatic Medicine 23:*493–507.

Gray, J. A. 1987. *Psychology of fear and stress.* Second edition. Cambridge University Press, Cambridge, England.

Grey, S., G. Sartory, and S. Rachman. 1979. "Synchronous and desynchronous changes during fear reduction." *Behaviour Research and Therapy 17:*137–147.

Grey, S. J., S. Rachman, and G. Sartory. 1981. "Return of fear: The role of inhibition." *Behaviour Research and Therapy 19:*135–143.

Griez, E., and M. A. van den Hout. 1986. "CO_2 inhalation in the treatment of panic attacks." *Behaviour Research and Therapy 24:*145–150.

Grinker, R., and J. Spiegel. 1945. *Men under stress.* Philadelphia: Blakiston; London: Churchills.

Groves, P., and R. Thompson. 1970. "Habituation: A dual-process theory." *Psychological Review* 77:419–450.

Grünbaum, A. 1977. "Is psychoanalysis a pseudo-science?" In R. Stern, L. Horowitz, and J. Lynes (Eds.), *Science and psychotherapy.* New York: Raven Press.

Grünbaum, A. 1984. *The foundations of psychoanalysis.* Berkeley: University of California Press.

Hagman, C. 1932. "A study of fear in pre-school children." *Journal of Experimental Psychology* 1:110–130.

Hallam, R. S. 1978. "Agoraphobia: A critical review of the concept." *British Journal of Psychiatry* 133:314–319.

Hallam, R. 1985. *Anxiety: Psychological perspectives on panic and agoraphobia.* London: Academic Press.

Hallam, R. S., and S. Rachman. 1976. "Current status of aversion therapy." In M. Hersen, R. Eisler, and P. Miller (Eds.), *Progress in behavior modification,* Vol. II. New York: Academic Press.

Hallam, R. S., S. Rachman, and W. Falkowski. 1972. "Subjective, attitudinal, and physiological effects of electrical aversion therapy." *Behaviour Research and Therapy* 10:1–14.

Hallowell, A. I. 1938. "Fear and anxiety as cultural and individual variables in a primitive society." *Journal of Social Psychology* 9:25–47.

Hamburg, D. (Ed.) 1967. *Report of an ad hoc committee on central factgathering data.* New York: American Psychoanalytic Association.

Hammersley, D. 1957. "Conditioned reflex therapy." In R. Wallerstein (Ed.), *Hospital treatment of alcoholism. Menninger Clinic Monographs 11.*

Hand, I., and H. Wittchen (Eds.) 1986. *Panic and phobias.* Berlin: Springer.

Hare, R. D. 1982. "Psychopathy and physiological activity during anticipation of an aversive stimulus in a distraction paradigm." *Psychophysiology* 19:266–271.

Hare, R. D., J. Frazelle, and D. N. Cox. 1978. "Psychopathy and physiological responses to threat of an aversive stimulus." *Psychophysiology* 15:165–172.

Harlow, H. 1954. "Motivational forces underlying learning." *Learning theory, personality theory and clinical research — Kentucky symposium.* New York: Wiley.

Hastings, D., D. Wright, and B. Glueck. 1944. *Psychiatric experiences of the Eighth Air Force.* New York: Josiah Macy Foundation.

Haug, T., L. Brenne, B. H. Johnsen, D. Berntzen, and K. Hugdahl. 1987. "A three-systems analysis of fear of flying: A comparison of a consonant versus a non-consonant treatment method." *Behaviour Research and Therapy* 25:187–194.

Heide, F. J., and T. D. Borkovec. 1984. "Relaxation-induced anxiety: Mechanisms and theoretical implications." *Behaviour Research and Therapy 22*:1–13.

Hekmat, H. 1987. "Origins and development of human fear reactions." *Journal of Anxiety Disorders 1*:197–218.

Helzer, J. E., M. M. Weissman, H. Orvaschel, J. D. Burke, and D. A. Regier. 1984. "Life-life prevalence of specific psychiatric disorders in three sites." *Archives of General Psychiatry 41*:949–954.

Hepner, A., and N. Cauthen. 1975. "Effects of subject control and graduated exposure." *Journal of Consulting and Clinical Psychology 43*:297–304.

Hersen, M. 1973. "Self-assessment of fear." *Behavior Therapy 4*:241–257.

Hibbert, G. A. 1984. "Ideational components of anxiety: Their origin and content." *British Journal of Psychiatry 144*:618–624.

Himadi, W. G. 1987. "Safety signals and agoraphobia." *Journal of Anxiety Disorders 1*:345–360.

Himadi, W. G., R. Boice, and D. H. Barlow. 1985. "Assessment of agoraphobia: Triple response measurement." *Behaviour Research and Therapy 23*:311–323.

Hodgson, R., and S. Rachman. 1974. "II. Desynchrony in measures of fear." *Behaviour Research and Therapy 12*:319–326.

Holloway, W., and R. J. McNally. 1987. "Effects of anxiety sensitivity on the response to hyperventilation." *Journal of Abnormal Psychology 96*:330–334.

Hugdahl, K. 1981. "The three-systems model of fear and emotion—A critical examination." *Behaviour Research and Therapy 19*:75–85.

Jacobs, W. J., and L. Nadel. 1985. "Stress induced recovery of fears and phobias." *Psychological Review 92*:512–531.

Jacobson, N., Wilson, L., and Tupper, C. 1988. "The clinical significance of treatment gains resulting from exposure-based treatments for agoraphobia." *Behavior Therapy 19*:53–554.

Janis, J. L. 1951. *Air war and emotional stress.* New York: McGraw-Hill.

Janis, J. L. 1958. *Psychological stress.* New York: Wiley.

Janis, J. L. 1971. *Stress and frustration.* New York: Harcourt.

Jannoun, L., A. Jerremalm, and L. G. Ost. 1980. "One-year follow-up of agoraphobics after exposure in vivo or applied relaxation." *Behavior Therapy 11*:294–305.

Jerremalm, A., L. Jansson, and L. Ost. 1986. "Individual response patterns and the effects of different behavioural methods in the treatment of dental phobia." *Behaviour Research and Therapy 24*:587–596.

Johansson, J., and L. Ost. 1982. "Perception of autonomic reactions and actual heart rate in phobic patients." *Journal of Behavioral Assessment 4*:133–143.

John, E. 1941. "A study of the effects of evacuation and air raids on pre-school children." *British Journal of Educational Psychology* 11:173–179.

Jones, E. 1955. *Sigmund Freud: Life and works*. London: Hogarth Press.

Jones, M. C. 1924. "A laboratory study of fear." *Pedagogical Seminars* 31:308–315.

Jowett, B. (trans.). 1953. "Laches." *The dialogues of Plato, Vol. I*. Oxford: Oxford University Press.

Jung, C. G. 1959. *Collected works*, Vol. 9. London: Routledge & Kegan Paul.

Kazdin, A. E. 1978. *History of behaviour modification*. Baltimore: University Park Press.

Kazdin, A. E., and G. T. Wilson. 1978b. *Evaluation of behaviour therapy: Issues, evidence, and research strategies*. Cambridge, Mass.: Ballinger.

Kent, G. 1984. "Anxiety, pain, and type of dental procedure." *Behaviour Research and Therapy* 22:465–469.

Kent, G. 1985. "Memory of dental pain." *Pain* 21:187–194.

Kernberg, O., et al. 1975. "Psychotherapy and psychoanalysis: Final report of the Menninger psychotherapy research project." *Bull. Menninger Clinic* 36:1–2.

Kimmel, H. 1973. "Habituation, habituability, and conditioning." In H. Peeke and M. Herz (Eds.), *Habituation*. New York: Academic Press.

Kirkpatrick, D. R. 1984. "Age, gender, and patterns of common intense fears among adults." *Behaviour Research and Therapy* 22:141–150.

Klein, D. F. 1964. "Delineation of two drug-responsive anxiety syndromes." *Psychopharmacologia* 5:397–408.

Klein, D. 1987. "Anxiety reconceptualized. In D. Klein (Ed.), *Anxiety*. Basel: Karger.

Klein, D., and H. Klein. 1989. "The nosology of anxiety disorders: A critical review of hypothesis testing about spontaneous panic." In P. Tyrer (Ed.), *Psychopharmacology of Anxiety*. Oxford: Oxford University Press. In press.

Kleiner, L., and W. L. Marshall. 1987. "The role of interpersonal problems in the development of agoraphobia with panic attacks." *Journal of Anxiety Disorders* 1:313–323.

Kleinknecht, R., and D. Bernstein. 1978. "The assessment of dental fear." *Behavior Therapy* 9:626–634.

Kleinknecht, R. A. 1982. "The origins and remission of fear in a group of tarantula enthusiasts." *Behaviour Research and Therapy* 20:437–443.

Kleinknecht, R. A. 1987. "Vasovagal syncope and blood-injury fear." *Behaviour Research and Therapy* 25:175–179.

Klorman, R. 1974. "Habituation of fear: Effects of intensity and stimulus order." *Psychophysiology* 11:15–26.

Klosko, J., et al. 1988. "Comparison of alprazolam and cognitive behavior therapy in the treatment of panic disorder: A preliminary report." In I. Hand and H. Wittchen (Eds.), *Panic and phobias*, Vol. 2. Berlin: Springer.

Koenigsberg, H. W., C. Pollak, and T. Sullivan. 1987. "The sleep lactate infusion: Arousal and the panic mechanism." *Biological Psychiatry* 22:786–789.

Korchin, S., and G. Ruff. 1964. "Personality characteristics of the Mercury astronauts." In G. Grosser, H. Wechsler, and M. Greenblatt (Eds.), *The threat of impending disaster*. Cambridge: MIT Press.

Lader, M. H., and I. M. Marks. 1971. *Clinical anxiety*. London: Heinemann Medical.

Lader, M., and A. Mathews. 1968. "A physiological model of phobia anxiety and desensitization.: *Behaviour Research and Therapy* 6:411–418.

Lader, M., and L. Wing. 1966. *Physiological ameasures, sedative drugs and morbid anxiety*. London: Oxford University Press.

Lang, P. 1970. "Stimulus control, response control and desensitization of fear." In D. Levis (Ed.), *Learning approaches to therapeutic behaviour change*. Chicago: Aldine Press.

Lang, P. 1977. "Imagery in therapy: An information processing analysis of fear." *Behavior Therapy* 8:862–886.

Lang, P. 1985. "The cognitive psychophysiology of emotion: Fear and anxiety." In A. Tuma and J. Maser (Eds.), *Anxiety and the anxiety disorders*. Hillsdale, N.J.: Erlbaum.

Lang, P. 1986. "Anxiety and memory." In B. Shaw et al. (Eds.), *Anxiety Disorders*. New York: Plenum.

Lang, P. 1987. "Fear and anxiety: Cognition, memory and behaviour." In D. Magnusson and A. Ohman (Eds.), *Psychopathology*. New York: Academic Press.

Lang, P. 1988. "Fear, anxiety, and panic: Context, cognition and visceral arousal." In S. Rachman and J. Maser (Eds.), *Panic: Psychological perspectives*. Hillsdale, N.J.: Erlbaum.

Lang, P., and D. Lazowik. 1963. "The experimental desensitization of a phobia." *Journal of Abnormal and Social Psychology* 66:519–528.

Lang, P., D. Lazowik, and C. Reynolds. 1966. "Desensitization, suggestibility and pseudotherapy." *Journal of Abnormal and Social Psychology* 70:395–405.

Lang, P., B. Melamed, and J. Hart. 1970. "A psychophysiological analysis of fear modification using an automated desensitization technique." *Journal of Abnormal Psychology* 76:220–234.

Lang, P. J., D. N. Levin, G. A. Miller, and M. J. Kozak. 1983. "Fear behavior, fear imagery, and the psychophysiology of emotion: The problem of affective response integration." *Journal of Abnormal Psychology* 92:276–306.

Last, C. 1987. "Simple phobias." In L. Michelson and M. Ascher (Eds.), *Anxiety and stress disorders.* New York: Guilford Press.

Lautch, H. 1971. "Dental phobia." *British Journal of Psychiatry 119*:151–158.

Lawlis, G. F. 1971. "Response styles of a patient population in the fear survey schedule." *Behaviour Research and Therapy 9*:95–102.

Leitenberg, H., S. Agras, R. Butz, and J. Wincze. 1971. "Heart rate and behavioural change during treatment of phobia." *Journal of Abnormal Psychology 78*:59–64.

Lepley, W. (Ed.) 1947. Psychological research in the theaters of war. *USAAF aviation psychology research report,* No. 17, Washington D.C.: U.S. Government Printing Office.

Levis, D. J. 1985. "Implosive theory: A comprehensive extension of conditioning theory of fear/anxiety to psychopathology." In S. Reiss and R. Bootzin (Eds.), *Theoretical issues in behavior therapy,* pp. 49–74.

Lewis, A. 1942. "Incidence of neurosis in England under war conditions." *Lancet 2*:175–183.

Lewis, N., and B. Engle. 1954. *Wartime Psychiatry.* New York: Oxford University Press.

Liddell, H. 1944. "Conditioned reflex method and experimental neurosis." In J. McV. Hunt (Ed.), *Personality and behaviour disorders.* New York: Ronald Press.

Lidz, T. 1946. "Nightmares and the combat neuroses." *Psychiatry 9*:37–49.

Lydiard, R., and Ballenger, J. 1988. "Panic-related disorders: Evidence for efficacy of anti-depressants." *Journal of Anxiety Disorders 2*:77–94.

MacCurdy, J. 1943. *The structure of morale.* New York: Macmillan.

Mackay, W., and A. Liddell. 1986. "An investigation into the matching of specific agoraphobic characteristics with specific types of treatment." *Behaviour Research and Therapy 24*:361–364.

Mackintosh, N. J. 1974. *The psychology of animal learning.* London: Academic Press.

Mackintosh, N. J. 1983. *Conditioning and associative learning.* New York: Oxford University Press.

Mackintosh, M. J. 1987. "Neurobiology, psychology and habituation." *Behaviour Research and Therapy 25*:81–98.

Mackworth, J. F. 1969. *Vigilance and habituation.* London: Penguin Books.

MacMillan, H. 1966. *Winds of change.* London: Macmillans.

Maier, W., R. Buller, and J. Hallmayer. 1988. "Comorbidity of panic disorder and major depression: Results from a family study." In I. Hand and H. Wittchen (Eds.), *Panic and phobias,* Vol. 2. Berlin: Springer.

Malan, D. 1976. *Toward the validation of dynamic psychotherapy.* New York: Plenum Press.

Margraf, J., and A. Ehlers. 1986a. "Biological models of panic disorder and agoraphobia—a review." *Behaviour Research and Therapy 24:*553–568.

Margraf, J., A. Ehlers, and W. Roth. 1986b. "Panic attacks: Theoretical models and empirical evidence." In I. Hand and H. Wittchen (Eds.), *Panic and phobia.* Berlin: Springer.

Margraf, J., and A. Ehlers. 1988. "Panic attacks in nonclinical subjects." In I. Hand and H. Wittchen (Eds.), *Panic and phobias,* Vol. 2. Berlin: Springer.

Marks, I. 1969. *Fears and phobias.* London: Heinemann.

Marks, I. 1970. "The origin of phobic states." *American Journal of Psychotherapy 34:*652–676.

Marks, I. 1987a. *Fears, phobias, and rituals.* Oxford: Oxford University Press.

Marks, I. M. 1987b. "Behavioural aspects of panic disorder." *American Journal of Psychiatry 144:*1160–1165.

Marks, I. M., and M. Gelder. 1967. "Transvestism and fetishism: Clinical and psychological changes during faradic aversion." *British Journal of Psychiatry 117:*173–185.

Marks, I. M., and E. R. Herst. 1970. "A survey of 1,200 agoraphobics in Britain." *Social Psychiatry 5:*16–24.

Marks, I. M., and A. M. Mathews. 1979. "Brief standard self-rating for phobic patients." *Behaviour Research and Therapy 17:*263–267.

Marshall, S. L. A. 1963. *Battle at best.* New York: Morrow.

Marshall, W. L. 1988. "An appraisal of expectancies, safety signals and the treatment of panic disorder patients." In S. Rachman and J. D. Maser (Eds.), *Panic: Psychological perspectives.* Hillsdale, N.J.: Erlbaum.

Masserman, J. H. 1943. *Behaviour and neurosis.* Chicago: University of Chicago Press.

Masters, J., T. Burish, S. Hollon, and D. Rimm. 1987. *Behaviour therapy.* Orlando, Fla.: Harcourt Brace Jovanovich.

Mathews, A. 1971. "Psychophysiological approaches to the investigation of desensitization." *Psychological Bulletin 76:*73–83.

Mathews, A. 1978. "Fear-reduction research and clinical phobias." *Psychological Bulletin 85:*390–404.

Mathews, A. M., M. G. Gelder, and D. W. Johnston. 1981. *Agoraphobia: Nature and treatment.* New York: Guilford Press.

Matias, J. R., R. and S. M. Turner. 1986. "Concordance and discordance in speech anxiety assessment: The effects of demand characteristic in the tripartite assessment method." *Behaviour Research and Therapy 24:*537–545.

Mavissakalian, M. 1986. "Clinically significant improvement in agoraphobia research." *Behaviour Research and Therapy* 24:369–370.

Mavissakalian, M. 1988. "The relationship between panic, phobic and anticipatory anxiety in agoraphobia." *Behaviour Research and Therapy* 26:235–240.

Mavissakalian, M., and J. Perel. 1985. "Imipramine in the treatment of agoraphobia." *American Journal of Psychiatry* 142:1032–1036.

May, M. 1944. *A social psychology of war and peace.* New Haven: Yale University Press.

May, R. 1950. *The meaning of anxiety.* New York: Ronald Press.

McAllister, D. E., and W. R. McAllister. 1967. "Incubation of fear: An examination of the concept." *Journal of Experimental Research in Personality* 2:180–190.

McCutcheon, B., and A. Adams. 1975. "The physiological basis of implosive therapy." *Behaviour Research and Therapy* 13:93–100.

McNally, R. J. 1986. "Preparedness and phobias: A review. *Psychological Bulletin* 101:283–303.

McNally, R. J., and E. B. Foa. 1986. "Preparedness and resistance to extinction of fear-relevant stimuli: A failure to replicate." *Behaviour Research and Therapy* 24:529–535.

McNally, R. J., and G. S. Steketee. 1985. "The etiology and maintenance of severe animal phobias." *Behaviour Research and Therapy* 23:431–435.

McMillan, T. M., and S. J. Rachman. 1987. "Fearlessness and courage in paratrooper veterans of the Falklands War." *British Journal of Psychology* 78:375–383.

McMillan, T. M., and S. J. Rachman. 1988. "Fearlessness and courage in paratroopers undergoing training." *Personality and Individual Differences* 9:373–378.

Meichenbaum, D., and R. Cameron. 1982. "Cognitive behavior therapy." In G. Wilson and C. Franks (Eds.), *Contemporary behavior therapy.* New York: Guilford Press.

Melamed, B. 1977. "Psychological preparation for hospitalization." In S. Rachman (Ed.), *Contributions to medical psychology.* Oxford: Pergamon Press.

Melamed, B. G., and R. J. Siegel. 1980. *Behavioral medicine: Practical applications in health care.* New York: Springer.

Merckelbach, H., M. A. Hout, R. Hoekstra, and P. Oppen. 1988. "Are prepared fears less severe, but more resistant to treatment?" *Behaviour Research and Therapy* 26:527–530.

Michelson, L. 1986. "Treatment consonance and response profiles in agoraphobia: The role of individual differences in cognitive, behavioural and physiological treatments." *Behaviour Research and Therapy* 24:263–275.

Michelson, L. 1987. "Cognitive behavioural assessment and treatment of agoraphobia." In L. Michelson and M. Ascher (Eds.), *Anxiety and stress disorders.* New York: Guilford Press.

Michelson, L. 1988. "Cognitive, behavioral and psychophysiological treatments and correlates of panic." In S. Rachman and J. Maser (Eds.), *Panic: Psychological perspectives.* Hillsdale, N.J.: Erlbaum.

Milgram, N. 1982. "War-related stress in Israeli children and youth." In L. Goldberger and S. Breznitz (Eds.), *Handbook of stress.* New York: Free Press.

Miller, N. E. 1960. "Learning resistance to pain and fear." *Journal of Experimental Psychology 60:*137–142.

Miller, B., and D. Bernstein. 1972. "Instructional demand in a behaviour avoidance test for claustrophobic fears." *Journal of Abnormal Psychology 80:*206–210.

Miller, R., R. Rubin, B. Clark, W. Crawford, and R. Arthur. 1970. "The stress of aircraft carrier landings." *Psychosomatic Medicine 32:*581–588.

Miller, R., T. Murphy, and I. Mirsky. 1959. "Non-verbal communication of affect." *Journal of Clinical Psychology 15:*155–158.

Miller, S. 1979. "Controllability and human stress." *Behaviour Research and Therapy 17:*287–304.

Miller, W. R., and M. E. P. Seligman. 1976. "Learned helplessness, depression and the perception of reinforcement." *Behaviour Research and Therapy 14:*7–18.

Mineka, S. 1979. "The role of fear in theories of avoidance learning, flooding and extinction." *Psychological Bulletin 86:*985–1010.

Mineka, S. 1986. "The frightful complexity of the origins of fears." In J. Overmier and F. Brush (Eds.), *Affect, conditioning and cognition.* New Jersey: Erlbaum.

Mineka, S. 1988. "A primate model of phobic fears." In H. Eysenck and I. Martin (Eds.), *Theoretical foundations of behavior therapy.* New York: Plenum Press.

Mineka, S. 1985. "Animal models of anxiety-based disorders." In A. Tuma and J. Maser (Eds.), *Anxiety and the anxiety disorders.* Hillsdale, N.J.: Erlbaum.

Mineka, S., M. Davidson, M. Cook, and R. Kein. 1984. "Observational conditioning of snake fear in rhesus monkeys." *Journal of Abnormal Psychology 93:*355–372.

Mineka, S., M. Gunner, and M. Champoux. 1986. "Control and early emotional development: Infant rhesus monkeys reared in controllable versus uncontrollable environments." *Child Development 57:*1241–1256.

Mineka, S., and J. F. Kihlstrom. 1978. "Unpredictable and uncontrollable events: A new perspective in experimental neurosis." *Journal of Abnormal Psychology 87:*256–271.

Mineka, S., and K. Richard. 1983. "The effects of flooding on reducing snake fear in rhesus monkeys: Six-month follow-up and further flooding." *Behaviour Research and Therapy 21:*527–535.

Mowrer, O. H. 1939. "Stimulus response theory of anxiety." *Psychological Review 46:*553–565.

Mowrer, O. H. 1960. *Learning theory and behavior.* New York: Wiley.

Munjack, D. J. 1984. "The onset of driving phobias." *Journal of Behaviour Therapy and Experimental Psychiatry 15:*305–308.

Murray, E. J., and F. Foot. 1979. "The origins of fear of snakes." *Behaviour Research and Therapy 17:*489–493.

Myers, J. K., M. M. Weissman, G. L. Tischler, C. E. Holzer III, P. J. Lear, H. Orvaschel, J. C. Anthony, J. H. Boyd, J. D. Burke, M. Kramer, and F. R. Stoltzman. 1984. "Six-month prevalence of psychiatric disorders in three communities." *Archives of General Psychiatry 41:*959–967.

Neiger, S., L. Atkinson, and B. Quarrington. 1981. "A factor analysis of personality and fear variables in phobic disorders." *Canadian Journal of Behavioral Science 13:*336–348.

Newman, L., and R. Stoller. 1969. "Spider symbolism and bisexuality." *Journal of the American Psychoanalytic Association 17:*862–872.

Nisbett, R., and T. Wilson. 1977. "Telling more than we can know: Verbal reports on mental processes." *Psychological Review 84:*231–259.

Norton, G., S. Cairns, K. Wozney, and J. Malan. 1988. "Panic attacks and psychopathology in non-clinical panickers." *Journal of Anxiety Disorders 2:*319–331.

Norton, G. R., B. Harrison, J. Hauch, and L. Rhodes. 1986. "Characteristics of people with infrequent panic attacks." *Journal of Abnormal Psychology 94:* 216–221.

Noyes, Jr., R., et al. 1986. "Relationship between panic disorder and agoraphobia." *Archives of General Psychiatry 43:*227–232.

Noyes, R., et al. 1988. "Alprazolam in panic disorder and agoraphobia: Results from a multicenter trial. Patient acceptance, side effects and safety." *Archives of General Psychiatry 45:*423–428.

O'Connor, K., R. Hallam, and S. Rachman. 1985. "Fearlessness and courage: A replication experiment." *British Journal of Psychology 76:*187–197.

Ohman, A., G. Erixon, and I. Lofberg. 1975. "Phobias and preparedness: Phobic versus neutral pictures as continued stimuli for human autonomic responses." *Journal of Abnormal Psychology 84:*41–45.

Ohman, A. 1987. "Evolution, learning and phobias." In D. Magnusson and A. Ohman (Eds.), *Psychopathology.* New York: Academic Press.

Ohman, A., V. Dimberg, and L. G. Ost. 1985. "Animal and social phobias: Biological constraints on learned fear responses." In S. Reiss and R. R. Bootzin (Eds.), *Theoretical issues in behavior therapy.* New York: Academic Press.

O'Leary, D., and G. T. Wilson. 1987. *Behavior therapy,* Second edition. Englewood Cliffs, N.J.: Prentice-Hall.

Ollendick, T. H. 1983. "Reliability and validity of the revised fear survey schedule for children (FSSC-R)." *Behaviour Research and Therapy* 21:685–692.

Ollendick, T. H., J. L. Matson, and W. J. Helsel. 1985. "Fears in children and adolescents: Normative data." *Behaviour Research and Therapy* 23:465–467.

Öst, L. G. 1985. "Ways of acquiring phobias and outcome of behavioural treatments." *Behaviour Research and Therapy* 23:683–689.

Öst, L. G. 1987. "Age of onset in different phobias." *Journal of Abnormal Psychology* 96:223–229.

Öst, L. G. 1987. "Individual response patterns and the effects of different behavioural methods in the treatment of phobias." In D. Magnusson and A. Ohman (Eds.), *Psychopathology*. New York: Academic Press.

Öst, L. G. (1989). "One-session treatment for specific phobias." *Behaviour Research and Therapy* 27:1–8.

Öst, L. G., and K. Hugdahl. 1981. "Acquisition of phobias and anxiety response patterns in clinical patients." *Behaviour Research and Therapy* 19:439–447.

Öst, L. G., and K. Hugdahl. 1983. "Acquisition of agoraphobia, mode of onset and anxiety response patterns." *Behaviour Research and Therapy* 21:623–631.

Öst, L. G., and K. Hugdahl. 1985. "Acquisition of blood and dental phobia and anxiety response patterns in clinical patients." *Behaviour Research and Therapy* 23:27–34.

Öst, L. G., A. Jerremalm, and L. Jansson. 1984. "Individual response patterns and the effects of different behavioural methods in the treatment of agoraphobia." *Behaviour Research and Therapy* 22:697–707.

Öst, L. G., J. Johannson, and A. Jerremalm. 1982. "Individual response patterns and the effects of behavioural methods of treatment of claustrophobia." *Behaviour Research and Therapy* 20:445–460.

Öst, L. G., J. L. Lindahl, V. Sterner, and A. Jerremalm. 1984. "Exposure in vivo versus applied relaxation in the treatment of blood phobia." *Behaviour Research and Therapy* 22:205–216.

Öst, L. G., V. Sterner, and J. Fellenius. 1989. "The treatment of blood phobia." *Behaviour Research and Therapy* 27:109–122.

Öst, L. G., V. Sterner, and J. L. Lindahl. 1984. "Physiological responses in blood phobics." *Behaviour Research and Therapy* 22:109–117.

Panter-Downes, M. 1971. *London war notes*. New York: Farrar Straus and Giroux.

Parkinson, L., and S. Rachman. 1980. "Speed of recovery from an uncontrived stress." In S. Rachman (Ed.), *Unwanted intrusive cognitions*. Oxford: Pergamon Press.

Paul, G. 1966. *Insight versus desensitization in psychotherapy*. Stanford, Calif.: Stanford University Press.

Pavlov, I. P. 1941. *Conditioned reflexes and psychiatry.* Trans. by W. H. Gantt. New York: International Publishing.

Pecknold, J., et al. 1988. Alprazolam in panic disorder and agoraphobia: Results from a multicenter trial. Discontinuation effects. *Archives of General Psychiatry 45:* 429–436.

Peterson, C., and M. E. P. Seligman. 1984. "Causal explanations as a risk factor for depression: Theory and evidence." *Psychological Review 91:*347–374.

Philips, H. C. 1985. "Return of fear in the treatment of a fear of vomiting." *Behaviour Research and Therapy 23:*45–52.

Philips, C. 1987. "Avoidance behaviour and its role in sustaining chronic pain." *Behaviour Research and Therapy 25:*273–280.

Pitman, R. K., and S. P. Orr. 1986. "Test of the conditioning model of neurosis: Differential aversive conditioning of angry and neutral facial expressions in anxiety disorder patients." *Journal of Abnormal Psychology 95:*208–213.

Ploeger, A. 1977. "A 10-year follow-up of miners trapped for two weeks under threatening circumstances." In C. Spielberger and I. Sarason (Eds.), *Stress and Anxiety*, Vol. 4. New York: Wiley.

Pollack, M., and J. Rosenbaum. 1988. "Benzodiazepines in panic-related disorders." *Journal of Anxiety Disorders 2:*95–108.

Rachman, S. 1967. "Systematic desensitization." *Psychological Bulletin 67:*93–103.

Rachman, S. 1968. *Phobias: Their nature and control.* Springfield, Ill.: Thomas.

Rachman, S. 1974. *The meanings of fear.* Middlesex: Penguin Books.

Rachman, S. 1976a. "The passing of the two-stage theory of fear and avoidance: Fresh possibilities." *Behaviour Research and Therapy 14:*125–131.

Rachman, S. 1976b. "Courage, fearlessness and fear." *The New Scientist 24:*271–273.

Rachman, S. 1976. "Observational learning and therapeutic modeling." In M. Feldman and A. Broadhurst (Eds.), *Theoretical and experimental bases of behaviour therapy.* Chichester: Wiley, 1976.

Rachman, S. 1978. *Fear and courage.* San Francisco: W. H. Freeman and Company.

Rachman, S. (Ed.) 1978b. "Perceived self-efficacy." *Adv. Behaviour Research and Therapy 2.*

Rachman, S. 1979. "The concept of required helpfulness." *Behaviour Research and Therapy 17:*1–6.

Rachman, S. 1981. "The primacy of affect: Some theoretical implications." *Behaviour Research and Therapy 19:*279–290.

Rachman, S. 1983. "The modification of agoraphobic avoidance behaviour: Some fresh possibilities." *Behaviour Research and Therapy 21:*567–574.

Rachman, S. (Ed.) 1983. *Fear and courage in military bomb-disposal operators. Adv. Behaviour Research and Therapy 4*:99–165.

Rachman, S. 1984. "Agoraphobia: A safety signal perspective." *Behaviour Research and Therapy 22*:59–60.

Rachman, S. 1984. "Anxiety disorders: Some emerging theories." *Journal of Behavioural Assessment 6*:281–299.

Rachman, S. 1984. "Fear and Courage." *Behavior Therapy 15*:109–120.

Rachman, S. 1985. "The treatment of anxiety disorders: A critique of the implications for psychopathology." In A. Tuma and J. Maser (Eds.), *Anxiety and the anxiety disorders*. New Jersey: Erlbaum.

Rachman, S. 1985. "A note on the conditioning theory of fear acquisitions." *Behavior Therapy 16*:145–148.

Rachman, S. 1989. "The return of fear: Review and prospect." *Clinical Psychology Review 9*:147–168.

Rachman, S. 1988. "Biologically significant fears." *Behaviour Anal. Modif. 2*: 234–239.

Rachman, S. 1988. "Panics and their consequences." In S. Rachman and J. Maser (Eds.), *Panic: Psychological perspectives*. Hillsdale, N.J.: Erlbaum.

Rachman, S. In press, 1989. "The consequences of panic." *Journal of Cognitive Psychotherapy*.

Rachman, S. 1989. "The return of fear: Review and prospect." *Clinical Psychology Review 9*:147–168.

Rachman, S., and C. Costello. 1961. "The aetiology and treatment of children's phobias." *American Journal of Psychiatry 118*:97–105.

Rachman, S., M. Craske, K. Tallman, and C. Solyom. 1986. "Does escape behaviour strengthen agoraphobic avoidance? A replication." *Behavior Therapy 17*: 366–384.

Rachman, S., and R. Hodgson. 1974. "Synchrony and desynchrony in fear and avoidance." *Behaviour Research and Therapy 12*:311–318.

Rachman, S., and R. Hodgson. 1980. *Obsessions and compulsions*. Englewood Cliffs, N.J.: Prentice Hall.

Rachman, S., and K. Levitt. 1985. "Panics and their consequences." *Behaviour Research and Therapy 23*:585–600.

Rachman, S. and K. Levitt. 1988. "Panic, fear reduction and habituation." *Behaviour Research and Therapy 26*:199–206.

Rachman, S., K. Levitt, and C. Lopatka. 1987. "Panic: The links between cognitions and bodily symptoms-1." *Behaviour Research and Therapy 25*:411–424.

Rachman, S., K. Levitt, and C. Lopatka. 1987. "A simple method for distinguishing between expected and unexpected panics." *Behaviour Research and Therapy* 25:149–154.

Rachman, S., K. Levitt, and C. Lopatka. 1988. "Experimental analyses of panic III—claustrophobic subjects." *Behaviour Research and Therapy* 26:41–52.

Rachman, S., and C. Lopatka. 1986a. "Match and mismatch in the prediction of fear-1." *Behaviour Research and Therapy* 24:387–393.

Rachman, S., and C. Lopatka. 1986b. "Match and mismatch in the prediction of fear-2." *Behaviour Research and Therapy* 24:395–401.

Rachman, S., and C. Lopatka. 1986c. "Do fears summate?" *Behaviour Research and Therapy* 24:653–660.

Rachman, S., and C. Lopatka. 1986d. "A simple method for determining the functional independence of two or more fears." *Behaviour Research and Therapy* 24:661–664.

Rachman, S., and C. Lopatka. 1988a. "Return of fear: Underlearning and overlearning." *Behaviour Research and Therapy* 26:99–104.

Rachman, S., and C. Lopatka. 1988b. "Accurate and inaccurate predictions of pain." *Behaviour Research and Therapy* 26:291–297.

Rachman, S., C. Lopatka, and K. Levitt, 1987. "Experimental analyses of panic-2. Panic patients." *Behaviour Research and Therapy* 25:33–40.

Rachman, S., and J. Maser (Eds.) 1988. *Panic: Psychological perspectives.* New Jersey: Erlbaum.

Rachman, S., and C. Philips. 1980. *Psychology and behavioral medicine.* New York: Cambridge University Press.

Rachman, S., S. Robinson, and C. Lopatka. 1987. "Is incomplete fear-reduction followed by a return of fear?" *Behaviour Research and Therapy* 25:67–70.

Rachman, S., and M. Seligman. 1976. "Unprepared phobias: Be prepared." *Behaviour Research and Therapy* 14:333–338.

Rachman, S., and J. Teasdale. 1969. *Aversion therapy and the behavior disorders.* London: Routledge & Kegan Paul.

Rachman, S., and M. L. Whittal. 1987. Unpublished data.

Rachman, S., and G. T. Wilson. 1980. *The effects of psychological therapy, second edition.* Oxford: Pergamon Press.

Rakos, R., and H. Schroeder. 1976. "Fear reduction in help-givers as a function of helping." *Journal of Counseling Psychology* 23:428–435.

Rapee, R. M., J. Ancis, and D. Barlow. 1988. "Emotional reactions to psychological sensations: Panic disorder patients and non-clinical subjects." *Behaviour Research and Therapy* 26:265–270.

Reid, D. 1979. "Some measures of the effect of operational stress on bomber crews." In E. Dearnaley and P. Warr (Eds.), *Aircrew stress in wartime operations.* New York: Academic Press.

Reiss, S. 1987. "Theoretical perspectives on the fear of anxiety." *Clinical Psychology Review* 7:585–596.

Reiss, S., R. A. Peterson, D. M. Gursky, and R. J. McNally. 1986. "Anxiety sensitivity, anxiety frequency and the prediction of fearfulness." *Behaviour Research and Therapy* 24:1–8.

Rescorla, R. A. 1969. "Pavlovian conditioned inhibition." *Psychological Bulletin* 72:77–94.

Rescorla, R. A. 1974. "Effect of inflation of the unconditioned stimulus value following conditioning." *Journal of Comparative and Physiological Psychology* 86: 101–106.

Rescorla, R. A. 1980. *Pavlovian second-order conditioning.* Hillsdale, N.J.: Erlbaum.

Rickman, J. 1938. "Panic and air-raid precautions." *The Lancet* 1:1291–1294.

Rimm, D. C., L. H. Janda, D. W. Lancaster, M. Nahl, and K. Dittmar. 1977. "An exploratory investigation of the origin and maintenance of phobias." *Behaviour Research and Therapy* 15:231–238.

Robins, L. N., J. E. Helzer, M. M. Weissman, et al. 1984. "Lifetime prevalence of specific psychiatric disorders in three sites." *Archives of General Psychiatry* 41:949–958.

Roper, G., S. Rachman, and I. Marks. 1975. "Passive and participant modeling in exposure and treatment of obsessive-compulsive neurotics." *Behaviour Research and Therapy* 13:271–279.

Rosenthal, T. L. 1978. "Bandura's self-efficacy theory: Thought is father to the deed." In S. Rachman (Ed.), *Perceived self-efficacy. Advances in behavior research and therapy, 12.* Oxford: Pergamon Press.

Rosenthal, T., and A. Bandura. 1978. "Therapeutic modeling." In A. Bergin and S. Garfield (Eds.), *Handbook of psychotherapy and behavior change.* Second edition. New York: Wiley.

Roth, M. 1959. "The phobic-anxiety-depersonalisation syndrome." *Proc. Roy. Soc. Med.* 52:8, 587–594.

Ruff, G., and S. Korchin. 1964. "Psychological responses of the Mercury astronauts to stress." In G. Grosser, H. Wechsler, and M. Greenblatt (Eds.), *The threat of impending disaster.* Cambridge, Mass.: MIT Press.

Sackett, G. 1966. "Monkeys reared in isolation with pictures as visual input." *Science* 154:1468–1472.

Saigh, P. A. 1984. "Pre- and post-invasion anxiety in Lebanon." *Behavior Therapy* 15:185–190.

Saigh, P. A. 1984. "An experimental analysis of delayed post-traumatic stress." *Behaviour Research and Therapy* 22:679–682.

Saigh, P. A. 1988. "Anxiety, depression, and assertion across alternating intervals of stress." *Journal of Abnormal Psychology*, in press.

Salkovskis, P., and D. Clark. 1986. "Cognitive and physiological processes in the maintenance and treatment of panic attacks." In I. Hand and H. Wittchen (Eds.), *Panic and phobias.* Berlin: Springer.

Salkovskis, P. M., D. R. O. Jones, and D. M. Clark. 1986. "Respiratory control in the treatment of panic attacks: Replication and extension with concurrent measurement of behaviour and pCO_2." *British Journal of Psychiatry* 148:526–532.

Salkovskis, P., and H. Warwick. 1986. "Morbid preoccupations, health anxiety and reassurance: A cognitive behavioral approach to hypochondriasis." *Behaviour Research and Therapy* 24:597–602.

Samsom, D., and S. Rachman. In press, 1989. "Mood and fear reduction." *British Journal of Clinical Psychology.*

Sanderson, R., S. Laverty, and D. Campbell. 1963. "Traumatically conditioned responses acquired during respiratory paralysis." *Nature* 196:1235–1236.

Sanderson, W. C., et al. 1988. "Panic induction via inhalation of 5.5% CO_2 enriched air." *Behaviour Research and Therapy* 26:333–337.

Sartory, G., S. Rachman, and S. Grey. 1977. "An investigation of the relation between reported fear and heart rate." *Behaviour Research and Therapy* 15:435–437.

Sartory, G., S. Rachman, and S. J. Grey. 1982. "Return of fear: The role of rehearsal." *Behaviour Research and Therapy* 20:123–133.

Schradle, S., and M. Dougher. 1985. "Social support as a mediator of stress." *Clinical Psychology Review* 5:641–661.

Seligman, M. 1970. "On the generality of the laws of learning." *Psychological Review* 77:406–418.

Seligman, M. 1971. "Phobias and preparedness." *Behavior Therapy* 2:307–320.

Seligman, M. 1975. *Helplessness.* San Francisco: W. H. Freeman and Company.

Seligman, M. E. P. 1988. "Competing theories of panic." In S. Rachman and J. D. Maser (Eds.), *Panic: Psychological perspectives.* Hillsdale, N.J.: Erlbaum.

Seligman, M., and J. Hager (Eds.). 1972. *Biological boundaries of learning.* New York: Appleton Century Crofts.

Seligman, M., and J. Johnston. 1973. "A cognitive theory of avoidance learning." In J. McGuigan and B. Lumsden (Eds.), *Contemporary approaches to conditioning and learning.* New York: Wiley.

Seligman, M., and S. Nolen-Hoeksema. 1987. "Explanatory style and depression." In

D. Magnusson and A. Ohman (Eds.), *Psychopathology*. New York: Academic Press.

Shaffer, L. 1947. "Psychological studies of anxiety reaction to combat." *USAAF aviation psychology research report no. 14*. Washington, D.C.: U.S. Government Printing Office.

Sharansky, N. 1988. *Fear no evil*. London: Wiedenfeld.

Shear, M. K., et al. 1988. "Cognitive behavioral treatment of panic." In I. Hand and H. Wittchen (Eds.), *Panic and phobias*, Vol. 2. Berlin: Springer.

Shils, E., and M. Janowitz. 1948. "Cohesion and disintegration in the Wehrmacht in World War II." *Public Opinion Quarterly 12*:280–315.

Skinner, B. F. 1938. *The behaviour of organisms: An experimental analysis*. New York: Appleton.

Sloan, B. R., F. Staples, A. Cristol, N. Yorkston, and K. Whipple. 1975. *Psychotherapy versus behaviour therapy*. Cambridge, Mass.: Harvard University Press.

Smith, M. B. 1949. "Combat motivations among ground troops." In Stouffer et al. (Eds.), *The American soldier*. Princeton, N.J.: Princeton University Press.

Solomon, J. 1942. "Reactions of children to black-outs." *American Journal of Orthopsychiatry 12*:361–364.

Sperling, M. 1971. "Spider phobias and spider fantasies." *Journal of the American Psychoanalytic Association 19*:472–498.

Stafford-Clark, D. 1949. "Morale and flying experience: Results of a wartime study." *Journal of Mental Science 95*:10–23.

Stampfl, T. 1970. "Implosive therapy." In D. Levis (Ed.), *Learning approaches to therapeutic behaviour change*. Chicago: Aldine Press.

Stengel, E. 1946. "Air-raid phobia." *British Journal of Medical Psychology 20*:135–143.

Stouffer, S., A. Lumsdaine, R. Williams, M. Smith, I. Janis, S. Star, and L. Cottrell. 1949. *The American soldier: Combat and its aftermath*. Princeton, N.J.: Princeton University Press.

Suarez, Y., H. Adams, and B. McCutcheon. 1976. "Flooding and systematic desensitization." *Journal of Consulting and Clinical Psychology 44*:872.

Symonds, C., and D. Williams. 1979. "Clinical and statistical study of neurosis precipitated by flying duties." In E. Dearnaley and P. Warr (Eds.), *Aircrew stress in wartime operations*. New York: Academic Press.

Tearnan, B. H., M. J. Telch, and P. Keefe. 1984. "Etiology and onset of agoraphobia: A critical review." *Comprehensive Psychiatry 25*:51–62.

Teasdale, J. 1974. Personal communication.

Teasdale, J. D. 1978. "Self-efficacy: Towards a unifying theory of behavioural change?" In S. Rachman (Ed.), *Perceived self-efficacy*. Oxford: Pergamon Press.

Teasdale, T. 1988. "Cognitive models and treatments for panic: A critical evaluation. In S. Rachman and J. Maser (Eds.), *Panic: Psychological perspectives*. Hillsdale, N.J.: Erlbaum.

Telch, M. 1988. "Combined pharmacological and psychological treatment for panic sufferers." In S. Rachman and J. Maser (Eds.), *Panic: Psychological perspectives*. Hillsdale, N.J.: Erlbaum.

Telch, M. J., W. S. Agras, C. B. Taylor, W. T. Roth, and C. C. Gallen. 1985. "Combined pharmacological and behavioural treatment for agoraphobia." *Behaviour Research and Therapy* 23:325–335.

Telch, M. J., M. Brouilard, and C. F. Telch. 1989. In press. "Role of cognitive appraisal in panic-related avoidance." *Behaviour Research and Therapy* 27.

Telch, M. J., B. H. Tearnan, and C. B. Taylor. 1983. "Antidepressant medication in the treatment of agoraphobia: A critical review." *Behaviour Research and Therapy* 21:505–517.

Thompson, J. 1989. "The King's Cross Fire: Psychological reactions." *Proceedings British Psychological Society Conference*: December.

Thompson, R. F., S. D. Berry, P. C. Rinaldi, and T. W. Berger. 1979. "Habituation and the orienting reflex: The dual-process theory revisited." In H. D. Kimmel, E. H. Van Olst, and J. F. Orlebeke (Eds.), *The orienting reflex in humans*. Hillsdale, N.J.: Erlbaum.

Thompson, R., P. Groves, T. Teyler, and R. Roemer. 1973. "A dual-process theory of habituation." In H. Pecke and M. Herz (Ed.), *Habituation*. New York: Academic Press.

Thompson, R. F., and W. Spencer. 1966. "Habituation." *Psychological Review* 73:16–42.

Thorpe, G., and L. Burns. 1983. *The agoraphobic syndrome*. Chichester: Wiley.

Thyer, B. A., and J. Himle. 1985. "Temporal relationship between panic attack onset and phobic avoidance in agoraphobia." *Behaviour Research and Therapy* 23:607–608.

Thyer, B. A., J. Himle, and G. C. Curtis. 1985. "Blood-injury-illness phobia: A review." *Journal of Clinical Psychology* 41:451–459.

Torgersen, S. 1983. "Genetic factors in anxiety disorders." *Archives of General Psychiatry* 40:1085–1089.

Torgersen, S. 1979. "The nature and origin of common phobic fears." *British Journal of Psychiatry* 134:343–351.

Turner, S., D. Beidel, and R. Jacob. 1988. "Assessment of panic." In S. Rachman and J. Maser (Eds.), *Panic: Psychological perspectives*. Hillsdale, N.J.: Erlbaum.

Turner, S. M., S. L. Williams, D. C. Beidel, and J. E. Mezzich. 1986. "Panic disorder and agoraphobia with panic attacks: Covariation along the dimensions of panic and agoraphobic fear." *Journal of Abnormal Psychology* 95:384–388.

Tversky, A., and D. Kahneman. 1974. "Judgement under uncertainty: Heuristics and biases." *Science 185*:1124–1131.

Tyrer, P. 1986. "Classification of anxiety disorders." *Journal of Affective Disorders 11*:99–104.

Uhde, T., et al. 1985. "Phenomenonology and neurobiology of panic disorder." In A. Tuma and J. Maser (Eds.), *Anxiety and the anxiety disorders*. Hillsdale, N.J.: Erlbaum.

Valentine, C. W. 1930. "The innate bases and fear." *Journal of Genetic Psychology 37*:394–419.

Valentine, C. W. 1946. *The psychology of early childhood*. Third edition. London: Methuen.

Van den Hout, M. 1988. "The explanation of experimental panic." In S. Rachman and J. Maser (Eds.), *Panic: Psychological perspectives*. Hillsdale, N.J.: Erlbaum.

Van den Hout, M., and E. Griez. 1986. "Experimental panic." In I. Hand and H. Wittchen (Eds.), *Panic and phobias*. Berlin: Springer.

Vermilyea, J. A., R. Boice, and D. H. Barlow. 1984. "Rachman and Hodgson (1974) a decade later: How do desynchronous response systems relate to the treatment of agoraphobia?" *Behaviour Research and Therapy 22*:615–621.

Vernon, P. 1941. "Psychological effects of air raids." *Journal of Abnormal and Social Psychology 36*:457–476.

Walk, R. 1956. "Self-ratings of fear in a fear-evoking situation." *Journal of Abnormal and Social Psychology 52*:171–178.

Wallen, R. 1945. "Food aversions of normal and neurotic males." *Journal of Abnormal and Social Psychology 40*:77–81.

Wardle, J. 1984. "Dental pessimism: Negative cognitions in fearful dental patients." *Behaviour Research and Therapy 22*:553–556.

Watson, J., and R. Rayner. 1920. "Conditioned emotional reactions." *Journal of Experimental Psychology 3*:1–22.

Watts, F. N. 1979. "Habituation model of systematic desensitization." *Psychological Bulletin 86*:627–637.

Weiner, H. 1987. "Human relationships in health, illness and disease." In D. Magnusson and A. Ohman (Eds.), *Psychopathology*. New York: Academic Press.

Weissman, M. W., J. F. Leckmann, K. R. Merikangas, et al. 1984. "Depression and anxiety disorders in parents and children." *Archives of General Psychiatry 41*:845–852.

Weissman, M. W., P. J. Leaf, C. E. Holzer, and K. R. Merikangas. 1985. "Epidemiology of anxiety disorders." *Psychopharmacological Bulletin 26*:543–545.

Wickert, F. (Ed.) 1947. "Psychological research on problems of redistribution." *USAAF aviation psychology program research report no. 14.* Washington, D.C.: U.S. Government Printing Office.

Wilson, G. T. 1978. "The importance of being theoretical: A commentary on Bandura's 'Self-efficacy: towards a unifying theory of behavioural change.'" In S. Rachman (Ed.), *Perceived self-efficacy. Advances in behaviour research and therapy, 2.*

Wilson, G. T. 1982. "Adult disorders." In G. Wilson and C. Franks (Eds.), *Contemporary behavior therapy.* New York: Guilford Press.

Wilson, G. T. 1986. "Psychosocial treatment of anxiety disorders." In B. Shaw et al. (Eds.), *Anxiety disorders.* New York: Plenum Press.

Wilson, H. 1942. "Mental reactions to air raids." *The Lancet* 1:284–287.

Wittchen, H. 1986. "Epidemiology of panic attacks and panic disorders." In I. Hand and H. Wittchen (Eds.), *Panic and phobias.* Berlin: Springer.

Wittchen, H. 1988. "Natural course and spontaneous remissions of untreated anxiety disorders." In I. Hand and H. Wittchen (Eds.), *Panic and phobias,* Vol. 2. Berlin: Springer.

Wittchen, H., and G. Semler. 1986. "Diagnostic reliability and epidemiology of DSMIII Anxiety Disorders." In I. Hand and H. Wittchen (Eds.), *Panic and phobias.* Berlin: Springer.

Wolpe, J. 1954. "Reciprocal inhibition as the main basis of psychotherapeutic effects." *Archives Neurology and Psychiatry* 72:205–214.

Wolpe, J. 1958. *Psychotherapy by reciprocal inhibition.* Stanford: Stanford University Press.

Wolpe, J. 1982. *The practice of behaviour therapy.* Third edition. Oxford: Pergamon Press.

Wolpe, J., and P. Lang. 1964. "A fear-survey schedule for use in behaviour therapy." *Behaviour Research and Therapy* 2:27–34.

Wolpe, J., and S. Rachman. 1960. "Psychoanalytic evidence: A critique based on Freud's case of Little Hans." *Journal of Nervous and Mental Diseases* 131:135–145.

Wolpe, J., and V. Rowan. 1988. "Panic disorder: A product of classical conditioning." *Behaviour Research and Therapy* 26:441–450.

Zafiropoulou, M., and F. M. McPherson. 1986. "Preparedness and the severity and outcome of clinical phobias." *Behaviour Research and Therapy* 24:221–222.

Zajonc, R. 1980. "Feeling and thinking." *American Psychologist* 35:151–175.

Zitrin, C. 1986. "New perspectives on the treatment of panic and phobic disorders." In B. Shaw et al. (Eds.), *Anxiety disorders.* New York: Plenum.

NAME INDEX

SUBJECT INDEX